Advanced Techniques
in dBASE III PLUS

D1603969

Advanced Techniques in dBASE III PLUS™

Alan Simpson

San Francisco • Paris • Düsseldorf • Soest

Cover design by Thomas Ingalls + Associates

dBASE II, dBASE III, dBASE III PLUS, Framework, and RunTime+ are trademarks of Ashton-Tate.
IBM PC is a registered trademark of International Business Machines Corporation.
Clipper is a trademark of Nantucket Inc.
dBIII Compiler is a trademark of WordTech Systems Inc.
Lotus 1-2-3 is a trademark of Lotus Development Corporation.
PFS:FILE is a trademark of Software Publishing Corporation.
VisiCalc is a trademark of Software Arts Inc.
Paradox is a trademark of Ansa Software.
R:base 5000 is a trademark of Microrim, Inc.
MailMerge and WordStar are trademarks of MicroPro International.
Microsoft Word and Multiplan are trademarks of Microsoft Corporation.
SYBEX is a registered trademark of SYBEX, Inc.

SYBEX is not affiliated with any manufacturer.

Every effort has been made to supply complete and accurate information. However, SYBEX assumes no responsibility for its use, nor for any infringements of patents or other rights of third parties which would result.

Library of Congress Card Number: 86-61590
ISBN 0-89588-369-4
Manufactured in the United States of America
20 19 18 17 16 15 14 13

To Susan

Acknowledgments

Thanks to everyone at SYBEX who contributed to this book and produced it, including Karl Ray (managing editor), Barbara Gordon (supervising editor), Michael L. Wolk (line editor), Joel Kroman (technical reviewer), David Clark and Olivia Shinomoto (word processors), Dawn Amsberry (typesetter), and Jon Strickland (proofreader).

Many thanks to the clinical psychologist (whose name and location escape me) for tips on the updating in the Accounts Receivable System.

Many thanks to Bill and Cynthia Gladstone for being great literary agents and friends.

And of course thanks to my wife and best friend Susan, for being there.

Contents

Introduction   xix

    Structure of the Book   xix

    The Dot Prompt   xx

    The Config.SYS File   xxi

    How to Buy the Programs in this Book   xxii

    Typographical Conventions   xxii

Chapter One

dBASE III PLUS   1
Database
Designs

    Single Database   1

    Single Database with Memo Field   3

    Relational Databases   8

    Master-File/Transaction-File Database System   13

Chapter Two

Index Power   19

    Database Indices   19

    Trimming Minutes down to Seconds   20

        Displaying Records in Sorted Order   21

        Faster Searching   24

Faster Math   31

Faster Reports   32

Faster Copying   32

Faster Editing   32

Faster Sorting   34

Managing Multiple Index Files   35

Points to Remember   37

Chapter Three

Programming in dBASE III PLUS

41

Creating Command Files   41

Interacting with the User   44

ACCEPT   44

INPUT   44

WAIT   45

READ   45

Looping with DO WHILE . . . ENDDO   46

Making Decisions with IF . . . ELSE . . . ENDIF   48

Making Decisions with DO CASE . . . ENDCASE   51

Structured Programming   52

Debugging Techniques   56

DISPLAY Commands   57

HISTORY   59

CLOSE and CLEAR   59

SET TALK ON   60

SET ECHO ON   60

SET STEP ON   60

SET DEBUG ON   61

Connect the Clauses   61

The Most Common Programming Errors   61

Chapter Four

Turning Ideas into Working Software: System Design   **67**

Problem Definition   68

Input-Output (I/O) Specification   70

Database Design   71

Modular Program Design   73

Writing and Testing Program Modules   75

Chapter Five

Membership System Main Menu   **77**

Getting Started: Writing the Pseudocode   77

Writing the Command File   78

Will It Work? Testing the Program   81

Chapter Six

Membership System Append Program   **85**

Creating the Form   85

Moving Information on the Blackboard   87

Inserting Blank Lines   87

Repositioning Field Highlights   89

Improving Field Labels   90

Deleting Labels   90

Boxed Titles   91

Saving the Form   94

Testing the Form   94

Modifying a Screen   95

Adding Picture Templates   96

Files Created by the Screen Painter   98

The AddNew Command File   100

   Writing the Pseudocode   100

   Writing the Command File   100

   Testing the Program   101

Using Graphics Characters   102

Chapter Seven

Membership Mailing Labels and Directory — 107

Mailing Labels   107

Custom dBASE III PLUS Reports   110

   Using the Report Form with a Word Processor   115

Modifying the Report Format   115

Chapter Eight

Membership System Sorting and Querying — 119

Writing the Pseudocode   122

Writing the Command File   123

   Sort orders   125

   Querying   126

   Displaying and Printing   126

Testing the Program   131

Chapter Nine

Membership System Editing and Deleting

133

Custom Screen for Editing and Deleting   133

The EditDel Command File   135

Writing the Pseudocode   135

Writing the Command File   137

Testing the Program   141

Chapter Ten

Membership System Enhancements

143

Checking for Duplicate Members   143

Mailing Labels Alignment Check   148

The Directory Program   149

Stopping the Printer   154

Chapter Eleven

Inventory System Design

161

General Design of Inventory Systems   161

Key Fields   163

Inventory System Problem Definition   164

Inventory System I/O Specifications   164

Inventory System Database Design   166

The Master File   166

The Sales File   167

The NewStock File   168

Inventory System Software Design   168

Inventory System Main Menu   170

Writing the Pseudocode   170

Writing the Command File   170

Testing the Program   174

Chapter Twelve

The Master   **177**
Inventory File

Master-File Software Design   177

Master-File Menu   179

Adding Unique Part Numbers   181

Creating the Custom Screen   181

Writing the Pseudocode   183

Writing the AddNumbs Command File   184

Inventory Master-File Reports   187

The Current-Stock Report   187

The Reorder Report   189

The Open-Order Report   191

The Purchase Orders   192

Writing the Command Files   193

The Reports   193

The Purchase Orders   197

Editing the Master File   203

Chapter Thirteen

Inventory Sales   **209**
System

Sales System Software Structure   209

Sales System Menu   210

Point-of-Sale Data Entry   212

    Writing the Pseudocode   215

    Writing the Command File   216

    Automatic Selling Price   226

Sales System Reports   227

    Writing the Pseudocode   230

    Writing the Command File   231

Chapter Fourteen

Inventory New Stock System   239

New Stock System Software Structure   239

New Stock System Menu   241

New Stock Data-Entry Program   242

    Writing the Pseudocode   242

    Creating the Command File   243

New Stock System Reports   246

Chapter Fifteen

Inventory System Updating   253

Updating the Master File   253

    Writing the Pseudocode   254

    Writing the Command File   255

Editing the Sales File   259

    Writing the Pseudocode   261

    Writing the Command File   262

Editing the NewStock File   269

Chapter Sixteen

Accounts Receivable System Design   **279**

Accounts Receivable Problem Definition   *279*

Accounts Receivable I/O Specifications   *280*

Accounts Receivable Database Design   *281*

     The Main System   282

     Historical Data   284

Accounts Receivable Software Structure   *285*

Chapter Seventeen

Procedures and Parameters   **289**

The A/R System Procedure File   *289*

     Standardizing Title Formats   290

     Standardizing Error Messages   291

     Customer-Number Validation Procedure   292

Creating the Procedure File   *293*

Using the Procedure File   *295*

A Note on Parameter Passing   *296*

The GetCust Procedure   *298*

Chapter Eighteen

Main Menu, Data Entry, and Editing   **303**

A/R System Main Menu   *303*

Adding New Customers   *306*

Adding New Charges   *310*

xvi

Adding New Payments   312
A/R System Edit Programs   315
Editing the Customer Database   317
Editing Current Charges   319
Editing Payments   322

Chapter Nineteen

A/R System Reports   377

Accounts Receivable Report Menu   327
Printing Invoices   329
The BillProc Procedure File   330
The Monthly Billing Cycle   333
Status Checks and Duplicate Invoices   333
Summary and Aging Reports   336
History Reports   339

Chapter Twenty

Monthly System Updates   345

Chapter Twenty-One

Useful Programs and Techniques   351

Modifying Existing Software   351
Minor Modifications   352
Major Modifications   353
An Inventory/Accounts Receivable Linker   356
A Debugging Tool   359
A Check-Writing Procedure   365

A Word-Wrap Procedure   370

Handy Business Formulas   372

Statistical Procedures   374

Light-Bar Menus   370

Appendix A

RunTime + and Compilers   *387*

RunTime +   388

Creating the Directories   388
Copying the Command Files   389
Creating a Response File   391
Copying RunTime +   391
Using dBCODE   392
Verifying the Encryption   392
Using dBLINKER   393
Testing the Encrypted File   394
Marketing Your Creation   395
RunTime + Limitations   395

Compilers   397

High-Level Languages, Low-Level Languages, and
   Compilers   398
The In-Between Languages   401
The Clipper Compiler   402
dBlll Compiler   408
Performance Comparisons   411
Conclusions   415

Appendix B

Interfacing with Other Software Systems   *417*

Interfacing with PFS:FILE   417

Interfacing with Spreadsheets   418

Interfacing with Word Processors   420

Appendix C

dBASE III PLUS   425
Vocabulary

Index   448

Introduction

If you want to write a custom software system in dBASE III PLUS, this book is for you. The emphasis of the book is on practical business programming: writing programs that get the job done quickly and efficiently. The book presents working business systems that not only perform useful business tasks but also demonstrate programming techniques that can be used in many business applications.

Unlike most programming books, this book provides step-by-step descriptions of virtually every technique used in every program. Therefore, you don't have to try to figure out "what's going on" from a mass of dBASE commands—it's already been done for you. As the rationale for each routine in a large software system is revealed, the mystery of programming dwindles. And as the mystery dwindles, your own ability to create custom software systems grows.

This book is not intended for the computer novice. However, familiarity with the basic commands used in either dBASE II, dBASE III, or dBASE III PLUS will be sufficient background. No prior programming experience is necessary.

Structure of the Book

The book is divided into six major sections. The first four chapters discuss general programming considerations and emphasize techniques for maximizing the speed and performance of a software system. These chapters also provide firm advice for planning ahead and getting the most out of dBASE III PLUS's many capabilities.

The second part (Chapters 5–10) presents a custom software system for managing a single database. We will be working with a membership database as our example, but the techniques we present can be used to manage any single database. In this part, specifically designed for the novice programmer, you will learn the basics of creating user-friendly, "menu-driven" systems; creating and using custom screens and reports; using index files for maximum speed; and other basic programming techniques universal to all business applications.

Chapters 11–15 present an inventory-management system and demonstrate more advanced techniques for managing multiple databases.

Chapters 16–20 discuss an accounts-receivable software system. This system demonstrates additional techniques for managing multiple databases, as well as advanced programming techniques that are unique to dBASE III PLUS.

Chapter 21 discusses some handy programs that are useful when working with dBASE, and also presents some advanced "tips and techniques" for solving tricky programming problems and tailoring existing software to your needs.

The last part consists of appendices. Appendix A describes software packages that can help you market your custom systems, including Ashton-Tate's RunTime+ and the Clipper and dBlll Compilers. Appendix B discusses techniques for interfacing dBASE III PLUS data with other software systems. Appendix C presents a summary of dBASE commands for quick reference.

For consistency, the book assumes that you are using an IBM PC or similar computer with two floppy-disk drives, A and B. In drive A you should store the dBASE III PLUS System Disk, and in drive B you should store the databases and programs you develop. To ensure that the files you create are always stored on drive B, you might want to set up a Config.DB file, as discussed in Appendix A.

If you are using a hard-disk system, you'll want to store both dBASE III PLUS and the files you create on the same directory. In this case, you don't need to change the default drive as long as you access dBASE from the DOS C> prompt and the appropriate directory.

The Dot Prompt

Since you've reached the level of "dBASE programmer" (based on the fact that you are reading this book), we'll dispense with the dBASE III PLUS Assistant and work directly from the dot prompt instead. While the Assistant is fine for building and managing a database, it offers little aid to the programmer. Besides that, things just move along at a quicker pace when you work from the dot prompt, and we have lots of material to cover here.

To leave the Assistant menu and get to the dot prompt, press the Esc key while the Assistant menu is displayed. To make dBASE III PLUS start up at the dot prompt, remove the lines

STATUS = ON
COMMAND = ASSIST

from the Config.DB file on your dBASE III PLUS System Disk 1. You can use any word processor or text editor (including the dBASE MODIFY COMMAND editor) to remove these lines.

The Config.SYS File

Chances are that you may have gotten away without using a Config.SYS file on your boot-up disk for a long time. But in this book, we'll develop more advanced applications that will eventually generate the error message

Too many files are open

if you don't have the proper Config.SYS file on your boot-up disk.

You can quickly see the contents of the Config.SYS file using the DOS TYPE command. Log onto the disk you usually boot your computer from (the root directory on your hard disk, or the DOS disk you insert before turning on your computer). This is usually *not* one of the dBASE III PLUS disks. At the DOS A > or C: > prompt, enter this command:

TYPE Config.SYS

Then press Return. If you do not see a configuration such as

FILES = 20
BUFFERS = 15

you need to create a Config.SYS file. You can use any word processor (with a nondocument mode), the dBASE MODIFY COMMAND editor, or just the DOS COPY command. To use the COPY command, leave the boot-up disk in place and type the following command at the DOS

A> or C> prompt:

COPY CON Config.SYS

Press Return. Type in the lines

FILES = 20
BUFFERS = 15

pressing Return once after each line. Next press F6 (or Ctrl-Z, whichever displays the ^Z on the screen) and Return. When the DOS A> or C> prompt reappears, you're done. To verify that you've created the file, enter this command once again at the A> or C> prompt:

TYPE Config.SYS

You should see the FILES and BUFFERS commands in the file exactly as you typed them. Next time you boot up your computer, DOS will read the Config.SYS file and set aside enough memory to hold open 20 files and 15 buffers simultaneously. This means you can have lots of dBASE database and command files open simultaneously without seeing the "Too many files are open" error message.

How to Buy
the Programs in this Book

If you would like to try out the sample programs in this book but don't want to take the time to type them in yourself, see the last page of this book for instructions on purchasing a disk containing all the sample programs.

Typographical Conventions

The following typographical conventions are used throughout the book:

- dBASE III PLUS commands are entirely capitalized (CREATE).

- The first letters of variables and field names are capitalized (Memo field).

- Keyboard keys are upper- and lowercase (PgUp).

- Control-key commands are indicated with the caret (^) symbol. ^C means: hold down Control and C at the same time.

dBASE III PLUS
Database Designs

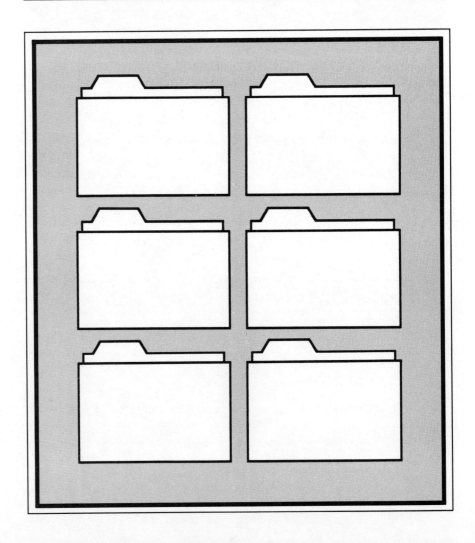

Deciding what to store in a database is one of the first steps in designing any software system. Many systems, such as mailing lists, involve only a single database and perhaps an index file or two. More sophisticated systems may use several databases interactively.

In this chapter we'll discuss the four most commonly used database designs: single database, single database with Memo field, relational databases, and master-file/transaction-file database systems.

Single Database

The simplest database design is the single database. There are just two steps in designing a single-database system:

1. Decide what fields to put in the database.

2. Identify key fields for sorting and searching.

A simple mailing list might have the database structure shown in Figure 1.1.

Notice that the first and last names are in two separate fields. This is so the database can be sorted by last name. If there were just a single name field and the data were stored like this,

Mr. James L. Bower
Andy Zappleby
Claudia Allen

there would be no way to sort the database by last name. By storing the first and last names in separate fields, you can sort by last name (or last name plus first name), and use the sorted file to locate records quickly.

Also notice that the address information is separated into distinct fields: City, State, and Zip. Once again, this is so that the data can be sorted or accessed easily on the basis of any of these independent pieces of information. In general, always break the information in a database into as many distinct fields as possible, since this allows the greatest freedom in sorting and searching.

To create the mailing-list database we've just discussed, type the CRE-ATE command with the name of the file:

CREATE Mail

(If you are using a computer with two floppy disks, first enter the command SET DEFAULT TO B.) dBASE III PLUS displays a form on which to enter the name, data type, width, and decimal places for each field in the database. When you've completed this screen, enter several sample records so you can test the index files we'll be creating next.

```
Structure for database : C:Mail.DBF

Field   Field name   Type         Width   Dec
    1    LNAME        Character      20
    2    FNAME        Character      20
    3    COMPANY      Character      20
    4    ADDRESS      Character      25
    5    CITY         Character      20
    6    STATE        Character       5
    7    ZIP          Character      10
    8    EXP_DATE     Date            8
```

Figure 1.1 – A sample mailing-list database

Now we need to identify key fields for sorting and searching. Mailing lists generally require two sort orders: by last and first names for printing a directory or looking up individual records, and by zip code for bulk mailing. To maintain these sort orders permanently, we'll store them in index files. First create an Index file of last and first names:

```
USE Mail
INDEX ON LName + FName to NAMES
```

Then create the index file of zip codes:

```
USE Mail
INDEX ON Zip TO Zips
```

Whenever you add new records to the database or make changes to the database through the EDIT, DELETE, PACK, or BROWSE commands, make sure both index files are active:

```
USE Mail INDEX Names, Zips
```

If the Mail database is already open, you can also use the command

```
SET INDEX TO Names, Zips
```

Since Names is the first-listed index file in this example, a DISPLAY, LIST, or REPORT FORM command will display the records in alphabetical order by last and first names. To display the records in zip-code order, just make Zips the first-listed index file:

```
USE Mail INDEX Zips, Names
```

See Chapter 2 for a more detailed discussion of multiple index files.

The membership system we'll develop later in the book uses a file similar to the one we've designed here to explore programming techniques for managing a single database with index files.

Single Database with Memo Field

A slight variation in the single-database structure is the addition of a Memo field for long passages of text within the database. A library-reference system provides a good opportunity to demonstrate the use of a Memo field. Suppose you wanted to create a database of journal references, and you wanted each reference to include author, title, journal, publication date, pages, keywords (topics), and an abstract. One method would be to design a single database like Figure 1.2.

Notice that the Abstract field in Lib.DBF uses the maximum dBASE field length of 254 characters. This structure is fine if you can keep the length of all abstracts to 254 characters, but this constraint can easily be eliminated by assigning the Abstract field a Memo rather than a Character data type. The structure in Figure 1.3 shows the same library reference database with the Abstract field as a Memo data type.

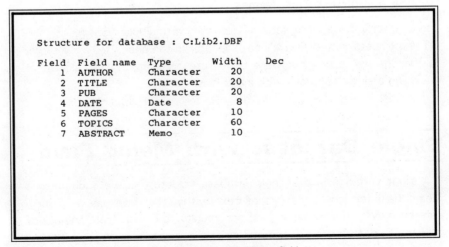

```
Structure for database : C:Lib.DBF

Field   Field name   Type        Width     Dec
   1    AUTHOR       Character      20
   2    TITLE        Character      20
   3    PUB          Character      20
   4    DATE         Date            8
   5    PAGES        Character      10
   6    TOPICS       Character      60
   7    ABSTRACT     Character     254
```

Figure 1.2 – A library-referencing database

```
Structure for database : C:Lib2.DBF

Field   Field name   Type        Width     Dec
   1    AUTHOR       Character      20
   2    TITLE        Character      20
   3    PUB          Character      20
   4    DATE         Date            8
   5    PAGES        Character      10
   6    TOPICS       Character      60
   7    ABSTRACT     Memo           10
```

Figure 1.3 – A library-referencing database with Memo field

Even though dBASE automatically assigns a width of ten characters to this field, each abstract can actually contain up to 4,000 characters. This is because data typed into Memo fields are physically stored in an auxiliary database with the extension .DBT. Only the location of each memo in the .DBT file is stored in the Lib2 database itself.

Go ahead and create Lib2, so you can test the Memo field. When you use the APPEND command to add records to the database or the EDIT command to modify existing data, the screen displays an entry form like Figure 1.4.

To enter data in the Abstract field, position the cursor in the field and press ^PgDn (the field will first show the word Memo). The screen will clear and you'll automatically be in the dBASE text editor. Then you can just type your abstract, using the dBASE editing commands to help compose and edit. When you're done typing or editing the abstract, press ^End (or ^W) to return to the APPEND or EDIT screen.

When you use the LIST command to view the records, the word Memo is displayed in the listing (see Figure 1.5), instead of the contents of the Abstract field.

However, if you specify the field names by typing

LIST OFF Author, Title, Pub, Date, Pages, Abstract

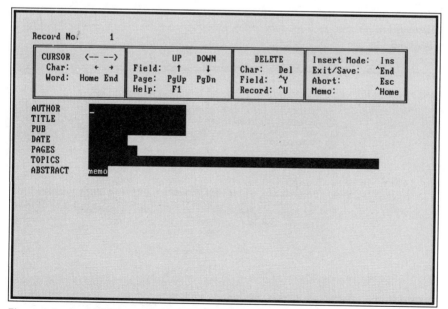

Figure 1.4 – An APPEND screen with Memo field

the contents of the Abstract field are included, as in Figure 1.6. You can gain some control over the appearance of the Memo field by using the SET MEMOWIDTH command. For example, to confine the width of the Memo field to 40 characters (the default width is 50), enter the following command at the dot prompt:

SET MEMOWIDTH TO 40

Another way to gain control over the appearance of the Memo field is to

```
Aronson, G.      Decisions Support Systems  Byte Magazine
05/01/85  45-48  Memo     Decision Support, EDP

Carlson, D.A.    Management By Objectives    MBO Quarterly
06/01/85  64-78  Memo     MBO, Management, Objectives
```

Figure 1.5 – Listing of Lib2 database

```
Garton, J.T.     Decision Support Systems         Byte Magazine
03/01/85  22-45  This article discusses automated Decision
                 Support Systems used in modern business mini- and
                 microcomputer systems.  Includes a review and
                 comparison of several currently available systems,
                 such as dSupport, Knowledge Master, Mind Games,
                 and Decisive.

Franklin, B.W.   Automated MBO                    MBO Monthly
05/01/85  44-51  Describes several automated systems that support
                 Management by Objectives (MBO).  The basic theory
                 of MBO is discussed, then several popular
                 automated MBO systems are reviewed.
```

Figure 1.6 – Lib2 database with Memo field displayed

use a command file. For example, Figure 1.7 shows a command file that displays data, including the Memo field, from the Lib2 database. Figure 1.8 shows how the data appear when printed by the sample command file.

```
******************************************** Library.PRG
* --- Sample program to print database with Memo field.
USE Lib2
GO TOP
DO WHILE .NOT. EOF()
   ? "Author     : ",Author
   ? "Title      : ",Title
   ? "Publication: ",Pub
   ? "Date       : ",Date,"            Pages: ",Pages
   ? "Keywords   : ",Topics
   ?
   ? Abstract
   ?
   ?
   SKIP
ENDDO (while not eof)
```

Figure 1.7 – Sample program to print a database with Memo field

```
Record no.       1
Author     :  Cusey, J.A.
Title      :  Management Theory
Publication:  Am. Jour. of Mngmt.
Date       :  04/01/85              Pages:  121-353
Keywords   :  Management, MBO, Microcomputer software

An in-depth analysis of management by objectives.
The use of microcomputer database management and
graphics packages as aids to the management
process.


Record no.       2
Author     :  Tobin, Cecilia
Title      :  DBMS Programming
Publication:  Micro DBMS Journal
Date       :  02/15/85              Pages:  68-75
Keywords   :  DBMS, Programming, Design, Development

Program design and development considerations when
working in a high-level database-management
language.  Discusses programming techniques with
dBASE II and III as well as other microcomputer
database-management systems.
```

Figure 1.8 – Sample printout from the Library.PRG command file

. One disadvantage of Memo fields is that you cannot perform searching functions on them. For example, the command

LIST FOR "dBASE" $ Abstract

simply returns this error message:

Operation with Memo field invalid.

However, there's a way around this problem. In the referencing database above, we've included a Character field called Keywords to store a list of topics discussed in each article. So to view all the references on the subject of dBASE, just look in the Keywords field. Type

LIST FOR "dBASE" $ Keywords

Another limitation of the Memo field is that it cannot be used for sorting or indexing. For example, you cannot ask dBASE to INDEX ON Abstract TO Abs. However, it's pretty unlikely that you'd want to index on a Memo field anyway. In this particular library example, you'd be more likely to index on the Author field for alphabetical listings by author, or the Date field for chronological listings by publication date.

Both the single-database and Memo-field designs are useful for situations where all of the data can be stored in a single database. Generally speaking, any type of data that can be stored on a Rolodex card file or in a file box with index cards can be stored in a single database. But some applications are better handled with multiple databases.

Relational Databases

Relational databases are files that are related to one another through a common field. They are used mainly to avoid unnecessary duplication of data, thereby using less disk storage space and speeding up data access.

An accounts-receivable system provides a good example of relational database design. Notice the structure of the accounts-receivable database in Figure 1.9.

For each record there is a billing date, an amount, and the name, address, city, state, and zip code of the vendor. Now this isn't a particularly good design for this application: there may be only a dozen or so individual vendors, but hundreds of billings to each. Hence the vendor name, address, city, state, and zip code could be repeated unnecessarily in hundreds of records, as in Figure 1.10.

```
Structure for database : C:AR.DBF

Field  Field name  Type        Width   Dec
  1    BILL_DATE   Date           8
  2    AMOUNT      Numeric        9      2
  3    VENDOR      Character     20
  4    ADDRESS     Character     20
  5    CITY        Character     20
  6    STATE       Character     20
  7    ZIP         Character     20
```

Figure 1.9 – The AR.DBF database structure

```
BILL_DATE    AMOUNT VENDOR              ADDRESS           CITY           STATE   ZIP
06/01/85     734.75 American Iceberg Co. 345 No. Pole St.  Nome           AL    00001
06/01/85    8456.32 Thompson Twins, Inc. 466 Chesapeake Way San Francisco  CA    91121
06/01/85    2956.70 Logitek Microcode   256 Eprom Blvd.   Van Nuys       CA    93323
06/01/85     624.88 DBMS Software       256 K. St.        Solana Beach   CA    93221
06/05/85    1115.60 Antioch Petroleum   8776 Fossil St.   Denver         CO    55555
06/15/85     534.94 Hockleed Aeronautics 1777 Cannard Blvd. Augusta       GA    32212
07/01/85    4236.54 Hockleed Aeronautics 1777 Cannard Blvd. Augusta       GA    32212
07/01/85    2352.54 DBMS Software       256 K. St.        Solana Beach   CA    93221
07/06/85    3426.43 Thompson Twins, Inc. 466 Chesapeake Way San Francisco  CA    91121
07/15/85    8351.76 American Iceberg Co. 345 No. Pole St.  Nome           AL    00001
07/15/85    6342.75 Logitek Microcode   256 Eprom Blvd.   Van Nuys       CA    93323
07/20/85     946.38 Antioch Petroleum   8776 Fossil St.   Denver         CO    55555
08/01/85     684.34 Logitek Microcode   256 Eprom Blvd.   Van Nuys       CA    93323
08/12/85   12354.34 DBMS Software       256 K. St.        Solana Beach   CA    93221
08/15/85    1234.56 American Iceberg    345 No. Pole St.  Nome           AL    00001
08/15/85     232.12 Thompson Twins, Inc. 466 Chesapeake Way San Francisco  CA    91121
08/15/85     877.43 Antioch Petroleum   8776 Fossil St.   Denver         CO    55555
08/21/85    3214.45 Hockleed Aeronautics 1777 Cannard Blvd. Augusta       GA    32212
```

Figure 1.10 – Listing from a sample accounts-receivable database

A better approach would be to store the billing date and amount in one database and the individual vendor names and addresses in another. Then use a code to relate the two databases to one another.

For example, you could create a database called AR1 to store vendor codes, billing dates, and amounts, as in Figure 1.11. A listing of the data in this database might appear as in Figure 1.12.

```
Structure for database : C:AR1.DBF

Field   Field name   Type        Width   Dec
   1    BILL_DATE    Date           8
   2    AMOUNT       Numeric        9      2
   3    VEND_CODE    Character      5
```

Figure 1.11 – The AR1.DBF database structure

```
Record#   BILL_DATE     AMOUNT VEND_CODE
      1   06/01/85      734.75 AIC
      2   06/01/85     8456.32 TTI
      3   06/01/85     2956.70 LM
      4   06/01/85      624.88 DBMS
      5   06/05/85     1115.60 AP
      6   06/15/85      534.94 HA
      7   07/01/85     4236.54 HA
      8   07/01/85     2352.54 DBMS
      9   07/06/85     3426.43 TTI
     10   07/15/85     8351.76 AIC
     11   07/15/85     6342.75 LM
     12   07/20/85      946.38 AP
     13   08/01/85      684.34 LM
     14   08/12/85    12354.34 DBMS
     15   08/15/85     1234.56 AIC
     16   08/15/85      232.12 TTI
     17   08/15/85      877.43 AP
     18   08/21/85     3214.45 HA
```

Figure 1.12 – Accounts-receivable database with vendor code

Then you could create a second database called AR2 to store vendor names and addresses, as in Figure 1.13. The only duplicate field in these two databases is the small Vend_Code field, so the space wasted by repeating vendor names and addresses is eliminated. A listing of the AR2 database might appear as in Figure 1.14.

This second database is sometimes called a lookup table for the first database, because dBASE looks up the vendor name and address in the second database, using the Vend_Code field created to relate the two

```
Structure for database : C:AR2.DBF

Field   Field name   Type        Width     Dec
    1   VEND_CODE    Character        5
    2   VENDOR       Character       20
    3   ADDRESS      Character       20
    4   CITY         Character       20
    5   STATE        Character       20
    6   ZIP          Character       20
```

Figure 1.13 – The AR2.DBF database structure

```
    VEND_CODE VENDOR                 ADDRESS              CITY        STATE   ZIP
  1 AIC       American Iceberg Co. 345 No. Pole St.    Nome            AL    00001
  2 AP        Antioch Petroleum    8776 Fossil St.     Denver          CO    55555
  3 DBMS      DBMS Software        256 K. St.          Solana Beach    CA    93221
  4 HA        Hockleed Aeronautics 1777 Cannard Blvd.  Augusta         GA    32212
  5 LM        Logitek Microcode    256 Eprom Blvd.     Van Nuys        CA    93323
  6 TTI       Thompson Twins, Inc. 466 Chesapeake Way  San Francisco   CA    91121
```

Figure 1.14 – Listing from AR2.DBF database

files. To set up the relationship between the two databases, the lookup database must first be indexed on the key field (the field that relates the two databases):

USE AR2
INDEX ON Vend_Code TO Vendor

Next, both databases must be opened simultaneously with the SELECT command, and the relationship set up with the SET RELATION TO command:

SELECT 1
USE AR1
SELECT 2
USE AR2 INDEX Vendor
SELECT 1
SET RELATION TO Vend_Code INTO AR2

If you were to type the LIST command now, you'd still see the records from the AR1 database, as in Figure 1.12. To see the associated vendor names and addresses, use the LIST command again, but specify field names from the AR2 database, using the B→ specification. (AR2 is the B database because it was selected second. A third file would be the C → database, a fourth would be the D→ database, and so forth.)

LIST Bill_date, Amount B→Vendor, B→Address

The listing on the screen or printer would now appear as in Figure 1.15.

```
 #  BILL_DATE   AMOUNT  B->VENDOR              B->ADDRESS
 1  06/01/85    734.75 American Iceberg Co.  345 No. Pole St.
 2  06/01/85   8456.32 Thompson Twins, Inc.  466 Chesapeake Way
 3  06/01/85   2956.70 Logitek Microcode     256 Eprom Blvd.
 4  06/01/85    624.88 DBMS Software         256 K. St.
 5  06/05/85   1115.60 Antioch Petroleum     8776 Fossil St.
 6  06/15/85    534.94 Hockleed Aeronautics  1777 Cannard Blvd.
 7  07/01/85   4236.54 Hockleed Aeronautics  1777 Cannard Blvd.
 8  07/01/85   2352.54 DBMS Software         256 K. St.
 9  07/06/85   3426.43 Thompson Twins, Inc.  466 Chesapeake Way
10  07/15/85   8351.76 American Iceberg Co.  345 No. Pole St.
11  07/15/85   6342.75 Logitek Microcode     256 Eprom Blvd.
12  07/20/85    946.38 Antioch Petroleum     8776 Fossil St.
13  08/01/85    684.34 Logitek Microcode     256 Eprom Blvd.
14  08/12/85  12354.34 DBMS Software         256 K. St.
15  08/15/85   1234.56 American Iceberg Co.  345 No. Pole St.
16  08/15/85    232.12 Thompson Twins, Inc.  466 Chesapeake Way
17  08/15/85    877.43 Antioch Petroleum      8776 Fossil St.
18  08/21/85   3214.45 Hockleed Aeronautics  1777 Cannard Blvd.
```

Figure 1.15 – Joint listing from the AR1 and AR2 databases

The information is readily available from both databases simultaneously, but no space has been wasted by repeating the vendor information in each record of the AR1 file.

The accounts-receivable system we'll develop later in the book will explore programming techniques for relational databases in more detail.

Master-File/Transaction-File Database System

The fourth commonly used database design involves master files and transaction files. These are most often used in inventory and bookkeeping applications, where one data file contains up-to-the-minute information about stock on hand or account balances, and additional databases contain records of individual transactions, such as goods sold and received or individual income and expense transactions.

A simple inventory system might use a master file and two transaction files, in a structure similar to that shown in Figure 1.16. In this example,

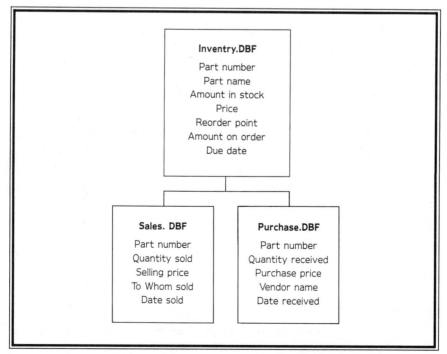

Figure 1.16 – Typical structure for master-file/transaction-file database design

Inventry.DBF is the master file. It contains current information about the stock on hand. It gets its information on individual sales transactions and new stock transactions from the transaction files Sales.DBF and Purchase.DBF. In a sense, Inventry.DBF is a summary of the Sales and Purchase files. The benefit of this database structure is that it allows you to keep abreast of the exact stock on hand at any given moment, while at the same time it provides a separate, permanent record of every item sold and received.

The master file, Inventry.DBF, might be structured like Figure 1.17. A listing of this database would display the stock numbers and item descriptions, as well as current status information, as in Figure 1.18.

```
Structure for database : C:Inventry .DBF

Field   Field name   Type        Width    Dec
    1   PART_NO      Character       5
    2   TITLE        Character      20
    3   ON_HAND      Numeric         4
    4   COST         Numeric         9      2
    5   REORDER      Numeric         4
```

Figure 1.17 – Sample inventory master-file structure

```
Record#   PART_NO TITLE          ON_HAND      COST REORDER
      1   AAA     Icebergs            10    120.00      10
      2   BBB     Tomatoes            10      0.35      10
      3   CCC     Floppy disks        10     12.00      10
      4   DDD     Bike pedals         10      7.77      10
      5   EEE     Modems              10     67.87      10
      6   FFF     Cantaloupes         10      0.77      10
```

Figure 1.18 – Listing from master inventory file

The Sales database contains information about individual sales transactions, and might have the structure shown in Figure 1.19. Using the LIST command on the data in the Sales file produces the output in Figure 1.20, indicating that seven of item AAA have been sold, and five each of items BBB and EEE.

Notice that both the Sales and Inventry files have a field called Part _No. This common field allows dBASE to relate records in the two files.

dBASE uses the UPDATE command to keep the master file current. First,

```
Structure for database : C:Sales.DBF

Field  Field name  Type       Width    Dec
    1   PART_NO     Character     5
    2   INVOICE_NO  Numeric       6
    3   CLERK       Character    12
    4   CUSTOMER    Character    12
    5   QTY         Numeric       4
    6   PRICE       Numeric       9       2
    7   DATE        Date          8
```

Figure 1.19 – The inventory sales-transactions database

```
Record#  PART_NO INVOICE_NO CLERK   CUSTOMER    QTY    PRICE DATE
     1   AAA        3453    ZTD     A.P. Smith    5   750.00 12/12/85
     2   BBB        3453    JAC     R.W. Jones    5     2.50 12/12/85
     3   EEE        5436    RAK     R. Jackson    5   339.35 12/12/85
     4   AAA        5476    ZTD     Q. Thomas     2   300.00 12/13/85
```

Figure 1.20 – A listing from the inventory sales database

index each database on the Part_No field:

USE Inventry
INDEX ON Part_No TO Master
USE Sales
INDEX ON Part_No TO Sales

Then open both databases with the SELECT command, and use the UPDATE command to transfer information from the Sales file to the Inventry file:

CLEAR ALL
SELECT 2
USE Sales INDEX Sales
SELECT 1
USE Inventry INDEX Master
UPDATE ON Part_No FROM Sales REPLACE On_Hand WITH;
On_Hand – B→Qty

(Note: In this book, commands that are too long to fit on one line in the text will be broken by a semicolon, as in the command above. You, however, should enter these commands as a single line without the semicolon.) This translates as "Update the Inventry file from the Sales file by replacing the On_Hand quantity with its current value minus the quantity (B →Qty) from the Sales file."

After the update is completed, you can issue the USE command on the Inventry file and list the records to see the current stock information, which looks like Figure 1.21. Notice that there are now three of item AAA

Record#	PART_NO	TITLE	ON_HAND	COST	REORDER
1	AAA	Icebergs	3	120.00	10
2	BBB	Tomatoes	5	0.35	10
3	CCC	Floppy disks	10	12.00	10
4	DDD	Bike pedals	10	7.77	10
5	EEE	Modems	5	67.87	10
6	FFF	Cantaloupes	10	0.77	10

Figure 1.21 – Listing from the master database after updating

in stock, because the Sales file recorded seven sold. There are five each of items BBB and EEE, since the Sales file recorded sales of five of each of these.

The update procedure from the Purchase file would be the same, except that the goods received would be added to the current stock:

UPDATE ON Part_No FROM Purchase REPLACE On_Hand;
WITH On_Hand + B→Qty

The inventory system we'll develop later in the book demonstrates programming techniques for managing databases in a master/transaction relationship.

As you can see from this discussion, there are many ways to design databases and database systems. Which design you use depends on what you need to do and the limits imposed by your hardware (floppy disk versus hard disk, amount of RAM, and so forth). By the time we've finished developing the three business systems in this book, you should feel comfortable with each design and have no difficulty deciding which to use when you begin developing systems on your own.

Index Power

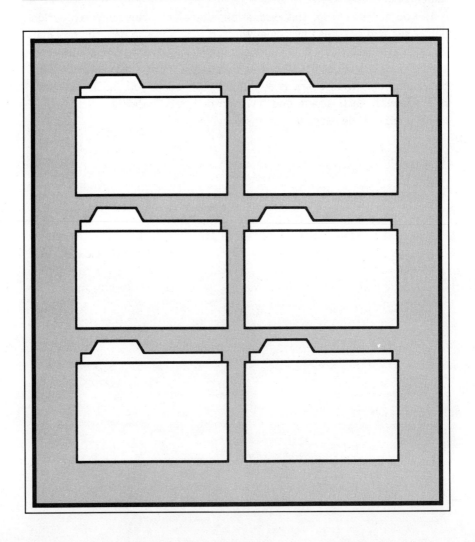

We all want to get the most out of our computers. So, although it's great that computers can trim to minutes what humans usually need hours to perform, who would complain if those computer minutes could be trimmed down to seconds? This chapter discusses and compares techniques for maximizing the speed of dBASE III PLUS applications through the use of index files. We'll trim some of those long dBASE processing minutes down to quick dBASE seconds!

Now keep in mind that we're not talking about saving a second or two of processing time here and there. Some of these techniques can actually trim hours from a program's processing time. The best example I can give you involves one of my consulting assignments. I was called in to work on a dBASE II program that produced 35 custom reports each month. Unfortunately, it took five solid work days to print the reports. With a couple of hours' programming effort I was able to trim those five days of processing time to a neat 27 minutes! And all I did was set up the appropriate index files to handle the job properly.

Database Indices

The best analogy for explaining how using a dBASE III PLUS index file helps a program run faster is the index in a book. Suppose you were reading a book about California fruit trees and wanted to find out about avocado trees. One way to look up the information in the book would simply be to start at page 1 and thumb through each and every page, scanning for the word avocados. If the book you were using had 500 pages, this wouldn't be a very efficient way to find the information you need.

A better approach would be to flip to the back of the book, look up the word Avocados in the alphabetical index, and then turn directly to the page number listed. The topics are in alphabetical order, so you can easily find the one you want (and know when to stop looking).

Obviously, using the index to look up information in a book is far faster and more efficient than scanning all the pages. The same holds true for dBASE III PLUS databases. There are two ways that you can go about looking up information in a database. One is to have dBASE read through every single record in the file (like reading every page in a book) to locate the desired information. Quite inefficient! The second is to create an *index file* based on one kind of information (such as last name or zip code) in the database, look up the information you want in that index, and go directly to the database records that contain the desired information.

In dBASE III PLUS you create indices by using the INDEX ON command. You make an index active (accessible) by specifying the index name in the USE command (for example, USE Mail INDEX Names). Then you can use the FIND or SEEK command to locate the specific information you need. The increase in speed and efficiency using this method is of about the same magnitude as the increase using a book index instead of thumbing through pages individually. In general, you'll find that processing goes anywhere from 10 to 100 times faster with the proper use of index files.

Index files can also vastly improve the speed with which a database is put into physically sorted order on the disk (using the COPY command). But before we get into any more theoretical discussions about index files, let's look at and compare some practical techniques for using index files to maximize the speed of a dBASE III PLUS application.

Trimming Minutes down to Seconds

We'll begin by comparing a few techniques for performing some basic tasks with dBASE III PLUS. We'll use a simple mailing-list database as an example, as shown in Figure 2.1.

Let's assume that this database already has 1,000 records in it. We'll test a number of methods for displaying these records in sorted order, as well as some techniques for searching through the database.

Displaying Records in Sorted Order

There are four methods you can use to display the records in a database in sorted order. We'll compare these methods using Test.DBF with the last-name field (LName) as our key field. (Note: processing times will vary on different computers.)

The SORT Method

The first and most frequently used method (and by far the slowest, if you have more than 50 records) is simply to use the SORT command to create a new physically sorted file. For example, suppose you had already sorted the database and then added some new records with the commands

USE Test
APPEND

To get the records back into alphabetical order using SORT, you would

```
Structure for database : C:Test.DBF
Number of data records :     1000

Field  Field name  Type        Width   Dec
    1  LNAME       Character      20
    2  FNAME       Character      20
    3  COMPANY     Character      20
    4  ADDRESS     Character      25
    5  CITY        Character      20
    6  STATE       Character       5
    7  ZIP         Character      10
    8  DATE        Date            8
    9  AMOUNT      Numeric         9      2
```

Figure 2.1 – Sample database for benchmarking performance

need to type in these commands:

```
SORT ON LName TO Temp
CLOSE DATABASES
ERASE Test.DBF
RENAME Temp.DBF TO Test.DBF
USE Test
LIST
```

The procedure to sort the 1,000-record database back into last-name order will take an estimated 6 minutes on a floppy-disk system and about 4½ minutes on a hard-disk system.

If you sort to the same disk on a floppy-disk system, the original data file must use less than half the total disk space, or dBASE won't be able to complete the sort.

The APPEND and INDEX Method

A second method would be to use the USE Test command, append the new records, then index the file on the LName field with these commands:

```
USE Test
APPEND
INDEX ON LName TO Names
LIST
```

This procedure requires about 45 seconds to resort the 1,000-record data-base back into last-name order on a floppy-disk system, and about 23 seconds on a hard-disk system.

The LOCATE and INSERT Method

A third method would be to locate the position in the sorted database where each new record belongs and insert the new records directly into their proper alphabetical locations, using these commands:

```
USE Test
LOCATE for LName = "Miller"
INSERT
LIST
```

The time required would be however long it takes you to find the appropriate place to insert each new record, plus about 50 seconds for each separate INSERT command to insert the record on a floppy-disk system, or about 30 seconds on a hard-disk system.

Creating an Index and Appending Files to It

The fourth method is to create an index file of the field you want to sort on and keep that index file active while you add new records. To make the index file active for automatic resorting, just specify its name in the USE command:

USE Test INDEX Names

Then any changes to the database, whether they are made through APPEND, EDIT, BROWSE, DELETE, REPLACE, PACK, or READ, are made to the index file as well, and the index is automatically resorted and adjusted.

To add new records and view the data in sorted order using an active index file, you use only the following commands:

USE Test INDEX Names
APPEND
LIST

dBASE automatically puts the index back into last-name order in less than 1 second, on either a hard-disk or floppy-disk system, and the LIST command immediately displays the records in last-name order.

Figure 2.2 shows resorting times for the four techniques just described. Clearly, the fourth method, using an active index file while adding the new records, is by far the fastest.

You can use this last method only with an index file that has *already* been created using the INDEX ON command, but you can create the index

```
-----------------------------------------------------------------
                                          Time Required

Method       Commands Used            Hard Disk     Floppy Disk

   1     USE, APPEND and SORT        270 seconds    360 seconds
   2     USE, APPEND and INDEX ON     23 seconds     45 seconds
   3     USE, LOCATE and INSERT       30 seconds     50 seconds
   4     USE INDEX file and APPEND     1 second       1 second
-----------------------------------------------------------------
```

Figure 2.2 – Sorting times using four different approaches

at any time after you create the database, even if there are no records in the database at all.

Faster Searching

Sorting is generally the most time-consuming step in managing a database, but searching the database for all records that meet a certain condition (for example, last name Miller or dates between 01/01/85 and 03/31/85) is also a slow process. An index file can also help speed up the searching process.

We've assumed that the Test database already has 1,000 records in it. Let's also assume that ten individuals in this database have the last name (LName) Miller. Just how long would it take to LIST, COUNT, or COPY all the Millers to another database? How long would it take to print a formatted report form with only Millers, or to add up the amounts for the Millers? It all depends, of course, on how you do it.

For our benchmark comparisons, we'll use the Test database with the Names index. Let's begin by comparing processing times using two different command files and two different approaches.

The first method uses the standard LIST FOR approach to pull out all the Millers, so the first command file looks like Figure 2.3. When you execute this command file (DO Test), it clears the screen and displays this prompt:

List all people with what last name?

```
**************************** Method 1: LIST FOR approach.
CLEAR
USE Test INDEX Names
ACCEPT " List all people with what last name? " TO Search
LIST FOR LName=Search
```

Figure 2.3 – Sample program using the LIST FOR approach

Now suppose you type in the name Miller and press the Return key. The program displays the records for all ten Millers on the screen. The time required for the command file to display the Millers and return to the dot prompt is a little over 2 minutes on a floppy-disk system and about 32 seconds on a hard-disk system.

A second approach to this same problem is to use the FIND or SEEK commands to look up the first Miller in the Names index, then use the WHILE option to display the remaining Millers in the database, as in Figure 2.4.

Processing time for this second method of displaying all ten Millers, then redisplaying the dot prompt on the screen, is about 5 seconds on a floppy-disk system and less than 4 seconds with a hard disk.

Figure 2.5 compares the processing times for the two different methods. Both methods perform exactly the same task, but as you can see, the speeds differ dramatically.

```
***************** Method 2: FIND and LIST WHILE Approach.
CLEAR
USE Test INDEX Names
ACCEPT " List all people with what last name? " TO Search
SEEK Search
LIST WHILE LName = Search
```

Figure 2.4 – Sample program using the LIST WHILE approach

		Time Required	
Method	Commands Used	Hard Disk	Floppy Disk
1	LIST FOR	32 seconds	120 seconds
2	SEEK and LIST WHILE	3.79 seconds	5.57 seconds

Figure 2.5 – Comparison of searching time using two methods

Searching for Ranges

You can also use index files with the WHILE command to select ranges of data from the database. For example, to create a smaller database of only those individuals whose names begin with the letters M through P, you could use these commands:

USE Test
COPY TO Temp FOR LName >= "M" .AND. LName <= "P"

Depending on how many records fall within this range of letters, the copy process could take anywhere from 1 to 2 minutes. An index file speeds this up considerably:

USE Test INDEX Names
FIND M
COPY TO Temp WHILE LName <= "P"

Since the COPY command begins at the record pointer, which is now at M rather than A, this approach will take only 1 to 3 seconds, again depending on how many records are to be copied.

Now suppose you wanted to create a command file to let you view all records that fall within a range of dates. Figure 2.6 shows a small program that lets you do so without the use of an index file. This command file will require several minutes to list all the records within the specified range of dates.

```
**************************************** Date1.PRG
* --- Pull out records within a range of dates.

USE Test
CLEAR
STORE "        " TO Start,Finish
@ 10,2 SAY "Enter start date " GET Start PICTURE "99/99/99"
@ 12,2 SAY "Enter ending date " GET Finish PICTURE "99/99/99"
READ
*---------- Convert Character dates to Date types.
STORE CTOD(Start) TO Start
STORE CTOD(Finish) TO Finish

LIST FOR Date >= Start .AND. Date <= Finish
```

Figure 2.6 – Sample program to pull out records by date

As an alternative, you could create an index of the Date field with the following commands:

USE Test
INDEX ON Date TO Dates

Then you could use the second command file, shown in Figure 2.7, to display all records within a range of dates. This will cut the searching time down dramatically, to under 5 seconds in most cases (again depending on how many records fall within the specified range).

There is one problem with using the FIND or SEEK commands to locate the first occurrence of a record within a range of values: if the command doesn't find an exact match for the first value in the range, the rest of the program won't find *any* values within the range. Then you'll have to revert to the FOR method of locating records within a range, even though the process will probably take longer. But as you'll see in the systems we develop in later chapters, there are techniques for having the program "decide" for itself which method to use. For those of you who are already pretty sophisticated programmers, Figure 2.8 shows a sample. As you can see, if the program has no success with the SEEK command, it automatically drops into the FOR mode to locate the specified records.

Technical Aspects of Index Files

Let's take a minute to discuss the technical side of indices, to see why the FIND and WHILE approach always dramatically outperforms the FOR approach.

```
**************************************** Date2.PRG
* --- Sample program to pull out records by date.
USE Test INDEX Dates
CLEAR
STORE "          " TO Start,Finish
@ 10,2 SAY "Enter start date " GET Start PICTURE "99/99/99"
@ 12,2 SAY "Enter ending date " GET Finish PICTURE "99/99/99"
READ
*---------- Convert Character dates to Date types.
STORE CTOD(Start) TO Start
STORE CTOD(Finish) TO Finish

SEEK Start
LIST WHILE Date <= Finish
```

Figure 2.7 – Sample program to pull out all records in a range of dates

When you use the FOR option to search a database, dBASE always starts accessing the records from record 1 and reads every single record in the database directly from the disk. For example, if you have a small database with 11 names in it, three of which are Miller, dBASE performs 11 disk accesses to display the three Millers. Schematically, Figure 2.9 shows how the search process looks using a command with the FOR option.

```
***************************************** Date2.PRG
USE Test INDEX Dates
CLEAR
STORE "          " TO Start,Finish
@ 10,2 SAY "Enter start date " GET Start PICTURE "99/99/99"
@ 12,2 SAY "Enter ending date " GET Finish PICTURE "99/99/99"
READ
*---------- Convert Character dates to Date types.
STORE CTOD(Start) TO Start
STORE CTOD(Finish) TO Finish


SEEK Start

*------------------- Decide whether to proceed with SEEK approach
*------------------- or revert to the slower, safer FOR approach.
IF FOUND ()
    LIST WHILE Date <= Finish
ELSE
    LIST FOR Date >= Start .AND. Date <= Finish
ENDIF (not found)
```

Figure 2.8 – Range search with safety catch for "no-find" condition

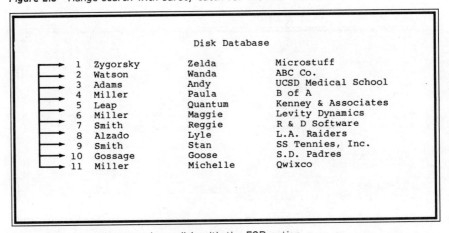

Figure 2.9 – Accessing records on disk with the FOR option

This approach is much like trying to find all occurrences of the topic "avocados" in a book without using an index. You'd have to start at page 1, read every page, and mark each occurrence of the word, even if the book contained 1,000 pages.

The dBASE INDEX command lets you do the equivalent of adding an index to that book. Furthermore, much (usually all) of that index is stored in the computer's RAM memory when the index is active, and RAM performs work at the speed of light compared with the pedestrian speeds of hard- or floppy-disk access. A dBASE index file stores key-field values and their record numbers in RAM in much the same way as an index in a book. For example, if you create an index of last names with the command INDEX ON LName TO Names, then the command USE Test INDEX Names, the computer's RAM will contain an index that looks something like Figure 2.10.

Like a book index, the names are sorted into alphabetical order. Next to each last name is the number of the record in which that name appears.

When you ask dBASE to find Miller, it goes directly to the first Miller in the index file in RAM. At that point, dBASE "knows" where the first Miller is in the database, because the record number (6) is stored right next to the name, as in Figure 2.11.

Now you can use the WHILE option rather than the FOR option to search for records; dBASE will start accessing the database at the current pointer position (record 6). Then it will skip to the next Miller (record 11),

```
        Last Name        Record Number

            Adams              3
            Alzado             8
            Gossage           10
            Leap               5
            Miller             6
            Miller            11
            Miller             4
            Smith              7
            Smith              9
            Watson             2
            Zygorsky           1
```

Figure 2.10 – An index file in RAM

and then the next (record 4). When it encounters the next entry in the index, it finds Smith. Since the WHILE option simply means "as long as," when dBASE encounters Smith, it stops accessing the database (the condition WHILE LName = "Miller" is no longer true). Hence it takes only 3 disk accesses, rather than 11, to pull out 3 Millers, as Figure 2.12 illustrates.

In this small database there won't be a dramatic improvement in processing speeds, but if you had an unindexed database with 10,000 records in it, 10 of which had the last name Miller, the command

LIST FOR LName = "Miller"

```
        Adams          3
        Alzado         8
        Gossage       10
        Leap           5
   ───▶ Miller         6   (FIND or  SEEK  positions
        Miller        11   pointer to the first Miller
        Miller         4   in RAM without accessing
        Smith          7   the disk.   dBASE  "knows"
        Smith          9   the first Miller is in
        Watson         2   record # 6).
        Zygorsky       1
```

Figure 2.11 – Pointer at the first Miller after FIND or SEEK commands

```
        Adams          3
        Alzado         8
        Gossage       10
        Leap           5
   ┌──▶ Miller         6   WHILE only accesses records "as long as"
   ├──▶ Miller        11   the last name is still Miller, hence
   └──▶ Miller         4   only three disk accesses in this example.
        Smith          7
        Smith          9
        Watson         2
        Zygorsky       1
```

Figure 2.12 – WHILE only accesses records as long as search condition is true

would require 10,000 disk accesses, which could take well over 30 minutes. If you use an index file to find and list only the records in which the last name is Miller, dBASE will make only 10 disk accesses, thereby eliminating 9,990 unnecessary ones and about 29 minutes and 55 seconds of wasted time!

Faster Math

The FIND and WHILE approach with an indexed database can offer significant time savings with other dBASE commands as well. For example, if you want dBASE to count the number of Millers in the database, you can use the following commands:

```
USE Test
COUNT FOR LName = "Miller"
```

This method requires about 15 seconds to display the fact that there are 10 Millers in the database, then redisplay the dot prompt. You can cut this time down significantly using these commands:

```
USE Test INDEX Names
FIND Miller
COUNT WHILE LName = "Miller"
```

Now dBASE performs the same task in about 1 second—quite a significant time saving!

The same technique can be used with the SUM and AVERAGE commands. To add up the Amount field for just the Millers, you can use the commands

```
USE Test
SUM Amount FOR LName = "Miller"
```

which would require over 17 seconds to accomplish. But the commands

```
USE Test INDEX Names
FIND Miller
SUM Amount WHILE LName = "Miller"
```

cut that down to about 2 seconds. Similarly, you can use the commands

```
FIND Miller
AVERAGE Amount WHILE LName = "Miller"
```

to determine the average of the Amount field in about 2 seconds.

Faster Reports

You can also use the WHILE command with the REPORT FORM command. For example, suppose you've already created a formatted report called MaiList with the CREATE REPORT command (or the Create Report option from the Assistant menu). To present the records for all the Millers in the report format, use these commands:

    USE Test INDEX Names
    REPORT FORM MaiList FOR LName = "Miller"

dBASE takes about 30 seconds to display all the Millers, then redisplay the dot prompt. But if you use the commands

    USE Test INDEX Names
    FIND Miller
    REPORT FORM MaiList WHILE LName = "Miller"

the same job can be completed in a slim 6 seconds!

Faster Copying

To copy portions of the Test database to a database called Temp, the commands

    USE Test INDEX Names
    COPY TO Temp FOR LName = "Miller"

require about 30 seconds to process on a hard disk. You can perform the same job using the commands

    USE Test INDEX Names
    FIND Miller
    COPY TO Temp WHILE LName = "Miller"

and trim the copying time down to a comfortable 2 seconds on a hard-disk system.

Faster Editing

Indexed files can also speed up the editing process. For example, suppose you want to browse through the database to edit data for one of the Millers. One approach would be to type the following commands:

    USE Test
    BROWSE

These commands set up the dBASE BROWSE screen with the names and addresses in their original order, as displayed in Figure 2.13. You'd have to press PgDn many times to scroll through the file and find the Millers. There's no telling how long it would take you to find the particular Miller you wish to edit, because the Millers are distributed randomly throughout the database.

If, on the other hand, you use the commands

USE Test INDEX Names
FIND Miller
BROWSE

the BROWSE screen displays the first Miller in the database, and all the remaining Millers immediately beneath it, as in Figure 2.14. There is no need to scroll through pages and pages of BROWSE screens to find the Miller you wish to edit, because dBASE displays all ten Millers immediately and simultaneously on one screen.

The disadvantage of this technique is that if you edit data in the key field, the entire BROWSE screen is instantly resorted, making it hard to track the cursor. However, you can type ^Home to call up the BROWSE menu, select Find, and enter a new last name to move to quickly.

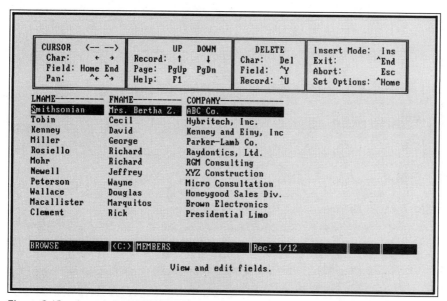

Figure 2.13 – An unindexed BROWSE screen

Similarly, if you wish to use the EDIT command to change the data for a particular Miller, you can use the following commands to quickly display the first Miller in the database on the EDIT screen:

USE Test INDEX Names
FIND Miller
EDIT

Each press of the PgDn key will immediately position you at the next Miller in the database, so once again you save a great deal of time by not having to scroll through the entire database searching for the individual Millers.

Faster Sorting

In some cases, a database should be physically sorted rather than indexed. For example, the UPDATE command works best if the file from which you are updating is presorted physically (that is, the entire database is already sorted without the use of an index file).

You could use the SORT command to create a sorted database called Temp from the Test database:

USE Test
SORT ON LName TO Temp

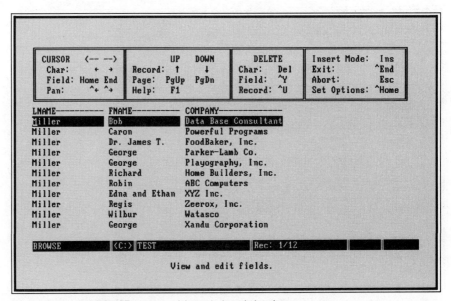

Figure 2.14 – A BROWSE screen with an indexed database

This can take anywhere from three to seven minutes with a 1,000-record database. But if the Names index file already exists, you can achieve the same result using these commands:

```
USE Test INDEX Names
COPY TO Temp
```

This approach is about 30 to 40 percent faster. When you copy an indexed file, with the index active, to another database, the records in the new database are sorted physically, just as though you'd used the SORT command.

Managing Multiple Index Files

In the previous examples, we compared processing times using an index file called Names. This index file contains only the LName field. But realistically, a mailing list will probably need to be accessed in two orders: by last and first names for printing a directory listing, and by zip code for bulk mailings.

To create an index file of last and first names, you need to use the Test database and enter the INDEX ON command like this:

```
USE Test
INDEX ON LName + FName TO Names
```

This causes dBASE to index the file on last names and then, if there is more than one record with the same last name, on first names.

A second index file, which we'll call Zips, maintains zip-code order for handling bulk mailings. To create this index file, simply type these commands:

```
USE Test
INDEX ON Zip TO Zips
```

The Test.DBF file now has two index files associated with it: Names.NDX and Zips.NDX. You can keep both index files active by using this command:

```
USE Test INDEX Names, Zips
```

With both index files specified in this fashion, all future modifications to the database with the APPEND, EDIT, BROWSE, READ, DELETE, PACK, or

REPLACE commands automatically update both indices, and once again you avoid having to resort or reindex the database.

The order in which you list active index files in the USE command plays an important role in how dBASE behaves. The first-listed index file is called the *primary* or *master* index. Whenever you use the LIST or REPORT commands or in any other way access the records in the database, dBASE displays them in the sorted order of the primary index file. Also, the FIND and SEEK commands work only with the primary index file. So when you use the databases with the active index files listed with the Names file first, the records will always appear sorted in last and first name order, and you will be able to use the FIND or SEEK command only to locate an individual by name. However, if you modify the database in any way, whether it be through the APPEND, EDIT, BROWSE, READ, DELETE, PACK, or any other command, both index files will automatically be updated and resorted.

Suppose you reverse the order of the active index-file names by using the command

USE Test INDEX Zips, Names

Whenever you display the records in the database, they will appear in zip-code order, and you will only be able to use the FIND or SEEK commands to locate a zip code. Again, of course, any changes that you make to the database through APPEND, EDIT, BROWSE, and so forth, will instantly update and resort both index files.

The ability to use multiple index files greatly increases speed and power in working with a database. If you use the SORT command on an unindexed file, every time you add new records to the database or edit the data, you need to sort twice to get the records in both alphabetical and zip-code order. In a database with 5,000 records, this can easily take 30 minutes or more. But by using two active index files, you can make changes without having to take any extra steps to maintain sort orders, eliminating 30 minutes of unnecessary sorting.

dBASE III PLUS allows a total of seven active index files with any given database, and they're all updated simultaneously when you make changes to the database. But for practical reasons, you may want to limit yourself to only two or three, as we'll discuss next.

There are some trade-offs we need to consider when using multiple index files. First, the more index files you have active at any given moment, the longer it generally takes to perform an APPEND, EDIT, or REPLACE procedure. For example, suppose you get carried away and decide to create five index files and keep them all active, like this:

USE Test INDEX Names, Zips, Cities, States, Amounts

You'll notice a definite delay between the time you fill one APPEND screen and the appearance of the next blank screen. In a database with over 1,000 records in it, the delay can be as much as 20 seconds, depending on how many fields are in each index file and the RAM capacity of your computer.

Second, each index takes up additional disk space, an especially important consideration with a floppy-disk system, where workspace is at a premium.

Two or three active index files are usually sufficient for most databases. The delays caused by a couple of active indices are relatively insignificant and are more than offset by the time saved using the FIND and WHILE commands and avoiding reindexing.

Points to Remember

There are some important points to keep in mind about indices and the SEEK and FIND commands.

First, the FIND command works only on an indexed field. Also, if a database is in use with multiple index files, the FIND command works only with the primary index file. For example, if you open the Test database with its two index files, using the command

USE Test INDEX Zips, Names

the FIND command can be used only to locate a zip code.

Second, if the data you want to look up are stored in a variable, you should use SEEK, rather than FIND, to locate the data in the index:

ACCEPT "Look up Whom? " TO Search
SEEK Search

However, you can optionally use FIND with a macro symbol (&) to tell dBASE you're looking for the contents of a memory variable:

ACCEPT "Look up whom? " TO Search
FIND &Search

Third, the FIND and SEEK commands do not support operators. For example, you cannot use commands such as these:

FIND Miller .OR. Smith
SEEK LNAME > Search

For this reason, FIND and SEEK limit you to fairly simple searches.

Fourth, there are situations where an index file can be used only to display records in sorted order, not to search with the FIND, SEEK, and WHILE commands. For example, suppose you want to produce a magazine-mailing list in zip-code order that includes only individuals whose subscriptions expire in July. To ensure zip-code order for the display, you need to use the command

USE Mail INDEX Zips

or

USE Mail INDEX Zips, Names

Now, to limit the display to expiration dates in July, you can't use the command FIND 07, because the Dates index is not in use. What you have to do is set up a filter condition instead, then print the mailing labels:

SET FILTER TO MONTH(Date) = 7
LABEL FORM TwoCol

This approach is not as fast as the FIND and WHILE approach, but there is no alternative, since the Zips index must be used to maintain the sort order.

Finally, if you add or modify data in the database without all of the index files being active, the unopened index files will be *corrupted* (temporarily ruined). Later, when you use the database with a corrupted index file, dBASE will display an error message such as RECORD OUT OF RANGE or END OF FILE FOUND UNEXPECTEDLY. If that occurs, you'll need to recreate the index files. To do so, use the database and make all index files active, then issue the REINDEX command:

USE Test INDEX Names, Zips
REINDEX

This will get everything back in shape, but your best bet is to avoid the problem entirely by always keeping all index files active when working with an indexed database.

We'll use index files frequently throughout this book, to maximize performance in the business systems we design. I'll discuss the rationale for each index at the time we create it, and we'll develop a number of techniques for putting indices to work for us, to reduce processing time.

Programming in
dBASE III PLUS

Many people tend to wince when they hear the term *programming*. The wince is probably caused by memories (or rumors) of unpleasant experiences with FORTRAN, COBOL, or BASIC: experiences that ended all interest in programming once and for all. Well, you'll be happy to hear that dBASE III PLUS makes programming relatively easy (some even say fun). A dBASE III PLUS program, or *command file,* is simply a series of commands stored in a file. The MODIFY COMMAND text editor allows you to create and edit these files; the DO command allows you to run them.

Let's take a look at some simple examples to give you a feel for the dBASE programming process. (If you already know how to program in dBASE II or III, you might want just to skim this chapter.)

Creating Command Files

dBASE III PLUS has a built-in *text editor* for creating command files. To use the text editor, type MODIFY COMMAND and the name of the file you want to create or edit. For our first example, we'll create a command file called Test.PRG.

If you're using a floppy-disk system, you might want to use the command SET DEFAULT TO B before creating the command file. Then, at the dot prompt, type

MODIFY COMMAND Test

and press the Return key. The screen displays a blank area for composing your command file, with a menu of control keys at the top. The control keys are described in Table 3.1.

Key	Function
↑ or ^E	Moves cursor up one line
↓ or ^X	Moves cursor down one line
← or ^S	Moves cursor left one character
→ or ^D	Moves cursor right one character
Del or ^G	Deletes character over cursor
Ins or ^V	Toggles INSERT mode on/off
End or ^F	Moves cursor right one word
Home or ^A	Moves cursor left one word
^N	Inserts blank line at cursor position
^T	Erases one word to right of cursor
^Y	Deletes entire line over cursor
^End or ^W	Saves command file
Esc or ^Q	Returns to dot prompt without saving edited command file
^KB	Reformats block of text (usually used only to format Memo field data)
^KF	Locates first occurrence of any word(s) you request
^KL	Locates next occurrence of word(s) specified with ^KF
^KR	Reads external command file (stored on disk) into current command file, starting at cursor position
^KW	Writes current command file to other file with different name

Table 3.1 – Screen control commands for MODIFY COMMAND

Now type in this simple two-line program:

CLEAR
? "Hi! I'm a test program."

Press the Return key after every line. If you make a mistake, use the arrow keys on the numeric keypad to move the cursor around and make changes. When you've typed both lines of the command file, press ^End or ^W to save the file. dBASE briefly displays a message stating that it is saving the command file, and then it returns to the dot prompt. dBASE also automatically adds the extension .PRG (program) to the file name.

To run your command file, type

DO Test

and press the Return key. The screen clears, displays the message

Hi! I'm a test program.

at the top of the screen, and returns to the dot prompt. Notice that dBASE obeyed both lines in the command file. First, it cleared the screen (CLEAR); then it printed the message "Hi! I'm a test program." (because of the ? command).

Now suppose you want to change something in your program. Just use MODIFY COMMAND again to make the changes. From the dot prompt, type

MODIFY COMMAND Test

dBASE displays the existing program on the screen, with the cursor under the first letter of the first line:

CLEAR
? "Hi! I'm a test program."

Using the cursor commands, change Hi to Hello. Then press ^End (or ^W) to save the edited program. When the dot prompt reappears, type the command DO Test and press the Return key. At this command, the new Test command file runs and displays the message

Hello. I'm a test program.

Now I realize this is not a very powerful program, but if you've never written a command file in your life, it's a good idea to start out simply. As we go along we'll be writing more complex programs, and in later chapters we'll actually develop very powerful systems of interrelated command files.

Interacting with the User

Our simple Test program only displayed information on the screen. But often a program needs to ask for information and then wait for an answer from the user. For example, a program that prints an inventory report might ask the user if the report should be displayed on the screen or sent to the printer, then display the report according to the user's answer. Several dBASE III PLUS commands will present a question to the user, wait for a response, and store that answer to a field or a file to try out these commands.

ACCEPT

The ACCEPT command presents a question to the user, waits for a response (followed by a press on the Return key), and stores that response to a Character-type memory variable. For example, the command

ACCEPT "Send report to printer? (Y/N) " TO YN

displays the message "Send report to printer? (Y/N) " on the screen and waits for an answer of any length. When the user presses Return, the answer is stored in a Character memory variable named YN. Since the ACCEPT command always stores information as Character data, it may not be the best choice when the program needs to ask about Numeric data.

INPUT

Like ACCEPT, the INPUT command displays a prompt on the screen and waits for the user's response (and a Return), but the type of data entered determines the type of variable created. For example, the command

INPUT "Enter your age " TO Age

presents the prompt "Enter your age" and stores the user's answer to a Numeric memory variable named Age. If data are to be stored as Character type, INPUT requires that the response be enclosed in quotation marks.

Be careful not to use the INPUT command to get Date information from the user. The command

INPUT "Enter today's date " TO Date

accepts information in date format (MM/DD/YY) but actually stores the entered date as a quotient. For example, 03/31/85 would be stored as the quotient of 3 divided by 31 divided by 85!

WAIT

The WAIT command presents a prompt and waits for a single keystroke (without a carriage return). If WAIT is used without a prompt or a memory variable specified, as in

WAIT

dBASE presents the message

Press any key to continue . . .

and waits for any key to be pressed (the keystroke is not stored in this case). However, if a prompt and memory variable are included in the command, as in

WAIT "Send data to printer? (Y/N) " TO YN

the program displays the message "Send data to printer? (Y/N)" and waits for a key to be pressed. In this case, the keystroke is stored in the memory variable YN as Character data.

The WAIT command always stores data as Character data. If you want to use WAIT to ask for a number, you must use the VAL function to convert the Character data to Numeric data:

WAIT "Enter your choice (1–5) " TO Choice
Choice = VAL(Choice)

In this example, the WAIT command accepts a single character, and the VAL function converts it to Numeric data.

READ

The READ command can be used to get field or memory-variable data. It is always used in conjunction with the @ . . . SAY . . . GET commands. Unlike ACCEPT, INPUT, and WAIT, READ works only with field or memory-input variable names that already exist. For example, to use the READ command to get information for a menu choice and store that information in a memory variable named Choice, you must create the Choice memory variable before using the READ command:

```
Choice = 0
@ 9,5 SAY "Enter choice " GET Choice
READ
```

This sequence of commands first creates a Numeric memory variable named Choice (Choice = 0), then displays the prompt "Enter choice" on row 9, column 5 of the screen. Then the program waits for an answer to the prompt (GET Choice) and stores that answer to the variable Choice (READ).

Looping with
DO WHILE . . . ENDDO

One of the most frequently used command structures in dBASE programming is the DO WHILE loop. A loop tells dBASE to repeat a series of commands as long as some condition exists. The DO WHILE command marks the start of the loop, and the ENDDO command marks the end of the loop.

Let's create an example to make this clearer. From the dot prompt, type

MODIFY COMMAND Count

to create a command file called Count.PRG. When the dBASE text editor appears, type the command lines exactly as in Figure 3.1. Then press ^End to save the file.

```
********************************************** Count.PRG
*---- Test of DO WHILE loop.

CLEAR
SET TALK OFF

STORE 1 TO X
DO WHILE X <= 20
   ? X
   X = X + 1
ENDDO

? "All Done"
```

Figure 3.1 – The Count command file

Let's discuss what each line in the program does. The first two lines are programmer comments. Since they are preceded by asterisks, dBASE does not attempt to process them as commands. The comments are useful, however, because they remind the programmer of the purpose of the command file. The CLEAR command simply clears the screen. SET TALK OFF keeps extraneous dBASE messages from appearing on the screen as the program is running. The STORE command creates a memory variable named X that contains the number 1 (an alternative form for this command is X = 1).

The next line begins the loop. DO WHILE X $<$ = 20 tells dBASE to start a loop that will repeat as long as X is either less than or equal to 20. The command ? X simply prints the current value of the memory variable X. Then the command X = X + 1 increments the current value of memory variable X by one. The ENDDO command marks the end of the DO WHILE loop. The last line prints the message "All Done" on the screen when the program is done (X $>$ 20). As long as X is less than or equal to 20, all commands within the loop are executed repeatedly. Every DO WHILE command in a program must have an ENDDO command associated with it.

To run this program, type

DO Count

The command file clears the screen and prints the increasing values of X until X is greater than 20. Then it prints the message "All Done". When the program is finished, the screen looks like Figure 3.2.

Figure 3.2 – Results of the Count command file

If you were to change the program so that the loop repeated as long as X was less than or equal to 40, and so that the values of X were printed on the same line (as in Figure 3.3), dBASE would count to 40 before display-ing the "All Done" message.

One of the most common uses for the DO WHILE command is to step through each record in a database and perform some action on every record. The command DO WHILE .NOT. EOF() is often used for this type of loop. In plain English, the command translates as "Do the following proce-dure as long as the last record in the database (EOF()) has not been encountered." We'll see many instances of this command in later chapters.

Making Decisions with IF . . . ELSE . . . ENDIF

A command file can also make decisions about what to do next, based on new information. If the choices are simple, the dBASE IF . . . ELSE . . . ENDIF commands can be used to handle the decision.

Again, let's create an example to help clarify the logic of the commands. From the dot prompt, type

MODIFY COMMAND IfTest

```
************************************************** Count.PRG
*---- Test of DO WHILE loop.

CLEAR
SET TALK OFF

STORE 1 TO X
DO WHILE X <= 40
    ?? X
    X = X + 1
ENDDO

? "All Done"
```

Figure 3.3 – The modified Count command file

When the dBASE text editor appears, type the command lines exactly as shown in Figure 3.4. Then save the file by pressing ^End.

Now let's look at each line in the command file. The first command after the programmer comments, CLEAR, simply clears the screen. The second line, ACCEPT "Turn on printer? (Y/N) " TO YN, presents the prompt

Turn on printer? (Y/N)

on the screen and waits for the user to type an answer and press the Return key. Whatever the user types is stored in a memory variable named YN. The next line, IF UPPER(YN) = "Y", checks to see if the upper-case equivalent of the user's answer is a capital Y (so it won't matter whether the user enters Y or y). If it is, dBASE performs all the lines between the IF and the ELSE statements. If the user's answer is not Y or y, dBASE skips the lines between the IF and ELSE statements and processes all lines between the ELSE and ENDIF statements instead.

To test the command file, type the command DO IfTest. The screen clears and the prompt

Turn on printer? (Y/N)

appears. If you type a Y and press the Return key, the program turns on the printer (SET PRINT ON), writes the message

You chose the printer.

```
************************************* IfTest.PRG
* --- Program to test the IF command.
CLEAR
ACCEPT "Turn on printer? (Y/N) " TO YN

* --- If answer is Yes, then...
IF UPPER(YN)="Y"
   SET PRINT ON
   ? "You chose the printer."
   EJECT
   SET PRINT OFF
* --- If answer is not yes, then...
ELSE
   CLEAR
   ? "You chose the screen."
ENDIF (End of IF clause)
```

Figure 3.4 – The IfTest command file

on paper, ejects the page from the printer (EJECT), and turns off the printer (SET PRINT OFF). If you type in any letter other than Y or y, the program clears the screen (CLEAR) and presents the message

You chose the screen.

In either case, the program returns to the dot prompt when done.

The last line in the command file, ENDIF, marks the end of the commands to be included within the IF clause. Every IF statement in a command file must have an ENDIF associated with it, but the ELSE statement is optional. For example, if you just want the program to turn on the printer when the user answers Yes to a prompt, you can use an IF . . . ENDIF clause without the ELSE, as in Figure 3.5.

An abbreviated form of the IF command is the IIF function, which can be used in a command line or even in a column definition in a report format or label format. The basic syntax for IIF is

IIF(this is true, do this, otherwise do this)

For example, the IIF command below prints the words Less Than if a memory variable named X is less than 10. Otherwise, the command line prints the words Greater Than:

? IIF(X<10,"Less Than","Greater Than")

The following IF command clause performs exactly the same task:

IF X < 10
    ? "Less Than"
ELSE

```
*************************** IfTest2.PRG
* --- Modified version of IfTest program.
CLEAR
WAIT "Turn on printer? (Y/N) " TO YN

IF UPPER(YN)="Y"
   SET PRINT ON
ENDIF

? "Hello Hello Hello"
SET PRINT OFF
```

Figure 3.5 – A program with an IF . . . ENDIF clause but no ELSE condition

? "Greater Than"
ENDIF

Notice that the big difference is that with the IIF function the ? (print) command begins the line, and the IIF function determines how to finish the command line. The IF command requires two separate ? commands to achieve the same goal.

Generally speaking, the IIF function is used where one condition leads to a single "either/or" result. The IF . . . ELSE . . . ENDIF commands can perform any number of steps based on the result of a condition.

Making Decisions with DO CASE . . . ENDCASE

A DO CASE . . . ENDCASE clause tells a program what to do based on any one of several mutually exclusive possibilities. A simple example is shown in Figure 3.6. If you want to try it out, type MODIFY COMMAND CaseTest to create the command file. After you've entered the program, save the file with ^End.

```
******************************* CaseTest.PRG
* --- Test the DO CASE command.
CLEAR
INPUT "Enter a number from 1 to 4 " TO X

DO CASE

   CASE X = 1
      ? "You entered one."

   CASE X = 2
      ? "You entered two."

   CASE X = 3
      ? "You entered three."

   CASE X = 4
      ? "You entered four"

   OTHERWISE
      ? "I said from one to four!"

ENDCASE
```

Figure 3.6 – The CaseTest command file

The first line of the program after the header, CLEAR, simply clears the screen. The next line, INPUT, presents the message

Enter a number from 1 to 4

on the screen and waits for the user to enter a response and press the Return key. The user's response is stored to a numeric memory variable named X. The next line, DO CASE, marks the beginning of the conditional clause. Beneath this, the lines CASE X = 1 and ? "You entered one." tell dBASE that if the user's answer is a 1 (X = 1), it should print the message "You entered one." The next CASE statement, CASE X = 2, prints the message "You entered two." if a 2 is typed in, and so forth for CASE X = 3 and CASE X = 4. The optional OTHERWISE command is used to cover all other possibilities. For example, if you run this command file and type in a number like 37 in response to the prompt, the program displays the message "I said from one to four!"

The ENDCASE statement must be used to mark the end of a DO CASE clause in a program; the OTHERWISE command is entirely optional.

The DO CASE command is most commonly found in menu programs, where the program displays a list of options to the user, waits for a response, then decides what to do next based on the user's menu choice. We'll see plenty of applications of the DO CASE . . . ENDCASE clause in the chapters that follow.

Structured Programming

You've probably noticed that all of the program examples so far have used many indentations. These aren't necessary from the computer's standpoint; the programs will run without them. They're used instead to make the program more readable and therefore easier to edit and debug.

Indenting commands within DO WHILE, IF, and DO CASE clauses is a structured programming technique, a concept popularized in the early 1970s to speed and simplify the design and development of large custom software systems.

The basic goal of structured programming is to create programs that are *self-documenting*. In less technical terms, the goal is to create programs that are easy for you and other programmers to read and therefore easy to debug or modify in the future. Naturally, programs are easier to read if they follow some basic structural techniques. For programming in dBASE III PLUS, the following rules of thumb can help make your command files easier to read and work with:

1. Use highly visible programmer comments in the program, to make it easy to locate the portions of the program that perform specific tasks.

2. Indent program lines within loops and decision-making routines, so you can see the beginning and ending points of these routines.

3. Try to select commands and variable names that are descriptive rather than cryptic.

These rules can best be demonstrated by comparing a program that doesn't use structured-programming techniques to one that does. Both programs perform exactly the same job: they present a main menu for a hypothetical library-management system, ask the user for his choice from the menu, then perform the task that the user requests.

Figure 3.7 presents a main-menu program that does not follow structure-programming rules of thumb. Let's look at it more closely.

```
*************************************** LibMenul.PRG
* --- Example of an unstructured menu program.
USE B:LIBRARY
DO WHILE .T.
CLEAR
@ 1,20 SAY "Library Management System"
@ 3,25 SAY "1. Add New Records"
@ 4,25 SAY "2. Print Reports"
@ 5,25 SAY "3. Edit Data"
@ 6,25 SAY "4. Exit"
STORE 0 TO CHOICE
@ 8,20 SAY "Enter choice (1-6) " GET CHOICE
READ
* BRANCH ACCORDINGLY
IF CHOICE=1
APPEND
ELSE
IF CHOICE=2
REPORT FORM LIBRARY
ELSE
IF CHOICE=3
EDIT
ELSE
* EXIT
IF CHOICE=4
RETURN
ENDIF
ENDIF
ENDIF
ENDIF
ENDDO
```

Figure 3.7 – *An unstructured main-menu program*

First of all, while there are some programmer comments in the program (lines preceded by a single asterisk), they are not highly visible. You need to skim through many lines of dBASE code to find the comment that reads * EXIT.

Second, there are no indentations in the program, making it difficult to figure out what's going on in this command file; the list of seemingly disconnected ENDIF commands near the bottom of the file is particularly daunting. If for some reason this program didn't work, it would not be easy to dig around and figure out why.

Third, there are some commands that are not very descriptive or even logical in a programming sense. For example, the fourth line reads

DO WHILE .T.

In the dBASE language, .T. means True. In fact, .T. is a value in the Logical data type, and is always true. Therefore, this line suggests that the loop will run forever. However, if you examine the lines below, you'll find that the loop won't truly run forever. When the user selects option 4 from the menu, dBASE executes a RETURN command, bypassing the loop and returning to the dot prompt.

At the bottom of the command file is the ENDDO command. There are no comments associated with it. If this were a larger program with many DO WHILE commands, it would be difficult to determine which DO WHILE this ENDDO belongs to. The same is true for the many ENDIF commands.

The program in Figure 3.8 performs exactly the same task as the previous program, but it is written using the rules for structured programming.

This structured command file is much easier to read than the preceding one. To begin with, all of the programmer's comments are visible at a glance. Furthermore, they're written in plain English syntax and upper- and lowercase. You don't have to dig around for them; they practically jump out at you. Also, there is a header at the top of the program that gives the name of the program and a brief description of what it does.

All the lines within the DO WHILE . . . ENDDO loop are indented four spaces. It is easy to find the beginning and ending points of the loop simply by running your finger down the margin from the DO WHILE command until you encounter an ENDDO in the same column.

This program also uses the DO CASE . . . ENDCASE commands to decide which task to perform, based on the user's request. This eliminates those confusing ENDIFs in the first program, making the program easier to read. The commands within the DO CASE . . . ENDCASE lines are also evenly indented, which makes the entire DO CASE . . . ENDCASE clause stand out.

Finally, some of the commands chosen are, in and of themselves, more descriptive than the commands in the first program. The command DO WHILE Choice # 4 immediately informs us that this loop is not going to repeat itself forever. It is going to stop when the memory variable Choice equals 4. So we need not dig around in the program to find the mysterious end to a seemingly infinite loop. In addition, the ENDDO command at the bottom of the program has a comment after it: (while Choice # 4). This simple comment pinpoints which DO WHILE command is associated with this ENDDO (many programs have more than one such loop) and makes the program easier to read and work with at a later date. In the dBASE programming language, anything that you type to the right of an ENDDO, ENDIF, or ENDCASE command is assumed to be a programmer's comment (it does not affect how the program runs). Therefore, you can do yourself a big favor by including these reminders about which particular DO WHILE, IF, or DO CASE each ENDDO, ENDIF, or ENDCASE command belongs to.

```
***************************************** Library.PRG.
* --------------------------- Library system main menu.
USE B:Library
STORE 0 TO Choice

DO WHILE Choice # 4
   CLEAR
   @ 1,20 SAY "Library Management System"
   @ 3,25 SAY "1. Add New Records"
   @ 4,25 SAY "2. Print Reports"
   @ 5,25 SAY "3. Edit Data"
   @ 6,25 SAY "4. Exit"
   @ 8,20 SAY "Enter choice (1-6) " GET Choice
   READ

   * ---------- Perform according to user's request.
   DO CASE

      CASE Choice = 1
           APPEND

      CASE Choice = 2
           REPORT FORM B:Library

      CASE Choice = 3
           EDIT

   ENDCASE
ENDDO (while Choice # 4)
* ------------------ When choice = 4, exit.
RETURN
```

Figure 3.8 – A structured main-menu program

While this may seem like a lot of bother for one small program, keep in mind that most systems are made up of many programs, not all of them small, and that can add up to a lot of code. Highly visible, descriptive comments make it much easier to spot a specific routine in a mass of program lines, and therefore make the program much easier to debug or modify later.

Debugging Techniques

Murphy's Law dictates that the total number of programs in the universe that run correctly the first time is always less than 1. A program can "crash" because of a simple error, such as a misspelled command or field name. These errors are very common and are quickly discovered when you run the program. Other common errors, such as a missing or misplaced ENDDO, ENDIF, or ENDCASE command, aren't always so easy to find, and the less common "logical" errors, with which the program runs without crashing but doesn't do exactly what you had in mind, can be really tough to identify.

dBASE III PLUS provides *debugging* tools that can be used to help find errors and correct them, thereby making the overall programming task a bit easier. For instance, when dBASE encounters a blatant error in a program, it displays the line with the error in it, the program in which the error occurred, and a warning message:

Cancel, Ignore, or Suspend? (C, I, or S)

These options have the following effects:

- Cancel terminates the program and returns to the dot prompt. Any private memory variables (those created within the command file) are erased.

- Suspend temporarily terminates the command file and returns to the dot prompt displaying the message "Do suspended". Private variables are not erased. The command file can be resumed at any time by entering the command RESUME at the dot prompt.

- Ignore ignores the error and attempts to continue processing at the next line in the command file.

(You can also force the Cancel, Ignore, and Suspend options to appear by pressing the Esc key while the command file is running. You need not wait for an error to occur.) For the rest of this chapter we'll discuss techniques you can use to help isolate and correct the error.

DISPLAY Commands

The various DISPLAY commands allow you to view the status of memory variables, open files, active index files, and other useful items of information that may be the cause of the error. If you suspend the program (rather than cancel it or ignore the error) you can enter the command

DISPLAY MEMORY

at the dot prompt to see the names, contents, and data types of all active memory variables. If the error message "Variable not found" accompanied your program error, you may have misspelled a variable name or attempted to use a nonexistent memory variable. Check for the existence and correct spelling of the variable name. If necessary, use the RESUME command to rerun the command file, then press Esc to terminate the program, then use MODIFY COMMAND to edit the command file so it creates the appropriate memory variable. (The "Variable not found" error can also be caused by attempting to access a field in an unopened database. DISPLAY STATUS and DISPLAY STRUCTURE will help determine that.)

DISPLAY MEMORY might also help uncover a "Data type mismatch" error. For example, the line

IF Today = "12/31/86"

will generate a "Data type mismatch" error if the Today variable is the Date data type (because "12/31/86" is Character data). Check the data types of variables using DISPLAY MEMORY and make corrections if necessary. (DISPLAY STRUCTURE will show the data types of fields in the active database.)

For a hard copy of the memory variables, you can use the command

DISPLAY MEMORY TO PRINT

The TO PRINT option also works with DISPLAY STRUCTURE and DISPLAY STATUS, discussed below.

The DISPLAY STRUCTURE command displays the structure of the database, including field names. Use this command to check for the existence (and correct spelling) of field names used in the program.

The DISPLAY STATUS command displays the names of all open databases, as well as the names and contents of all active (open) index files, as shown in Figure 3.9.

In this example, the currently selected database, in Select area 2, is C:Sales.DBF. It has no alias, other than the file name SALES in uppercase. The active index file associated with it is C:Sales.NDX, which is an index of the key field Part_ No. After you press any key to continue, the DISPLAY STATUS command also shows the status of all dBASE SET parameters (SET TALK, SET SAFETY, and so forth), function key assignments, the left margin setting for the printer, and the default disk drive.

Use these DISPLAY commands to look for clues when a programming error occurs. Perhaps you've simply misspelled a field or variable name, or attempted to use a nonexistent field or variable. Perhaps the wrong data-base or the wrong index file is in use. Or perhaps your data file is not on the default drive (or you forgot to set the default drive). The DISPLAY commands will help you find out. Fortunately, many of the problems identified in the debugging process are of this type, rather than being errors in program logic, and are therefore easily corrected.

```
. DISPLAY STATUS

Select area: 1, Database in Use: C:Master.DBF   Alias: MASTER
     Master index file: C:Master.NDX  Key: part_no

Currently Selected Database:
Select area: 2, Database in Use: C:Sales.DBF   Alias: SALES
     Master index file: C:Sales.NDX  Key: part_no

File search path:
Default disk drive: C:
Print destination: PRN:
Margin =     0
Current work area =    2

Press any key to continue..._
```

Figure 3.9 – Example of results of DISPLAY STATUS command

HISTORY

At any time in your work with dBASE III PLUS, you can enter the command

DISPLAY HISTORY

to view the last 20 commands you've entered at the dot prompt. These 20 commands will not include lines from a command file, unless you perform certain steps first.

First of all, at the dot prompt, you can use the SET HISTORY command to determine how many lines will be recorded. When recording from a program, you may want to increase the default value of 20 to perhaps 50 or more, as in the command below:

SET HISTORY TO 50

Next, before you run your program, enter the following command:

SET DOHISTORY ON

This ensures that command file lines are recorded in the history file.

When a program error occurs, you can suspend operation and from the dot prompt enter the command

DISPLAY HISTORY

or

LIST HISTORY

to view the last 50 commands. (DISPLAY pauses the screen every 22 lines; LIST does not. You can use the TO PRINT option with either command.)

The SET DOHISTORY ON command will slow a program's performance dramatically. Therefore, when not debugging, be sure to enter the command

SET DOHISTORY OFF

at the dot prompt.

CLOSE and CLEAR

If a program that has several files open at once crashes, chances are the files will still be open when you attempt to run the program again. If you get the error message "File already open" when rerunning a command file, just enter the command CLEAR ALL or CLOSE DATABASES at the dot prompt, then try again. This will allow you to test the program from "neutral ground."

SET TALK ON

The command SET TALK OFF is often used in program files to keep dBASE's feedback messages from appearing on the screen as the program is running. But if you're having a problem getting a program to run correctly, these messages can be very helpful, so just remove the SET TALK OFF command from the program temporarily, or put an asterisk in front of it to make dBASE ignore it. Then, from the dot prompt, type SET TALK ON before you run the command file. Watch the various messages that appear on the screen for clues to what might be amiss.

SET ECHO ON

The SET ECHO ON command allows you to see each line in a command file as the program is running. To see the entire program echoed, just type SET ECHO ON from the dot prompt before running the program. Or, if you know that an error is somewhere in a small part of the program, put the SET ECHO ON command right before that spot in the command file. (Remember to use SET ECHO OFF when you've finished debugging.)

SET STEP ON

If SET ECHO ON presents commands too quickly to be read or analyzed, use the SET STEP ON command to slow things down. With both ECHO and STEP ON, dBASE displays each line of the command file as it is being processed, pauses after each line, and displays this message:

Press SPACE to step, S to suspend, or Esc to cancel . . .

Just press the Space bar to watch the next program line being processed, press the S key to suspend the command file, or press the Esc key to stop the program and return to the dot prompt.

The STEP option allows you to control the progress of the program, so you can watch the logic of the program unfold as dBASE executes each command. This is a good technique for finding those logical errors that let a program run without crashing, but also without doing exactly what you had in mind. If the STEP option doesn't let you solve the problem, you can break out the heavy artillery with the DEBUG command.

SET DEBUG ON

The SET DEBUG ON command sends every echoed statement in the program to the printer. (With DEBUG, it's best to use SET ECHO ON and SET STEP OFF.) You can use the printed copy of the echoed lines to study each step in the program in a concentrated fashion.

Connect the Clauses

Perhaps the best overall debugging technique is to make a hard copy of the command file and then draw lines to connect all the IF, DO CASE, and DO WHILE commands with their ENDIF, ENDCASE, and ENDDO commands. As an instructor, I've found that a large percentage of the most stubborn and mysterious program errors are caused by missing or misplaced ENDDO, ENDIF, and ENDCASE commands.

You can use the dBASE TYPE command with the TO PRINT option to create a hard copy of the command file:

TYPE Test.PRG TO PRINT

Once you get the printed copy, use a pen or pencil to draw the connecting arrows, as in Figure 3.10.

Once you have the arrows drawn, check to make sure there are no left-over DO CASE, ENDCASE, DO WHILE, ENDDO, IF, or ENDIF commands. (The Debug command file in Chapter 21 rewrites command files so that the indentations are correct and informs you of any missing ENDDO, ENDIF, or ENDCASE commands.) Also, look for lines that cross over one another, which may be indicative of a logic problem. For example, the program in Figure 3.11 with crossed-over arrows is likely to cause problems. Use MODIFY COMMAND to correct these logic problems and then be sure to test the program again.

The Most Common Programming Errors

To close this section, I'll summarize the most common programming errors and the best approaches to solving them.

Data Type Mismatches

These are caused by trying to treat Character data as Numeric or Date data as Character. For example, if you enter the command

LIST FOR Date = "01/01/85"

and the Date field is stored as Date data, dBASE responds with the message "Data type mismatch" because the quotation marks indicate that the date is Character data. Date will have to be converted to Character data, so that the types match (LIST FOR DTOC(Date) = "01/01/85"). A data-type mismatch occurs whenever two different data types are being compared or combined. Use the DISPLAY MEMORY and DISPLAY STRUCTURE commands to check the data types of the entries being compared.

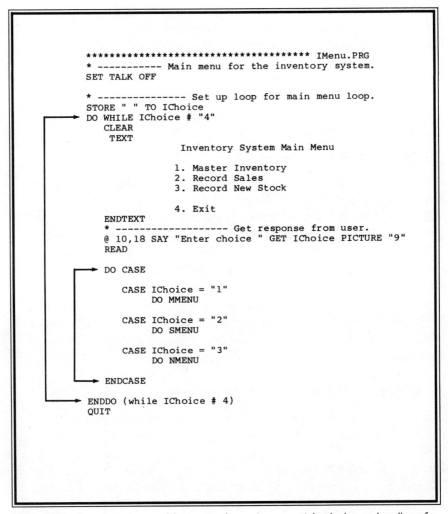

```
*************************************** IMenu.PRG
* ----------- Main menu for the inventory system.
SET TALK OFF

* --------------- Set up loop for main menu loop.
STORE " " TO IChoice
DO WHILE IChoice # "4"
     CLEAR
     TEXT
                    Inventory System Main Menu

                    1. Master Inventory
                    2. Record Sales
                    3. Record New Stock

                    4. Exit
     ENDTEXT
     * -------------------- Get response from user.
     @ 10,18 SAY "Enter choice " GET IChoice PICTURE "9"
     READ

     DO CASE

          CASE IChoice = "1"
               DO MMENU

          CASE IChoice = "2"
               DO SMENU

          CASE IChoice = "3"
               DO NMENU

     ENDCASE

ENDDO (while IChoice # 4)
QUIT
```

Figure 3.10 – Sample program with arrows drawn to connect beginning and ending of clauses

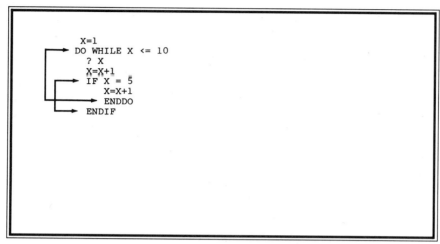

```
        X=1
    ┌→  DO WHILE X <= 10
    │     ? X
    │     X=X+1
    │ ┌→  IF X = 5
    │ │     X=X+1
    │ └──→  ENDDO
    └────→  ENDIF
```

Figure 3.11 – *Arrows show a cross-over, which might indicate a problem*

Invalid Function Argument

This error is also caused by confusing data types. For example, if memory variable X is a Numeric data type and you attempt to perform a command such as ? UPPER(X), you'll receive an error message, because the UPPER function converts only Character data to uppercase. dBASE will display the message "Invalid function argument" because the argument (X) is numeric, and the UPPER function requires Character data. Table 3.2 shows the dBASE functions and their "legal" argument data types.

Misspelled Commands and Field/Variable Names

This error prevents dBASE from finding the command or name in memory. If a program contains a misspelled command, dBASE responds with this message:

★ ★ ★ Unrecognized command verb.

You'll need to correct the spelling or syntax of the command in the program. If you attempt to use a memory variable or field name that does not exist (even if only because it's misspelled), dBASE will display the message

Variable not found.

Use the DISPLAY MEMORY commands to check the memory variables. Use the DISPLAY STATUS and DISPLAY STRUCTURE commands to see what files are in use and what fields are available.

Numeric	Character	Date	None
ABS(n)	ASC(c)	CDOW(d)	BOF( )
CHR(n)	AT(c,c)	CMONTH(d)	COL( )
EXP(n)	CTOD(c)	DOW( )	DATE( )
FIELD(n)	FILE(c)	DTOC(d)	DBF( )
FKLABEL(n)	GETENV(c)	MONTH(d)	DELETED( )
INT(n)	ISALPHA(c)	YEAR(d)	DISKSPACE( )
LOG(n)	ISLOWER(c)		EOF( )
MAX(n,n)	ISUPPER(c)		ERROR( )
MIN(n,n)	LEFT(c,n)		FKMAX( )
MOD(n,n)	LEN(c)		FOUND( )
NDX(n)	LOWER(c)		INKEY( )
ROUND(n,n)	LTRIM(c)		ISCOLOR( )
SPACE(n)	REPLICATE(c,n)		LUPDATE( )
SQRT(n)	RIGHT(c,n)		MESSAGE( )
STR(n,n,n)	RTRIM(c)		OS( )
	STUFF(c,n,n,c)		PROW( )
	SUBSTR(c,n,n)		READKEY( )
	TRIM(c)		RECCOUNT( )
	TYPE(c)		RECSIZE( )
	UPPER(c)		ROW( )
	VAL(c)		TIME( )
			VERSION

Table 3.2 – Functions and argument types

Record out of Range

This error is caused by attempting to go to a nonexistent record (for instance, GOTO 99 in a database with only 98 records). It often occurs when the index file in use has been corrupted. Use the INDEX ON or REINDEX command to reconstruct the index file.

Errors in Logic

When a program contains errors in logic, it continues to run but does not perform the tasks you had in mind. The logic of the program is simply not the logic you intended. In many cases, these errors are caused by missing or misplaced ENDDO, ENDIF, or ENDCASE commands. Make a hard copy of the program and connect all DO WHILE, IF, and DO CASE commands with their respective ENDDO, ENDIF, and ENDCASE commands. In some cases, logic errors are caused by simply putting the right command in the wrong place (for example, putting a command inside an IF . . . ENDIF clause when it belongs outside the clause). Use the ECHO, STEP, and DEBUG options to connect the clauses if you can't spot the problem readily.

Too Many Files Open

The "Too many files are open" error is usually caused by a missing Config.SYS file on the boot-up disk. See the introduction to this book for a discussion of Config.SYS.

In this chapter we've discussed some basic commands and techniques used in creating, structuring, editing, running, and debugging dBASE III PLUS command files. The programs presented throughout this book expand on these examples and give you many opportunities to practice dBASE programming techniques. Though all of the programs have been fully tested and debugged, there's a chance that you'll make some simple typographical errors or omissions when you copy a program, so remember to use the various debugging aids to help you locate and solve any problems that may arise.

Turning Ideas into Working Software: System Design

Writing a custom software system is much like writing a term paper or a book: it's a highly creative task that usually starts as a very general idea and finally grows into a polished working product. As with any creative product, the first question in writing custom software is always "Where do I begin?" And once you do get started, the next question, which pops up repeatedly, is "Where do I go from here?" If the project is to be successful, you'll need answers to these questions, so in this chapter we'll discuss program design and development: the art and science of turning great ideas into working software.

Any software project, large or small, can be broken into a series of steps, starting with a basic idea and ending with a finished product. These are the steps:

1. Define the goal of the project and the user level (problem definition).

2. Specify the input and output (I/O specification).

3. Design the database structure (database design).

4. Isolate specific program functions (modular program design).

5. Write the individual programs (module development).

6. Test and make corrections (testing and debugging).

We'll discuss each of these steps in more detail in the following sections.

Problem Definition

A software project is like a puzzle to be solved. Before you can begin, you need to decide just what it is you're trying to solve. In other words, you must *define* the problem.

Problem definition for a software project usually starts out as a vague description of the actual problem, such as "Create a membership-management system." We'll need, however, to be a bit more specific if we want project development to go smoothly. For instance, who is going to use this system? The experience level of the end user is also a key element in system design, so let's refine the problem definition to include it. For example, "Create a membership-management system that can be used by an individual with little or no computer experience."

We want to develop a mailing-list system for an inexperienced user, but what do we want it to do? To define the problem more specifically, it helps to think in terms of the specific tasks that a database-management system can perform:

- Add information to a database

- Sort data into a meaningful order

- Search for sets of data by type or range

- Display data in any report format desired, and include calculations and summaries

- Allow changes and deletions to a database

- Check for duplications in the database

With these basic database capabilities in mind, it becomes easier for us to define the task more specifically: Generate a membership-management system that allows an inexperienced user to do the following:

- Add new names and addresses to the database

- Sort the data into alphabetical order by last name and by zip code for bulk mailing

- Select specific data by zip code, name, city, or expiration date

- Print mailing labels and a directory, and make a merge file for printing form letters

- Make changes to the database, and delete names and addresses

- Check the database for duplicate records

This is much better. Now the large task of creating a membership system is clearly specified and, more importantly, broken down into smaller tasks that are relatively easy to accomplish.

But we can be even more specific: Generate a membership-management system that allows an inexperienced user these capabilities:

- Add new names and addresses to the database

- Use a custom screen, including instructions for controlling the cursor, rather than the usual APPEND screen

- Sort data into alphabetical order by last name and by zip code for bulk mailing

- Choose the sort order just before printing mailing labels or a directory or making a merge file

- Select specific data by zip code, name, city, or expiration date

- The option of specifying a field to search on (for example, zip code) and a value to search for (92122) just before printing mailing labels or a directory or making a merge file

- Print mailing labels and a directory, and make a merge file for printing form letters

- Display the labels and directory on the screen or the printer, or create a text file of data to be inserted in form letters

- Make changes to the database and delete names and addresses

- Look up information to edit or delete based on name rather than record number

- Check the database for duplicate records

- Compare last name, address, and zip code of each record with every other record in the database, and allow the user to remove duplicates

As the problem definition becomes more specific, our task becomes less overwhelming. Clearly defined goals are always easier to attain than vague, general ones.

Input-Output (I/O) Specification

The next step in developing a custom software system is to think about the problem in terms of what we want to go into the computer and what we want to come out. Let's not worry about what's in between just yet. In our Membership System, we want the computer to produce three items:

- Mailing labels
- A directory
- A file for form letters

Clear enough, but we need to refine the output definition still further:

- Mailing labels contain name, company, address, city, state, and zip code.
- A directory contains name, company, address, city, state, zip code, phone number, and expiration date.
- A form-letter file contains name, company, address, city, state, and zip code.

Now, defining the output really determines the input, so after we remove the redundancies in the output, we know what the input must be:

Name
Company
Address
City
State
Zip code
Phone number
Expiration date

This is a relatively simple application, so specifying the I/O requirements was easy.

Database Design

Now that we've decided what information needs to be stored, we can begin designing the database. We need to think about the type of data in each field and how much space the data require. We can break out the fields in our membership database as in Figure 4.1.

Notice that Zip code and Phone number are both Character data types rather than Numeric. Zip codes are best stored as characters because some foreign zip codes contain letters and spaces (such as AO7 331), and some American zip codes contain leading zeros (00123) or hyphens (92038-2892), which would not be handled properly by the Numeric data type.

Telephone numbers also are best treated as Character data, since they usually contain nonnumeric characters (for example, (800) 555-1212) that dBASE regards as mathematical operators if we assign a Numeric data type.

At this stage of the process, go ahead and load dBASE and create the database file. For this system, we'll name the database Members.DBF, so at the dot prompt type the commands

SET DEFAULT TO B
CREATE Members

and give the file the structure shown in Figure 4.2.

Field No.	Contents	Type	Width	Decimals
1	Last name	Character	20	0
2	First name	Character	20	0
3	Company	Character	20	0
4	Address	Character	25	0
5	City	Character	20	0
6	State	Character	5	0
7	Zip code	Character	10	0
8	Phone number	Character	13	0
9	Expiration Date	Date	8	0

Figure 4.1 – Database fields with space requirements

Now we need to consider what index files we need. The most important consideration here is what the most frequently used sort orders will be. In a mailing system this is pretty obvious: we need the records sorted by last and first names for directories and by zip code for bulk mailing.

The second consideration is the kinds of searches we're likely to do. Any type of searching that is to be performed regularly might justify the use of an index file. In the Membership System, we'll probably want to look up members by name fairly often, to make changes to their records, delete records, or find addresses and phone numbers. An index file of names would help us find this information quickly.

So we'll need just two index files for the Members database: one by last and first names and the other by zip code. We'll call the index file of names Names.NDX and use the following commands to create it:

USE Members
INDEX ON UPPER(LName) + UPPER(FName) TO Names

(We've used the UPPER function to make all the names uppercase, for more accurate sorting and easier searching. We've combined the LName and FName fields with the plus (+) sign to ensure that identical last names will be further sorted alphabetically by first name.) We'll call the index file of zip codes Zips.NDX and create it with these dBASE commands:

USE Members
INDEX ON Zip to Zips

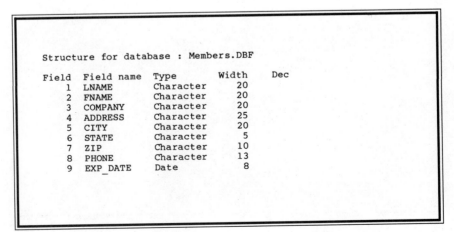

```
Structure for database : Members.DBF

Field   Field name  Type        Width   Dec
    1    LNAME       Character      20
    2    FNAME       Character      20
    3    COMPANY     Character      20
    4    ADDRESS     Character      25
    5    CITY        Character      20
    6    STATE       Character       5
    7    ZIP         Character      10
    8    PHONE       Character      13
    9    EXP_DATE    Date            8
```

Figure 4.2 – The Members database

Now that we've created the database and indices, we can start thinking about the command files (programs) we'll need to manage the Membership System.

Modular Program Design

As we discussed earlier, the easiest way to develop any software system is to break it down into small, manageable chunks. The problem-definition phase of the design has already helped us do this, but now we have to think in terms of how the user (in this case, one with little or no computer experience) is going to interact with the system.

To make the Membership System easy to use, we'll have the computer display a menu of options, as in Figure 4.3. All the user will have to do is select an option, and our program will take over from there. (Since we want the sorting and searching functions to be part of the printing program in this system, we'll just include those under option 2. That way, when the user asks to print mailing labels or a directory, the computer will simply ask how to sort the data and what information to select.)

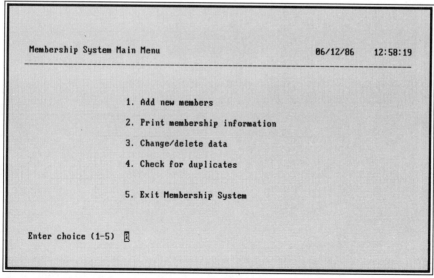

```
Membership System Main Menu                        06/12/86    12:58:19
--------------------------------------------------------------------------

                        1. Add new members

                        2. Print membership information

                        3. Change/delete data

                        4. Check for duplicates


                        5. Exit Membership System



Enter choice (1-5)  ▊
```

Figure 4.3 – Menu options for the Membership System

Now, rather than attempt to write one very large program to handle all these tasks, we'll create a separate, smaller program for each individual task. This modular design will make the programming task much simpler and the program logic much easier to follow.

In modular program design, we can draw the various tasks of the software system as boxes in a hierarchical structure. This allows us to see how the various parts of the system are related. Figure 4.4 shows the modular design for the Membership System software.

We can see from the diagram that the Membership System will consist of five programs: the main menu, a program to add new members, a program to select and print data in a chosen order and format, a program to allow changes and deletions, and a program to check for duplicates. The main menu program will be the master program that turns control over to the appropriate subprogram to perform the task the user requests.

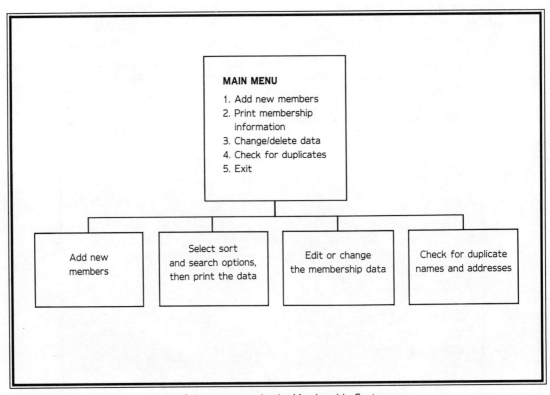

Figure 4.4 – Hierarchical structure of the programs in the Membership System

Writing and Testing Program Modules

The next step is to start developing the actual programs. It isn't very helpful to discuss this in general terms, so in the next chapters we'll use the Membership System design we've just developed to help us actually create the programs for an entire system. Then we'll test and debug the programs, to be sure they actually work.

Membership System
Main Menu

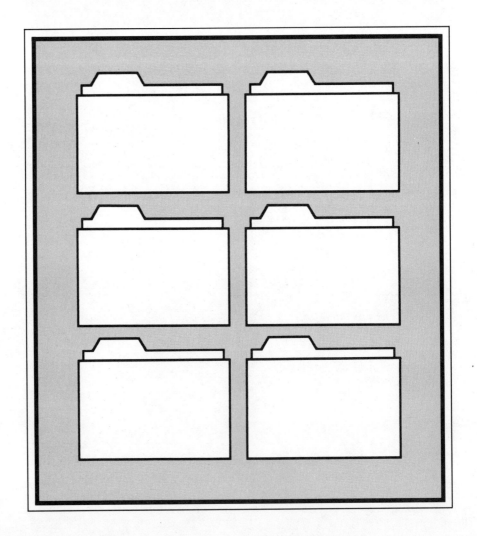

In Chapter 4 we defined the goals of our project, identified the information we need, created the database, and laid out the modular design for the Membership System. Now we can begin writing the command files that will make it all happen.

At the top of our hierarchy of programs is the main-menu program. We'll give that program the name Members.PRG and develop and test it first.

Getting Started: Writing the Pseudocode

The first step in writing a command file is to decide what the program needs to do and develop the plain English pseudocode that provides a working outline.

A menu program needs to perform three main tasks:

1. Set up system parameters

2. Present a list of options to the user and wait for a selection

3. Branch to the appropriate program to perform the task the user selected

So our pseudocode for the Members command file will look something like this:

Set up system parameters

Set up loop to perform tasks and then repeat menu

    Clear screen

    Present menu of options

        1. Add new members

        2. Print membership information

        3. Change/delete data

        4. Check for duplicates

        5. Exit Membership System

    Wait for user to select option

    Branch to appropriate program

        If choice = 1, branch to append program

        If choice = 2, branch to printing program

        If choice = 3, branch to editing program

        If choice = 4, branch to duplicates program

    On return to main program, redisplay menu

    Quit (if user selects exit)

Once we've mapped out the program in pseudocode, we can load dBASE and start writing the command file.

Writing the Command File

For the examples in this book, we'll use the dBASE MODIFY COMMAND editor, though you can use any text editor or word processor you like, as long as it has a "nondocument" mode for creating programs (see Appendix B for information on linking with word processors).

From the dBASE dot prompt, type in the command

MODIFY COMMAND Members

and press the Return key. An empty screen for creating the command file will appear on your monitor. At this point, just type each command line, using the arrow keys on the numeric keypad to move the cursor around and make changes.

We'll begin by putting in the name of the program and a brief description of what it does, then set the various dBASE parameters to be used in the Membership System. (Remember that the lines preceded by asterisks are programmer comments. These are just for our own information and do not affect the program in any way.)

```
* * * * * * * * * * * * * * * * * * * * *  Members.PRG
*
* Main menu for Membership System
*
SET STATUS OFF
SET DEFAULT TO B
SET TALK OFF
SET HELP OFF
SET BELL OFF
```

The SET commands control various system parameters. SET STATUS OFF removes the status bar from the bottom of the screen. SET DEFAULT TO B makes drive B the default drive for accessing the disk. For a system with a hard disk, this should be changed to SET DEFAULT TO C. The TALK, HELP, and BELL parameters control miscellaneous dBASE screen messages that won't be needed in our Membership System, so set them all OFF.

Now we'll create a variable called ULine, which we'll use throughout the Membership System to draw lines below the headings on menu screens:

```
*------------- Create underline variable, ULine.
ULine = REPLICATE ("_",80)
```

We need to set up a loop in our program so the menu is displayed each time a task is completed, until the user requests to exit. First we create a variable called Choice where we can store the user's menu selection. Then we can set up a loop that says "Repeat all the steps in this loop until the user selects option 5 to exit."

```
*------------------ Display menu and get user's choice.
Choice = 0
DO WHILE Choice # 5
```

Within the loop, we want the program to clear the screen, create a heading, display the menu, and wait for a response from the user. The next lines of code handle those tasks:

```
CLEAR
@ 2,1 SAY "Membership System Main Menu"
@ 2,50 SAY DTOC(DATE( )) + "     " + TIME( )
@ 3,0 SAY ULine
?
?
TEXT
          1. Add new members
          2. Print membership information
          3. Change/delete data
          4. Check for duplicates

          5. Exit Membership System
ENDTEXT
@ 24,1 SAY "Enter choice (1–5) " GET Choice;
    PICTURE "9" RANGE 1,5
READ
```

The first three @ . . . SAY statements create a screen heading to identify the menu and display the current system date (DTOC(DATE( ))) and time (TIME( )). The TEXT segment displays the actual menu choices. The user's response is stored in the memory variable Choice (GET Choice). The PICTURE statement ensures that only a single numeral will be accepted by the program, and the RANGE option ensures that the number will be between 1 and 5 (inclusive). The READ command activates the GET Choice command and waits for the user to enter a number.

Once the user selects a menu option, the Members program must branch to another program to perform the selected task. (Though we haven't created any of these other programs yet, I've gone ahead and given them names here, just to get this program written.) A DO CASE clause can handle this best:

```
*-------------------- Branch to appropriate program.
    DO CASE
        CASE Choice = 1
            DO AddNew
        CASE Choice = 2
            DO Reports
```

```
        CASE Choice = 3
            DO EditDel
        CASE Choice = 4
            DO DupCheck
ENDCASE
```

When the user enters a menu choice, the command file will branch to the appropriate program, perform the selected task, and return to the menu program. At that point, we want to redisplay the menu, so we need to close the DO WHILE loop:

ENDDO (while Choice # 5)

Once the user decides to exit from the Membership System (option 5), the program can close the database files, clear the screen, and quit dBASE. So the last three lines in the program are

CLOSE DATABASES
CLEAR
*QUIT

I placed an asterisk in front of the QUIT command to inactivate it for now, since it will be more convenient during development of the system to return to the dBASE dot prompt than all the way to the operating system A> (or C>) prompt. After all the programs are written and tested, we can come back and remove the asterisk.

Figure 5.1 shows our entire Members command file. Once you've proof-read it, you can save it by pressing ^End or ^W. The dBASE dot prompt then reappears.

Will It Work?
Testing the Program

Since we haven't developed any other command files yet, we really can't test this program thoroughly, but let's do what we can.

From the dot prompt, type this command:

DO Members

The screen clears and the main menu appears as in Figure 5.2.

```
************************************************** Members.PRG
*
*   Main menu for Membership System
*
SET STATUS OFF
SET DEFAULT TO B
SET TALK OFF
SET HELP OFF
SET BELL OFF

*------------------ Create underline variable, ULine.
ULine = REPLICATE ("_",80)

*------------------ Display menu and get user's choice.
Choice = 0
DO WHILE Choice # 5
    CLEAR
    @ 2,1 SAY "Membership System Main Menu"
    @ 2,60 SAY DTOC(DATE()) + "     " + TIME()
    @ 3,0 SAY ULine
    ?
    ?
    TEXT
                    1. Add new members

                    2. Print membership information

                    3. Change/delete data

                    4. Check for duplicates


                    5. Exit Membership System
    ENDTEXT
    @ 24,1 SAY "Enter choice (1-5) " GET Choice;
        PICTURE "9" RANGE 1,5
    READ

*------------------ Branch to appropriate program.
    DO CASE
        CASE Choice = 1
            DO AddNew
        CASE Choice = 2
            DO Reports
        CASE Choice = 3
            DO EditDel
        CASE Choice = 4
            DO DupCheck
    ENDCASE

ENDDO (while Choice # 5)

CLOSE DATABASES
CLEAR
*QUIT
```

Figure 5.1 – The completed Members command file

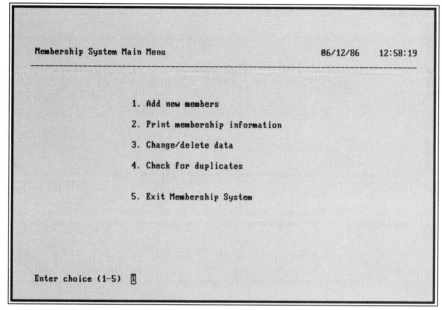

Figure 5.2 – Main menu shown from Members command file

Now try selecting a number beyond the acceptable range of menu choices, such as 9. dBASE displays this message at the upper right of the screen:

RANGE is 1 to 5 (press SPACE)

Press the Space bar and try again. This time, select option 5 to exit the menu and go back to the dot prompt, so we can develop some more programs.

Membership System
Append Program

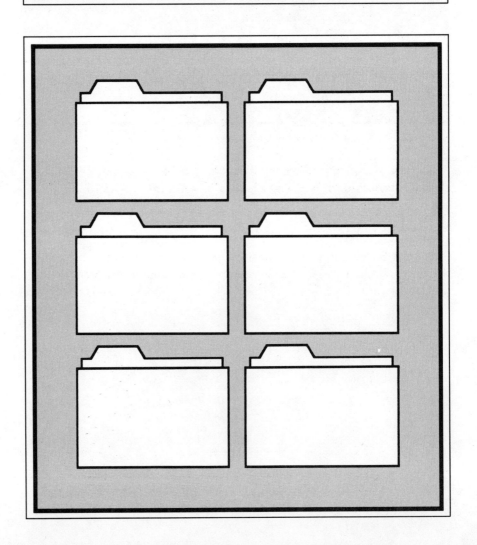

In this chapter we'll use the dBASE III PLUS Screen Painter to develop a custom form (or screen) for entering data into the Members database. Then we'll develop a program to display the screen so the user can add some records and be returned to the main menu automatically when done.

Creating the Form

We'll develop a custom form named AddNames.FMT for the Membership System. To begin, enter the following command at the dot prompt:

CREATE SCREEN AddNames

This brings up the Screen Painter menu, as shown in Figure 6.1.

First, you need to tell dBASE which database this form will be used for. Follow these steps:

1. Choose the Select Database File option.

2. Specify Members.DBF.

Now, as a shortcut to developing a form, we can have the Screen Painter put together a general purpose form, which we, in turn, will modify. (This is easier than trying to create the form completely from scratch.)

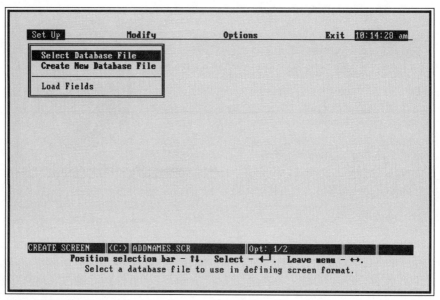

Figure 6.1 – The Screen Painter menu

Follow these steps:

1. Select Load Fields.
2. Highlight each field and press Return.

You'll notice that as you press ↓, the highlight moves through each field name on the menu. If you press Return while a field name is highlighted, a triangle appears next to it, indicating that the field is selected for inclusion on the custom form. In this exercise, you want to select all the fields in this fashion. Press ← after all the field names have triangles next to them, so your screen looks like Figure 6.2.

Notice that there are field *labels* (such as LNAME, FNAME, and so on). There are also field *highlights,* which show where the reverse video portion of the screen will appear when the form is used for entering and editing data. The Xs inside the field highlights show the number of characters in each field. The 9s show where numeric (or date) values will be entered.

The portion of the screen where the field labels and highlights appear is called the *Blackboard,* because it's easy to add, erase, and move things around. I suspect that you already have some experience with the Blackboard. But just in case you don't, we'll go over the basic steps used in creating a custom form here.

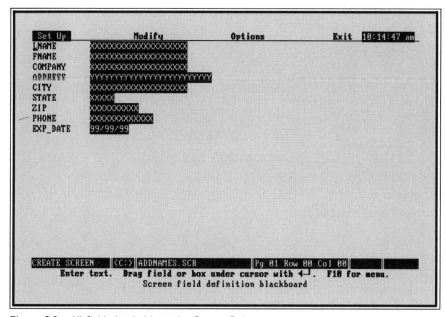

Figure 6.2 – *All fields loaded into the Screen Painter*

Moving Information on the Blackboard

It's pretty easy to move information around on the Blackboard once you've practiced a bit. Take a moment to review the basic editing keys listed in Table 6.1.

When moving the cursor around, look to the lower-right corner of your screen for the cursor's current position. When the cursor is in the upper-left corner, the screen will display Row 00 Col 00.

Inserting Blank Lines

Now let's start shifting some things around to create a better-looking screen. First of all, let's put some blank lines at the top of the screen for a title (which we'll add later). Make sure the cursor is in the upper-left corner of the screen and the field names and highlights are still displayed on the screen. If not, press F10 to switch from the menu to the Blackboard. Then

Key	Effects
F10	Switches between menu and Blackboard.
←	Moves cursor left one character.
→	Moves cursor right one character.
↑	Moves cursor up one line.
↓	Moves cursor down one line.
Ins or ^V	Turns the Insert mode on and off if cursor is not in a field highlight. Otherwise, extends the length of the field highlight.
^N	Adds a blank line between two lines.
End or ^F	Moves cursor to beginning of next word.
Home or ^A	Moves cursor to beginning of current or previous word.
↵ or ^M	(Return key.) Inserts a new line if Insert mode is on. Otherwise, just moves down a line. Also used for moving field highlights and boxes.
Del or ^G	Deletes character or space over cursor if cursor is inside a field highlight.
Backspace	Deletes character to left of cursor.
^T	Deletes word to right of cursor.
^Y	Deletes an entire line from form.
^U	Deletes a field highlight or box.
PgDn or ^C	Scrolls down 18 lines on screen.
PgUp or ^R	Scrolls up 18 lines on screen.

Table 6.1 – Keys used with the Screen Painter Blackboard

follow these steps:

1. Put Insert mode on (first make sure that the cursor is *not* inside a field highlight, then press the Ins key).

2. Press Return four times.

This should move the entire group of field names and field highlights down four lines (same effect as typing ^N four times).

Repositioning Field Highlights

Next, let's move the field highlight for the LNAME field over next to the FNAME field. To do so, follow these steps:

1. Put the cursor inside the LNAME field highlight (press the End key).

2. Press Return to enter Drag mode.

3. Press → 14 times to move the cursor 14 spaces to the right (Row 4 Col 45).

4. Press ↓.

5. Complete the move by pressing Return.

The LNAME field highlight will now be next to the FNAME field highlight, as shown in Figure 6.3.

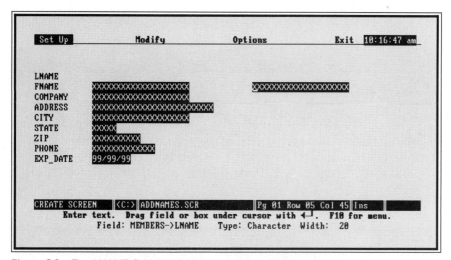

Figure 6.3 – The LNAME field highlight in a new location

Note the steps we used to move the field highlight. First, we put the cursor inside the field highlight that we wanted to move. Then we pressed the Return key to enter the Drag mode. The following message was displayed at the bottom of the screen:

Move field with ↑ ↓ ← →. Complete with ↵.

We used the → and ↓ keys to move the cursor to the new location, then pressed Return to complete the move.

Improving Field Labels

There is no need to use the abbreviated LNAME and FNAME field names on the form. You can simply type in new ones following these steps:

1. Press Home twice so the cursor is on the F in the word FNAME.

2. Press Ins until Ins disappears from the bottom of the screen.

3. Type in the new field prompt:

   First Name:

4. Press → four times to Row 05 Col 34.

5. Enter the new field prompt:

   Last Name:

Deleting Labels

You no longer need the LNAME label above the current row, so follow these steps to delete it:

1. Press ↑ and Home to move the highlight to the L in LNAME.

2. Type ^T.

Notice that ^T deletes the word to the right, but it does not delete the entire line. If you had used ^Y rather than ^T, the entire line would have been deleted, and all rows beneath would have moved up a row. Your screen should now look like Figure 6.4.

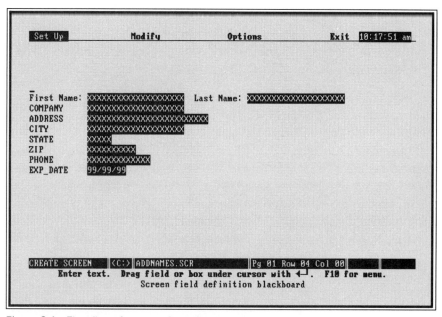

Figure 6.4 – *First line of custom form is in shape*

Boxed Titles

Now we'll add a boxed title to the top of the screen using the "Double bar" option from the Screen Painter menu. Here are the steps:

1. Move the cursor to Row 01 Col 00.

2. Press F10 to call up the menu.

3. Highlight Options.

4. Select Double bar and press Return.

5. Press Return to start the box at the cursor position.

6. Press ↓ twice.

7. Hold down → until the cursor reaches the opposite corner, Row 03 Col 79.

8. Press Return to complete the move.

The double-bar box will appear on the screen. Now, to put the title inside, move the cursor to Row 02 Col 34 and type in this title:

Membership System: Add New Names

Now the custom screen will look like Figure 6.5.

Using these basic techniques, you should be able to complete the custom screen for the Membership System. Of course, you can design the screen however you wish. The completed screen in Figure 6.6 is only a suggestion. The help box at the bottom of the screen was created with a double-bar box around it, and the "Single bar" option was used to create the thin lines dividing the box into sections. The locations of boxes, field highlights, and

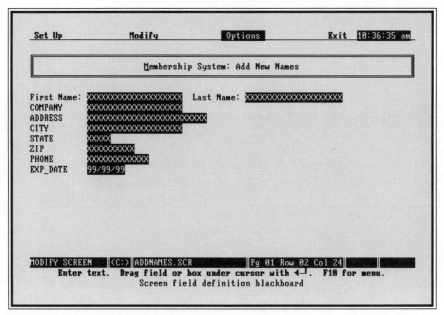

Figure 6.5 – Boxed title added to the screen

field prompts are summarized below:

Field Highlights:

Row	Col	Field Highlight
5	45	LNAME
5	12	FNAME
7	12	COMPANY
7	45	ADDRESS
9	12	CITY
9	41	STATE
9	58	ZIP
11	12	PHONE
11	51	EXP_DATE

Field Prompts:

Row	Col	Field Prompt
5	34	Last Name:
5	00	First Name:
7	00	Company:
7	34	Address:
9	00	City:
9	34	State:
9	48	Zip Code:
11	00	Phone:
11	34	Expiration Date:

Boxes:

Start Row	Col		End Row	Col	Type
1	0	TO	3	79	Double
13	0	TO	19	78	Double
14	27	TO	18	27	Single
14	50	TO	18	50	Single

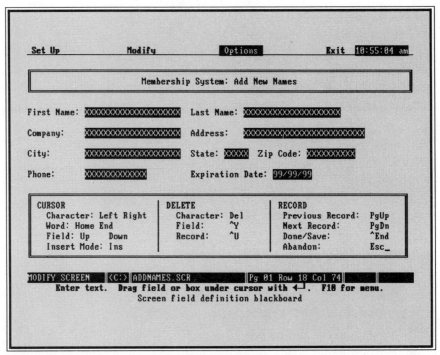

Figure 6.6 – Completed screen on the Blackboard

Saving the Form

When your form looks good, save it by calling up the menu (F10) and highlighting the Exit option. Select Save. You'll then be returned to the dot prompt.

Testing the Form

To test the form, use the database and the SET FORMAT command. In this example, enter these commands:

```
USE Members INDEX Names, Zips
SET FORMAT TO AddNames
```

Then enter either the APPEND or EDIT command to view the form. (If there are no records in the database, you'll have to use the APPEND command.) You'll see the form appear, ready for adding or editing data, as in Figure 6.7.

When you've finished testing the screen and the dot prompt reappears, enter this command to return dBASE to its normal screen:

CLOSE FORMAT

(You can also use the command

SET FORMAT TO

without a file name to close a format file.)

```
                    Membership System: Add New Names

First Name: Mrs. Bertha Z.      Last Name: Smithsonian

Company:    ABC CO.             Address:   333 Grape St.

City:       San Diego          State: CA    Zip Code: 92122

Phone:      (800)555-1212       Expiration Date: 12/31/86


 CURSOR                    DELETE              RECORD
   Character: Left Right      Character: Del      Previous Record:  PgUp
   Word: Home End            Field:     ^Y       Next Record:      PgDn
   Field: Up    Down         Record:    ^U       Done/Save:        ^End
   Insert Mode: Ins                              Abandon:          Esc
```

Figure 6.7 – AddNames screen in use

Modifying a Screen

Creating custom screens is usually a trial-and-error process. To modify an existing screen, make sure the associated database is in use, then enter the MODIFY SCREEN command with the name of the form. In this example, you would enter the following commands:

USE Members INDEX Names, Zips
MODIFY SCREEN AddNames

When the Screen Painter menu appears, press F10 to see the custom screen. Use the usual editing keys to make changes. When you're finished making changes, call up the menu once again (F10), highlight Exit, and select the Save option. You'll be returned to the dot prompt.

Adding Picture Templates

Templates are used to reduce the likelihood of errors being typed into forms, as well as to simplify data entry. For example, we can add a template to the Phone field that looks like this:

:( ) - :

The template encourages a standardized format and simplifies entry, because the parentheses and hyphen are added to the field contents automatically.

To add this template to the AddNames form, bring the form back onto the screen using the MODIFY SCREEN command. Press F10 to view the Blackboard.

Next, move the cursor to the first character in the Phone field highlight. Then call up the menu (F10) and highlight the Modify option. At the bottom of the pull-down menu you'll see these options:

Picture Function
Picture Template
Range

Select the Picture Template option. You'll see a menu of the following special characters that you can use in your picture template:

Special Character	Meaning
A	Allows only letters to be entered
L	Allows only logical data (T, F, Y, or N)

Special Character	Meaning
N	Allows alphabetic and numeric characters
X	Allows entry of any character
#	Allows numbers, + and − signs, spaces, and periods
9	Allows only numeric digits
!	Converts entry to uppercase
other	Any other character is added to the entry

You'll see that the screen is also asking for the template. Type in the template as

(999)999-9999

Notice that we've specified that only numbers can be entered into the field by placing the special character 9 into the template. Therefore, the template also helps ensure that faulty data are not entered into the field.

Let's discuss a few other tricks that you can do with picture templates. For example, if you were to put the template

!AAAAAAAAAAAAAAAAA

in the LNAME field highlight, and the template

!AAAAAAAAAAAAAAAAAA

in the FNAME field highlight, both of these fields would automatically switch the first letter of the entry to uppercase. The A special character after the ! will allow any letter, without switching its case.

Placing the template

#########

into the Zip field highlight allows only numbers, spaces, periods, and + and − signs in the zip code. (If your mailing list includes foreign zip codes, however, you'll want to stay with the XXXXXXXXX template already in the field highlight, because it will allow any characters.) Figure 6.8 shows how the AddNames form looks with some new picture templates typed in.

When you're done adding the picture templates to the AddNames form, highlight the Exit option and select Save.

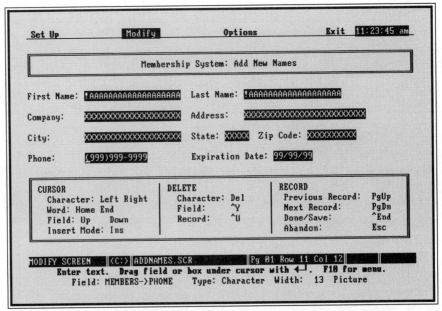

Figure 6.8. – Picture templates added to the AddNames form

Files Created
by the Screen Painter

Whenever you create a screen with the Screen Painter, it automatically creates two files. One, with the extension .SCR (for instance, Add-Names.SCR), is the file used only by the Screen Painter. A second file, with the extension .FMT (for instance, AddNames.FMT), is the one actually used by the SET FORMAT command in dBASE. The .FMT file contains the @, SAY, GET, and PICTURE commands that actually draw the custom screen. Figure 6.9 shows the AddNames.FMT *format file,* created by the Screen Painter in this chapter. You can modify the .FMT file directly with any text editor, including the dBASE MODIFY COMMAND editor.

You can also create a *text file* of your custom screen by highlighting the Options option on the Screen Painter menu and selecting "Generate text file image". This will create a file with the extension .TXT. The text file is readily accessible from any word processor, and it can come in handy for developing documentation. Figure 6.10 shows a text file generated for the AddNames screen.

```
@ 2, 24  SAY "Membership System: Add New Names"
@ 5,  0  SAY "First Name:"
@ 5, 12  GET  MEMBERS->FNAME  PICTURE "!AAAAAAAAAAAAAAAAAAA"
@ 5, 34  SAY "Last Name:"
@ 5, 45  GET  MEMBERS->LNAME  PICTURE "!AAAAAAAAAAAAAAAAAAA"
@ 7,  0  SAY "Company:"
@ 7, 12  GET  MEMBERS->COMPANY
@ 7, 34  SAY "Address:"
@ 7, 45  GET  MEMBERS->ADDRESS
@ 9,  0  SAY "City:"
@ 9, 12  GET  MEMBERS->CITY
@ 9, 34  SAY "State:"
@ 9, 41  GET  MEMBERS->STATE
@ 9, 48  SAY "Zip Code:"
@ 9, 58  GET  MEMBERS->ZIP
@ 11,  0  SAY "Phone:"
@ 11, 12  GET  MEMBERS->PHONE  PICTURE "(999)999-9999"
@ 11, 34  SAY "Expiration Date:"
@ 11, 51  GET  MEMBERS->EXP_DATE
@ 14,  2  SAY "CURSOR                      DELETE              RECORD"
@ 15,  4  SAY "Character: Left Right    Character: Del     Previous Record: PgUp"
@ 16,  4  SAY "Word: Home End           Field:     ^Y      Next Record:     PgDn"
@ 17,  4  SAY "Field: Up   Down         Record:    ^U      Done/Save:       ^End"
@ 18,  4  SAY "Insert Mode: Ins                             Abandon:         Esc"
@ 1,  0  TO 3, 79      DOUBLE
@ 13,  0  TO 19, 78    DOUBLE
@ 14, 27  TO 18, 27
@ 14, 50  TO 18, 50
```

Figure 6.9 – The AddNames.FMT format file

```
Field definitions for Screen : addnames .scr

Page  Row  Co   Data Base   Field         Type        Width Dec
 1     5   45   MEMBERS     LNAME         Character      20
PICTURE !AAAAAAAAAAAAAAAAAAA
 1     5   12   MEMBERS     FNAME         Character      20
PICTURE !AAAAAAAAAAAAAAAAAAA
 1     7   12   MEMBERS     COMPANY       Character      20
 1     7   45   MEMBERS     ADDRESS       Character      25
 1     9   12   MEMBERS     CITY          Character      20
 1     9   41   MEMBERS     STATE         Character       5
 1     9   58   MEMBERS     ZIP           Character      10
 1    11   12   MEMBERS     PHONE         Character      13
PICTURE (999)999-9999
 1    11   51   MEMBERS     EXP_DATE      Date            8


Content of page :  1

                    Membership System: Add New Names


First Name: XXXXXXXXXXXXXXXXXXX  Last Name: XXXXXXXXXXXXXXXXXXX

Company:    XXXXXXXXXXXXXXXXXXX  Address:   XXXXXXXXXXXXXXXXXXXXXXXXX

City:       XXXXXXXXXXXXXXXXXXX  State: XXXXX  Zip Code: XXXXXXXXXX

Phone:      XXXXXXXXXXXXX        Expiration Date: XXXXXXXX

  CURSOR                      DELETE              RECORD
    Character: Left Right       Character: Del       Previous Record:  PgUp
    Word: Home End              Field:     ^Y        Next Record:      PgDn
    Field: Up   Down            Record:    ^U        Done/Save:        ^End
    Insert Mode: Ins                                 Abandon:          Esc
```

Figure 6.10 – Text file image AddNames.TXT

The AddNew Command File

Now that we have a custom screen for adding new records to the Members database, we can create a command file that uses it. We'll call the file AddNew.PRG.

Writing the Pseudocode

The pseudocode for this program is very simple:

Use Members database with both index files
Set format to custom screen AddNames
Append new records
Set format back to normal dBASE III PLUS screen
Return to main-menu program

Writing the Command File

To create the command file, type

MODIFY COMMAND AddNew

from the dBASE dot prompt. When the word processing screen appears, enter a couple of lines of descriptive comments, then put in the command to open the Members database with both the Names and Zips index files:

```
* * * * * * * * * * * * * * * * * * * * * * * *  AddNew.PRG
*
* Add new members using the AddNames screen.
* Called from Membership main menu.
*
USE Members INDEX Names,Zips
```

Next, we'll have the program set up the AddNames custom screen and go into the APPEND mode:

```
SET FORMAT TO AddNames
APPEND
```

When the user is done entering new data, we want the program to return to normal screen mode and loop back to the main-menu program, so we'll enter the following commands to complete AddNew.PRG:

CLOSE FORMAT
RETURN

Save the file with ^End (or ^W). Figure 6.11 shows the entire AddNew command file.

Testing the Program

To test the AddNew program, run the Members command file by typing

DO Members

at the dot prompt. The main menu appears. Now select option 1, and you'll see the custom screen.

Go ahead and type in a few records, so you'll have some data in the database when you test future programs. You might want to purposely type some duplicate names and addresses to help test the "Check for duplicates" program we'll develop in Chapter 10. When you're done adding members, press Return rather than typing a last name, and you'll be returned to the Members main menu.

```
*********************************************** AddNew .PRG
*
*   Add new members using the AddNames screen.
*   Called from Membership main menu.
*
USE Members INDEX Names,Zips

SET FORMAT TO AddNames
APPEND
CLOSE FORMAT

RETURN
```

Figure 6.11 - The completed AddNew command file

Using Graphics Characters

You can use graphics characters (such as arrow keys) in your custom screens by editing the .FMT file and using the appropriate CHR code. For example, to print a ←, use CHR(27). The → is CHR(26). CHR(24) is a ↑, and CHR(25) is a ↓. You can create a reasonable facsimile of the Return (or Enter) key using CHR(17) + "−'". The main trick is to place these special characters in the format (.FMT) file without disrupting the original alignment of things.

To add arrow keys to the AddNames.FMT file, first enter these commands:

CLOSE FORMAT
MODIFY COMMAND AddNames.FMT

When the format file appears, use PgDn to work your way down to the bottom of the format file. Replace the words Left and Right with CHR(27) and CHR(26) respectively. (You'll also need to break up the line, as shown in Figure 6.12.) Replace the words Up and Down with the arrows, CHR(24) and CHR(25). Figure 6.12 shows the modified portion of AddNames.FMT.

After making the change, save the format file (using ^End). To test the new version, use the usual commands:

USE Members INDEX Names, Zips
SET FORMAT TO AddNames

```
@ 14,  2  SAY "CURSOR                          DELETE                  RECORD"
@ 15,  4  SAY "Character: "+CHR(26)+" "+CHR(27)
@ 15, 31  SAY "Character: Del        Previous Record:  PgUp"
@ 16,  4  SAY "Word: Home End              Field:      ^Y      Next Record:  PgDn"
@ 17,  4  SAY "Field: "+CHR(24)+" "+CHR(25)
@ 17, 31  SAY "Record:      ^U          Done/Save:        ^End"
```

Figure 6.12 – Graphics characters added to AddNames.FMT

Then enter either EDIT or APPEND. Figure 6.13 shows the modified screen. Note the arrow keys in the help box near the bottom of the screen.

You should add graphics characters as the very last step, because if you use MODIFY SCREEN to change the format file, it will erase any changes you made with MODIFY COMMAND.

For a quick look at all the ASCII characters available on your screen, you can key in the program shown in Figure 6.14. Use the MODIFY COMMAND editor to create the command file with a name such as ASCII.PRG. Save the command file with ^W, and enter the command DO ASCII at the dot prompt to run it.

```
                       Membership System: Add New Names

   First Name: Mrs. Bertha Z.         Last Name: Smithsonian

   Company:    ABC CO.                 Address:   333 Grape St.

   City:       San Diego               State: CA    Zip Code: 92122

   Phone:      (800)555-1212           Expiration Date: 12/31/86

  CURSOR                  DELETE                  RECORD
    Character: → ←          Character: Del          Previous Record:  PgUp
    Word: Home End          Field:     ^Y           Next Record:      PgDn
    Field: ↑ ↓              Record:    ^U           Done/Save:        ^End
    Insert Mode: Ins                                Abandon:          Esc
```

Figure 6.13 – Custom screen with graphics characters

```
    *---------------------- ASCII.PRG
    *---------------------- Display all ASCII codes.
SET TALK OFF
Counter = 0
DO WHILE Counter <= 255
   ?? STR(Counter,3),CHR(Counter)+" "
   Counter = Counter + 1
ENDDO (Counter = 0)
```

Figure 6.14 – Program to show ASCII characters

Now that you've had a chance to become comfortable with custom screens, let's use the dBASE label and report generators to develop formats for the mailing labels and directory produced by the Membership System.

Membership Mailing Labels and Directory

One of the primary functions of our Membership System is to create mailing labels and a current directory. In this chapter, we'll develop the format files for the labels and directory; then in Chapter 8 we'll use these formats in a command file that allows presorting and searching. (Notice that we don't need to write pseudocode for these files, since they're actually going to be created by the dBASE label and report generators.)

Mailing Labels

To create a mailing-label format for the Membership System, we must first open the Members database. Then we need to give the format file a name. In this example, we're going to create a two-across label format (two columns of labels on each sheet), so I've chosen the name TwoCol. Just type the following commands to create the TwoCol.LBL format file for the Members database:

USE Members
CREATE LABEL TwoCol

A screen displaying the label-format parameters appears, as in Figure 7.1.

We can change any of the parameters on the screen to modify the appearance of the labels. Most printers print ten characters to the inch

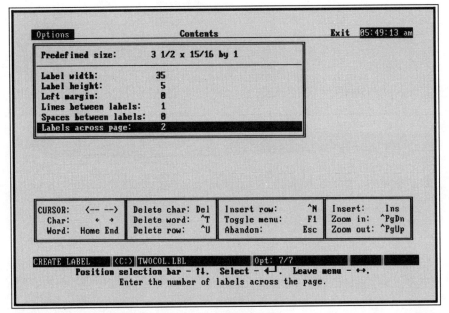

Figure 7.1 – Label format for two-across mailing labels

(cpi) across and six lines to the inch (lpi) down. So for two-across mailing labels 3.5 inches wide, we need only change the "Labels across page" option to 2. Use the arrow keys to move the cursor around the label screen and make changes. (Of course, you can set up the label parameters in any way you like.)

Figure 7.2 shows the Label Contents screen that appears after you've changed the appropriate format settings and pressed →

Notice that the lines are numbered 1 through 5. With the highlight on line 1, press Return, type the following, and then press the Return key again:

    TRIM(FName), LName

This causes the first name (with trailing blanks trimmed off) and the last name to be displayed at the top of the mailing label. On line 2, enter the field name Company. On line 3, type the field name Address.

The fourth line of the mailing label is a little more complicated. It needs to contain the city, followed by a comma and a blank space, then the state followed by a blank space and the zip code. So fill in the fourth line like this:

    TRIM(City) + "," , State, Zip

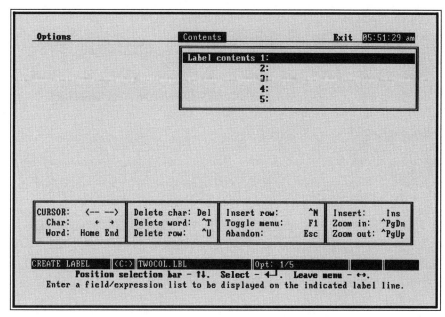

Figure 7.2 – Label Contents screen

If you make mistakes while typing data, you can use the usual cursor-control keys to make changes. The arrows on the numeric keypad, as well as the ^E, ^D, ^X, and ^S key combinations, move the cursor. The ← and → keys flip back and forth between the first and second pages of the label format generator. You can use ^N to add a blank line between two existing lines, ^U to delete a line, or ^Y to delete all characters to the right of the cursor. Our completed Label Contents screen looks like Figure 7.3.

When you've finished filling in the Label Contents portion of the screen, highlight Exit and select Save.

To display the labels, type the command

LABEL FORM TwoCol

and the labels will appear on the screen in the two-across format, as in the example in Figure 7.4.

To send the label output to your printer, just type

LABEL FORM TwoCol TO PRINT

We'll use both versions of the LABEL FORM command in the Reports program in Chapter 8.

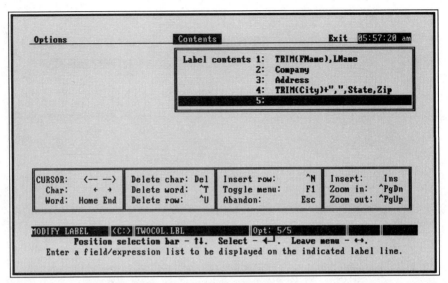

Figure 7.3 – Label contents for the Members database

```
Bertha Smith                    Julie Bucey
ABC Co.                         XYZ Co.
333 Grape St.                   111 Sorrento Valley Blvd.
San Diego, CA   92122           San Diego, CA   92111
```

Figure 7.4 – Some mailing labels with the TwoCol.LBL format

Custom dBASE III PLUS Reports

The Membership System will print a directory of customers using the dBASE III PLUS report generator. A sample of the directory appears in Figure 7.5.

As you'll soon see, it takes a bit of trickery to get the dBASE III PLUS report generator to display three lines for each customer. (In Chapter 10 we'll see an alternative technique for printing the directory, using a command file instead of the report generator.)

I assume that you are fairly familiar with the report generator, since you're reading an advanced book. Nonetheless, I'll describe the somewhat elaborate contents of the various fields.

```
Page No.      1
04/30/86

                          Membership Directory


**   Adams, Ruth                      Zeerox Electronics
     1142 Jackson Dr.
     Los Angeles, CA  91234      (800)555-0101    01/01/86

**   Appleby, Andy T.                   Quality Insurance
     345 Oak St.
     Los Angeles, CA  92123      (800)555-9999    12/31/86

**   Smithsonian, Mrs. Bertha Z.        AlphaBetics, Inc.
     333 Grape St.
     San Diego, CA  92122        (800)555-1212    12/31/86

**   Watson, Wilbur G.                    Data Ventures
     9111 Baldy Vista Ct.
     Los Angeles, CA  91234      (800)555-6543    06/01/86
```

Figure 7.5 – Sample directory of customers

To start designing the report, which we'll name Director.FRM, enter these commands at the dot prompt:

USE Members INDEX Names,Zips
CREATE REPORT Director

Highlight the "Page title" option, press Return, and enter this title on the third line of the title box, as shown in Figure 7.6:

Membership Directory

Also, highlight and select the "Left margin" setting, change it to 4, and press Return.

Next press → to highlight the Groups option on the top menu. Select the "Group on expression" option by highlighting it and pressing Return. Enter the following expression:

TRIM(LName) + ",   " + TRIM(FName) + SPACE(40 −
(LEN(TRIM(LName)) + LEN(TRIM(FName)) + 2)) + Company

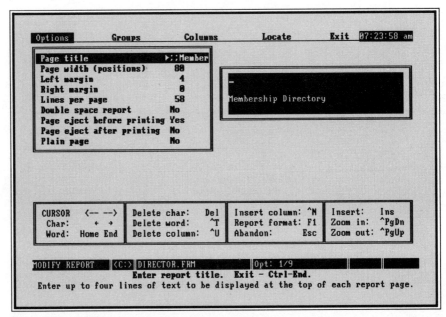

Figure 7.6 – *Page title for the directory*

(NOTE: Even though the expression is broken to fit in the book, you must type it as one long line.) While typing in the expression, you can press Ctrl-PgDn to zoom in and see more of the formula at the bottom of the screen. Press Ctrl-PgUp to zoom back out, and press Return after entering the formula.

Let's discuss this expression. First of all, we aren't especially concerned with grouping at all in the directory. However, since group titles appear on a separate line, this gives us one of the three lines we need for each name and address on the directory. The portion in the grouping expression that reads

TRIM(LName) + '', '' + TRIM(FName)

prints the last name, with trailing blanks removed, followed by a comma and a space, then the first name with blanks removed, as below:

Adams, Ruth

The middle portion of the expression,

+ SPACE(40 – (LEN(TRIM(LName)) + LEN(TRIM(FName)) + 2))

ensures that the company name always starts on the fortieth column of the report. How? By adding a certain number of spaces, calculated by subtracting the combined length of the Last and First names (with blanks removed) plus two for the comma and space. Hence, if a person's name contains 30 characters (with comma and space), this portion of the expression places 10 spaces (40 minus 30) after the person's name. The last portion of the expression,

+ Company

prints the company name to the right of the name and calculated number of spaces (always beginning in the fortieth column).

The advantage of lining up the company names in an even column is that you can run your finger down the right side of the printed report to scan company names. (If you index the Members database on the Company field, then print the report, the companies will be listed in alphabetical order.)

The one disadvantage of using the grouping expression for a line on the report is that it always displays preceding asterisks. The only way around this is to create a command file to print the report. We'll explore this alternative in Chapter 10.

Next, you need to define the columns in the report. Press → to highlight the Columns option on the top menu. With the highlight on the Contents option, press Return and enter this expression:

Address + SPACE(5) + TRIM(City) + ", "
+ TRIM(State) + " " + TRIM(Zip)

(Once again, the expression is split in two, only to fit in the book—you must enter it as a single line.) Press Return after entering the expression, then highlight the Width option and press Return. Specify 30 as the column width.

The column displays the Address, City, State, and Zip on two separate lines of the report. The portion that reads

Address + SPACE(5)

prints the Address (25 characters) and five blank spaces, for a total width of 30 characters. Since the column width is defined as 30, anything beyond the thirtieth character will wrap around to the second line. Hence, the City, State, and Zip, printed with the following portion of the expression,

+ TRIM(City) + ", " + TRIM(State) + " " + TRIM(Zip)

appear beneath the address, as in this example:

1142 Jackson Dr.
Los Angeles, CA 91234

Figure 7.7 shows the first column defined for the report. (The full column expression appears in the "zoom" portion above the Status line at the bottom of the screen.)

After entering the expression and width for the first column, press PgDn to define the second column. Select the Contents option and enter this expression:

SPACE(15) + Phone

Press Return, select Width, and specify 16 as the column width. This expression prints nothing on the top line of the column (except 15 spaces, plus the additional space dBASE automatically places between columns) and the Phone number on the second line.

Finally, press PgDn to define the third column, and enter this expression:

SPACE(7) + DTOC(Exp_Date)

Press Return, select Width, and enter a width of 8. This expression places blanks on the first line of the column and a series of seven spaces followed by the expiration date on the second line. The DTOC function is necessary so that the date can be concatenated to the spaces: you can't add a date onto a character string unless you first convert it to a character string.

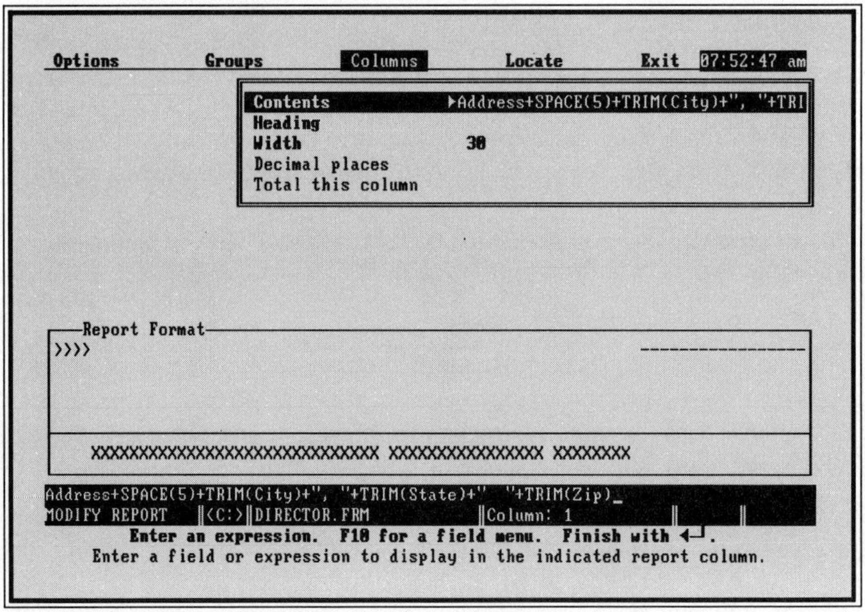

Figure 7.7 – First column defined for the directory

Now that you've defined the report format, highlight the Exit option and select Save. To test the report, enter these commands:

USE Members INDEX Names
REPORT FORM Director

You should see the directory, similar to the example presented in Figure 7.5, displayed on the screen.

To display the report on the printer rather than on the screen, use this command:

REPORT FORM Director TO PRINT

You can also specify that only certain records be included in the report. For example, to display the Director report for people whose membership expires in December, use the following command:

REPORT FORM Director FOR MONTH(Exp_Date) = 12

Using the Report Form
with a Word Processor

To use the report in a word processing document, type this command:

REPORT FORM Director TO MemText

You can use the dBASE or DOS TYPE command to verify that the report was stored on disk. For example, either the command

TYPE MemText.TXT

or

TYPE B:MemText.TXT

will work from either DOS or the dBASE dot prompt. You can also read the report into any word processor, including the dBASE MODIFY COMMAND editor. (Just remember to include the .TXT extension.)

Modifying the Report Format

Once you've created a report format, you can change it at any time by using the appropriate database and entering the MODIFY REPORT command. For example, to change the format of the Director report, enter these commands:

USE Members INDEX Names,Zips
MODIFY REPORT Director

You can use all the same techniques used to create the report. Use ^N to insert new columns between existing columns. ^U deletes columns from the report. Remember to highlight Exit and select Save after making any changes to the report format.

Membership System
Sorting and Searching

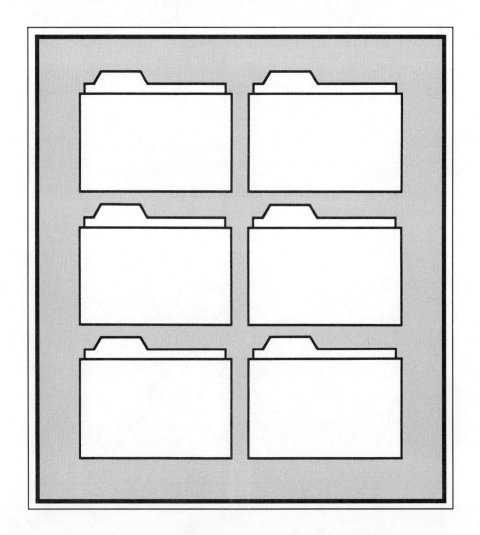

Now that we've created the format files for our labels and directory, we can develop the Reports command file. This program, accessed by selecting option 2 in the main menu, needs to perform many functions.

First we want the program to display a menu of report options on the screen, as in Figure 8.1. Option 1 creates mailing labels based on the format we created in the TwoCol label file. Option 2 displays or prints membership information using the Director report form we created in the last chapter. Option 3 creates a special file that can be used with the WordStar MailMerge and Microsoft Word programs to create form letters.

Once the user selects a report format, we want a second menu to appear on the screen asking how to organize the report, as in Figure 8.2. If the user selects option 1, the members' records are displayed in alphabetical order by last and first names. Option 2 presents data sorted in zip-code order. Option 3 displays data in whatever order they were originally entered, unsorted.

After the user selects a sort order, the screen displays this prompt:

(A)ll records or (Q)uery?

If the user types the letter A to select All, all records from the database will be displayed on the report. If the user types the letter Q to select Query, a dBASE III PLUS query form appears on the screen. The user can select the Field Name, Operator, Constant/Expression, and Connect options

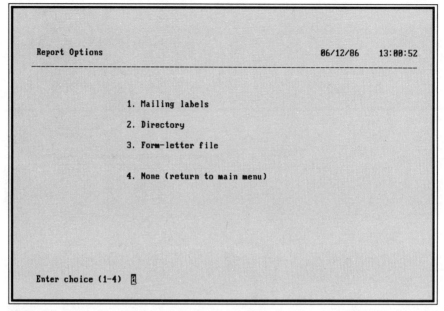

Figure 8.1 – Menu for selecting report format

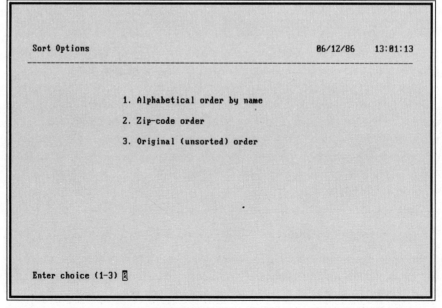

Figure 8.2 – Menu for selecting sort order

in the usual manner to create a filter condition. For example, the query form shown in Figure 8.3 will display only those records that have expiration dates in March 1986. Highlighting Exit on the top menu and selecting Save completes the query and filters out all records that do not match the query criteria. (Our program will use the query temporarily to print the mailing labels, directory, or form-letter file, then immediately "unfilter" the database.)

Finally, we want the program to ask the user whether the data (either mailing labels or the directory) should be displayed on the screen or printed:

Send data to printer? (Y/N)

Once the last question is answered, we want the program to display the requested data in the requested sort order and in the requested format (for instance, mailing labels in zip-code order for everyone whose membership expires in July).

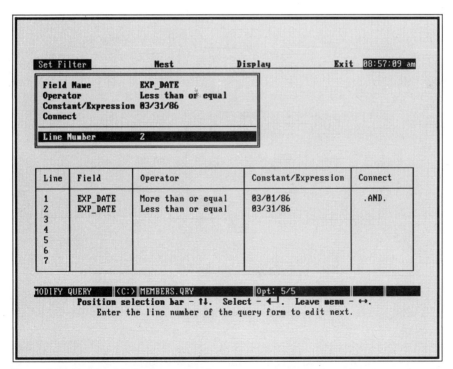

Figure 8.3 – Membership System query form

Writing the Pseudocode

The pseudocode for this command file looks more complicated than for our earlier programs, because so many more tasks must be performed to achieve our goals. But the approach is identical: use short statements in simple English to create a step-by-step outline of what you want the program to do:

> Clear screen
>
> Display menu of report options
>
>> Select report format
>>
>>> 1. Mailing labels
>>>
>>> 2. Directory
>>>
>>> 3. Form-letter file
>>>
>>> 4. None (return to main menu)
>
> Get user's menu choice
>
> If option 4 requested
>
>> Return to main menu
>
> Otherwise
>
>> Display menu of sort options
>>
>>> Specify sort order
>>>
>>>> 1. Alphabetical order by name
>>>>
>>>> 2. Zip-code order
>>>>
>>>> 3. Original (unsorted) order
>>
>> Get user's menu choice
>>
>>> If option 1 selected
>>>
>>>> Use index of last and first names
>>>
>>> If option 2 selected
>>>
>>>> Use index of zip codes
>>>
>>> If option 3 selected
>>>
>>>> Use Members database without index file

Ask if (A)ll or (Q)uery

If Query

　　　Modify query form

Ask about hard copy

　　If going to printer

　　　　　Have user prepare printer

　　　　　Set up macro for sending report to printer

　　　　　Leave out records marked for deletion

　　　　　Execute the selection

　　If mailing labels requested

　　　　　Print mailing labels

　　If directory report requested

　　　　　Print directory

　　If form-letter file requested

　　　　　Ask for name of form-letter file

　　　　　Make form-letter file

Done, pause screen

Set up Names and Zips index files again for future use

Remove filters

Return to main menu

Now let's use this outline to develop the Reports command file.

Writing the Command File

From the dBASE dot prompt, type the following command to start building the Reports program:

MODIFY COMMAND Reports

Once again we'll begin by putting in the file name and a brief description of the program, then opening the database and index files:

```
* * * * * * * * * * * * * * * * * * * * * * * * * * * * * * * *  Reports.PRG
* Set up sort orders and search conditions,
*      then print the appropriate report.
* Called from Membership main menu.
*------- Open Members database and index files.
USE Members INDEX Names, Zips
```

Next, we'll write commands to clear the screen, set up a heading, and display the menu of report-format options:

```
CLEAR
@ 2,1 SAY "Report Options"
@ 2,60 SAY DTOC(DATE()) + "      " + TIME()
@ 3,0 SAY ULine
?
?
TEXT
        1. Mailing labels
        2. Directory
        3. Form-letter file

        4. None (return to main menu)
ENDTEXT
```

Then we'll create a variable called MChoice for the user's format choice, and we'll use the @ . . . SAY . . . GET and READ commands to get and store the selection:

```
MChoice = 0
@ 24,1 SAY "Enter choice (1–4) " GET MChoice PICT "9";
    RANGE 1,4
READ
```

Now, if the user selects option 4 (not to print a report), we want the command file to return to the main menu:

```
IF MChoice = 4
    RETURN
ENDIF
```

If the user makes any other selection, we'll need to add routines to handle the sort orders and query (filter) conditions.

Sort Orders

First we want the command file to clear the screen, create a heading, and display a menu of sort options:

```
*------------------ Ask about sort order.
CLEAR
@ 2,1 SAY "Sort Options"
@ 2,60 SAY DTOC(DATE()) + "      " + TIME()
@ 3,0 SAY ULine
?
?
TEXT
          1. Alphabetical order by name
          2. Zip-code order
          3. Original (unsorted) order
ENDTEXT
```

We'll set up a memory variable called SChoice for the user's menu choice, then use the @ . . . SAY . . . GET and READ commands to get and store the selection:

```
SChoice = 0
@ 24,1 SAY "Enter choice (1–3) " GET SChoice PICT "9";
   RANGE 1,3
READ
```

Now we can have the program set up the selected sort order simply by using the appropriate index file. A DO CASE clause will handle this job for us:

```
*------------------ Set up appropriate sort order.
DO CASE
   CASE SChoice = 1
     SET INDEX TO Names
   CASE SChoice = 2
     SET INDEX TO Zips
   CASE SChoice = 3
     USE Members
ENDCASE
```

Querying

Next the program needs to ask the user if he wants all the records in the database to be displayed or if he wants to set up a query, such as California residents or members with expiration dates in March. The command lines below display the prompt

(A)ll records or (Q)uery?

and store the user's answer in the memory variable named AllSome:

```
*------------------ Ask about query.
CLEAR
AllSome = " "
@ 5,2 SAY "(A)ll records or (Q)uery? " ;
   GET AllSome PICT "!"
READ
```

If the user selects Query, the IF clause below allows him to modify (or create) a query form named Members.QRY. After the query form is filled in and saved, dBASE III PLUS automatically sets up the requested filter condition:

```
*------------------ Respond to query choice.
IF AllSome = "Q"
   MODIFY QUERY Members
ENDIF
```

If the user selected All, the program bypasses the query form, thereby not filtering any records from the database.

Displaying and Printing

Now that the sort order and search filter are set up, we want the program to display or print the appropriate report. First the program clears the screen and sets up two memory variables, Printer and PMacro, which are needed in conjunction with printing:

```
*------------------ Print report based on previous MChoice.
CLEAR
STORE " " TO Printer, PMacro
```

If the user is not making a form-letter file, we want the program to ask whether the report should be sent to the printer. The answer to this question is stored in the memory variable Printer. If the report is indeed being sent to the printer (Printer = "Y"), the program must store the words TO PRINT to the memory variable PMacro (for use when the LABEL FORM or REPORT FORM command is actually executed) and then pause to allow the user to prepare the printer:

```
*------- If not making a form-letter file, ask about printer.
IF MChoice < 3
    @ 15,5 SAY "Send data to printer? (Y/N) " GET Printer;
        PICT "!"
    READ
    IF Printer = "Y"
        PMacro = "TO PRINT"
        WAIT "Prepare printer, then press any key to;
        continue . . . "
    ENDIF
ENDIF
```

To ensure that records marked for deletion are not included in any reports, we'll use the SET DELETED ON command and then have the program clear the screen to display the report:

```
*------- Leave out records marked for deletion.
SET DELETED ON
CLEAR
```

Finally, the program will use a DO CASE clause to print the appropriate report, based on the initial report-format request (MChoice). If MChoice is 1, mailing labels are displayed using the TwoCol format:

```
DO CASE
    *------- Print mailing labels.
    CASE MChoice = 1
        LABEL FORM TwoCol &PMacro
```

If the user requested that the labels be sent to the printer, the PMacro variable is already set equal to "TO PRINT"; hence the command line for printing labels becomes, by macro substitution, LABEL FORM TwoCol TO PRINT. The SET INDEX command issued earlier in the program ensures that labels are printed in sorted order, and the MODIFY QUERY command ensures that they are printed for only certain records.

If MChoice is 2, the directory is displayed using the Director report format. Again, the PMacro variable is used to send the directory to the printer, if requested, and the SET INDEX and MODIFY QUERY commands issued earlier in the program ensure proper sort order and searching.

```
*------- Print directory.
CASE MChoice = 2
     REPORT FORM Director &PMacro
```

If the user requests option 3, to create a form-letter file, the program must ask for a name for the file, then copy the selected contents of the Members database to a text file with the appropriate format for interfacing with Word or WordStar. The SET INDEX and MODIFY QUERY commands have already taken care of the sort and search requirements; the DELIMITED WITH " option used with the COPY command will ensure the appropriate format. The third case statement handles these tasks:

```
*------- Make a form-letter file.
CASE MChoice = 3
   Filename = SPACE(14)
   SET CONFIRM ON
   @ 5,0 CLEAR
   @ 15,5 SAY "Enter name of form-letter file (e.g.,;
      B:MMerge.TXT)" GET Filename
   READ
   SET CONFIRM OFF
   COPY TO &Filename DELIMITED WITH "
ENDCASE
```

Notice that the variable Filename is set to 14 spaces to allow for a drive specifier and an extension, and that CONFIRM is set on to give the user a chance to double-check the file name before proceeding.

Once the appropriate report has been printed, we want the program to pause, to allow the user to read information on the screen, and turn off the MODIFY QUERY and DELETED conditions so the user once again has access to all records in the database. The last few lines in the Reports program take care of these tasks before returning control to the Report

Options menu:

```
*------------------ Done. Return to Reports menu.
IF Printer = "Y"
   EJECT
ENDIF
WAIT "Press any key to return to Reports menu . . . "
SET DELETED OFF
SET FILTER TO
RETURN
```

Figure 8.4 shows the entire Reports.PRG file. It is a fairly large program, but it provides extensive sorting and searching capabilities to even the most novice user, because all procedures are selected from single menus.

```
****************************************************** Reports.PRG
*   Set up sort orders and search conditions,
*      then print the appropriate report.
*   Called from Membership main menu.

*------- Open Members database and index files.
USE Members INDEX Names, Zips

CLEAR
@ 2,1 SAY "Report Options"
@ 2,60 SAY DTOC(DATE()) + "      " + TIME()
@ 3,0 SAY ULine
?
?
TEXT
                    1. Mailing labels

                    2. Directory

                    3. Form-letter file


                    4. None (return to main menu)
ENDTEXT

MChoice = 0
@ 24,1 SAY "Enter choice (1-4) " GET MChoice PICT "9" RANGE 1,4
READ

IF MChoice = 4
   RETURN
ENDIF

*------------------ Ask about sort order.
CLEAR
@ 2,1 SAY "Sort Options"
@ 2,60 SAY DTOC(DATE()) + "      " + TIME()
@ 3,0 SAY ULine
?
?
```

Figure 8.4 – The completed Reports command file for the Membership System

```
      TEXT
                            1. Alphabetical order by name

                            2. Zip-code order

                            3. Original (unsorted) order
      ENDTEXT

      SChoice = 0
      @ 24,1 SAY "Enter choice (1-3)" GET SChoice PICT "9" RANGE 1,3
      READ

      *------------------- Set up appropriate sort order.
      DO CASE
          CASE SChoice = 1
              SET INDEX TO Names
          CASE SChoice = 2
              SET INDEX TO Zips
          CASE SChoice = 3
              USE Members
      ENDCASE

      *------------------- Ask about query.
      CLEAR
      AllSome = " "
      @ 5,2 SAY "(A)ll records or (Q)uery? " ;
        GET AllSome PICT "!"
      READ

      *------------------ Respond to query choice.
      IF AllSome = "Q"
          MODIFY QUERY Members
      ENDIF

      *------------------- Print report based on previous MChoice.
      CLEAR
      STORE " " TO Printer, PMacro

      *------- If not making a form-letter file, ask about printer.
      IF MChoice < 3
          @ 15,5 SAY "Send data to printer? (Y/N) " GET Printer PICT "!"
          READ
          IF Printer = "Y"
              PMacro = "TO PRINT"
              WAIT "Prepare printer, then press any key to continue..."
          ENDIF
      ENDIF

      *------- Leave out records marked for deletion.
      SET DELETED ON
      CLEAR

      DO CASE

          *------- Print mailing labels.
          CASE MChoice = 1
              LABEL FORM TwoCol &PMacro

          *------- Print directory.
          CASE MChoice = 2
              REPORT FORM Director &PMacro
```

Figure 8.4 – The completed Reports command file for the Membership System (continued)

```
      *------- Make a form-letter file.
      CASE MChoice = 3
           Filename = SPACE(14)
           SET CONFIRM ON
           @ 5,0 CLEAR
           @ 15,5 SAY "Enter name of form-letter file (e.g., B:MMerge.TXT)";
             GET Filename
           READ
           SET CONFIRM OFF
           COPY TO &Filename DELIMITED WITH "

      ENDCASE

      *------------------- Done.  Return to Reports menu.
      IF Printer = "Y"
           EJECT
      ENDIF
      WAIT "Press any key to return to Reports menu..."
      SET DELETED OFF
      SET FILTER TO
      RETURN
```

Figure 8.4 – The completed Reports command file for the Membership System (continued)

Testing the Program

After the program is all typed and saved, you can execute Members from the dot prompt and select option 2 from the main menu to test the program. Try out various sorting and searching options, as well as all three reports. Since this is such a large program, you may have to do a little debugging. If you have trouble debugging, remember to use the SET ECHO ON command from the dot prompt to watch the program run (see Chapter 3).

Membership System Enhancements

In addition to adding names to our Members database, we'll need to make changes and delete records, so in this chapter we'll develop the EditDel program to handle these tasks. As with the program for adding new records to the database, we'll first design a custom editing screen and then develop a command file to make the process as easy as possible for the user.

Custom Screen for Editing and Deleting

Figure 9.1 shows the custom screen we'll use in the Membership System for editing and deleting member records. Since this screen is so similar to the AddNames screen we developed earlier, we can just modify the Add-Names.SCR file. First, make a copy of AddNames.SCR and name it EdNames.SCR by entering this command at the dBASE dot prompt:

COPY FILE AddNames.SCR TO EdNames.SCR

On a floppy-disk system, you may need to use the command below:

COPY FILE B:AddNames.SCR TO B:EdNames.SCR

Now you can use the Screen Painter to change this new EdNames

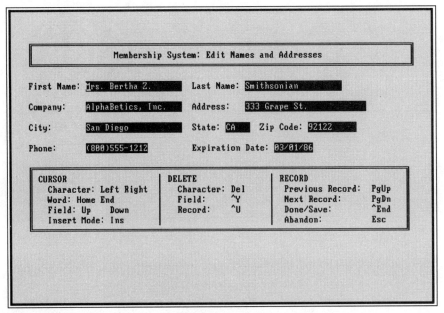

Figure 9.1 – *Custom screen for editing membership data*

screen. First, enter these commands at the dot prompt:

USE Members INDEX Names,Zips
MODIFY SCREEN EdNames

When the Screen Painter menu appears, press F10 to see the screen. Change the screen title inside the box to

Membership System: Edit Names and Addresses

To center the new heading, position the cursor at Row 02 Col 18 and type ^T. When you're done, the modified screen should look like Figure 9.2. Press F10 to call up the Screen Painter menu, highlight Exit, and select Save to save the new screen and generate the EdNames format file.

To test the EdNames.FMT file, load dBASE and at the dot prompt type

USE Members INDEX Names, Zips

Then type these commands:

SET FORMAT TO EdNames
EDIT 1

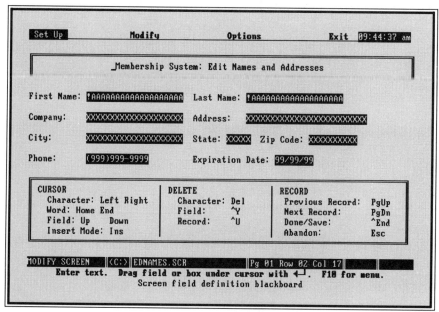

Figure 9.2 – *The EdNames custom screen on the Blackboard*

Data from record number 1 in the Members database file appears on the custom screen. Type ^U a few times and watch the Del symbol appear and disappear from the top of the screen. Move to other records and make some changes to the data. When you've finished testing, press ^End to return to the dot prompt. Then reset the normal dBASE screen by typing the command

CLOSE FORMAT

The EditDel Command File

Now let's create the EditDel command file that will use the EdNames screen.

Writing the Pseudocode

We want the EditDel command file to ask the user for the name of the individual whose record is to be edited or deleted, as in Figure 9.3. The

```
Edit/Delete Records                              06/12/86   13:01:59
_____




              Last name  : ████████████████
              First name : ████████████████




          ** Enter name of member to edit/delete **
```

Figure 9.3 – The EditDel opening screen

user can type just the last name or both the last and first names of the member. If the program finds the member's record, we want the data to be displayed on the custom edit screen. If the record cannot be found in the database, we want the computer to beep, briefly display the message

Not found!

and then allow the user to try again.

When the user has finished editing and presses ^End (or just presses Return when the program asks for another name), we want the Membership System main menu to reappear on the screen.

The pseudocode for the EditDel command file looks like this:

Use Members database with both index files

Set up loop for editing names

    Clear screen

    Get last and first name of record to edit

    If no name entered, return to main menu

    If name entered, try to find member's record to edit

If record found, allow edit

If record not found, beep and warn user

Continue to allow editing (until user requests to exit)

When user is done editing, ask whether records marked for deletion should be removed

If user requests deletion, pack database

Return to main menu

Writing the Command File

Now let's begin developing the program. As usual, start from the dBASE dot prompt and type this command:

MODIFY COMMAND EditDel

We'll have the first few lines of the program present the program name and function and then execute the Members data file with the Names and Zips index files. It's especially important to use both index files here, so that any changes to the database are entered in both indices simultaneously. Here are the first few lines of the EditDel file:

```
* * * * * * * * * * * * * * * * * * * * * * * * * * * * * * * * EditDel.PRG
*
* Edit and delete members using EdNames screen format.
* Called from Membership main menu.
*
USE Members INDEX Names, Zips
```

Next we'll set up a loop in the program so the user can continue to edit as many members' records as desired before returning to the main menu. We'll use a logical variable called More to control the loop:

```
*------------------ Set up loop for editing.
More = .T.
DO WHILE More
```

Now we want the program to clear the screen, display a heading, set up memory variables for storing the search criteria, and then ask the user to enter the name to search for:

```
CLEAR
@ 2,1 SAY "Edit/Delete Records"
@ 2,60 SAY DTOC(DATE()) + "      " + TIME()
@ 3,0 SAY ULine
STORE SPACE(20) TO Mem_LName, Mem_FName
@ 15,5 SAY "Last name :" GET Mem_LName
@ 17,5 SAY "First name :" GET Mem_FName
@ 24,1 SAY "* * Enter name of member to edit/delete * *"
READ
```

If the user does not enter a last name to search for, we want the program to set the More variable that controls the loop to False, then skip all remaining lines down to ENDDO by using the LOOP command:

```
*------- Exit if no last name entered.
IF Mem_LName = " "
   More = .F.
   LOOP
ENDIF
```

If the user enters a name to search for, we need to have the program set up a search string. First, we store the uppercase equivalent of the last name to a variable called Search. If a first name was also specified, we add that to the Search memory variable:

```
*------- If name entered, create search string.
Search = UPPER(Mem_LName)
IF Mem_FName # " "
   Search = Search + TRIM(UPPER(Mem_FName))
ENDIF
```

The program attempts to find the appropriate record. Since the database is indexed on UPPER(LName) + UPPER(FName), and the Names index is the first-listed active index file, we can use the SEEK command to look up the record to edit:

```
*------- Try to find that individual.
SEEK Search
```

If the SEEK command finds the name the user requested, we want the program to set the format to the custom EdNames screen and allow editing. If the name was not found, we want the program to beep (CHR(7)) and display the message "Not found!". The following lines take care of these tasks:

```
*------- If found, edit. Otherwise, warn user.
  IF FOUND()
     SET FORMAT TO EdNames
     EDIT RECNO()
     SET FORMAT TO
  ELSE
     @ 5,0 CLEAR
     @ 15,5 SAY "Not found!"
     ? CHR(7)
  ENDIF
```

After the editing is completed for this record, the program loops back and asks for another name:

```
  ENDDO (while More)
```

When the user is finished editing, the program can return to the main menu. But first we want to ask the user about packing the records that have been marked for deletion. Since the packing process is usually pretty slow and removes records from the database permanently, it's a good idea to give the user some control over when (or whether) packing occurs. The last routine in the program takes care of packing, if selected, before returning to the main menu:

```
*------------------ Done editing. Ask about packing the database.
@ 5,0 CLEAR
YesNo = " "
@ 15,5 SAY "Pack records marked for deletion now? (Y/N) ";
  GET YesNo PICTURE "!"
READ
IF YesNo = "Y"
  SET TALK ON
  PACK
  SET TALK OFF
ENDIF
RETURN
```

Notice that we set the TALK parameter back on briefly in the above routine. dBASE normally presents a counter while the database is being packed, and since the PACK process takes some time to complete, displaying the count by setting TALK on reassures the user that progress is being made.

Figure 9.4 shows the entire EditDel.PRG file.

```
****************************************************** EditDel.PRG.
*
*   Edit and delete members using EdNames screen format.
*   Called from Membership main menu.
*

USE Members INDEX Names, Zips

*------------------- Set up loop for editing.
More = .T.
DO WHILE More
    CLEAR
    @ 2,1 SAY "Edit/Delete Records"
    @ 2,60 SAY DTOC(DATE()) + "     " + TIME()
    @ 3,0 SAY ULine

    STORE SPACE(20) TO Mem_LName, Mem_FName
    @ 15,5 SAY "Last name  :" GET Mem_LName
    @ 17,5 SAY "First name :" GET Mem_FName
    @ 24,1 SAY "** Enter name of member to edit/delete **"
    READ

    *------- Exit if no last name entered.
    IF Mem_LName = "  "
        More = .F.
        LOOP
    ENDIF

    *------- If name entered, create search string.
    Search = UPPER(Mem_LName)
    IF Mem_FName # "  "
        Search = Search + TRIM(UPPER(Mem_FName))
    ENDIF

    *------- Try to find that individual.
    SEEK Search

    *------- If found, edit.  Otherwise, warn user.
    IF FOUND()
        SET FORMAT TO EdNames
        EDIT RECNO()
        SET FORMAT TO
    ELSE
        @ 5,0 CLEAR
        @ 15,5 SAY "Not found!"
        ? CHR(7)
    ENDIF

ENDDO (while More)
```

Figure 9.4 – *The completed EditDel command file*

```
*------------------- Done editing. Ask about packing the database.
@ 5,0 CLEAR
YesNo = " "

@ 15,5 SAY "Pack records marked for deletion now? (Y/N) ";
   GET YesNo PICTURE "!"
READ

IF YesNo = "Y"
    SET TALK ON
    PACK
    SET TALK OFF
ENDIF

RETURN
```

Figure 9.4 – *The completed EditDel command file (continued)*

Testing the Program

Once the EditDel program is keyed in and saved, you can test it by typing

DO Members

Then select option 3 from the main menu to edit data. The screen asks for the name of the member whose record is to be edited. To test the program fully, try entering names of people who aren't in the database, as well as names of people who are. Try typing just a last name, a first and last name, and even a last name and a first initial. (Remember that while the EDIT screen is displayed you can use the PgUp and PgDn keys to move around the database and make changes to other members' data.)

We've developed an easy-to-use system that allows us to add members, update their data, and delete members, and also to create labels, form letters, and directories. But there are some other things we can do to make this a really streamlined package: for instance, add a program to check for duplicate names and addresses in the Members database. We'll develop several of these enhancements in Chapter 10.

Membership System
Editing and Deleting

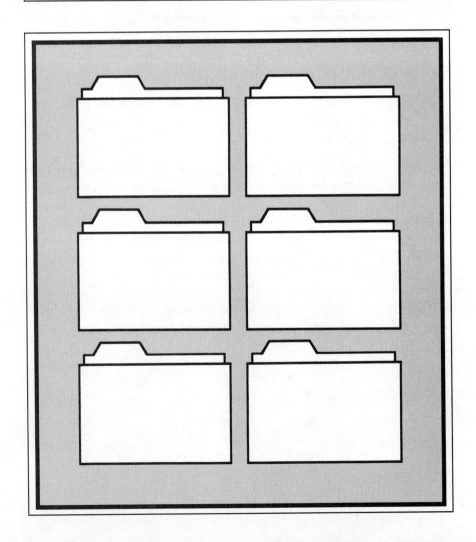

In this chapter we'll develop the final program in the Membership System, DupCheck.PRG, which checks for duplicate records in the database. In addition, we'll discuss some more advanced programming techniques to enhance the Membership System.

Checking for Duplicate Members

The final program in the Membership System checks the database for duplicate records based on identical zip codes, addresses, and last names. Rather than actually deleting records, the program displays a report of possible duplications, as in Figure 10.1.

The easiest way to check for duplicates in a database is to first sort the data into some order, then check for matching pairs. For this example, we'll have the program index the Members database based on zip code, address, and last name. Then the program will display all records that match on these fields.

```
Possible Duplications                                06/01/85


     Kenney, Dave  371 Brill St. 92112
     Kenney, David  371 Brill St. 92112
     Kenney, D. 371 Brill St. 92112

     Tobin, Cecilia  280 Z St. 92038
     Tobin, Ralph  280 Z St. 92038
```

Figure 10.1 – Membership System duplications report

The pseudocode for the DupCheck command file is displayed below:

Set dBASE parameters

Use the Members database

Create an index of zip code and address

Ask about the printer

Set printer on, if necessary

Clear the screen

Print report title

Loop through database

    Store Zip, Address, and Name

    Skip down one record

    See if identical match occurs. If so,

        skip back one record and

        list records with identical match

    Otherwise

        continue at next record

Continue loop

When done, reset parameters

Return to main menu

As usual, we'll use the dBASE MODIFY COMMAND editor to create the program. To begin, enter this command next to the dot prompt:

MODIFY COMMAND DupCheck

Then start the program with the usual identifying lines and some SET parameters, as below:

```
* * * * * * * * * * * * * * * * * * * * * * * * * * * DupCheck.PRG
* Scan database for possible duplicates.
* Called from Members.PRG
*
SET HEADING OFF
SET DELETED ON
SET SAFETY OFF
```

The HEADING command is used to keep headings from being printed with the LIST command used later in the program. The DELETED parameter keeps records that have already been marked for deletion from being displayed in the duplicates report. The SAFETY setting keeps dBASE from asking for permission to write the temporary index file later in the program.

The next routines we'll set up ask the user whether the duplicates report should be sent to the printer and set the printer on if the answer is yes.

```
* * * * * * * * * * * * * * * * * * * * * * * * * * Ask about printer.
CLEAR
Printer = " "
@ 15,5 SAY "Send possible duplicates to printer? (Y/N) ";
   GET Printer PICTURE "!"
READ
* * * * * * * * * * * * * * * * * * * * * Set printer on, if necessary.
IF Printer = "Y"
   WAIT "Prepare printer, then press any key to continue . . . "
   SET PRINT ON
ENDIF
```

Next, we want the command file to create an index of zip codes and addresses. This index file could be treated as the Names and Zips indices are; that is, created once and kept active throughout all appending and editing. However, since you probably won't perform duplication checks very often, it is wiser to just create a new index file each time you need it. The routine below creates the temporary index file named Temp.NDX:

```
* * * * * * * * * * * Display resorting message and create index file.
CLEAR
@ 5,10 SAY "Resorting: Please wait . . . "
USE Members
INDEX ON Zip + Address + LName TO Temp
```

The next routine clears the screen and prints the report title:

```
*------------------ Clear screen and print title.
CLEAR
? "Possible Duplications" + SPACE(30) + DTOC(DATE())
?
?
```

Next, we need a DO WHILE loop that reads through every record in the database. In the loop, the zip code, address, and last name are stored in a variable named Compare. Then the program skips to the next record in the database and compares the new zip code, address, and last name to those in the previous record. If they match, the program skips back to the original record and displays all duplicate records with a LIST WHILE command. Then the program continues through the database, checking each record for matching adjacent records.

```
* * * * * * * * * * * * * Loop through database until end of file, and
* * * * * * * * * * * * * compare last name, address, and zip code.
DO WHILE .NOT. EOF()
   Compare = UPPER(Zip) + UPPER(Address) + ;
   UPPER(LName)
   SKIP
   IF UPPER(Zip) + UPPER(Address) + UPPER(LName) = ;
   Compare
      SKIP - 1
      LIST WHILE UPPER(Zip) + UPPER(Address) + ;
        UPPER(LName) = Compare;
        TRIM(LName) + ", " + TRIM(FName) ;
        + " " + TRIM(Address) + " " + Zip OFF
      ?
   ENDIF (Equal records)
ENDDO (while not eof)
```

When the duplication check is done, the program ejects the printer page and sets the printer off, then erases the temporary index file and returns to the main menu, as shown below:

```
* * * * * * * * * * * * * * * * * * * * * * * * Turn off printer, if necessary.
IF Printer = "Y"
   EJECT
   SET PRINT OFF
ENDIF (printer)
* * * * * * * * * * * * * * * * * * * Done. Erase temporary index file.
CLOSE DATABASE
ERASE Temp.NDX
* * * * * * * * * * * * * * * * * * * * Pause, then return to main menu.
@ 24,1
WAIT "Press any key to return to main menu . . . "
SET DELETED OFF
SET SAFETY ON
RETURN
```

Figure 10.2 shows the entire DupCheck command file.

```
****************************************************** DupCheck.PRG
*   Scan database for possible duplicates.
*   Called from Members.PRG
*
SET HEADING OFF
SET DELETED ON
SET SAFETY OFF

******************** Ask about printer.
CLEAR
Printer = " "
@ 15,5 SAY "Send possible duplicates to printer? (Y/N) ";
   GET Printer PICTURE "!"
READ

******************** Set printer on, if necessary.
IF Printer = "Y"
    WAIT "Prepare printer, then press any key to continue..."
    SET PRINT ON
ENDIF

******** Display resorting message and create index file.
CLEAR
@ 5,10 SAY "Resorting: Please Wait..."
USE Members
INDEX ON Zip + Address + LName TO Temp
```

Figure 10.2 – The DupCheck command file

```
******************* Clear screen and print title.
CLEAR
? "Possible Duplications" + SPACE(30) + DTOC(DATE())
?
?

******** Loop through database until end of file, and
******** compare last name, address, and zip code.

DO WHILE .NOT. EOF()
    Compare = UPPER(Zip)+UPPER(Address)+UPPER(LName)
    SKIP
    IF UPPER(Zip)+UPPER(Address)+UPPER(LName)= Compare
        SKIP -1
        LIST WHILE UPPER(Zip)+UPPER(Address)+UPPER(LName)=Compare;
          TRIM(LName) + ", " + TRIM(FName) ;
          + "   " + TRIM(Address) + " " + Zip OFF
        ?
    ENDIF (Equal records)
ENDDO (while not eof)

******************* Turn off printer, if necessary.
IF Printer = "Y"
    EJECT
    SET PRINT OFF
ENDIF (printer)

****************** Done. Erase temporary index file.
CLOSE DATABASE
ERASE Temp.NDX

****************** Pause, then return to main menu.
@ 24,1
WAIT "Press any key to return to main menu..."
SET DELETED OFF
SET SAFETY ON
RETURN
```

Figure 10.2 – The DupCheck command file (continued)

Mailing Labels Alignment Check

You can have the Reports program check the alignment of labels in the printer before printing. Load Reports.PRG with the MODIFY COMMAND editor and change the routine that reads

```
*------- Print mailing labels.
CASE MChoice = 1
    LABEL FORM TwoCol &PMacro
```

to this one:

```
*------- Print mailing labels.
CASE MChoice = 1
     LABEL FORM TwoCol SAMPLE &PMacro
```

Then save the command file with the usual ^W or ^End keys.

When you run the Reports program and ask to print mailing labels, the SAMPLE option will display two false labels as rows of asterisks. These show how the actual labels will be printed. The prompt

Do you want more samples? (Y/N)

will appear on the screen.

If the labels are not properly aligned, adjust them in the printer and select Y to print more samples. Repeat this process until the labels are properly aligned, then select No to quit printing samples. The program will then print all the mailing labels in the system.

The Directory Program

One problem you may find with dBASE III PLUS is that the REPORT command is sometimes unwieldy when formatting a report from a large database with many fields. In this section, we'll develop a program, named PrintDir.PRG, to print a formatted report without the use of the REPORT command. Figure 10.3 shows a sample report printed by the PrintDir program.

The pseudocode for the PrintDir command file is displayed below:

Set up LineCount, PageCount, and Title

Start at top of database

Set printer on if requested

Print report title

Loop through each record in database

    Print last and first name

    Print company

    Print address and phone number

Format city, state, zip

Print city, state, zip, and expiration date

Print a blank line

Increment line counter by 5

If report is being printed, handle pagination

Start on new page

Increment page counter

Print report title

Reset line counter

Skip to next database record

When done, handle printer and return to Reports menu.

The PrintDir program is fairly large, so we'll take it a step at a time. First, the program begins with the usual opening lines and sets up three

```
Membership Directory                          05/15/85   Page  1
----------------------------------------------------------------

Smithsonian, Mrs. Bertha Z.
ABC Co.
333 Grape St.                         (938)402-9312
San Diego, CA      92122                 12/31/85

Kenney, Dave
Kenney and Einy, Ltd
371 Brill St.                         (800)555-1212
Los Angeles, CA      92112               04/01/85

Rosielli, Richard
Raydontics, Inc.
444 Scotch Dr.                        (293)842-0932
Glendora, CA      91740                  12/31/85

Stark, Robin
QSA Computers
771 Mt. Alifan Dr.                    (892)374-2912
San Diego, CA      92111                 12/31/85

Eprom, Edna and Ethan
Liquid Crystal, Inc.
471 Archibald Way                     (387)837-4912
Las Vegas, NE      88888                 01/30/86
```

Figure 10.3 – *Sample report printed by the PrintDir program*

memory variables: LineCount (line counter), PageCount (page counter), and Title (report title). Then the program positions the record pointer to the top of the database, as shown below:

```
* * * * * * * * * * * * * * * * * * * * * * * * * * * * * * * * PrintDir.PRG
* Print directory for Membership System.
* Called from modified Reports.PRG.
*
* ------- Initialize LineCount and Title variables.
LineCount = 4
PageCount = 1
Title = "Membership Directory"
* ------- Start at top of database.
GO TOP
```

Next, the program turns on the printer if the Printer variable (from Reports.PRG) has been set to "Y":

```
* ------- Set printer on if requested.
IF Printer = "Y"
   SET PRINT ON
ENDIF (Printer = "Y")
```

Then the program prints the report heading, which includes the title, 35 blank spaces, the current date (DTOC(DATE())), and the page number (PageCount).

```
* ------- Print title.
? Title + SPACE(35) + DTOC(DATE()) + "    Page " +;
STR(PageCount,2)
? ULine
?
?
```

Now we'll set up a loop that moves through the entire database:

```
* ------- Loop through each record in database.
DO WHILE .NOT. EOF()
```

At this point the actual printing begins. First the name, company, address, and phone number are printed on the report:

```
? TRIM(LName) + ", " + FName
? Company
? Address + SPACE(10) + Phone
```

Then, to ensure proper formatting, we assign the city (with trailing blanks trimmed off) followed by a comma and a space, the state, and the zip code to a variable named FullCSZ:

```
FullCSZ = TRIM(City) + ", " + State + " " + Zip
```

The next line ensures that the program prints the expiration date in column 40 (adds 40 spaces and the expiration date, minus the length of FullCSZ, to the FullCSZ variable). Then the program prints FullCSZ and a blank line:

```
FullCSZ = FullCSZ + SPACE(40 – LEN(FullCSZ)) + ;
DTOC(Exp_Date)
? FullCSZ
?
```

The line counter is then incremented by 5:

```
LineCount = LineCount + 5
```

If the report is being sent to the printer, the program has to notice when it is time to start a new page (LineCounter > = 55). At this time the page advances (EJECT), the page counter increases by 1, the title is printed, and the line counter resets to 4. This is set up in the following routine:

```
* ------- If report is being printed, handle pagination.
IF Printer = "Y" .AND. LineCount > = 55
   EJECT
   PageCount = PageCount + 1
   ? Title + SPACE(35) + DTOC(DATE()) + "    Page " + ;
     STR(PageCount + 1)
   ? ULine
   ?
   ?
   LineCount = 4
ENDIF
```

Next, the program skips to the next record in the database and continues printing records until it encounters the end of the file:

```
SKIP
ENDDO (while not eof)
```

After the directory is printed, the program simply turns the printer off and returns control to the Reports program:

*------ Done. Return to Reports program.
SET PRINT OFF
RETURN

Figure 10.4 displays the entire PrintDir program.

```
**************************************************** PrintDir.PRG
* Print directory for Membership System.
* Called from modified Reports.PRG.
* ------ Initialize LineCount and Title variables.
LineCount = 4
PageCount = 1
Title = "Membership Directory"

* ------ Start at top of database.
GO TOP

* ------ Set printer on if requested.
IF Printer = "Y"
   SET PRINT ON
ENDIF (Printer = "Y")

* ------ Print title.
? Title + SPACE(35) + DTOC(DATE()) + "   Page " + STR(PageCount,2)
? ULine
?
?
* ------ Loop through each record in database.
DO WHILE .NOT. EOF()
    ? TRIM(LName) + ", " + FName
    ? Company
    ? Address+SPACE(10)+Phone
    FullCSZ = TRIM(City) + ", " + State+" "+Zip
    FullCSZ = FullCSZ + SPACE(40-LEN(FullCSZ))+DTOC(Exp_Date)
    ? FullCSZ
    ?
    LineCount = LineCount + 5

    * -------- If report is being printed, handle pagination.
    IF Printer = "Y" .AND. LineCount >= 55
        EJECT
        PageCount = PageCount + 1
        ? Title + SPACE(35) + DTOC(DATE()) + "   Page " + ;
          STR(PageCount+1)
        ? ULine
        ?
        ?
        LineCount = 4
    ENDIF
    SKIP
ENDDO (while not eof)
* ------ Done. Return to Reports program.

SET PRINT OFF
RETURN
```

Figure 10.4 – The PrintDir program

To use the PrintDir program, you need to modify the Reports command file. At present, Reports.PRG accesses the Director.FRM file to print a report, as shown in the following lines:

```
*------- Print directory.
CASE MChoice = 2
   REPORT FORM Director &PMacro
```

Use the commands MODIFY COMMAND REPORT to change these lines so that they access the PrintDir program:

```
*------- Print directory.
CASE MChoice = 2
DO PrintDir
```

To test the program, execute Members from the dot prompt, and select menu options to print the directory.

Stopping the Printer

If you use a command file rather than REPORT FORM to print a report, you can also add a feature to stop the printer by pressing any key. In this example, the screen displays this message while the report is being printed:

Press any key to abort print job

Pressing any key displays the message

Print job aborted . . .

and returns control to the Membership System main menu.

To add this feature to the PrintDir program, you need to use the MODIFY COMMAND editor to change the routine that reads

```
*------- Set printer on if requested.
IF Printer = "Y"
   SET PRINT ON
ENDIF (Printer = "Y")
```

to this:

```
* ------- Set printer on if requested.
IF Printer = "Y"
   * ----------------- Allow for printer abort.
   CLEAR
   @ 23,1 SAY "Press any key to abort print job"
   CLEAR TYPEAHEAD
   ON KEY DO PrinStop
   SET CONSOLE OFF
   SET PRINT ON
ENDIF
```

The CLEAR command clears the screen, and the @ displays the "Press any key to abort print job" message. Then the CLEAR TYPEAHEAD command clears out any extraneous keystrokes from the typeahead buffer. (Every time you press a key, it first goes into a "holding tank" called the typeahead buffer. To ensure that the next command in the program, ON KEY, works, it's best to make sure the typeahead buffer is clear.)

The command ON KEY DO PrinStop will run a program named PrinStop-.PRG (which we'll write in a moment) that, in turn, will stop all printing, get the database and index files back in shape, and return to the main menu. The command SET CONSOLE OFF keeps the printed report from appearing on the screen so that the "Press any key to abort print job" message doesn't disappear.

At the bottom of the PrintDir program, you need to change the last lines from

```
* ------- Done. Return to Reports program.
SET PRINT OFF
RETURN
```

to

```
* ------- Done. Return to Reports program.
SET CONSOLE ON
ON KEY
CLEAR TYPEAHEAD
SET PRINT OFF
RETURN
```

These commands will be executed after the entire report is printed, only if the user does *not* press any key to abort printing. The SET CONSOLE ON command returns the screen back to normal. (Forgetting this command leaves the screen permanently blank, unless you successfully type in the command SET CONSOLE ON without being able to see what you're typing.) The ON KEY command disables the previous ON KEY DO PrinStop command, so the next keypress does not run the PrinStop program. CLEAR TYPEAHEAD again clears out any extraneous keystrokes, which is just a precautionary measure in this case.

Once you've modified the PrintDir program and saved it, you need to create the PrinStop program using the usual MODIFY COMMAND editor. Figure 10.5 shows the PrinStop program.

The PrinStop program is run only if the user presses any key to abort printing. PrinStop.PRG immediately sets the console back on, turns off the printer, and clears the screen. Then it displays the message "Print job aborted . . . ", as shown in the lines below:

```
*------------------ PrinStop.PRG
*------- Halt printer and return to main menu.
SET CONSOLE ON
SET PRINT OFF
CLEAR
? "Print job aborted . . . "
```

```
*-------------------------------- PrinStop.PRG
*--------- Halt printer and return to main menu.
SET CONSOLE ON
SET PRINT OFF
CLEAR
? "Print job aborted..."
SET FILTER TO
SET DELETED OFF
SET INDEX TO Names,Zips
CLEAR TYPEAHEAD
ON KEY
RETURN TO MASTER
```

Figure 10.5 – The PrinStop program

The SET FILTER TO command removes any filter conditions set by the query form (back in the Reports program). The SET DELETED OFF command "unhides" the records marked for deletion, and the SET INDEX command reactivates the Names and Zips index files, as shown in the lines below:

SET FILTER TO
SET DELETED OFF
SET INDEX TO Names,Zips

Finally, the program clears the typeahead buffer, disables the previous ON KEY DO PrinStop command, and returns all the way back to the main menu, Members.PRG, using the commands below:

CLEAR TYPEAHEAD
ON KEY
RETURN TO MASTER

In essence, PrinStop.PRG performs the same tasks that the closing lines in PrintDir.PRG and Reports.PRG perform. However, PrinStop.PRG performs them without first printing the entire report. Figure 10.6 shows the entire modified PrintDir command file.

```
************************************************* PrintDir.PRG
*
*   Print directory for Membership System.
*   Called from modified Reports.PRG.

*------- Initialize LineCount and Title variables.
LineCount = 4
PageCount = 1
Title = "Membership Directory"

*------- Start at top of database.
GO TOP

*------- Set printer on if requested.
IF Printer = "Y"
   *---------------- Allow for printer abort.
   CLEAR
   @ 23,1 SAY "Press any key to abort print job"
   CLEAR TYPEAHEAD
   ON KEY DO PrinStop
   SET CONSOLE OFF
   SET PRINT ON
ENDIF
```

Figure 10.6 – PrintDir.PRG modified for printer abort

```
      *------- Print title.
      ? Title + SPACE(35) + DTOC(DATE()) + "    Page " + STR(PageCount,2)
      ? ULine
      ?
      ?

      *------- Loop through each record in database.
      DO WHILE .NOT. EOF()
          ? TRIM(LName)+" " + FName
          ? Company
          ? Address+SPACE(10)+Phone
          FullCsz = TRIM(City) + ", "+State+" "+Zip
          FullCSZ = FullCSZ + SPACE(40-LEN(FullCSZ))+DTOC(Exp_Date)
          ? FullCSZ
          ?
          LineCount = LineCount + 5

          *--- If report is being printed, handle pagination.
          IF Printer = "Y" .AND. LineCount >= 50
              EJECT
              PageCount = PageCount + 1
              ? Title + SPACE(35) + DTOC(DATE()) + "    Page " + ;
                STR(PageCount,2)
              ? ULine
              ?
              ?
          LineCount = 4
          ENDIF·
          SKIP
      ENDDO (while not eof)

      *------- Done. Return to Reports program.
      SET CONSOLE ON
      ON KEY
      CLEAR TYPEAHEAD
      SET PRINT OFF
      RETURN
```

Figure 10.6 – PrintDir.PRG modified for printer abort (continued)

Inventory System Design

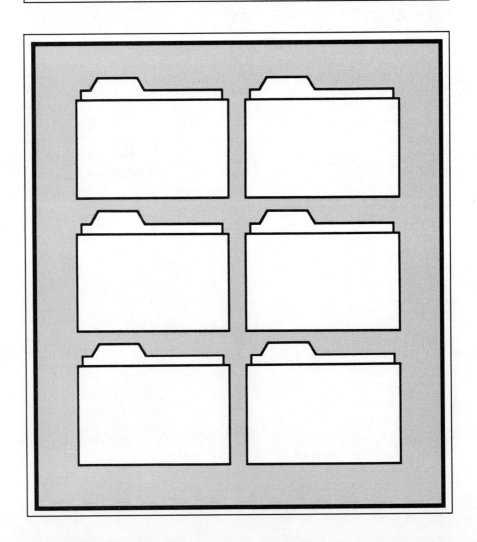

Most modern businesses require some method of inventory control, whether they are involved in outside sales or need to monitor equipment and supplies for internal use. Beginning with this chapter, we'll develop such an inventory system for a retail sales enterprise. This will give us an opportunity to use a software system with a master file and two transaction files (see Chapter 1). Then, in Chapter 21, we'll discuss how the Inventory System can be linked with the Accounts Receivable System we'll develop later in the book to create a complete sales management package.

General Design of Inventory Systems

Inventory systems generally require the use of several data files. One file, usually referred to as the *master file*, keeps track of the quantity of each item presently in stock. In addition, it may also keep track of the location of each item in the warehouse, the cost of the item, the reorder point, the quantity currently on order, and the name and address of the vendor the item is purchased from. This allows the user of the system to locate an item quickly, get a listing of goods that need to be ordered, automatically create and print new orders, and perform other similar stock-control tasks.

Most businesses also like to keep track of each individual transaction that occurs within the business. Information on these individual transactions is usually maintained in separate data files called *transaction files.* One such file might keep track of individual sales transactions: to whom items were sold, when, for how much, and the invoice or receipt number. A second transaction file might maintain an ongoing record of all new stock received. We can see the relationship between the master file and two such transaction files in Figure 11.1.

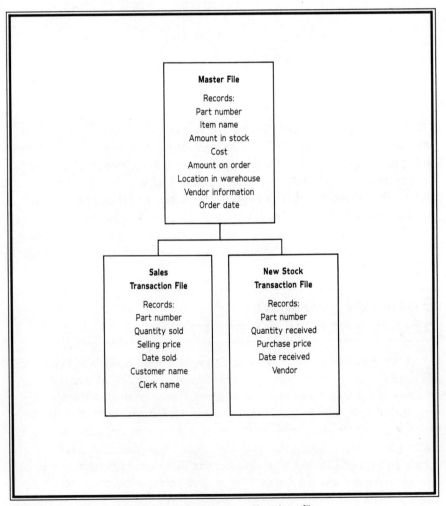

Figure 11.1 – Relationship of typical inventory system data files

The transaction files maintain a *history* of all individual transactions involving the sale and receipt of goods, while the master file maintains the *current* status of goods in stock at any given moment by using information supplied directly from the two transaction files. In a sense, the master file is an up-to-date summary of all activities in the two transaction files.

Key Fields

Whenever we design a system involving multiple data files such as these, it is very important to define a *key field* that can be used to relate the various files to one another. A dBASE III PLUS key field has the following characteristics:

- It is unique for every record (item) in the master file.

- It exists in the master file *and* in the transaction files with the identical field name, type, and width.

The key field in most software systems is an identifying code. In an inventory system such as the one we're designing here, this code is usually a part number: each item the store carries has a unique part number. The government uses the social security number column in its IRS database as a key field, since every employed individual has a unique social security number. The Department of Motor Vehicles issues each licensed driver a unique driver's license number, and banks issue each account a unique account number; this is also true for credit-card accounts. All of these are used as key fields in computerized systems.

Without the use of key fields, data can be very difficult to manage. For example, suppose the government did not use social security numbers. Well, there are probably several thousand Alan Simpsons in the country. When I pay my taxes and the IRS wishes to record this fact, they can either dig through thousands of files on people with my name to make sure they find the right Alan Simpson, or they can just enter my social security number in their computer to update my tax file. Obviously, the latter is much easier and less error prone. So by simply assigning each individual a unique code and using that code as a key field, the government's job has become easier and more efficient.

Even on as small a scale as our Inventory System, key fields are necessary. The reasons will become apparent as we develop the system.

Inventory System Problem Definition

Our Inventory System will be designed to allow a small business to keep track of all goods in stock, goods on order, and the location of the goods in the store. Whenever the store decides to carry a new item, the item will be assigned a unique part number and added to the master database. The system will provide the user with reports of all goods in stock, items that need to be reordered, and items on order, and it will automatically produce purchase orders.

The system will also allow the user to keep track of all individual sales transactions: item sold, to whom sold, salesperson, date of sale, and invoice number. Similarly, the user will be able to keep track of all incoming goods as stock is replenished. The individual transaction records from sales and goods received will be used to update the stock status records in the master file automatically.

Inventory System I/O Specifications

The primary output from the Inventory System master file will be reports concerning the status of the inventory and purchase orders for restocking. A current inventory report will display the part number, part description, quantity on hand, purchase price, location in warehouse, and quantity on order for each item in stock. A reorder report will list all those items that need to be reordered, and an on-order report will list all items currently on open order. Finally, the system will actually print the purchase orders when the user is ready to restock.

We'll need at least the following input in the master database to develop all these reports:

Part number
Item description
Quantity in stock
Purchase price
Reorder point

Quantity on order
Location in warehouse
Vendor name
Vendor address
Date of last update
Date of last order
Quantity to order

The system should produce a receipt for each sales transaction. The receipt should contain the part number, quantity, invoice (receipt) number, salesperson's name, customer's name, selling price, and date. So the sales transaction file will need to include the following:

Part number
Invoice number
Salesperson's name
Customer's name
Quantity sold
Selling price
Date sold
Whether posted

And finally, the system must keep track of goods received and produce a report showing the part number, quantity received, purchase price, date received, and name of vendor. So the new-stock transaction file will need to include the following:

Part number
Quantity
Purchase price
Date received
Vendor name
Whether posted

Now that we have a basic idea of the information we want the Inventory System to manage, we can begin designing the database structure.

Inventory System Database Design

We'll use three data files to manage the inventory: the master file, called Master.DBF, and two transaction files, called Sales.DBF and NewStock.DBF.

The Master File

The structure of Master.DBF, with a brief description of each field's contents, is shown in Figure 11.2. You can use this information to build the Master database with the dBASE CREATE command:

CREATE Master

(Remember to set the default to the appropriate disk drive before you begin developing your files. As usual in this book, we'll use drive B as the default drive. If you're using a hard-disk system, set the default to C.)

To keep the data file in part-number order, as well as to speed up the processes of looking up and updating items, we'll create an index file of the Part_No field and call it Master.NDX. To do this, simply type in these commands:

USE Master
INDEX ON Part_No TO Master

```
Structure for the Master data file

    Field name     Type      Width  Dec        Contents
    ================================================================

  1 PART_NO        Character    5              Part number (key field)
  2 TITLE          Character   20              Item description
  3 QTY            Numeric      4     0        Quantity in stock
  4 COST           Numeric      9     2        Purchase price
  5 REORDER        Numeric      4     0        Reorder point
  6 ON_ORDER       Numeric      4     0        Quantity on order
  7 LOCATION       Character    5              Location in warehouse
  8 VENDOR         Character   25              Vendor name
  9 VENDOR_ADD     Character   25              Vendor address
 10 VENDOR_CSZ     Character   25              Vendor city, state, zip
 11 DATE           Date         8              Date of last update
 12 ORDER_DATE     Date         8              Date of last order
 13 NEW_ORDER      Numeric      4     0        Quantity to order
```

Figure 11.2 – Structure for the Master data file

The Sales File

Next we'll create a data file to keep track of individual sales transactions. Notice that in the Master.DBF file we just created, the key field is named Part_No, has a Character data type, and is five characters wide. Since this will be the field used for updating the Master file, the Sales transaction file must have an identical key field. The structure of Sales.DBF is shown in Figure 11.3. Field 8, Posted, is a special field that will be used to determine whether a given transaction has already been recorded in (or posted to) the Master inventory file, to keep transactions from accidentally being posted twice. Notice that its data type is Logical. A logical field can be either .T. (for True) or .F. (for False). We'll design our system so that when dBASE updates the Master file, the Posted field becomes True (.T.) for the records that have been updated.

Go ahead and create the Sales file on the same disk as the Master file, using the field names, types, widths, and decimal places shown in Figure 11.3. Then use the commands

USE Sales
INDEX ON Part_No TO Sales

to create the Sales index file, which arranges the Sales database by part number.

```
Structure for the Sales data file

    Field name      Type      Width  Dec        Contents
    ======================================================================

  1 PART_NO         Character   5               Part number (key field)
  2 INVOICE_NO      Numeric     6       0       Invoice number
  3 CLERK           Character  12               Salesperson's name (or code)
  4 CUSTOMER        Character  12               Customer name
  5 QTY             Numeric     4       0       Quantity sold
  6 PRICE           Numeric     9       2       Selling price
  7 DATE            Date        8               Date sold
  8 POSTED          Logical     1               Posted to Master file yet?
```

Figure 11.3 – Structure for the Sales data file

The NewStock File

The third file in the system will be used to keep track of goods received to replenish stock. Again, since the Master file will be receiving information from this file, we'll need to include the key field Part_No. The structure of NewStock.DBF is shown in Figure 11.4.

Use the field names, types, widths, and decimal places shown in Figure 11.4 to create the NewStock file, and index it on Part_No to an index file called NewStock.NDX:

USE NewStock
INDEX ON Part_No TO NewStock

The overall database for our Inventory System now consists of six files: three data (.DBF) files and three index (.NDX) files. The system will also create and use some temporary files, but we need not be concerned with those now.

```
Structure for the NewStock data file

    Field Name    Type      Width Dec        Contents
    ==================================================================

  1  PART_NO     Character    5            Part number (key field)
  2  QTY         Numeric      4     0      Quantity received
  3  COST        Numeric      9     2      Purchase price
  4  DATE        Date         8            Date received
  5  VENDOR      Character   25            Vendor name
  6  POSTED      Logical      1            Posted to Master file yet?
```

Figure 11.4 – Structure for the NewStock data file

Inventory System Software Design

Now that we've designed the database for our Inventory System, we need to design the software structure. Obviously, this is going to be a fairly large system, so preplanning is very important.

We want to design the system to allow different individuals to perform the various major tasks. That is, the store manager will be responsible for managing the master inventory, placing orders, checking the status of goods, and so forth. Individual sales transactions will be entered by sales clerks at the point of sale, and incoming stock will be recorded by a stock room clerk. In a sense, we'll be developing three separate but related systems, with the overall structure shown in Figure 11.5.

The IMenu.PRG file will be the overall Inventory System menu. Depending on the user's choice, it will branch to either MMenu.PRG to manage the master file, SMenu.PRG to handle individual sales transactions, or NMenu.PRG to handle incoming stock transactions. Each of the submenus in Figure 11.5 will further branch to other command files, but we'll cross those bridges when we come to them.

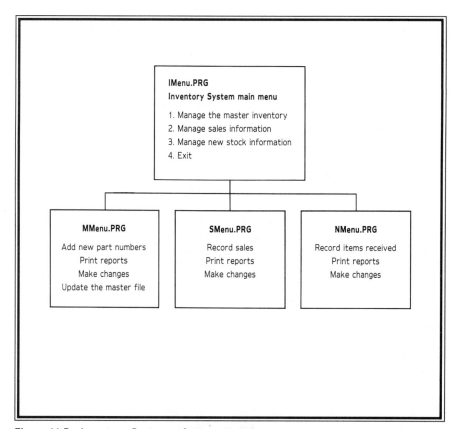

Figure 11.5 – Inventory System software structure

Inventory System Main Menu

Let's begin developing the Inventory System with the overall main menu. We'll develop each of the submenu command files in separate chapters.

Writing the Pseudocode

The main menu for the Inventory System performs two basic tasks. First, it assigns the system date (DATE( )) to a memory variable called T_Date. Then it displays that date and asks the user for confirmation or correction. (We'll use the T_Date variable in various procedures through-out the system.) Next the program asks the user which file to work with: the Master file, the Sales transaction file, or the NewStock transaction file. Then it branches to the appropriate command file, based on the user's request. The pseudocode for the main-menu program looks like this:

Clear existing memory variables

Set parameters for dBASE environment

Clear screen

Create memory variable for today's date

Set up loop for main menu

    Clear screen

    Display options

        Manage the master inventory

        Manage sales information

        Manage new stock information

        Exit

    Get user's menu selection

    Branch to appropriate program

Continue loop (until user requests exit)

Quit dBASE

Writing the Command File

Now we can develop the main-menu command file, IMenu.PRG, using the MODIFY COMMAND editor. The first job, as usual, is to put some identifying comments at the top of the program, set up the dBASE parameters, and clear the screen:

```
* * * * * * * * * * * * * * * * * * * * * * * * * * * * * * * * * * * * * * * IMenu.PRG
* Main menu for the Inventory System.
*
SET STATUS OFF
CLEAR ALL
SET TALK OFF
SET BELL OFF
SET SAFETY OFF
SET HEADING OFF
CLEAR
```

Next we'll enter the underscore routine we used for headings in the Membership System:

```
*------- Create underline variable, ULine.
ULine = REPLICATE ("_", 80)
```

Then we want the program to store the system date (DATE()) to T_Date (today's date), display today's date on the screen, and allow the user to make a change, if necessary. These lines handle that task:

```
*------- Create memory variable for today's date.
T_Date = DATE()
@ 17,5 SAY "*** To change date, type new date and press;
    Return ***"
@ 15,5 SAY "Today's date = " GET T_Date PICT "99/99/99"
READ
```

The T_Date memory variable will be used later to fill in the Date fields in the Sales and NewStock databases automatically.

The next step is to set up a loop to clear the screen, create a heading, and display the menu. We've already created several menus, and this one isn't any different:

```
*------- Set up loop for presenting main menu.
IChoice = 0
DO WHILE IChoice # 4
    CLEAR
    @ 2,1 SAY "Inventory System Main Menu"
    @ 2,60 SAY DTOC(T_Date) + "      " + TIME()
```

```
    @ 3,0 SAY ULine
    ?
    ?
    TEXT
            1. Manage master inventory
            2. Record sales
            3. Record new stock

            4. Exit
    ENDTEXT
    *------- Wait for answer.
    @ 24,1 SAY "Enter choice: " GET IChoice PICT "9";
        RANGE 1,4
    READ
```

Now the program branches to the appropriate command file, based on the user's request, as shown in this DO CASE clause:

```
    DO CASE
        CASE IChoice = 1
            DO MMenu
        CASE IChoice = 2
            DO SMenu
        CASE IChoice = 3
            DO NMenu
    ENDCASE
```

(MMenu is the menu program for managing the Master file; SMenu and NMenu are the menu programs for the Sales and NewStock portions of the Inventory System.)

Finally, the program closes the DO WHILE loop, clears the screen, and tells dBASE to quit, should the user decide to exit. These next three lines handle that job:

```
    ENDDO (while IChoice # 4)
    *------- When done, exit dBASE.
    CLEAR
    *QUIT
```

The completed IMenu command file is shown in Figure 11.6.

```
*************************************************** IMenu.PRG
*   Main menu for the Inventory System.
*
SET STATUS OFF
CLEAR ALL
SET TALK OFF
SET BELL OFF
SET SAFETY OFF
SET HEADING OFF
CLEAR

*------- Create underline variable, ULine.
ULine = REPLICATE ("_", 80)

*------- Create memory variable for today's date.
T_Date = DATE()
@ 17,5 SAY "*** To change date, type new date and press Return ***"
@ 15,5 SAY "Today's date = " GET T_Date PICT "99/99/99"
READ

*------- Set up loop for presenting main menu.
IChoice = 0
DO WHILE IChoice # 4
    CLEAR

    @ 2,1 SAY "Inventory System main menu"
    @ 2,60 SAY DTOC(T_Date) + "      " + TIME()
    @ 3,0 SAY ULine
    ?
    ?
    TEXT

                1. Manage master inventory

                2. Record sales

                3. Record new stock


                4. Exit

    ENDTEXT

    *------- Wait for answer.
    @ 24,1 SAY "Enter choice: " GET IChoice PICT "9" RANGE 1,4
    READ

    DO CASE
        CASE IChoice = 1
            DO MMenu
        CASE IChoice = 2
            DO SMenu
        CASE IChoice = 3
            DO NMenu
    ENDCASE

ENDDO (while IChoice # 4)

*------- When done, exit dBASE.
CLEAR
*QUIT
```

Figure 11.6 – The completed IMenu command file

Testing the Program

As usual at this stage, there is very little to test, but it's still a good idea to try out what you've got by typing

DO IMenu

and entering an out-of-range choice to be sure there are no typographical errors in your program. Then select option 4 to return to the DOS prompt. Now we'll design and develop the command files to manage the Master inventory file.

The Master Inventory File

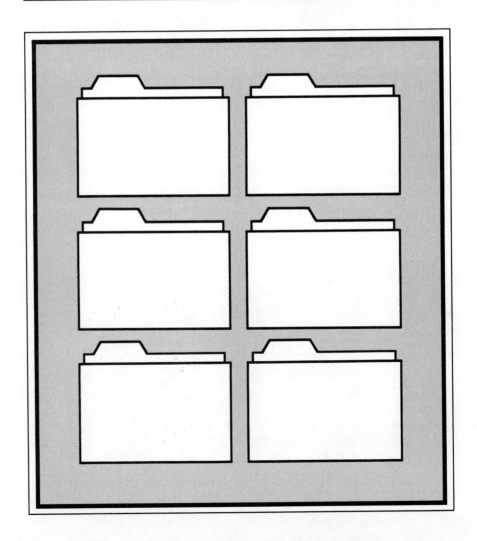

The Master file for the Inventory System that we created in Chapter 11 keeps track of the current status of goods in stock. (See Figure 11.2.) We've already indexed the file on the Part _No field to Master.NDX. Now we need to design and develop command files to manage the information in the Master database.

Master-File Software Design

You'll recall from Chapter 11 that the user enters the Inventory System through the IMenu command file, which presents the options shown in Figure 12.1. If the user selects option 1, IMenu.PRG branches to MMenu.PRG, which is the submenu for managing the Master database. The MMenu command file, in turn, presents additional options to the user, as in Figure 12.2.

The structure of the system used to manage these functions for the Master inventory database is displayed in Figure 12.3.

```
Inventory System Main Menu                          06/27/86    02:43:57
-------------------------------------------------------------------------

                1. Manage master inventory

                2. Record sales

                3. Record new stock

                4. Exit




Enter choice:  ▓
```

Figure 12.1 – *Inventory System main-menu options*

```
Manage Master Inventory                             06/27/86    04:09:18
-------------------------------------------------------------------------

                1. Add new part numbers

                2. Print reports

                3. Make changes

                4. Update from sales and new stock

                5. Return to main menu




Enter Choice (1-5) ▓
```

Figure 12.2 – *Inventory Master-file menu*

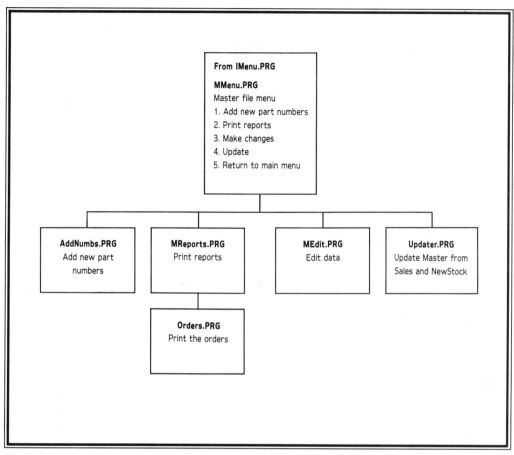

Figure 12.3 – Software structure for managing the Master database

Master-File Menu

Let's begin by developing the MMenu command file. Since this is simply another menu program with the same basic structure as previous menu programs, we can use the same pseudocode we used in the Membership System and bypass the tutorial. The MMenu command file is displayed in Figure 12.4. You'll see immediately how similar it is to our previous menu programs.

```
******************************************************* MMenu.PRG
*   Menu for Master portion of Inventory System.
*   Called from Inventory System main menu.
*

*------- Set up loop for presenting menu.
MChoice = 0
DO WHILE MChoice # 5
    CLEAR

    @ 2,1 SAY "Manage Master Inventory"
    @ 2,60 SAY DTOC(T_DATE) + "      " + TIME()
    @ 3,0 SAY ULine
    ?
    ?
    TEXT
                     1. Add new part numbers

                     2. Print reports

                     3. Make changes

                     4. Update from sales and new stock


                     5. Return to main menu
    ENDTEXT

    @ 24,1 SAY "Enter Choice (1-5)" GET MChoice PICT "9" RANGE 1,5
    READ

    *------- Branch to appropriate program.
    DO CASE
        CASE MChoice = 1
             DO AddNumbs
        CASE MCHOICE = 2
             DO MReports
        CASE MChoice = 3
             DO MEdit
        CASE MChoice = 4
             DO Updater
    ENDCASE

ENDDO (while MChoice # 5)

*------- When done, return to main menu.
RETURN
```

Figure 12.4 – The MMenu command file

Adding Unique Part Numbers

The first option from the Master menu is to add new part numbers. This job is handled by the AddNumbs command file. When the user selects option 1, the screen displays the prompt

Enter part number (or press Return to exit)

Now, since Part_No is a key field, each number must be unique. To ensure this, the AddNumbs command file checks to make sure the new part number is not a duplicate. If it is a duplicate, the program tells the user

A-111 already exists!

(where A-111 is the existing number) and gives a warning beep. Then it allows the user to try another number.

Creating the Custom Screen

When the user does enter a unique part number, a custom data-entry screen like that in Figure 12.5 appears on the monitor.

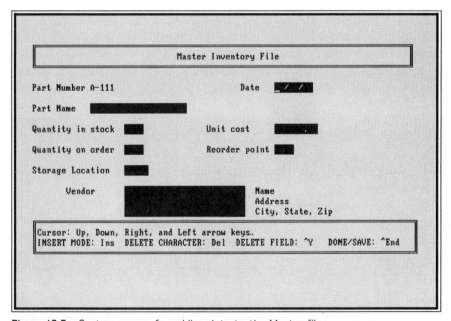

Figure 12.5 – *Custom screen for adding data to the Master file*

You can use the Screen Painter to create the custom screen. At the dot prompt enter this command:

CREATE SCREEN IScreen1

When the Screen Painter menu appears, choose the Select Database File option and specify Master.DBF as the database. Then select the Load Fields option. Recall that to select a field for the custom screen, you highlight it and press Return (a triangle appears next to the field name). In this case, you want to select all the fields except Order_Date and New_Order. Press ← after selecting fields.

When the Blackboard with the fields appears, move the cursor to the highlight for Part_No (the top XXXXX highlight), and change its action from Edit/GET to Display/SAY. (Press F10, then press Return to change Action to Display/SAY.) When you return to the Blackboard (F10), you'll notice that the highlight for the prompt disappears, but the XXXXX remains.

You can use the usual techniques for moving prompts and field highlights around the screen. The example shown in Figure 12.6 is just a suggestion. Highlight Exit and select Save when you have finished setting up the

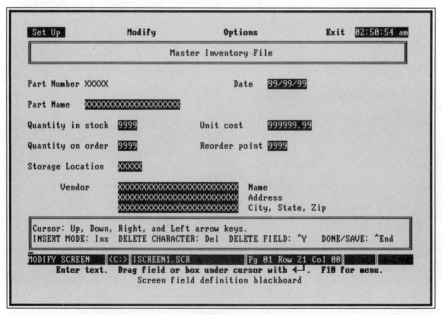

Figure 12.6 – IScreen1 screen on the Blackboard

screen. Figure 12.7 shows the format file (IScreen1.FMT) generated by the Screen Painter.

Writing the Pseudocode

Once the IScreen1.FMT file is created, you can begin developing AddNumbs.PRG. The pseudocode for AddNumbs looks like this:

Use Master file and Master index

Set up loop for adding new part numbers

    Clear screen

    Ask user for new part number

    Check to see if part number already exists

        If user did not enter part number

            Clear screen and return to Master menu

```
@  2, 30  SAY "Master Inventory File"
@  5,  0  SAY "Part Number"
@  5, 12  SAY  MASTER->PART_NO
@  5, 43  SAY "Date"
@  5, 50  GET  MASTER->DATE
@  7,  0  SAY "Part Name"
@  7, 12  GET  MASTER->TITLE
@  9,  0  SAY "Quantity in stock"
@  9, 19  GET  MASTER->QTY
@  9, 36  SAY "Unit cost"
@  9, 50  GET  MASTER->COST
@ 11,  0  SAY "Quantity on order"
@ 11, 19  GET  MASTER->ON_ORDER
@ 11, 36  SAY "Reorder point"
@ 11, 50  GET  MASTER->REORDER
@ 13,  0  SAY "Storage Location"
@ 13, 19  GET  MASTER->LOCATION
@ 15,  7  SAY "Vendor"
@ 15, 19  GET  MASTER->VENDOR
@ 15, 46  SAY "Name"
@ 16, 19  GET  MASTER->VENDOR_ADD
@ 16, 46  SAY "Address"
@ 17, 19  GET  MASTER->VENDOR_CSZ
@ 17, 46  SAY "City, State, Zip"
@ 19,  1  SAY "Cursor: Up, Down, Right, and Left arrow keys."
@ 20,  1  SAY "INSERT MODE: Ins  DELETE CHARACTER: Del  DELETE FIELD: ^Y   DONE/SAVE: ^End"
@  1,  0  TO  3, 79     DOUBLE
@ 18,  0  TO 21, 79     DOUBLE
```

Figure 12.7 – The IScreen1 format file generated by the Screen Painter

If part number exists

Notify user and allow another try

If part number not already taken

Let user add it, using IScreen1 format

Continue loop for adding part numbers (while user does not enter blank)

Return to Master menu

Writing the AddNumbs Command File

Now let's write AddNumbs.PRG. The first step is to put in the leading comments and designate Master.DBF with Master.NDX as the file to use:

```
* * * * * * * * * * * * * * * * * * * * * * * * * * * * * * * * * * * * * * * * AddNumbs.PRG
* Add new items to the Master file.
* Called from Master menu, MMenu.PRG.
USE Master INDEX Master
```

Next we need to set up a loop so that the program continues asking for part numbers as long as the user does not wish to exit. For ease of use, we'll make it possible to exit this program by simply pressing the Return key. To get the loop started, we need to store an arbitrary character to PartNumb—in this case, the letter X. Then we'll have the program clear the screen, display a heading, and use the standard @. . .SAY. . .GET and READ commands to ask the user for a part number:

```
*-------------- Set up loop for adding new part numbers.
PartNumb = "X"
DO WHILE PartNumb # " "
   CLEAR
   @ 2,1 SAY "Add New Part Numbers"
   @ 2,60 SAY DTOC(T_DATE) + "      " + TIME( )
   @ 3,0 SAY ULine
   ?
   ?
   *------- Get proposed part number.
   PartNumb = SPACE(5)
   @ 15,5 SAY "Enter part number (or press Return to exit) ";
      GET PartNumb
   READ
```

Next comes the task of checking to make sure the part number the user entered doesn't already exist. Since the Master file is indexed on the Part_No field, we can just use the SEEK command (first, we'll translate the part number to uppercase for consistency):

```
*------- Check to see if part number already exists.
PartNumb = UPPER(PartNumb)
SEEK PartNumb
```

Now the program has to decide what to do next. If the user did not even enter a part number, it just returns control to the Master menu (MMenu.PRG). The first statement in the DO CASE clause handles this situation:

```
DO CASE
     *------- If user did not enter a part number,
     *------- clear the screen and return to Master menu.
     CASE PartNumb = " "
          CLEAR
```

If a user entered a part number that already exists, the program displays a warning message and allows another try. The second CASE statement handles this situation:

```
     *------- If part number already exists,
     *------- notify user and allow another try.
     CASE FOUND( )
          @ 20,10 SAY PartNumb + " already exists!"
          ? CHR(7)
          WAIT
```

Notice the statement ? CHR(7). This causes most computers to beep, giving the user an audible feedback along with the written warning.

Finally, if the user entered a part number that doesn't already exist, the program displays the custom data-entry screen and allows the user to add the rest of the information about the part. The last case handles this situation:

```
     *------- If part number not already taken, let user add it.
     CASE .NOT. FOUND( )
          APPEND BLANK
          REPLACE Part_No WITH PartNumb
          REPLACE Date WITH T_DATE
```

```
    SET FORMAT TO IScreen1
    READ
    SET FORMAT TO
ENDCASE
```

Let's analyze the steps in the lines above. First, the CASE statement checks to make sure that the part number does not already exist (.NOT. FOUND( )). When this is the case, the program adds one new record to the database with all fields blank (APPEND BLANK). Since the user has already typed a part number (PartNumb) and the date has previously been set (in the IMenu program), the two REPLACE commands automatically fill in these two fields and the user need not retype them. Then the command file simply sets the format to the custom IScreen1 screen, reads in the data for the new record, and sets the format back to the regular dBASE III PLUS screen.

Now, if the user did not request to exit, the command file needs to loop around again. If the user does exit, the program just returns control to the MMenu command file:

```
ENDDO (while user does not enter blank for part number)
*------- Return to Master menu.
RETURN
```

The AddNumbs command file is shown in its entirety in Figure 12.8.

```
***************************************************** AddNumbs .PRG
*   Add new items to the Master file.
*   Called from Master menu, MMenu.PRG.

USE Master INDEX Master

*--------------- Set up loop for adding new part numbers.
PartNumb = "X"
DO WHILE PartNumb # " "
    CLEAR
    @ 2,1 SAY "Add New Part Numbers"
    @ 2,60 SAY DTOC(T_DATE) + "      " + TIME()
    @ 3,0 SAY ULine
    ?
    ?

    *------- Get proposed part number.
    PartNumb = SPACE(5)
    @ 15,5 SAY "Enter part number (or press Return to exit)" GET PartNumb
    READ
```

Figure 12.8 – The completed AddNumbs command file

```
*------- Check to see if part number already exists.
PartNumb = UPPER(PartNumb)
SEEK PartNumb

DO CASE

     *------- If user did not enter a part number,
     *------- clear the screen and return to Master menu.
     CASE PartNumb = " "
          CLEAR

     *------- If part number already exists,
     *------- notify user and allow another try.
     CASE FOUND()
          @ 20,10 SAY PartNumb + " already exists!"
          ? CHR(7)
          WAIT

     *------- If part number not already taken, let user add it.
     CASE .NOT. FOUND()
          APPEND BLANK
          REPLACE Part_No WITH PartNumb
          REPLACE Date WITH T_DATE
          SET FORMAT TO IScreen1
          READ
          SET FORMAT TO

  ENDCASE
ENDDO (while user does not enter blank for part number)

*------- Return to Master menu.
RETURN
```

Figure 12.8 – The completed AddNumbs command file (continued)

Inventory Master-File Reports

When the user selects option 2 to print reports from the Master inventory, MMenu.PRG branches to the MReports command file, which displays the menu of report options shown in Figure 12.9. Before we begin writing MReports.PRG, let's look at samples of the various reports and study their formats.

The Current-Stock Report

If the user selects option 1 on the Reports menu, the program displays an entire inventory report on the screen. You can create the report by typing

USE MASTER
CREATE REPORT AllMast

at the dBASE dot prompt and assigning the general format parameters as shown in Figure 12.10.

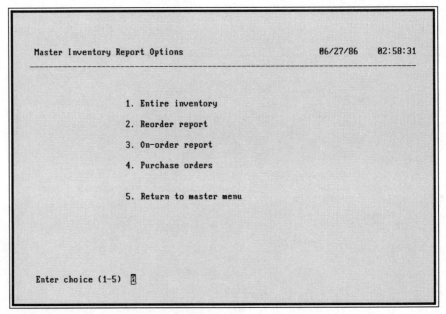

```
Master Inventory Report Options                    06/27/86   02:58:31
──────────────────────────────────────────────────────────────────────



                    1. Entire inventory

                    2. Reorder report

                    3. On-order report

                    4. Purchase orders


                    5. Return to master menu




Enter choice (1-5)  █
```

Figure 12.9 – The Master report menu

```
      Page title              Current Stock
      Page width (positions)  74
      Left margin             1
      Right margin            0
      Lines per page          58
      Double space report     No
```

Figure 12.10 – Format parameters for the AllMast format file

Now include the information in Figure 12.11 in column format. Then use the dBASE REPORT FORM command to print the report, so that it appears as in Figure 12.12.

The Reorder Report

If the user selects option 2 from the Reports menu, the program displays the reorder report shown in Figure 12.13. For this to happen, you must

```
Column No.      Contents        Heading     Width    Decimals    Total?
     1          Part_No         Part          6
     2          Title           Description  20
     3          Qty             On-Hand       5         0           N
     4          Cost            Unit Cost     9         2           N
     5          Reorder         Reorder       8         0           N
     6          Location        Loc.          9
     7          Date            Last Update   9
```

Figure 12.11 – Structure for the AllMast format file

```
Page No.      1
10/29/85
                        Current Stock

              On-        Unit                     Last
Part  Description  Hand   Cost Reorder   Loc.    Update

AAA    Icebergs        10    120.00      10 A-111 10/08/85
BBB    Tomatoes        10      0.35      10 T-224 10/09/85
CCC    Floppy disks    10     12.00      10 R-991 10/09/85
K-222  Cantaloupes     12      0.77      15 C-333 10/10/85
TTT    Tamales         10      0.10      10 T-999 10/09/85
ZZZ    Bike pedals     10     23.00      10 B-228 10/09/85
```

Figure 12.12 – The current-stock report produced by AllMast.FRM

first design the reorder report using the CREATE REPORT Reorders command with the parameters shown in Figure 12.14. You must then set up the information in Figure 12.15 in column format.

```
Page No.        1
10/29/85
                        Goods to be Reordered

Part   Description  On-Hand  On-Order  Reorder    Vendor Name


BBB    Tomatoes         5        5        10     Juicy Tomatoes, Inc.
K-222  Cantaloupes      5        5        15     American Cantaloupe
ZZZ    Bike pedals      5        5        10     American Bicycle Co.
```

Figure 12.13 – *The reorder report printed by Reorders.FRM*

```
Page title                 Goods to be Reordered
Page width (positions)     77
Left margin                 1
Right margin                0
Lines per page             58
Double space report        No
```

Figure 12.14 – *Report settings for the Reorders format file*

Column No.	Contents	Heading	Width	Decimals	Total?
1	Part_No	Part	6		
2	Title	Description	15		
3	Qty	On-Hand	7	0	N
4	On_Order	On-Order	9	0	N
5	Reorder	Reorder	8	0	N
6	Vendor	Vendor Name	25		

Figure 12.15 – *Structure for the Reorders format file*

The Open-Order Report

When the user selects option 3 from the Reports menu, a report of the goods currently on order is displayed, as in Figure 12.16. The command CREATE REPORT OnOrder is used to create this report, with the parameters shown in Figure 12.17.

Then the column format is set up to include the information in Figure 12.18. Notice that we've used a mathematical expression here, rather than

```
Page No.       1
10/29/85
                        Items Currently on Order

Order   Part Description    On-      Unit      Total Vendor Name
Date    No.                 Order    Cost      Cost


10/10/85 AAA  Icebergs        5     120.00     600.00 American Iceberg Co.
10/10/85 BBB  Tomatoes        5       0.35       1.75 Juicy Tomatoes, Inc.
10/10/85 CCC  Floppy disks    5      12.00      60.00 Diamond Disks
10/10/85 K-222 Cantaloupes    5       0.77       3.85 American Cantaloupe
10/10/85 TTT  Tamales         5       0.10       0.50 American Hot Tamale
10/10/85 ZZZ  Bike pedals     5      23.00     115.00 American Bicycle Co.
*** Total ***
                                                781.10
```

Figure 12.16 – *The on-order report printed by OnOrder.FRM*

```
Page title               Items Currently on Order
Page width (positions)   80
Left margin              1
Right margin             0
Lines per page           58
Double space report      No
```

Figure 12.17 – *Report settings for the OnOrder format file*

Column No.	Contents	Heading	Width	Decimals	Total?
1	Order_Date	Order Date	8		
2	Part_No	Part No.	5		
3	Title	Description	15		
4	On_Order	On-Order	5	0	N
5	Cost	Unit Cost	9	2	N
6	Cost * On_Order	Total Cost	9	2	Y
7	Vendor	Vendor Name	20		

Figure 12.18 – *Structure for the OnOrder format file*

just a field name, to create the values for the Total Cost column.

The Purchase Orders

Option 4 from the Reports menu allows the user to place orders and have the purchase orders printed automatically. When the user selects this option, the screen (shown in Figure 12.19) displays some basic information about each item in stock that has fallen below the reorder point.

The user can quickly see how many pairs of snowshoes are in stock, how many are on order, and what the reorder point is for the item. To order more, the user simply fills in the quantity to order at the "Order how many?" prompt. After the program has gone through the entire list of items that need to be reordered, it prints the purchase orders. Figure 12.20 shows a sample purchase order created by the Inventory System.

```
Part number A-111  Snowshoes
On hand        10
On order       10
Reorder        20
Unit Cost         12.11

Order how many?  █
```

Figure 12.19 – Screen for ordering items

```
Zeppo's Custom Dog Supplies
1234 Canine Way
San Juan Capistrano, CA 91234

Please send us the following items...

   10 Dog Biscuits        2.50        25.00
   10 Dog Bones           2.50        25.00
   10 Dog Blankets        2.50        25.00

   Total cost:                        75.00

      Mail to:   My Company, Inc.
                 123 A St.
                 Anywhere, CA  91234
```

Figure 12.20 – Sample purchase order created by the Inventory System MReports program

Writing the Command Files

The task of presenting the report options to the user and then printing the appropriate report is handled by the MReports command file. MReports is basically a simple menu program, but it has a few unique features that deserve some discussion.

The Reports

MReports.PRG begins with the usual comments, but this time the program opens the Master database and index before it begins the loop to display the menu, since the same index is used for all REPORT FORM options:

```
* * * * * * * * * * * * * * * * * * * * * * * * * * * * * * * * * * * * * MReports.PRG
* Present report options for Master file.
* Called from Master menu, MMenu.PRG.
USE Master INDEX Master
*------- Set up loop for presenting menu.
RepChoice = 0
DO WHILE RepChoice # 5
   CLEAR
   @ 2,1 SAY "Master Inventory Report Options"
   @ 2,60 SAY DTOC(T_DATE) + "      " + TIME()
   @ 3,0 SAY ULine
   ?
   ?
   TEXT
            1. Entire inventory
            2. Reorder report
            3. On-order report
            4. Purchase orders

            5. Return to master menu
   ENDTEXT
   @ 24,1 SAY "Enter choice (1–5) " GET RepChoice PICT;
      "9" RANGE 1,5
   READ
```

Before branching to the appropriate report routine, MReports asks whether the user wants a hard copy of the report—unless the user is placing orders, in which case the program assumes the printer will be used:

```
*------- If not placing orders, ask about printer.
CLEAR
STORE " " TO YN, Printer
IF RepChoice < 4
    @ 5,5 SAY "Send report to printer? " GET YN PICT "!"
    READ
    CLEAR
```

If the user does request the printer, the program stores the command TO PRINT to a memory variable called Printer, to be used later as a macro with the REPORT FORM command:

```
*------- Set up for printer.
    IF YN = "Y"
        Printer = "TO PRINT"
    ENDIF
ENDIF (RepChoice < 4)
```

Now the program can print the report. If one of the first three reports was chosen, the program simply selects the appropriate report-form file and uses the &Printer macro to determine whether the report will be sent to the printer or simply displayed on the screen. The CASE statements below handle the first three report options:

```
DO CASE
    CASE RepChoice = 1
        REPORT FORM AllMast &Printer
    CASE RepChoice = 2
        REPORT FORM Reorders FOR;
        (Qty + On_Order) < = Reorder &Printer
    CASE RepChoice = 3
        REPORT FORM OnOrder FOR On_Order > 0 &Printer
```

Notice that the first case displays all data from the Master file. The second case displays only those records whose on-hand quantity (Qty) plus on-order quantity (On_Order) is less than the reorder amount (< = Reorder), whereas the third case displays only those items already on order (On_Order > 0).

The fourth option, placing orders, is handled by a separate command file called Orders.PRG, which we'll discuss in a moment. The fourth CASE statement handles this choice:

```
CASE RepChoice = 4
     DO Orders
ENDCASE
```

If the report is not going to the printer (and the user is not exiting), we want the program to pause momentarily to allow the user to view the report on the screen. To cause the program to pause, type the following lines:

```
*------- If report not going to printer,
*------- and not exiting program, pause.
IF YN # "Y" .AND. RepChoice # 5
    ?
    ?
    WAIT "Press key to return to the Reports menu. . ."
ENDIF
```

Then the program can simply close the DO WHILE loop and return to the Master menu:

```
ENDDO (RepChoice # 5)
*------- Return to Master menu.
RETURN
```

Figure 12.21 shows the entire MReports command file.

```
************************************************* MReports.PRG
*  Present report options for Master file.
*  Called from Master menu, MMenu.PRG.

USE Master INDEX Master

*------- Set up loop for presenting menu.
RepChoice = 0
DO WHILE RepChoice # 5
    CLEAR

    @ 2,1 SAY "Master Inventory Report Options"
    @ 2,60 SAY DTOC(T_DATE) + "     " + TIME()
    @ 3,0 SAY ULine
    ?
    ?
```

Figure 12.21 – The completed MReports command file

```
        TEXT
                              1. Entire inventory

                              2. Reorder report

                              3. On-order report

                              4. Purchase orders


                              5. Return to master menu
        ENDTEXT
        @ 24,1 SAY "Enter choice (1-5) " GET RepChoice PICT "9" RANGE 1,5
        READ

        *------- If not placing orders, ask about printer.
        CLEAR
        STORE " " TO YN, Printer

        IF RepChoice < 4
            @ 5,5 SAY "Send report to printer? " GET YN PICT "!"
            READ
            CLEAR

            *------- Set up for printer.
            IF YN = "Y"
                Printer = "TO PRINT"
            ENDIF
        ENDIF (RepChoice < 4)

        DO CASE

            CASE RepChoice = 1
                REPORT FORM AllMast &Printer

            CASE RepChoice = 2

                REPORT FORM ReOrders FOR;
                  (Qty + On_Order) <= Reorder &Printer

            CASE RepChoice = 3
                REPORT FORM OnOrder FOR On_Order > 0 &Printer

            CASE RepChoice = 4
                DO Orders


        ENDCASE

        *------- If report not going to printer,
        *------- and not exiting program, pause.
        IF YN # "Y" .AND. RepChoice # 5
            ?
            ?
            WAIT "Press key to return to the Reports menu..."
        ENDIF

    ENDDO (RepChoice # 5)

    *------- Return to Master menu.
    RETURN
```

Figure 12.21 – The completed MReports command file (continued)

The Purchase Orders

To place and print orders, MReports.PRG branches to the Orders command file. Orders.PRG must perform several tasks. First, it must step through each record in the Master file and determine which items are due for reordering (by checking whether the amount on hand plus the amount on order is below the reorder point). Then, each time it finds an item that needs reordering, it must ask the user how many to reorder. Once all the orders are entered, the program must print the orders and update the On_Order field in the Master file. The pseudocode for Orders.PRG looks like this:

Clear screen

Use Master file with Master index

Start loop through Master file

If on-hand plus on-order quantity is less than reorder point

Clear screen

Show status of item to be reordered

Ask user how many to order

Update New_Order and Order_Date fields

Skip to next record

Continue loop until end of file

When all orders have been entered

Clear screen

Make temporary file of items to be ordered (Temp)

Update On_Order field in Master file with new orders

Set New_Order field back to zero in Master file

Use the temporary file (which contains only new orders)

Index by vendor name

Set printer on

For each vendor in Temp

Print vendor name and address

For each item to order from this vendor

Print quantity to order, item, and cost

> When done with this vendor
>
> > Print total cost of order
> >
> > Print shipping name and address
> >
> > Start a new page
> >
> > Go to next vendor
>
> Continue for each vendor in Temp file
>
> When done, turn printer off and return to MReports

We can build the Orders command file as follows. First, we enter the usual opening lines:

```
* * * * * * * * * * * * * * * * * * * * * * * * * * * * * * * * * * * * Orders.PRG
* Create purchase orders for reordering.
* Called from Reports menu, MReports.PRG.
CLEAR
USE Master INDEX Master
```

Then we have the program loop through the Master file, displaying data for those items whose total on-hand plus on-order quantities are below the reorder point. For each of these items, the program asks the user how many to order:

```
*------- Loop through and display goods below reorder point
*------- and ask user how many of each to order.
GO TOP
DO WHILE .NOT. EOF( )
    *------- Find out if on-hand plus on-order quantity
    *------- is less than reorder point.
    IF (Qty + On_Order) <= Reorder
        CLEAR
        *------- Show status of item to be reordered.
        @ 5,5 SAY "Part number" + Part_No + "     " + Title
        @ 6,5 SAY "On hand     " + STR(Qty,4)
        @ 7,5 SAY "On order    " + STR(On_Order,4)
        @ 8,5 SAY "Reorder     " + STR(Reorder,3)
        @ 9,5 SAY "Unit Cost   " + STR(Cost,9,2)
```

```
*------- Ask user how many to order.
@ 12,5 SAY "Order how many? " GET New_Order;
    PICT "9999"
REPLACE Order_Date WITH T_Date
READ
ENDIF (Qty + On_Order < Reorder)
SKIP
ENDDO (continue loop until end of file)
```

Notice that the amount to be ordered is stored in the New_Order field. Also, Order_Date is automatically changed to today's date (T_Date), which was set when the user first entered the Inventory System.

Once all of the orders are placed, the program copies the items to be ordered to a separate temporary file called Temp:

```
*------- When all orders have been placed,
*------- make a temporary file (Temp) of items to be ordered.
CLEAR
? "Preparing files . . . please wait"
?
? "(Prepare printer while waiting)"
COPY TO Temp FOR New_Order > 0
```

Now that the items to be ordered are stored in a separate file, the program can make some changes to the Master file. First of all, the On_Order field needs to be incremented to show the actual quantity of each item on order (the previous quantity plus the quantity just ordered). Then the New_Order field can be set back to zero. The following lines handle these tasks:

```
*------- Update On_Order field in Master file with new orders,
*------- then set the New_Order field back to zero.
REPLACE ALL On_Order WITH On_Order + New_Order
REPLACE ALL New_Order WITH 0
```

Before printing the orders, the program needs to use the Temp file and sort it into order by vendor:

```
*------- Use Temp file (which contains new orders), indexed by
*------- vendor.
USE Temp
INDEX ON UPPER(Vendor) TO Temp
```

Once the Temp file is indexed, the program asks the user to make sure the printer is ready:

```
*------- Files ready, inform user.
CLEAR
? CHR(7)
WAIT "Ready printer and press any key to print orders"
```

Now, to produce orders for individual vendors, the program needs to step through the entire Temp file. For each vendor, we want to print only one order. This requires two nested loops. The first loop goes record by record through the Temp file:

```
SET PRINT ON
GO TOP
*------- Loop through Temp file.
DO WHILE .NOT. EOF()
```

Within this first loop, the program stores the name of the current vendor to the memory variable This_Loop and initializes a memory variable called MTotal for calculating the grand total of the order. Then it prints the vendor name and address at the top of the invoice:

```
*------- For each vendor, print name and address.
This_Loop = Vendor
MTotal = 0
? Vendor
? Vendor_Add
? Vendor_CSZ
?
? "Please send us the following items . . ."
?
```

Now, as long as the vendor name does not change (Vendor = This_Loop), the program continues through the file, printing the quantity (New_Order), description (Title), and total cost (New_Order x Cost) for each item to be ordered. It also keeps a running total of the overall order (MTotal). This second loop handles these jobs:

```
*------- For each item to be ordered from this vendor,
*------- print quantity, item, and price.
DO WHILE Vendor = This_Loop .AND. .NOT. EOF()
    ? New_Order, Title, Cost, New_Order    * Cost
```

```
    MTotal = New_Order * Cost + MTotal
    SKIP
ENDDO
```

When it's finished with the current vendor (vendor name no longer matches This_Loop), the program prints the total cost of the order and the address to ship the order to. Then it advances the printer to a new page:

```
*------- When done with this vendor, print total cost
*------- and shipping name and address.
?
? "Total cost:                    ", MTotal
?
? "Mail to:    My Company, Inc."
? "            123 A St."
? "            Anywhere, CA 91234"
EJECT
```

The main loop through the entire file continues until all orders have been placed:

```
ENDDO (continue for each vendor in Temp file)
```

When all orders have been printed, the program sets the PRINT parameter OFF and returns control to MReports.PRG:

```
*------- Done. Turn off printer and return to Reports menu.
SET PRINT OFF
RETURN
```

The Orders command file is a bit more abstract than others we've developed, and it may take some study to grasp fully. However, it presents several techniques that will be useful in a variety of programming situations, so it's worth the extra effort. Figure 12.22 shows the complete Orders command file.

```
*************************************************** Orders.PRG
*  Create purchase orders for reordering.
*  Called from Reports menu, MReports.PRG.

CLEAR
```

Figure 12.22 – The completed Orders command file

```
USE Master INDEX Master

*------- Loop through and display goods below reorder point
*------- and ask user how many of each to order.
GO TOP
DO WHILE .NOT. EOF()

    *------- Find out if on-hand plus on-order quantity
    *------- is less than reorder point.
    IF (Qty + On_Order) <= Reorder
        CLEAR

        *------- Show status of item to be reordered.
        @ 5,5 SAY "Part number " + Part_No + "     " + Title
        @ 6,5 SAY "On hand      " + STR(Qty,4)
        @ 7,5 SAY "On order     " + STR(On_Order,4)
        @ 8,5 SAY "Reorder      " + STR(Reorder,3)
        @ 9,5 SAY "Unit Cost    " + STR(Cost,9,2)

        *------- Ask user how many to order.
        @ 12,5 SAY "Order how many? " GET New_Order PICT "9999"
        REPLACE Order_Date WITH T_Date
        READ

    ENDIF (Qty + On_Order < Reorder)
    SKIP

ENDDO (continue loop until end of file)

*------- When all orders have been placed,
*------- make a temporary file (Temp) of items to be ordered.
CLEAR
? "Preparing files... please wait"
?
? "(Prepare printer while waiting)"
COPY TO Temp FOR New_Order > 0

*------- Update On_Order field in Master file with new orders,
*------- then set the New_Orders field back to zero.
REPLACE ALL On_Order WITH On_Order + New_Order
REPLACE ALL New_Order WITH 0

*------- Use Temp file (which contains new orders), indexed by vendor.
USE Temp
INDEX ON UPPER(Vendor) TO Temp

*------- Files ready, inform user.

CLEAR
? CHR(7)
WAIT "Ready printer and press any key to print orders"
SET PRINT ON
GO TOP

*------- Loop through Temp file.
DO WHILE .NOT. EOF()

    *------- For each vendor, print name and address.
    This_Loop = Vendor
    MTotal = 0
    ? Vendor
    ? Vendor_Add
    ? Vendor_CSZ
    ?
```

Figure 12.22 – The completed Orders command file (continued)

```
    ? "Please send us the following items..."
    ?

    *------- For each item to be ordered from this vendor,
    *       print quantity, item, and price.
    DO WHILE Vendor = This_Loop .AND. .NOT. EOF()
        ? New_Order, Title, Cost, New_Order * Cost
        MTotal = New_Order * Cost + MTotal
        SKIP
    ENDDO

    *------- When done with this vendor, print total cost
    *------- and shipping name and address.
    ?
    ? "Total cost:                    ", MTotal
    ?
    ? "Mail to:   My Company, Inc."
    ? "           123 A St."
    ? "           Anywhere, CA  91234"
    EJECT

ENDDO (continue for each vendor in Temp file)

*------- Done. Turn off printer and return to Reports menu.
SET PRINT OFF
RETURN
```

Figure 12.22 – The completed Orders command file (continued)

Editing the Master File

Option 3 from the Master menu allows the user to edit the Master file. The command file that performs this task is named MEdit.PRG, and here is its pseudocode:

Use Master file and Master index

Start loop for performing edits

    Find out what part number to edit

    Try to find that part number

        If no part number entered

            Return to menu

        If part number found

            Edit the record, using IScreen1 format

        If part number not found

            Warn user and allow another try

Continue editing until user requests exit

When done, return to Master menu

Since we've already created the IScreen1 format file, we'll use it for editing purposes also. This makes development of the MEdit command file relatively quick. First we enter the usual comments and use the Master file and index:

```
* * * * * * * * * * * * * * * * * * * * * * * * * * * * * * * * * * * * * * * * MEdit.PRG
* Edit the Inventory Master file.
* Called from Master menu, MMenu.PRG.
*
USE Master INDEX Master
```

Then we set up a loop that will allow the user to make several edits, or to exit by not entering a part number:

```
*------- Start loop for performing edits.
PartNumb = "X"
DO WHILE PartNumb # " "
```

Now the program displays a screen heading and asks the user for the part number of the record to edit:

```
*------- Find out what part number to edit.
CLEAR
@ 2,1 SAY "Edit Inventory Master File"
@ 2,60 SAY DTOC(T_DATE) + "      " + TIME( )
@ 3,0 SAY ULine
?
?
PartNumb = SPACE(5)
@ 15,5 SAY "Edit for what part number? " GET PartNumb
READ
```

Then it converts PartNumb to uppercase for consistency and tries to find the number requested:

```
*------- Try to find that part number.
PartNumb = UPPER(PartNumb)
SEEK PartNumb
```

At this point, the program must decide what to do next. If no part number was entered, it can just clear the screen and bypass the other CASE statements, but if a valid part number was entered, it must allow the user to edit, using the IScreen1 format file. If an invalid part number was entered, the program must warn the user and allow another try. A DO CASE clause handles these three possibilities:

```
DO CASE
    *------- If no part number entered, return to Master menu.
    CASE PartNumb = " "
        CLEAR
    *------- If part number found, edit using IScreen1 format.
    CASE FOUND( )
        SET FORMAT TO IScreen1
        READ
        SET FORMAT TO
    *------- Otherwise, warn user and allow another try.
    CASE .NOT. FOUND( )
        @ 17,5 SAY "There is no part " + PartNumb
        @ 24,5 SAY "Press any key to try again . . ."
        WAIT " "
ENDCASE
```

An ENDDO command closes the loop that keeps asking the user for another part number:

```
ENDDO (continue editing until user requests exit)
```

When the user is done editing, the program returns control to MMenu.PRG:

```
*------- Return to Master menu.
RETURN
```

Figure 12.23 displays the entire MEdit command file.

The last option from the Master menu allows the user to update the Master file from information held in the Sales and NewStock files. Since we haven't developed those files yet, we can't test the update option at this stage. So we'll develop the Sales and NewStock portions of the Inventory System in the next two chapters, and then we'll create the programs for updating and editing in Chapter 15.

```
********************************************** MEdit.PRG
*   Edit the Inventory Master file.
*   Called from Master menu, MMenu.PRG.
*

USE Master INDEX Master

*------- Start loop for performing edits.
PartNumb = "X"
DO WHILE PartNumb # " "

    *------- Find out what part number to edit.
    CLEAR
    @ 2,1 SAY "Edit Inventory Master File"
    @ 2,60 SAY DTOC(T_DATE) + "     " + TIME()
    @ 3,0 SAY ULine
    ?
    ?
    PartNumb = SPACE(5)
    @ 15,5 SAY "Edit for what part number? " GET PartNumb
    READ

    *------- Try to find that part number.
    PartNumb = UPPER(PartNumb)
    SEEK PartNumb

    DO CASE

        *------- If no part number entered, return to Master menu.
        CASE PartNumb = " "
            CLEAR

        *------- If part number found, edit using IScreen1 format.
        CASE FOUND()
            SET FORMAT TO IScreen1
            READ
            SET FORMAT TO

        *------- Otherwise, warn user and allow another try.
        CASE .NOT. FOUND()
            @ 17,5 SAY "There is no part " + PartNumb
            @ 24,5 SAY "Press any key to try again..."
            WAIT " "

    ENDCASE

ENDDO (continue editing until user requests exit)

*------- Return to Master menu.
RETURN
```

Figure 12.23 – The completed MEdit command file

Inventory Sales System

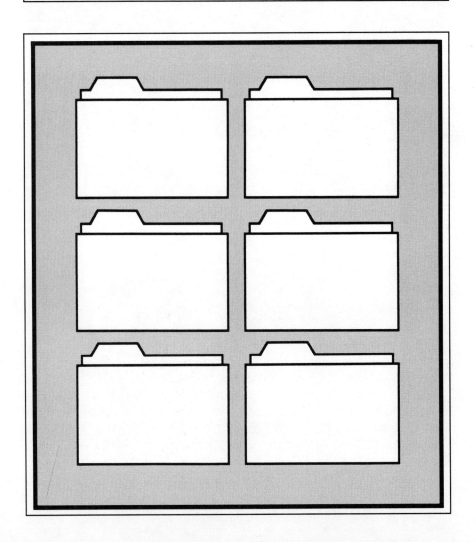

The Sales portion of the Inventory System keeps track of individual sales transactions. The data are stored in Sales.DBF, which we created in Chapter 11 (see Figure 11.3).

In this chapter we'll create command files that allow the user to add data to the Sales file and print reports based on invoice number or date. The data-entry program will be a powerful *point-of-sale* routine using a screen that resembles an actual page from an invoice book. As an added convenience to the user, the program will automatically fill in the item description, based on the part number the user enters. If the part number does not exist, the screen will warn of this and allow another try. The program will automatically calculate and display subtotals and totals as the user is entering data, and it will also automatically create and store invoice numbers.

Sales System Software Structure

The Sales system command files are linked to SMenu.PRG. There are three programs: Pos.PRG, which allows the user to add new data at the point of sale; SalReps.PRG, which prints reports from the Sales transaction file; and SalEdit.PRG, which allows the user to edit the Sales file. Figure 13.1 shows the structure of the command files.

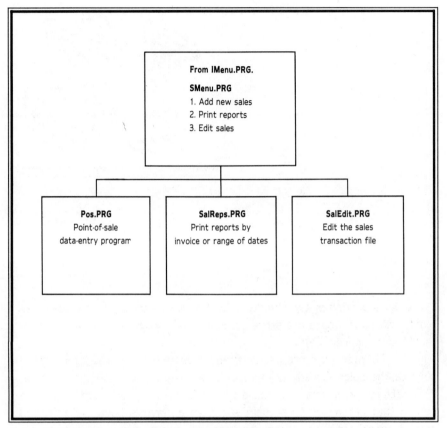

Figure 13.1 – Software structure for the Sales system

We'll design and develop SMenu, Pos, and SalReps now, but we'll wait until Chapter 15 to write the SalEdit program, because the editing procedures will be affected by the updating program developed there.

Sales System Menu

When the user chooses option 2 from the Inventory System main menu, the Sales menu appears on the screen as in Figure 13.2. The SMenu command file then branches to the program indicated by the user's selection. Since this is a simple menu program, we'll use the pseudocode from MMenu.PRG again and just present the completed program in Figure 13.3.

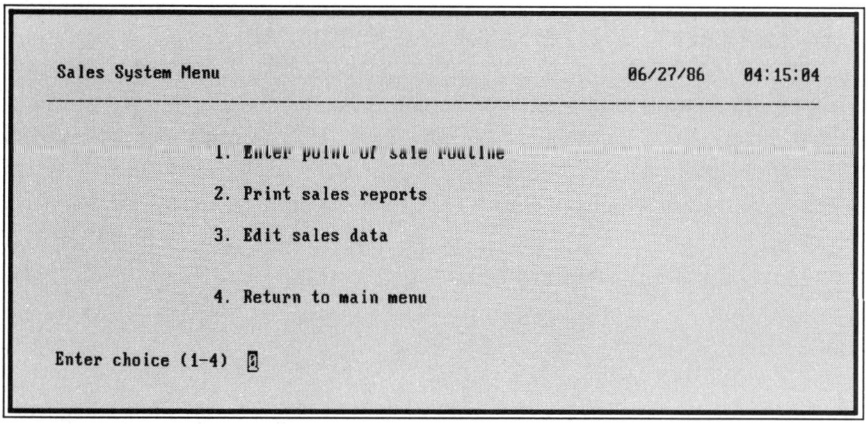

Figure 13.2 – The Sales menu

```
**************************************************** SMenu.PRG
*   Menu for Sales portion of the Inventory System.
*   Called from Inventory System main menu.

*------- Set up loop for presenting menu.
SChoice = 0
DO WHILE SChoice # 4

    CLEAR
    @ 2,1 SAY "Sales System Menu"
    @ 2,60 SAY DTOC(T_Date) + "     " + TIME()
    @ 3,0 SAY ULine
    ?
    ?
    TEXT
                1. Enter point-of-sale routine

                2. Print sales reports

                3. Edit sales data


                4. Return to main menu
    ENDTEXT

    @ 24,1 SAY "Enter choice (1-4) " GET SChoice PICT "9"
    READ

    *------- Branch to appropriate program.
    DO CASE
        CASE SChoice = 1
            DO Pos
        CASE SChoice = 2
            DO SalReps
        CASE SChoice = 3
            DO SalEdit
    ENDCASE

ENDDO (while SChoice # 4)

*------- When done, return to main menu.
RETURN
```

Figure 13.3 – The completed SMenu command file

Point-of-Sale Data Entry

The program to add new data to the Sales database presents a screen that looks like an invoice. Using that screen, it prompts the user through the data-entry process. The top portion of the invoice form is displayed on the screen when the user enters the point-of-sale system (see Figure 13.4).

The program automatically fills in the date and invoice number, and the user types the salesperson's name (Clerk) and the customer's name. Then a highlight for entering the part number appears on the screen, as in Figure 13.5.

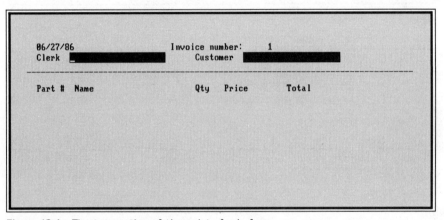

```
06/27/86                    Invoice number:      1
Clerk   ▮                   Customer  ▮

_____

Part #  Name                   Qty    Price       Total
```

Figure 13.4 – The top portion of the point-of-sale form

```
06/27/86                    Invoice number:      1
Clerk   ACS                 Customer  Jane Doe

_____

Part #  Name                   Qty    Price       Total
        ▮
```

Figure 13.5 – Pos.PRG screen with highlight for part number

The user enters the part number of the item sold. If that number does not exist, the screen provides the warning

No such part!!!

and the user can try again. When a valid number is entered, the name of the part appears automatically, as in Figure 13.6, along with prompts for filling in the quantity and selling price.

If the user types 5 as the quantity sold and $10.00 as the selling price, the program automatically fills in the transaction total and awaits the next part number, as in Figure 13.7.

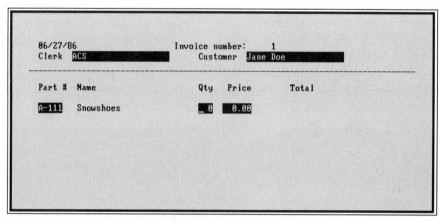

Figure 13.6 – Pos.PRG screen with part number filled in

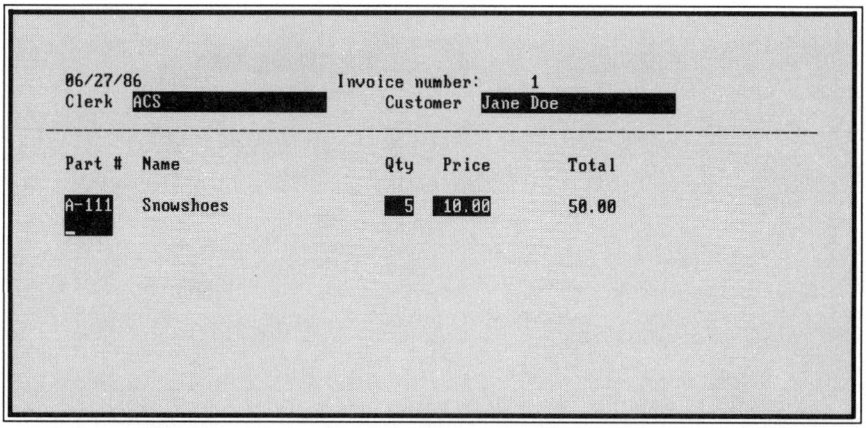

Figure 13.7 – Pos.PRG screen awaiting next part number

Now suppose the user enters another valid transaction with the quantity sold and the selling price. Again, the program calculates the transaction total and displays it on the screen, as shown in Figure 13.8.

If the user enters a valid but incorrect part number (based on the part name displayed automatically), he can just press ← (or Return twice) rather than enter a quantity. Pressing Return twice works because a quantity of zero tells the program that the part number the user entered is valid but incorrect; the program then lets him enter a new part number.

When there are no more items to add to this invoice, the user simply presses Return, and the screen displays the total of the invoice, as well as a prompt to print the invoice, as shown in Figure 13.9.

If the user enters Y in response to the prompt, the program prints the invoice. Then the screen asks the user whether he wants to enter another invoice. The user enters Y to do another invoice with a new invoice number. He enters N to stop entering invoices and return to the Sales menu.

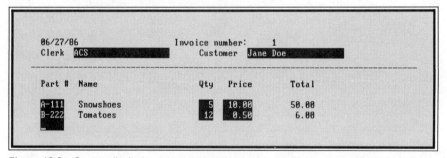

Figure 13.8 – Screen displaying two transactions

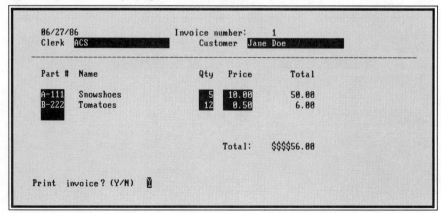

Figure 13.9 – Screen displaying the grand total of the invoice and prompt to print the invoice

Writing the Pseudocode

The name of the point-of-sale command file is Pos.PRG; its pseudocode looks like this:

Get last-used invoice number from the Sales file

Set up temporary file for new transactions

Open Master and temporary files

Set up relationship between Master and Sales

Set up loop for displaying invoice forms

    Set up top portion of invoice on the screen

    Set up loop for each item on the invoice

        Set up loop to check validity of part number

            Set up invoice memory variables

            Ask for part number

            Make sure part number exists

                If exiting, end program

                If no such part number, warn

                If part number exists, display it

                    Get quantity and selling price

                    If quantity is zero, try again

                        Otherwise, display total

                        Increment grand total

                    Store transaction on temporary file

        Continue loop for checking for valid part numbers

        Increment row counter

        If nearing bottom of screen

            Scroll everything up a line

    Continue loop for adding transactions

    Display grand total

    Ask about printing invoice

    If print requested, print invoice

Ask about another transaction

Continue loop to add transactions

Close databases and update the Sales file

Clear out temporary file

Return to menu

Writing the Command File

Before you begin entering the Pos command file, be forewarned that it barely fits into the MODIFY COMMAND editor. If you must use MODIFY COMMAND, you can conserve memory by leaving out programmer comments, blank lines, and even indentations if necessary. (The program might also run a little faster if you do so.)

The first step in the Pos program is to open the Sales database and determine the invoice number of the last transaction entered by the user. This is accomplished by simply going to the bottom of the file and storing the invoice number of that transaction to a memory variable called MInvoice:

```
* * * * * * * * * * * * * * * * * * * * * * * * * * * * * * * * * * * * * * * * * * * * Pos.PRG
* Point-of-sale data entry program for Sales.
* Called from Sales menu, SMenu.PRG.
*------- Get last-used invoice number from the Sales file.
USE Sales
GO BOTT
MInvoice = Invoice_No
```

In the interest of maximizing the speed of the Pos program, all new transactions will be stored in a temporary file named TempInv.DBF. Automatic updating on the Sales.NDX file takes a few seconds when the file is very large. By adding new transactions to a temporary file, the program will bypass this slight delay. After all new transactions have been entered, this program will add the new sales transactions to Sales.DBF and update Sales.NDX.

The commands to create an empty temporary file of new transactions are shown below:

```
*------- Add new transactions to a temporary file.
SET SAFETY OFF
COPY STRUCTURE TO TempInv
```

Next the program opens both the temporary file and the Master file and sets up a relationship between the two based on common part numbers. We need both files to be open so that the program can check for the existence of a part number entered in a transaction against part numbers in the Master database. The relationship is also necessary when printing the invoice later in the program. As you'll see later, the program uses the command A–>Part_No to display the part name on the invoice. The commands to open the files and set up the relationship are as follows:

```
*------- Open Master and temporary files.
SELECT A
USE Master INDEX Master
SELECT B
USE TempInv
SET RELATION TO Part_No INTO Master
```

When printing invoices in a later routine, the program will need to know the record number of the first transaction to be printed. This record number is stored in a variable named StartTrans. The StartTrans variable is initialized with a value of 1 in this line:

```
*------- Set pointer in temporary file.
StartTrans = 1
```

Now we'll set up a loop to continue adding invoices, and we'll use the variable Again to control the loop. Since each invoice must have a unique number, we'll have the program increment the variable MInvoice by one for each new invoice. The program also needs to initialize the memory variables MClerk and MCust, to store the salesperson's and customer's names. The grand total of the invoice is accumulated in the memory variable Total, which must be reset to zero for each new invoice. Then we'll have the program display the top portion of the invoice on the screen, for the user to fill out. This screen includes the new invoice number and the column headings to prompt the user through the data-entry process.

```
*------- Set up loop for displaying invoice forms.
Again = "Y"
DO WHILE Again = "Y"
    *------- Set up top portion of invoice on the screen.
    CLEAR
    MInvoice = MInvoice + 1
    STORE SPACE(20) TO MClerk, MCust
```

```
MTotal = 0
@ 1,2 SAY T_Date
@ 1,30 SAY "Invoice number: " + STR(MInvoice,5)
@ 2,2 SAY "Clerk " GET MClerk
@ 2,35 SAY "Customer " GET MCust
@ 3,0 SAY ULine
? "  Part #  Name",SPACE(20)
?? "Qty     Price          Total"
READ
```

Next, the program starts a loop for each individual line item on the invoice. The loop, controlled by the variable Adding, begins accepting transactions at line 7 on the screen. It will continue to accept transactions until the user doesn't enter a part number (PartNumb = " "). These lines set up the variables and begin the loop:

```
*------- Set up loop for each item on the invoice.
Row = 7
Adding = .T.
DO WHILE Adding
```

Then the program begins another loop to check the validity of the part numbers entered by the user. First the program creates a memory variable for storing the transaction part number (PartNumb). The variable OK becomes True when a valid part number (or request to quit adding line items) is entered; so to ensure that the loop occurs at least once, the program initializes OK as False. These lines set up that loop:

```
PartNumb = SPACE(5)
OK = .F.
*- Loop to check validity of part number.
DO WHILE .NOT. OK
```

The quantity and selling price of items sold are stored in the memory variables Quantity and Sel_Price, and these must be reset to zero after each entry:

```
*- Set up invoice memory variables.
Quantity = 0
Sel_Price = 0.00
```

Now the program can ask for the part number of the item sold, store the answer to the memory variable PartNumb, and use the SEEK command to make sure the part number exists:

```
*------- Ask for part number.
PartNumb = SPACE(5)
@ Row,2 GET PartNumb
READ
*------- Make sure part number exists.
PartNumb = UPPER(TRIM(PartNumb))
SELECT A
SEEK PartNumb
```

A DO CASE clause handles the next step, based on whether the user requests to exit, enters an invalid part number, or enters a valid part number. If no part number is entered, the variable OK becomes True, because this is a valid entry. The variable Adding becomes False, so that the command file quits asking for new transactions. The program skips the remaining CASE options, since the user is exiting:

```
*------- Decide next step based on
*------- existence of part number.
DO CASE
    *---- No part number was entered.
    CASE LEN(PartNumb) = 0
        OK = .T.
        Adding = .F.
```

However, if a nonexistent part number is entered, the command file displays a warning and loops around to allow the user to try again. This is accomplished by making the OK variable False, as in the following CASE statement:

```
*---- Part number does not exist.
CASE .NOT. FOUND()
    @ Row,10 SAY "No such part!!!  "
    OK = .F.
```

If the user enters a valid part number, the program must get the rest of the data for the transaction. First, it displays the description of the part (Title), then asks for the quantity sold (Quantity) and the selling price (Sel_Price). The following lines handle these tasks:

```
*------- Part number does exist.
CASE FOUND()
```

```
*- Say part description,
*- get quantity and price.
@ Row,10 SAY Title
@ Row,35 GET Quantity PICT "999"
@ Row,40 GET Sel_Price PICT "999.99"
READ
```

Then the program displays the total for the single line in the transaction and adds that amount to the grand total of the invoice (MTotal). The variable OK becomes True, since a valid part number was entered. However, if the quantity is zero (indicating that the user probably entered the wrong part number and wants to back up), the program just repeats the loop for entering the part number. The following routine handles these tasks:

```
*------- If quantity is zero, loop.
*------- Else, display total.
IF Quantity = 0
    LOOP
ELSE
    @ Row,50 SAY Quantity * Sel_Price;
        PICT "##,###.##"
    MTotal = MTotal + Quantity * Sel_Price
    OK = .T.
ENDIF
```

Once all the data for the transaction are entered, they must be stored in the TempInv (secondary) file. An APPEND BLANK command, followed by a series of REPLACE commands, will handle this job:

```
*------- Add a blank record to the TempInv file,
*------- and fill in the fields.
SELECT B
APPEND BLANK
REPLACE Date WITH T_Date
REPLACE Clerk WITH MClerk
REPLACE Invoice_No WITH MInvoice
REPLACE Customer WITH MCust
REPLACE Part_No WITH PartNumb
REPLACE Qty WITH Quantity
REPLACE Price WITH Sel_Price
REPLACE Posted WITH .F.
```

That ends the DO CASE clause as well as the loop for checking the validity of the part number, so the program can close those loops:

```
ENDCASE
ENDDO (continue loop while checking for valid part numbers)
```

Now the user is ready to enter the next line item. The variable Row is incremented by one, since it determines which line on the screen is used to enter the transaction. However, if the line items have reached row 19, the program scrolls all existing lines up a row to make room for new transactions. To scroll the screen up, the program moves the cursor to the bottom row (24) and prints a blank line. The row number for the line item remains constant (19):

```
Row = Row + 1
*----------- Scroll screen if nearing end.
IF Row >= 19
    @ 24,1
    ?
    Row = 19
ENDIF
ENDDO (while still adding transactions to invoice)
```

When the user has finished this invoice, the program displays the invoice total and asks whether it should be printed, as below:

```
*------- Display grand total and pause before next invoice.
@ Row+2,40 SAY "Total: "
@ Row+2,50 SAY MTotal PICT "$#,###.##"
Pinvoice = "Y"
@ 23,2 SAY "Print invoice? (Y/N) ";
    GET Pinvoice PICT "!"
READ
```

If the user chooses to print the invoice, the program sets the printer on, prints the heading, sets the record pointer to the first transaction for the current invoice (StartTrans), and lists all records to the end of the file. Then it prints the invoice total, ejects the paper in the printer, and sets the printer back off. The next transaction will be stored at the record below the current last record in the TempInv file, so the StartTrans variable is adjusted accordingly:

```
*------ Print invoice, reset StartTrans.
IF Pinvoice = "Y"
    SET PRINT ON
    ? "Date: ", T_Date
    ? "Invoice number: ",STR(MInvoice,5)
    ? "Customer: ",MCust,SPACE(20)
    ?? "Clerk: ",MClerk
    ? ULine
    ?
    SELECT B
    GOTO StartTrans
    LIST OFF WHILE .NOT. EOF();
        Part_No,A->Title,Qty,Price,Qty*Price
    ?
    ?
    ? " Total: ",SPACE(34),MTotal
    EJECT
    SET PRINT OFF
    StartTrans = RECCOUNT()+1
ENDIF
```

Next the program asks the user whether he wants to print another transaction, and it repeats the appropriate loop if the user answers Yes:

```
CLEAR
@ 23,2 SAY "Do another transaction? (Y/N) ";
    GET Again PICT "!"
READ
ENDDO (add invoices while user does not request to exit)
```

When the user is finished entering invoices, the program must add all the records from the TempInv file to the bottom of the Sales file, then update the Sales file index. To conserve disk space, the program also empties the TempInv file, then closes all databases and returns to the calling program:

```
*------- Close databases and update Sales file.
CLOSE DATABASES
CLEAR
? "Updating transaction file, please wait . . . "
SET TALK ON
```

```
USE Sales
APPEND FROM TempInv
USE TempInv
ZAP
USE Sales INDEX Sales
REINDEX
SET TALK OFF
CLOSE DATABASES
RETURN
```

The Pos program is complex, but it provides a great deal of convenience for the user. It also minimizes the likelihood of errors by checking the validity of the part numbers entered, as well as by immediately performing and displaying calculations for each transaction. It is, of course, a very general point-of-sale program, and it would probably need to be modified to suit each business's exact needs. But the overall procedures for looking up data in the master file, automatically calculating and filling in data, and storing the data in the sales transaction file will be the same for most such programs. Figure 13.10 shows the entire Pos command file.

```
**************************************** Pos.PRG
*   Point-of-sale data entry program for Sales.
*   Called from Sales Menu, SMENU.PRG.

*------- Get last-used invoice number from the Sales file.
USE Sales
GO BOTT
MInvoice = Invoice_No

*------ Add new transactions to a temporary file.
SET SAFETY OFF
COPY STRUCTURE TO TempInv

*------- Open Master and temporary files.
SELECT A
USE Master INDEX Master
SELECT B
USE TempInv
SET RELATION TO Part_No INTO Master

*------- Set pointer in temporary file.
StartTrans = 1

*------- Set up loop for displaying invoice forms.
Again = "Y"
```

Figure 13.10 – The completed Pos command file for recording sales transactions

```
DO WHILE Again = "Y"
    *------- Set up top portion of invoice on the screen.
    CLEAR
    MInvoice = MInvoice + 1
    STORE SPACE(20) TO MClerk, MCust
    MTotal = 0

    @ 1,2 SAY T_Date
    @ 1,30 SAY "Invoice number: " + STR(MInvoice,5)
    @ 2,2 SAY "Clerk " GET MClerk
    @ 2,35 SAY "Customer " GET MCust
    @ 3,0 SAY ULine
    ? "  Part #  Name",SPACE(20)
    ?? "Qty   Price        Total"
    READ

    *------- Set up loop for each item on the invoice.
    Row = 7
    Adding = .T.

    DO WHILE Adding
        PartNumb = Space(5)
        OK = .F.

        *- Loop to check validity of part number.
        DO WHILE .NOT. OK

            *- Set up invoice memory variables.
            Quantity = 0
            Sel_Price = 0.00

            *------- Ask for part number.
            PartNumb = SPACE(5)
            @ Row,2 GET PartNumb
            READ

            *------ Make sure part number exists.
            PartNumb = UPPER(TRIM(PartNumb))
            SELECT A
            SEEK PartNumb

            *------- Decide next step based upon
            *------- existence of part number.
            DO CASE

                *---- No part number was entered.
                CASE LEN(PartNumb) = 0
                    OK = .T.
                    Adding = .F.

                *---- Part number does not exist.
                CASE .NOT. FOUND()
                    @ Row,10 SAY "No such part!!!"
                    OK = .F.

                *------- Part number does exist.
                CASE FOUND()
                    *- Say part description,
                    *- get quantity and price.
                    @ Row,10 SAY Title
                    @ Row,35 GET Quantity PICT "999"
                    @ Row,40 GET Sel_Price PICT "999.99"
                    READ
```

Figure 13.10 – The completed Pos command file for recording sales transactions (continued)

```
                              *------- If quantity is zero, loop.
                              *------- Else, display total.
                              IF Quantity = 0
                                    LOOP
                              ELSE
                                    @ Row,50 SAY Quantity * Sel_Price;
                                       PICT "##,###.##"
                                    MTotal = MTotal + Quantity * Sel_Price
                                    OK = .T.
                              ENDIF

                              *------- Add a blank record to the TempInv file,
                              *------- and fill in the fields.
                              SELECT B
                              APPEND BLANK
                              REPLACE Date WITH T_Date
                              REPLACE Clerk WITH MClerk
                              REPLACE Invoice_No WITH MInvoice
                              REPLACE Customer WITH MCust
                              REPLACE Part_No WITH PartNumb
                              REPLACE Qty WITH Quantity
                              REPLACE Price WITH Sel_Price
                              REPLACE Posted WITH .F.

                       ENDCASE

                 ENDDO (continue loop while checking for valid part numbers)
                 Row = Row + 1
                 *----------- Scroll screen if nearing end.
                 IF Row >= 19
                    @ 24,1
                    ?
                    Row = 19
                 ENDIF
            ENDDO (while still adding transactions to invoice)

            *------- Display grand total, and pause before next invoice.
            @ Row+2,40 SAY "TOTAL: "
            @ Row+2,50 SAY MTotal PICT "$#,###.##"
            Pinvoice = "Y"
            @ 23,2 SAY "Print invoice? (Y/N) ";
              GET Pinvoice PICT "!"
            READ

            *------ Print invoice, reset StartTrans.
            IF Pinvoice = "Y"

                 SET PRINT ON
                 ? "Date: ", T_Date
                 ? "Invoice number: ",STR(MInvoice,5)
                 ? "Customer: ",MCust,SPACE(20)
                 ?? "Clerk: ",MClerk
                 ? ULine
                 ?
                 SELECT B
                 GOTO StartTrans
                 LIST OFF WHILE .NOT. EOF();
                    Part_No,A->Title,Qty,Price,Qty*Price
                 ?
                 ?
                 ? " Total: ",SPACE(34),MTotal
                 EJECT
                 SET PRINT OFF
                 StartTrans = RECCOUNT()+1
```

Figure 13.10 – The completed Pos command file for recording sales transactions (continued)

```
        ENDIF
        CLEAR
        @ 23,2 SAY "Do another transaction? (Y/N) ";
          GET Again PICT "!"
        READ

    ENDDO (add invoices while user does not request to exit)

    *------- Close databases and update Sales file.
    CLOSE DATABASES
    CLEAR
    ? "Updating transaction file, please wait..."
    SET TALK ON
    USE Sales
    APPEND FROM TempInv
    USE TempInv
    ZAP
    USE Sales INDEX Sales
    REINDEX
    SET TALK OFF
    CLOSE DATABASES
    RETURN
```

Figure 13.10 – The completed Pos command file for recording sales transactions (continued)

Automatic Selling Price

The Pos program assumes that the user enters the selling price for each transaction. As an alternative, you can store the selling price for each item on the Master file and have it come to the Pos screen automatically when the user enters the appropriate part number. The Pos program will still calculate the appropriate totals.

To add this automatic price feature, you need to modify the structure of the Master database so it includes a field for storing the selling price. In the example in Figure 13.11, the name of the new field is Sel_Price. You'll also need to modify the IScreen1 screen to allow entry and editing on this field.

Then you need to modify Pos.PRG so that it uses the selling price from the database. First, you'll want the program to display the selling price, not ask for it. Therefore, you need to change the line that reads

   @ Row,40 GET Sel_Price PICT "999.99"

to

   @ Row,40 SAY Sel_Price PICT "999.99"

Then you'll need to be sure that the Sel_Price variable contains the same amount as the Sel_Price field by adding the line Sel_Price = Sel_Price,

```
Structure for database: C:Master.DBF

Field  Field Name  Type       Width   Dec
    1  PART NO     Character       5
    2  TITLE       Character      20
    3  QTY         Numeric         4    0
    4  COST        Numeric         9    2
    5  SEL_PRICE   Numeric         9    2
    6  REORDER     Numeric         4    0
    7  ON_ORDER    Numeric         4    0
    8  LOCATION    Character       5
    9  VENDOR      Character      25
   10  VENDOR_ADD  Character      25
   11  VENDOR_CSZ  Character      25
   12  DATE        Date            8
   13  ORDER_DATE  Date            8
   14  NEW_ORDER   Numeric         4    0
```

Figure 13.11 – Modified structure of the Master database

as indicated below:

```
*------- If quantity is zero, loop.
*------- Else, display total.
IF Quantity = 0
    LOOP
ELSE
    *---- New line for automatic price.
    Sel_Price = Sel_Price
    @ Row,50 SAY Quantity * Sel_Price;
       PICT "##,###.##"
    MTotal = MTotal + Quantity * Sel_Price
    OK = .T.
ENDIF
```

Sales System Reports

Option 2 from the Sales menu allows the user to print reports from the Sales database. Reports can be based on either a single invoice number or sales transactions for a range of dates (for example, all sales transactions from 01/01/85 to 03/31/85). When the user decides to print a report of sales, the menu in Figure 13.12 appears on the screen.

If the user selects option 1, the program asks

Look for what invoice number?

The user types the invoice number and the screen (or printer) displays data from that invoice, as in Figure 13.13.

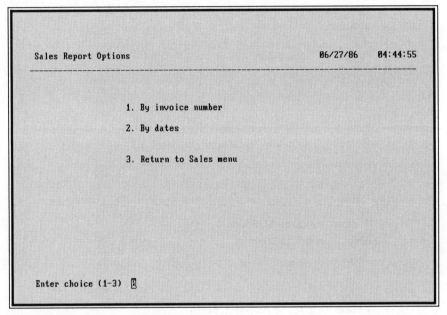

```
Sales Report Options                              06/27/86    04:44:55
----------------------------------------------------------------------------


                    1. By invoice number

                    2. By dates


                    3. Return to Sales menu







Enter choice (1-3)  ▓
```

Figure 13.12 – Sales Reports menu

```
Invoice number: 12345      Date  02/15/85
Clerk: ACS                 Customer: D. Jones

    Part #   Qty. Part Name      Price        Total
    Z-999    2    Penny loafers  12.00        24.00
    A-113    3    Sandals        15.00        45.00
    A-111    1    Wingtips       90.00        90.00
```

Figure 13.13 – Invoice report

If the user selects option 2 to display data for a range of dates, the program asks the user to

Enter start date : / / :
Enter end date : / / .

The user then enters the range of dates and the screen (or printer) displays a summary of all sales transactions for that period, as in Figure 13.14.

You can create the report format by using the dBASE MODIFY REPORT command

USE Sales
MODIFY REPORT Sales

and by setting the REPORT FORM parameters, as in Figure 13.15. Then set up the information in column format, as in Figure 13.16.

```
Page No.       1
02/15/85
                         Sales Transactions

 Date       Invoice Salesperson  Customer      Part    Qty Sale Price

 02/15/86   12345 ZTD            J. Jones      AAA      10      12.50
 02/15/86   12345 ZTD            J. Jones      BBB       7       0.55
 02/15/86   12346 ACS            G. Gossage    BBB       0       0.00
 02/15/86   12346 ACS            G. Gossage    TTT      12       0.66
 02/16/86   12347 ZTD            S. Garvey     TTT       5       0.40
 02/15/86   12346 ACS            G. Gossage    ZZZ       4      15.00
 02/16/86   12347 ZTD            S. Garvey     ZZZ       2      15.00
 *** Total ***

                                                              44.11
```

Figure 13.14 – Sample Sales transactions report for a range of dates

```
Page title                Sales Transactions
Page width (position)     75
Left margin                1
Right margin               0
Lines per page            58
Double space report       No
```

Figure 13.15 – REPORT FORM parameters

```
Column   Contents      Heading       Width   Decimals   Total?
  1      Date          Date            9
  2      Invoice_No    Invoice         7
  3      Clerk         Salesperson    14
  4      Customer      Customer       14
  5      Part_No       Part            6
  6      Qty           Qty             5        0          N
  7      Cost          Sale Price     10        0          Y
```

Figure 13.16 – Column format for Sales.FRM

Writing the Pseudocode

The command file that asks the user which report he wishes and displays the reports is called SalReps.PRG. Its pseudocode is as follows:

> Use the Sales and Master data files
>
> Set up relationship
>
> Start loop for menu
>
>> Present options
>>
>>> 1. By invoice number
>>>
>>> 2. By dates
>>>
>>> 3. Return to Sales menu
>>
>> Get user's choice
>>
>> If not exiting, ask about printer
>>
>>> Set up printer macro if requested
>>
>> Print appropriate report based on request
>>
>>> Case 1: Search by invoice number
>>>
>>>> Ask user for invoice number
>>>>
>>>> Locate first transaction with that invoice number

If found, print invoice

> If printer requested, set printer on

> Print header information from first record with

> that invoice number

> Print data from remaining records with that

> invoice number

> Set printer off

> Case 2: Search by dates

> Ask for starting and ending dates

> Convert dates to Date types

> Clear screen

> Print report for those dates, using Sales.FRM

If not going to printer and not exiting, pause the screen

Continue to loop through menu (while user does not request exit)

When done, return to Sales menu

Writing the Command File

The program starts by using the Sales file without an index. Recall that the index maintains order by part number. But for these reports we want the sales transactions grouped by date and invoice number. Because of the way the point-of-sale program automatically generates invoice numbers and fills in dates, the records will already be in the required order without the use of the index file.

To include part names on the Invoice report, we'll also open the Master file and set up a relationship between the two files using the SET RELA-TION command. The first few lines of the program are displayed below:

```
* * * * * * * * * * * * * * * * * * * * * * * * * * * * * * * * * * * SalReps.PRG
* Print reports from the Sales file.
* Called from Sales Menu, SMenu.PRG.
*----Open files and set up relationship.
SELECT 1
USE Sales
SELECT 2
```

```
USE Master INDEX Master
SELECT 1
SET RELATION TO Part_No INTO Master
```

Now we need to set up a loop for the menu. We'll have the program store the user's menu choice in the memory variable RepChoice. The following lines set up the variables and the loop, then display the menu and wait for a response:

```
RepChoice = 0
*------- Start loop for menu.
DO WHILE RepChoice # 3
    CLEAR
    @ 2,1 SAY "Sales Report Options"
    @ 2,60 SAY DTOC(T_Date) + "      " + TIME()
    @ 3,0 SAY ULine
    ?
    ?
    TEXT
              1. By invoice number
              2. By dates

              3. Return to Sales menu
    ENDTEXT
    @ 24,1 SAY "Enter choice (1–3) " GET RepChoice PICT;
        "9" RANGE 1,3
    READ
```

If the user did not request to return to the Sales menu (option 3), the program asks the user whether the report should be printed in hard copy, and, if so, sets up the printer macro with the variable Printer:

```
    *------- If not exiting, ask about printer.
    @ 5,0 CLEAR
    STORE " " TO YN, Printer
    IF RepChoice # 3
        @ 15,5 SAY "Send to printer? " GET YN PICT "!"
        READ
        *------- Set up printer macro.
        IF YN = "Y"
            Printer = "TO PRINT"
        ENDIF
    ENDIF
```

Now we'll have the program use a DO CASE clause to print the appropriate report. If the user wishes to print by invoice number, the program asks for the invoice to print, locates the first record with that number, and displays the basic heading information (invoice number, date, salesperson, and customer name). Then it uses the LIST WHILE command to print data from all transactions associated with that invoice number. The following lines handle these tasks:

```
*------- Print appropriate report based on request.
@ 5,0 CLEAR
DO CASE
    *------- Case 1: Search by invoice number.
    CASE RepChoice = 1
    @ 15,5
    INPUT "Look for what invoice number? " TO ISearch
    CLEAR
    LOCATE FOR Invoice_No = ISearch
    *------- If found, print invoice.
    IF FOUND()
        IF YN = "Y"
            SET PRINT ON
        ENDIF
        *------- Print header info from first record
        *------- with that invoice number.
        ? "Invoice number:", Invoice_No
        ?? "      Date:", Date
        ? "Clerk:", Clerk, "Customer:", Customer
        ?
        ? "Part #    Part Name    Qty    Price      Total"
        *------- Print data for all records
        *------- with that invoice number.
        LIST OFF WHILE Invoice_No = ISearch;
        Part_No, B->Title, Qty, Price, (Qty * Price)
        IF YN = "Y"
            EJECT
            SET PRINT OFF
        ENDIF
    ENDIF (found)
```

If the user requests report option 2, the program asks for the starting and ending dates and then uses Sales.FRM to print the report for all records that fall within the dates requested. The second CASE statement handles this report:

```
*------- Case 2: Search by dates.
CASE RepChoice = 2
    STORE SPACE(8) TO Start, End
    @ 15,5 SAY "Enter start date " GET Start PICT;
      "99/99/99"
    @ 17,5 SAY "Enter end date  " GET End PICT;
      "99/99/99"
    READ
    Start = CTOD(Start)
    End = CTOD(End)
    CLEAR
    *------- Print the report.
    REPORT FORM Sales;
      FOR Date >= Start .AND. Date <= End &Printer
ENDCASE
```

Note the use of the CTOD() (character-to-date) function in the routine above. Since the Start and End dates are entered as character strings, the CTOD() function is used to translate them to Date-type variables, so that the REPORT FORM condition FOR Date >= Start .AND. Date <= End will work properly.

The next routine in SalReps merely pauses the report on the screen if the user did not request to print the report or exit the program:

```
*------- If not going to printer, pause the screen.
IF YN # "Y" .AND. RepChoice # 3
    ?
    ?
    WAIT "Press any key to return to the Reports menu . . . "
ENDIF
```

The remaining lines close the DO WHILE loop, close the open databases, and return control to the SMenu command file:

```
ENDDO (while user does not request exit)
*------- When done, return to Sales menu.
SET RELATION TO
```

CLOSE DATABASES
RETURN

Figure 13.17 shows the complete SalReps command file. Note the use of the B-> to get the Title data from the Master file. You can also use the B-> pointer with fields in a REPORT FORM format file.

```
*****************************************************  SalReps.PRG
*   Print reports from the Sales file.
*   Called from Sales menu, SMenu.PRG.

*----- Open files and set up relationship.
SELECT 1
USE Sales
SELECT 2
USE Master INDEX Master

SELECT 1
SET RELATION TO Part_No INTO Master


RepChoice = 0
*------- Start loop for menu.
DO WHILE RepChoice # 3
    CLEAR
    @ 2,1 SAY "Sales Report Options"
    @ 2,60 SAY DTOC(T_Date) + "     " + TIME()
    @ 3,0 SAY ULine
    ?
    ?
    TEXT
                    1. By invoice number

                    2. By dates


                    3. Return to Sales menu
    ENDTEXT

    @ 24,1 SAY "Enter choice (1-3) " GET RepChoice PICT "9" RANGE 1,3
    READ

    *------- If not exiting, ask about printer.
    @ 5,0 CLEAR
    STORE " " TO YN, Printer
    IF RepChoice # 3
        @ 15,5 SAY "Send to printer? " GET YN PICT "!"
        READ

        *------- Set up printer macro.
        IF YN = "Y"
            Printer = "TO PRINT"
        ENDIF
    ENDIF

    *------- Print appropriate report based on request.
    @ 5,0 CLEAR
    DO CASE
```

Figure 13.17 – The completed SalReps command file

```
                  *------- Case 1: Search by invoice number.
              CASE RepChoice = 1
                  @ 15,5
                  INPUT "Look for what invoice number? " TO ISearch
                  CLEAR
                  LOCATE FOR Invoice_No = ISearch

                  *------- If found, print invoice.
                  IF FOUND()
                      IF YN = "Y"
                          SET PRINT ON
                      ENDIF

                      *------- Print header info from first record
                      *------- with that invoice number.
                      ? "Invoice number:", Invoice_No
                      ?? "     Date:", Date
                      ? "Clerk:", Clerk, "Customer:", Customer
                      ?
                      ? " Part #  Part Name   Qty       Price          Total"

                      *------- Print data for all records
                      *------- with that invoice number.
                      LIST OFF WHILE Invoice_No = ISearch;
                          Part_No, B->Title, Qty, Price, (Qty * Price)
                      IF YN = "Y"
                          EJECT
                          SET PRINT OFF
                      ENDIF
                  ENDIF (not eof)

              *------- Case 2: Search by dates.
              CASE RepChoice = 2
                  STORE SPACE(8) TO Start, End
                  @ 15,5 SAY "Enter start date " GET Start PICT "99/99/99"
                  @ 17,5 SAY "Enter end date   " GET End PICT "99/99/99"
                  READ
                  Start = CTOD(Start)
                  End = CTOD(End)
                  CLEAR

                  *------- Print the report.
                  REPORT FORM Sales;
                      FOR Date >= Start .AND. Date <= End &Printer

          ENDCASE

          *------- If not going to printer, pause the screen.
          IF YN # "Y" .AND. RepChoice # 3
              ?
              ?
              WAIT "Press any key to return to the Reports menu..."
          ENDIF

      ENDDO (while user does not request exit)

      *------- When done, return to Sales menu.
      SET RELATION TO
      CLOSE DATABASES
      RETURN
```

Figure 13.17 – The completed SalReps command file (continued)

Sales file editing, the third option in the SMenu program, will be developed in Chapter 15, since it's one of the updating functions for the Inventory System.

Inventory New Stock System

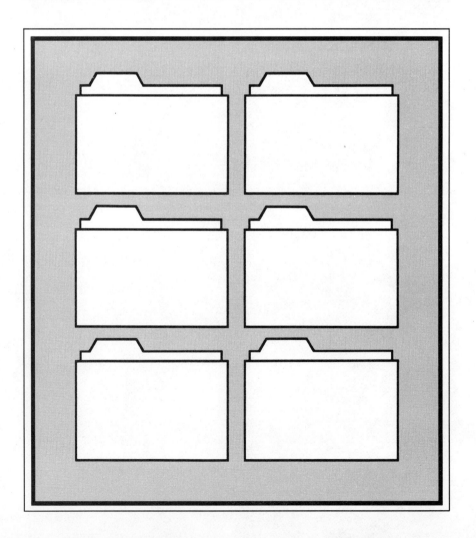

The New Stock portion of the Inventory System allows the user to record new items that come into the stockroom. These data are stored in NewStock.DBF, which we created in Chapter 11 (see Figure 11.4). We created an index file, NewStock.NDX, by typing this command:

INDEX ON Part_No TO NewStock

The user enters the New Stock menu by selecting option 3 from the Inventory System main menu. This brings up the screen shown in Figure 14.1. As with the Sales System, the menu allows the user to add transactions, print reports, edit data, or return to the Inventory System main menu.

New Stock System
Software Structure

The New Stock system consists of the following four command files:

1. NMenu, which presents the opening menu

2. NewStock, which allows the user to add new data

3. NewReps, which prints reports

4. NewEdit, which allows the user to edit existing data

Figure 14.2 shows the software structure for this portion of the Inventory System.

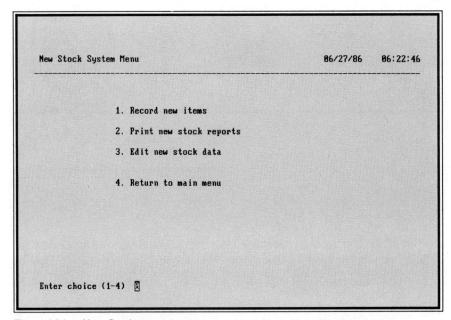

Figure 14.1 – *New Stock system menu*

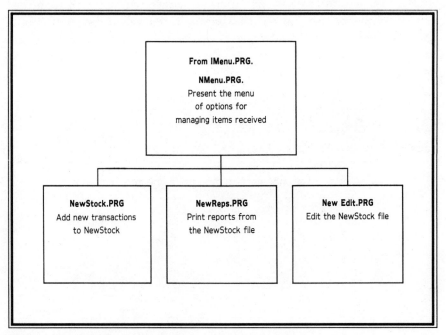

Figure 14.2 – *Software structure for the New Stock system*

New Stock System Menu

The menu for the New Stock portion of the Inventory System is handled by the NMenu command file. Because it is another simple menu program, the completed program is shown in Figure 14.3. We'll develop New-Stock.PRG and NewReps.PRG in this chapter, then create NewEdit.PRG in Chapter 15.

```
***************************************************** NMenu.PRG
*   Menu for managing New Stock portion of Inventory System.
*   Called from Inventory System main menu.

*------- Set up loop for presenting menu.
NChoice = 0
DO WHILE NChoice # 4

    CLEAR
    @ 2,1 SAY "New Stock System Menu"
    @ 2,60 SAY DTOC(T_Date) + "     " + TIME()
    @ 3,0 SAY ULine
    ?
    ?
    TEXT
                1. Record new items

                2. Print new stock reports

                3. Edit new stock data


                4. Return to main menu
    ENDTEXT

    @ 24,1 SAY "Enter choice (1-4) " GET NChoice PICT "9"
    READ

    *------- Branch to appropriate program.
    DO CASE
       CASE NChoice = 1
            DO NewStock
       CASE NChoice = 2
            DO NewReps
       CASE NChoice = 3
            DO NewEdit
    ENDCASE

ENDDO (while NChoice # 4)

*------- Return to main menu.
RETURN
```

Figure 14.3 – The completed NMenu command file

New Stock Data-Entry Program

When the user selects option 1 from the the New Stock system menu, the screen clears and the following prompt appears:

> **Enter data for goods received**
> **Part number :_   :**

If the user enters an invalid part number, the computer beeps and a warning appears on the screen:

> **Enter data for goods received**
> **Part number :_   : No such part!!!**

Then the user is given an opportunity to try again. If a part number is valid, the screen will display the name of the part, the date, and the vendor (which can be changed, if necessary), and prompts the user to fill in the quantity received and the purchase price, as below:

> **Enter data for goods received**
> **Part number A-111   Icebergs**
> **Quantity :_   :   Price :   . :**
> **Date 02/15/85   Vendor American Iceberg Co.**

When the user has filled in the blank fields and pressed Return, the program asks for the next transaction. After adding the transactions, the user just presses the Return key rather than typing another number. This brings back the New Stock system menu.

Writing the Pseudocode

The pseudocode for the NewStock command file will look like this:

> Open both the Master and NewStock databases
> Set up loop for recording goods received
>> Clear screen
>> Get part number for next transaction
>> If part number was entered,
>> Find it in Master

If part number cannot be found, warn user

and allow another try

If part number exists

Display description of part

Add blank record to NewStock.DBF

Fill in part number

Fill in date received

Fill in vendor name

Get quantity and cost of item received

Continue loop (while user does not quit)

Return to New Stock menu

Creating the Command File

The NewStock command file needs to use the Master data file to check the validity of part numbers as well as the NewStock data file to record individual transactions. The first lines of the program open these two files:

```
****************************** NewStock.PRG
* Data entry program for goods received.
* Called from New Stock menu, NMenu.PRG.
SELECT A
USE Master INDEX Master
SELECT B
USE NewStock INDEX NewStock
SELECT A
```

Next, the program sets up a loop for adding new transactions. The following lines handle this task:

```
*------- Set up loop for recording goods received.
PartNumb = "X"
DO WHILE PartNumb # " "
    @ 5,0 CLEAR
    PartNumb = SPACE(5)
    @ 10,2 SAY " Enter data for goods received"
    @ 12,4 SAY " Part number " GET PartNumb PICT "!!!!!"
    READ
```

If the user does not request to exit by leaving PartNumb blank, the program tries to find the part number in the Master file.

```
*------- If a part number was entered, find it in Master file.
IF PartNumb # " "
    SEEK PartNumb
```

Next, the command file must either warn the user of an invalid part number or continue with the transaction if the part number is valid. The first CASE statement in the DO CASE clause below handles invalid part numbers:

```
DO CASE
    ****** If part not found, warn user and try again.
    CASE .NOT. FOUND()
        @ 12,25 SAY "No such part!!!"
        ? CHR(7)
```

If the user enters a valid part number, the description of the part is presented on the screen and a blank record is added to the NewStock file. Now the user can enter data for the transaction. The Part_No, Date, and Vendor fields are filled in automatically with data already available to the program, and the user needs to provide only the quantity (Qty), price (Cost), and new vendor name (Vendor) if changed. The program then selects the Master (primary) file, in preparation for the next entry. The following lines handle these jobs:

```
*------- If found, append a new record to NewStock
*------- and get rest of data.
CASE FOUND()
    @ 12,25 SAY Title
    SELECT B
    APPEND BLANK
    REPLACE Part_No WITH PartNumb
    REPLACE Date WITH T_Date
    REPLACE Vendor WITH A->Vendor
    @ 14,2 SAY "Quantity " GET Qty
    @ 14,22 SAY "Price " GET Cost PICT "99999.99"
    @ 16,2 SAY "Date " GET Date PICT "99/99/99"
    @ 16,22 SAY "Vendor" GET Vendor
    READ
    SELECT A
```

The remainder of the program simply closes the DO CASE, IF, and DO WHILE statements. If the user elects to exit, the program then closes the open data files and returns control to the NMenu command file:

ENDCASE
  ENDIF (PartNumb # '' '')
ENDDO (while user does not ask to quit)
* * * * * * * * * * * * * * * Close files and return to NewStock menu.
CLOSE DATABASES
RETURN

Figure 14.4 shows the completed NewStock command file.

```
*************************************************** NewStock.PRG
*  Data entry program for goods received.
*  Called from New Stock menu, NMenu.PRG.

SELECT A
USE Master INDEX Master
SELECT B
USE NewStock INDEX NewStock
SELECT A

*------- Set up loop for recording goods received.
PartNumb = "X"
DO WHILE PartNumb # " "
    @ 5,0 CLEAR
    PartNumb = SPACE(5)
    @ 10,2 SAY " Enter data for goods received"
    @ 12,4 SAY " Part number " GET PartNumb PICT "!!!!!"
    READ

    *------- If a part number was entered, find it in Master file.
    IF PartNumb # " "
        SEEK PartNumb

        DO CASE

            *------- If part not found, warn user and try again.
            CASE .NOT. FOUND()
                @ 12,25 SAY "No such part!!!"
                ? CHR(7)

            *------- If found, append a new record to NewStock
            *------- and get rest of data.
            CASE FOUND()
                @ 12,25 SAY Title

                SELECT B
                APPEND BLANK
                REPLACE Part_No WITH PartNumb
                REPLACE Date WITH T_Date
                REPLACE Vendor WITH A->Vendor
```

Figure 14.4 – The completed NewStock command file

```
                   @ 14,2 SAY "Quantity " GET Qty
                   @ 14,22 SAY "Price " GET Cost PICT "99999.99"
                   @ 16,2 SAY "Date " GET Date PICT "99/99/99"
                   @ 16,22 SAY "Vendor" GET Vendor
                   READ
                   SELECT A

             ENDCASE

        ENDIF (PartNumb # " ")

     ENDDO (while user does not ask to quit)

     *------- Close files and return to New Stock menu.
     CLOSE DATABASES
     RETURN
```

Figure 14.4 – The completed NewStock command file (continued)

New Stock System Reports

The New Stock system allows the user to review, in report form, all stock received, by part number or for a range of dates. These reports are useful for resolving discrepancies with vendors or between the computer's report of stock and what is actually on hand. Also, these data allow a store manager to review the number of orders for a particular item over a given period of time and adjust reorder points accordingly.

When the user decides to print reports, another menu of options appears:

1. By part number
2. By dates

3. Return to New Stock menu

If the user selects option 1, the program asks whether the report should be sent to the printer and then displays this prompt:

Look for what part number? :_   :

The user enters a part number, and all transactions for goods received for that part number are displayed in a report, such as the one in Figure 14.5.

The user can also choose to view only transactions that occurred between two dates. When the user selects option 2 from the Reports menu, the program displays these prompts:

Enter start date :_ / / :
Enter end date : / / :

The user then types the starting and ending dates, and the program displays all transactions between those dates (inclusive) in a report, as in Figure 14.6.

```
Page No.      1
02/15/85
                  Inventory Items Received

Part  Part Name      Qty     Purchase  Date   Vendor Name
                              Price


A-111 Icebergs        10      120.00 02/15/85 American Iceberg Co.
A-111 Icebergs        10      120.00 03/15/85 American Iceberg Co.
A-111 Icebergs        10      120.00 04/20/84 American Iceberg Co.
A-111 Icebergs        10      130.00 05/20/85 American Iceberg Co.
A-111 Icebergs        10      130.00 06/10/85 American Iceberg Co.
```

Figure 14.5 – Report of items received, by part number

```
Page No.       1
02/15/85
                  Inventory Items Received

Part  Part Name      Qty     Purchase  Date   Vendor Name
                             Price


A-111 Icebergs        10      120.00 02/15/85 American Iceberg Co.
BBB   Tomatoes        10        0.35 02/15/85 Juicy Tomatoes, Inc.
CCC   Floppy disks    10       12.00 02/15/85 Diamond Disks
TTT   Tamales         10        0.10 02/16/85 American Hot Tamales
ZZZ   Bicycle seats   10       23.00 02/16/85 American Bicycle Co.
```

Figure 14.6 – Inventory New Stock file printed by date

Both report options use a REPORT FORM file called NewStock.FRM. You can create it by typing the commands

CLEAR ALL
SELECT 1
USE NewStock
SELECT 2
USE Master INDEX Master
SELECT 1
SET RELATION TO Part_No INTO Master
MODIFY REPORT NewStock

at the dBASE dot prompt and filling out the questionnaire with the information in Figure 14.7. (Note the use of the B-> pointer to get part names
from the Master database.)

The logic for NewReps.PRG is virtually identical to that for SalReps.PRG
in Chapter 13. Figure 14.8 presents the entire NewReps command file.

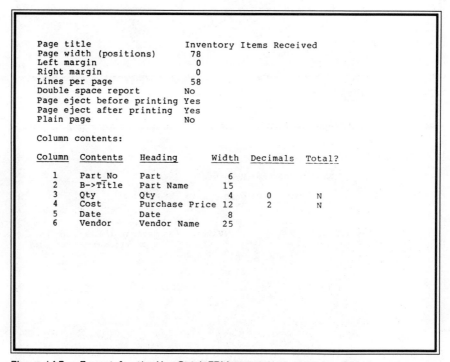

```
Page title                     Inventory Items Received
Page width (positions)         78
Left margin                    0
Right margin                   0
Lines per page                 58
Double space report            No
Page eject before printing     Yes
Page eject after printing      Yes
Plain page                     No

Column contents:

Column   Contents    Heading         Width   Decimals   Total?

   1     Part_No     Part               6
   2     B->Title    Part Name         15
   3     Qty         Qty                4       0          N
   4     Cost        Purchase Price    12       2          N
   5     Date        Date               8
   6     Vendor      Vendor Name       25
```

Figure 14.7 – Format for the NewStock.FRM report

```
**************************************************** NewReps.PRG
*  Print reports from the NewStock file.
*  Called from New Stock menu, NMenu.PRG.

*------- Open Newstock and Master databases.
SELECT 1
USE Newstock
SELECT 2
USE Master INDEX Master

*-------- Set up relationship.
SELECT 1
SET RELATION TO Part_No INTO Master

RepChoice = 0

*------- Start loop for menu
DO WHILE RepChoice # 3

    CLEAR
    @ 2,1 SAY "New Stock Report Options"
    @ 2,60 SAY DTOC(T_Date) + "     " + TIME()
    @ 3,0 SAY ULine
    ?
    ?
    TEXT
                    1. By part number

                    2. By dates


                    3. Return to New Stock menu
    ENDTEXT

    @ 24,1 SAY "Enter choice (1-3) " GET RepChoice PICT "9"
    READ

    *------- If not exiting, ask about printer.
    @ 5,0 CLEAR
    STORE " " TO YN, Printer
    IF RepChoice # 3
        @ 15,5 SAY "Send to printer? " GET YN PICT "!"
        READ

        *------- Set up printer macro.
        IF YN = "Y"
            Printer = "TO PRINT"
        ENDIF
    ENDIF

    *------- Print appropriate report based on request.
    @ 5,0 CLEAR
    DO CASE

        *------- Case 1: Search by part number.
        CASE RepChoice = 1
            SET INDEX TO NewStock
            NSearch = SPACE(5)
            @ 15,5 SAY "Look for what part number?: ";
              GET NSearch PICT "!!!!!"
            READ
            CLEAR
            SEEK NSearch
            REPORT FORM NewStock WHILE Part_No = NSearch &Printer
```

Figure 14.8 – The completed NewReps command file

```
            *------- Case 2: Search by dates.
            CASE RepChoice = 2
                SET INDEX TO
                STORE SPACE(8) TO Start, End
                @ 15,5 SAY "Enter start date " GET Start PICT "99/99/99"
                @ 17,5 SAY "Enter end date   " GET End PICT "99/99/99"
                READ
                Start = CTOD(Start)
                End = CTOD(End)
                CLEAR

                *------- Print the report.
                REPORT FORM NewStock;
                    FOR Date >= Start .AND. Date <= End &Printer

        ENDCASE

        *------- If not going to printer, pause the screen.
        IF YN # "Y" .AND. RepChoice # 3
            ?
            ?
            WAIT "Press any key to return to the Reports menu..."
        ENDIF

    ENDDO (while user does not request exit)

    *------- When done, return to New Stock menu.
    SET RELATION TO
    CLOSE DATABASES
    RETURN
```

Figure 14.8 – *The completed NewReps command file (continued)*

At this point, we've created all three major portions of the Inventory System. However, the final program, the one that gives the system its real power, remains to be written: a command file that can read data from both the Sales and NewStock files and update the Master file based on those data. We also need to develop programs to allow editing to the Sales and NewStock files after an update has taken place. We'll do all this in Chapter 15.

Inventory System Updating

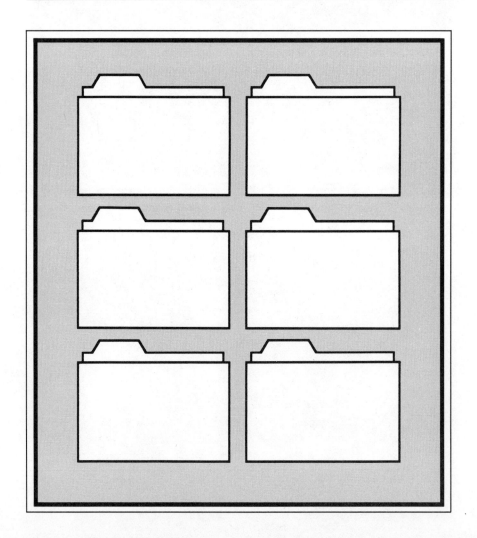

Now that we've developed the command files to manage the Master inventory file as well as the Sales and NewStock transaction files, we need to write the program to handle Master-file updates. This program needs to subtract the quantities in the Sales file from those in the Master file, since these items have been sold. Then it needs to add the quantities from the NewStock file to those in the Master file, since these items are now in stock.

Also, the updating command file must subtract the quantities in the New-Stock file from the on-order quantities in the Master file, since these have now been received, and replace the purchase price of items in the Master file with the purchase price in the NewStock file, since this is the most recent price. Finally, the program should replace the dates in the Master file with the dates in the transaction files, as a means of keeping track of when the last update occurred.

Updating the Master File

From the user's point of view, updating is performed by simply selecting option 4 from the Master menu, which we placed in the command file MMenu.PRG.

Writing the Pseudocode

The command file to perform the update is called Updater.PRG, and its pseudocode looks like this:

Clear screen

Display message that Master is being updated from Sales

Use Sales file indexed by part number

Copy all nonupdated records to a temporary file, Temp

    Use Temp file

    Make sure there are records in Temp

    If there are records

        Use Master file and index for updating

        Update from Temp, subtracting quantities and replacing dates

        Close databases for safety

        Use original Sales file

        Make all items in the Posted field True in Sales

    Close databases to free work areas

Display message that Master is being updated from NewStock

Use NewStock file indexed by part number

Copy all nonupdated records to Temp file

    Use Temp file

    Make sure there are records in Temp

    If there are records

        Use Master file and index for updating

        Update from Temp, adding quantities, replacing cost and date, and subtracting quantities from On _Order field

        Close databases for safety

        Use original NewStock file

        Make all items in the Posted field True in NewStock

Close databases to free work areas

Return to MMenu.PRG

Writing the Command File

The Updater command file begins by clearing the screen and asking the user to confirm the decision to update. If the user enters Y (Yes), the program displays a message so the user has something to read during what may be a fairly long process. Then the program opens the Sales file and index and copies all records that have not already been updated to a temporary data file called Temp, as shown in the following lines:

```
* * * * * * * * * * * * * * * * * * * * * * * * * * * * * * * * * * * * * * * Updater.PRG
* Update the Master file from Sales and NewStock.
* Called from Master menu, MMenu.PRG.
*------- Ask user if sure about updating.
YesNo = "Y"
@ 5,0 CLEAR
@ 15,4 SAY "Update Master file from Sales and NewStock?;
    (Y/N)" GET YesNo PICT "!"
READ
IF YesNo = "N"
RETURN
ENDIF
*------- Display message that Master is being updated from Sales
*------- file.
@ 5,0 CLEAR
@ 15,5 SAY "Updating from the Sales file . . . "
USE Sales INDEX Sales
*------- Copy all nonupdated records to Temp file.
COPY STRUCTURE TO Temp
COPY TO Temp FOR .NOT. Posted
```

At this point, Temp contains all the records that need to be used to update Master. Next, the program opens the Temp file in a separate work area (2, in this example) and makes sure there are records in it. Updating from an empty database file sometimes causes unpredictable results. Hence, dBASE programs should always check to make sure there are records in the Temp file to update from:

```
*------- Make sure there are records in Temp.
SELECT 2
USE Temp
IF RECCOUNT( ) > 0
```

Next, the Master file with the Master index is opened in work area 1.

```
*------- Use Master file and index for updating.
SELECT 1
USE Master INDEX Master
```

Then the update is performed by subtracting the quantities in the Temp file (Temp->Qty) from the quantities in the Master file (Qty), then replacing the Date field in the Master file with the appropriate date from the Temp file (Temp->Date):

```
*------- Update from the temporary sales file.
UPDATE ON Part_No FROM Temp;
   REPLACE Qty WITH Qty  –  Temp->Qty, Date WITH;
   Temp->Date
```

Finally, the records in the Sales file must be marked so that they're not accidentally updated again in the future. The Posted field acts as a flag for this purpose, and it is set to True (.T.) when the record has been posted (updated to the Master file).

```
*------- Use original Sales file, make all Posted fields "True".
CLOSE DATABASES
USE Sales
REPLACE ALL Posted WITH .T.
```

Now we can end the IF clause that was used to confirm that the Temp file had data in it, and then close all open databases:

```
ENDIF (record count > 0)
CLOSE DATABASES
```

Next the command file needs to perform a similar update from the New-Stock file. First, the program displays a new "Updating" message and opens the NewStock file and index. Then it copies all records that have not yet been posted to the Temp file (since we used the SET SAFETY OFF command in IMenu.PRG, the new Temp file will simply overwrite the previous one):

```
*------- Message that Master is being updated from the
*------- NewStock file.
@ 15,5 SAY "Updating from the NewStock file . . ."
USE NewStock INDEX NewStock
*------- Copy nonupdated records to Temp file.
COPY STRUCTURE TO Temp
COPY TO Temp FOR .NOT. Posted
```

Again, for safety and speed, the command file makes sure that there are records in Temp before proceeding with the update:

```
*------- Make sure there are records in Temp.
SELECT 2
USE Temp
IF RECCOUNT() > 0
```

Now the Master file and index are opened again with the following commands:

```
*------- Use Master file and index for updating.
SELECT 1
USE Master INDEX Master
```

The command file then updates from the Temp file, summing the quantities (Qty + Temp->Qty), replacing the Cost and Date fields, and subtracting the number of items received from the On_Order field (On_Order − Temp->Qty):

```
*------- Update from the temporary NewStock file.
UPDATE ON Part_No FROM Temp;
  REPLACE Qty WITH Qty + Temp->Qty,;
  Date WITH Temp->Date,;
  Cost WITH Temp->Cost,;
  On_Order WITH On_Order − Temp->Qty
```

Finally, the program sets all records in the Posted field in NewStock to True, to make sure the NewStock data are not accidentally updated again. Then it closes the IF clause that made sure there were records in the Temp file to use for updating:

```
*------- Use original NewStock file, make all Posted fields
*------- "True".
CLOSE DATABASES
USE NewStock
REPLACE ALL Posted WITH .T.
ENDIF (record number > 0)
```

That finishes the update procedure. All that's left to do now is close the data files again and return to the Master menu:

```
*------- Free up all work areas and return to Master menu. CLOSE
DATABASES
RETURN
```

Figure 15.1 shows the entire Updater command file.

```
******************************************************* Updater.PRG
*   Update the Master file from Sales and NewStock.
*   Called from Master menu, MMenu.PRG.

*------- Ask user if sure about updating.
YesNo = "Y"
@ 5,0 CLEAR
@ 15,4 SAY "Update Master file from Sales and NewStock? (Y/N)";
  GET YesNo PICT "!"
READ
IF YesNo = "N"
    RETURN
ENDIF

*------- Display message that Master is being updated from Sales file.
@ 5,0 CLEAR
@ 15,5 SAY "Updating from the Sales file..."
USE Sales INDEX Sales

*------- Copy all nonupdated records to Temp file.
COPY STRUCTURE TO Temp
COPY TO Temp FOR .NOT. Posted

*------- Make sure there are records in Temp.
SELECT 2
USE Temp
IF RECCOUNT() > 0

    *------- Use Master file and index for updating.
    SELECT 1
    USE Master INDEX Master

    *------- Update from the temporary sales file.
    UPDATE ON Part_No FROM Temp;
      REPLACE Qty WITH Qty - Temp->Qty, Date WITH Temp->Date
```

Figure 15.1 – The completed Updater command file

```
        *------- Use original Sales file, make all Posted fields "True".
        CLOSE DATABASES
        USE Sales
        REPLACE ALL Posted WITH  T

ENDIF (record count > 0)
CLOSE DATABASES

*------- Message that Master is being updated from the NewStock file.
@ 15,5 SAY "Updating from the NewStock file..."
USE NewStock INDEX NewStock

*------- Copy nonupdated records to Temp file.
COPY STRUCTURE TO Temp
COPY TO Temp FOR .NOT. Posted

*------- Make sure there are records in Temp.
SELECT 2
USE Temp
IF RECCOUNT() > 0

        *------- Use Master file and index for updating.
        SELECT 1
        USE Master INDEX Master

        *------- Update from the temporary NewStock file.
        UPDATE ON Part_No FROM Temp;
          REPLACE Qty WITH Qty + Temp->Qty,;
          Date WITH Temp->Date,;
          Cost WITH Temp->Cost,;
          On_Order WITH On_Order - Temp->Qty

        *------- Use original NewStock file, make all Posted fields "True".
        CLOSE DATABASES
        USE NewStock
        REPLACE ALL Posted WITH .T.

ENDIF (record number > 0)

*------- Free up all work areas and return to Master menu.
CLOSE DATABASES
RETURN
```

Figure 15.1 – The completed Updater command file (continued)

Editing the Sales File

Now we have a problem, though it's one that's easily solved. What happens if the user needs to edit a record in the Sales file *after* the update has already occurred? For example, suppose the user accidentally records 100 sales of part number A-111, and later he discovers it was only supposed to be 10. Simply editing the Sales file would leave the Master file off by 90 items. Or suppose the user records a sale of 10 of part number A-111, but later he discovers that they were part A-112? Again, when the user makes the correction to the Sales file, the Master file will be incorrect unless it too is changed.

The solution is to write a program that allows the user to make any changes he wishes to the Sales file and automatically makes the same corrections to the Master file. The logic for this process is as follows:

- Allow the user to change data for a record in Sales.

- If the user changed a part number, add the quantity to the quantity for the old part number, and subtract it from the quantity for the new part number in the Master file.

- If the user changed a quantity in Sales, find the difference between the old quantity and the new quantity, and subtract that difference from the quantity in Master.

(If the user changes the date, we could also change that in the Master file, but it is not necessary to do so. The date will still reflect the date of the last update, rather than the date of the edit.)

When the user chooses to edit the Sales file, we want the screen to clear and display this prompt:

Enter invoice number to edit (0 if none): _

When the user enters the invoice number, the program displays all the transactions on that invoice, for example:

```
 99  A-111  10  10.50  ACS  J. Smith  12/12/84
100  Z-999   3  12.99  ACS  J. Smith  12/12/84
101  B-232  14  11.99  ACS  J. Smith  12/12/84
```

Once the user selects a single transaction, the program displays the data for that transaction on the custom screen for editing or deleting, as in Figure 15.2.

The user can move the cursor around and change whatever data are incorrect, or he can type a Y into the field labeled

Delete this record? (Y/N)

to remove the transaction. The command file then handles all aspects of adjusting the Master file, if necessary, and allows the user to edit more sales transactions.

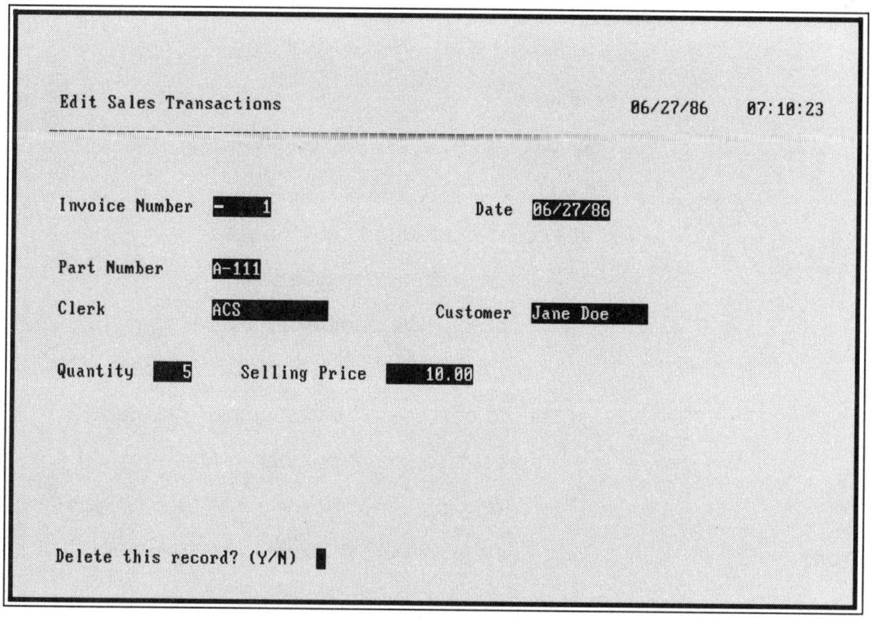

Figure 15.2 – Custom screen for editing sales transactions

Writing the Pseudocode

The command file to allow the user to edit the Sales file is called SalEdit-.PRG, and its pseudocode is as follows:

```
Set up memory variables
Set up loop for invoice numbers
    Get invoice number for data to edit
    If user does not request exit
        Use Sales file with Sales index
        Count records with that invoice number
        If invoice not found
            Warn user and allow another try
        If several records have that invoice number
            Display them and get record number from user
```

Otherwise just go to the record

Locate record and store original values to memory
  variables

Display data on edit screen and allow edit

After editing, adjust Master file

If record posted but now deleted

Mark record for deletion

Locate part number in Master file

Increment inventory quantity in Sales file

If record posted and part number changed

Locate old part number in Master file

Add old quantity back into Master file

Find new part number in Master file

Subtract new quantity from Master file

If record posted and quantity changed

Calculate difference between old and new
  quantities

Find part number in Master file

Subtract difference from Master quantity

Continue loop to allow user more edits

If records deleted, pack Sales data file

Return to SMenu.PRG

Writing the Command File

Now we can develop the SalEdit command file. We'll begin by setting up one variable to count how many records the user has deleted (No_Dels) and another to store the number of the invoice to be edited (Search):

```
********************************************* SalEdit.PRG
* Edit the Sales file and update Master.
* Called from Sales Menu, SMenu.PRG.
```

```
*------- Set up memory variables.
No_Dels = 0
Search  = 1
```

Next, we'll have the program begin a loop to ask the user for the number of the invoice that needs editing:

```
*------- Set up loop for invoice numbers.
DO WHILE Search # 0
    CLEAR
    @ 2,1 SAY "Edit Sales Transactions"
    @ 2,60 SAY DTOC(T_Date) + "      " + TIME( )
    @ 3,0 SAY ULine
    ?
    ?
    @ 15,5 SAY "Enter invoice number to edit (0 if none): ";
        GET Search PICT "9999"
    READ
```

If the user does not request to exit, the program opens the Sales database and index, counts the number of records with the requested invoice number, and stores the total to the memory variable HowMany:

```
*------- If user does not request exit, continue with edit.
IF Search > 0
    USE Sales INDEX Sales
    *------- Count records with that invoice number.
    COUNT FOR Invoice_No = Search TO HowMany
```

If there are no transactions with that invoice number, the program warns the user:

```
DO CASE
    *------- If invoice not found, warn user.
    CASE HowMany = 0
        @ 24,1 SAY "No such invoice number!!"
        ? CHR(7)
```

If several records have that invoice number, the program displays all transactions and asks the user for the number of the record to edit. Then the program can go to that record number:

```
*------- If invoice number found, proceed.
CASE HowMany > 0
    *------- If several records have that invoice number,
    *------- display them and get correct record number.
    IF HowMany > 1
        @ 5,0 CLEAR
        ? "  RecNo  Part#  Qty      Price  Clerk"
        ?? "             Customer      Date"
        ?
        LIST FOR Invoice_No = Search;
         Part_No, Qty, Price, Clerk, Customer, Date
        ?
        INPUT "Edit which record: " TO RecNo
        GOTO RecNo
```

If only one record has the requested invoice number, the program goes directly to that record:

```
    *------- Otherwise, just go to the record.
    ELSE
        LOCATE FOR Invoice_No = Search
    ENDIF
```

Next, the program stores the original part number and quantity to the memory variables Old_Part and Old_Qty, so that later it can detect whether these fields have been changed:

```
    *------- Store original field values to variables.
    Old_Part = Part_No
    Old_Qty = Qty
```

Then it initializes a variable to store the user's decision on deleting the record (Deleted) and sets up a screen so the user can edit the data in the record:

```
    *------- Display data on edit screen and allow edit.
    @ 5,0 CLEAR
    Deleted = " "
    @ 7,1 SAY "Invoice Number " GET Invoice_No
    @ 7,44 SAY "Date " GET Date PICT "99/99/99"
```

```
@ 10,1 SAY "Part Number       " GET Part_No PICT "!!!!!"
@ 12,1 SAY "Clerk            " GET Clerk
@ 12,40 SAY "Customer " GET Customer
@ 15,1 SAY "Quantity " GET Qty
@ 15,20 SAY  "Selling Price " GET Price
@ 24,1 SAY "Delete this record? (Y/N) ";
    GET Deleted PICT "!"
READ
```

Once the user has entered the record, the program checks to see whether the Master database needs updating. If the record was deleted, the program adds the quantity from the sales transaction back into Master.DBF and increments the No _Dels variable, which counts how many records have been marked for deletion:

```
*------- After editing, adjust Master file.
DO CASE
    *------- If transaction to be deleted, delete it and
    *------- add its quantity back to the Master file.
    CASE Posted .AND. Deleted = "Y"
        DELETE
        No_Dels = No_Dels + 1
        USE Master INDEX Master
        SEEK Old_Part
        IF FOUND( )
            REPLACE Qty WITH Qty + Old_Qty
        ENDIF
```

If the user changed the part number, the program adds the quantity from the Sales database back into the quantity for the old part number in Master.DBF (since it originally subtracted it). Then it subtracts the quantity of the sale from the quantity for the new part number in the Master database:

```
*------- If part number changed,
*------- add quantity to old part number,
*------- and subtract from new part number.
CASE Posted .AND. Part_No # Old_Part
    New_Qty = Qty
    New_Part = Part_No
    USE Master INDEX Master
```

```
                    SEEK Old_Part
                    IF FOUND()
                        REPLACE Qty WITH Qty + Old_Qty
                    ENDIF
                    SEEK New_Part
                    IF FOUND( )
                        REPLACE Qty WITH Qty - New_Qty
                    ENDIF
```

If the user changed only the quantity of the sale, the program adjusts the quantity in the Master database accordingly, by subtracting the old quantity from the new quantity, producing a variable called Diff, and then subtracting Diff from the current quantity in Master.DBF:

```
             *------- If quantity changed,
             *------- adjust the Master file quantity.
             CASE Posted .AND. Qty # Old_Qty
                 Diff = Qty - Old_Qty
                 USE Master INDEX Master
                 SEEK Old_Part
                 IF FOUND( )
                     REPLACE Qty WITH Qty - Diff
                 ENDIF
```

The updating is now complete, so the program can close all the conditional clauses:

```
                    ENDCASE (adjustments after editing)
                 ENDCASE (HowMany > 0)
              ENDIF (Search > 0)
           ENDDO (while still editing)
```

Before exiting to the Sales menu, the program rebuilds the Sales database, if necessary, without including the records marked for deletion:

```
             *------- If records deleted, pack the Sales data file.
             If No_Dels > 0
                 @ 5,0 CLEAR
                 ? "Deleting unwanted records from the Sales file . . . "
                 USE Sales INDEX Sales
                 PACK
             ENDIF
```

Then it closes the databases and returns to SMenu.PRG:

*------- Return to Sales menu.
CLOSE DATABASES
RETURN

Figure 15.3 shows the complete SalEdit command file.

```
**************************************************** SalEdit.PRG
*   Edit the Sales file and update Master.
*   Called from Sales Menu, SMenu.PRG.

*------- Set up memory variables.
No_Dels = 0
Search = 1

*------- Set up loop for invoice numbers.
DO WHILE Search # 0

    CLEAR
    @ 2,1 SAY "Edit Sales Transactions"
    @ 2,60 SAY DTOC(T_Date) + "      " + TIME()
    @ 3,0 SAY ULine
    ?
    ?
    @ 15,5 SAY "Enter invoice number to edit (0 if none): ";
      GET Search PICT "9999"
    READ

    *------- If user does not request exit, continue with edit.
    IF Search > 0
        USE Sales INDEX Sales

        *------- Count records with that invoice number.
        COUNT FOR Invoice_No = Search TO HowMany

        DO CASE

            *------- If invoice not found, warn user.
            CASE HowMany = 0
                @ 24,1 SAY "No such invoice number!!"
                ? CHR(7)

            *------- If invoice number found, proceed.
            CASE HowMany > 0

                *------- If several records have that invoice number,
                *------- display them and get correct record number.
                IF HowMany > 1
                    @ 5,0 CLEAR
                    ? "  RecNo  Part#  Qty     Price  Clerk"
                    ?? "          Customer      Date"
                    ?
                    LIST FOR Invoice_No = Search;
                      Part_No, Qty, Price, Clerk, Customer, Date
                    ?
                    INPUT "Edit which record: " TO RecNo
                    GOTO RecNo
```

Figure 15.3 – The completed SalEdit command file

```
*------- Otherwise, just go to the record.
ELSE
     LOCATE FOR Invoice_No = Search
ENDIF

*------- Store original field values to variables.
Old_Part = Part_No
Old_Qty = Qty

*------- Display data on edit screen and allow edit.
@ 5,0 CLEAR
Deleted = " "
@ 7,1 SAY "Invoice Number " GET Invoice_No
@ 7,44 SAY "Date " GET Date PICT "99/99/99"
@ 10,1 SAY "Part Number     " GET Part_No PICT "!!!!!"
@ 12,1 SAY "Clerk           " GET Clerk
@ 12,40 SAY "Customer " GET Customer
@ 15,1 SAY "Quantity " GET Qty
@ 15,20 SAY "Selling Price " GET Price
@ 24,1 SAY "Delete this record? (Y/N) ";
  GET Deleted PICT "!"
READ

*------- After editing, adjust Master file.
DO CASE

     *------- If transaction to be deleted, delete it and
     *------- add its quantity back to the Master file.
     CASE Posted .AND. Deleted = "Y"
         DELETE
         No_Dels = No_Dels + 1
         USE Master INDEX Master

         SEEK Old_Part
         IF FOUND()
              REPLACE Qty WITH Qty + Old_Qty
         ENDIF

     *------- If part number changed,
     *------- add quantity to old part number,
     *------- and subtract from new part number.
     CASE Posted .AND. Part_No # Old_Part
         New_Qty = Qty
         New_Part = Part_No
         USE Master INDEX Master

         SEEK Old_Part
         IF FOUND()
              REPLACE Qty WITH Qty + Old_Qty
         ENDIF

         SEEK New_Part
         IF FOUND()
              REPLACE Qty WITH Qty - New_Qty
         ENDIF
```

Figure 15.3 – The completed SalEdit command file (continued)

```
                    *------- If quantity changed,
                    *------- adjust the Master file quantity.
                    CASE Posted .AND. Qty # Old_Qty
                        Diff = Qty - Old_Qty
                        USE Master INDEX Master

                        SEEK Old_Part
                        IF FOUND()
                            REPLACE Qty WITH Qty - Diff
                        ENDIF

                ENDCASE (adjustments after editing)

        ENDCASE (HowMany > 0)

    ENDIF (Search > 0)

ENDDO (while still editing)

*------- If records deleted, pack the Sales data file.
IF No_Dels > 0
    @ 5,0 CLEAR
    ? "Deleting unwanted records from the Sales file..."
    USE Sales INDEX Sales
    PACK
ENDIF

*------- Return to Sales menu.
CLOSE DATABASES
RETURN
```

Figure 15.3 – The completed SalEdit command file (continued)

Editing the NewStock File

The procedure for editing the NewStock file and updating the Master file accordingly is very similar to the procedure used in SalEdit.PRG. The primary difference is that the edit program for the NewStock file has to take into consideration changes to the Master file Cost and On_Order fields, but these are just simple additions. Also, the user will look up records by part number in NewStock, since there is no invoice number field.

The NewEdit command file handles edits to the NewStock database. At the outset, it looks very similar to the SalEdit program, except that it asks the user for the part number, rather than the invoice number, of the transaction to edit. (Notice that Search is a character variable here, since part numbers include both letters and numerals, and that the UPPER function is used to handle upper/lowercase differences.)

```
* * * * * * * * * * * * * * * * * * * * * * * * * * * * * *   NewEdit.PRG
* Edit the NewStock file and update Master.
* Called from NMenu.
*------- Set up memory variables.
No_Dels = 0
Search = "1"
*------- Get part number for data to edit.
DO WHILE Search # "0"
    USE NewStock INDEX NewStock
    CLEAR
    @ 2,1 SAY "Edit New Stock Transactions"
    @ 2,60 SAY DTOC(T_Date) + "    " + TIME()
    @ 3,0 SAY ULine
    ?
    ACCEPT "Enter part number to edit (0 if none) " TO Search
    Search = UPPER (Search)
```

The program counts the number of records in the NewStock file with the requested part number:

```
    *------- If user did not request exit, continue with edit.
    IF Search # "0"
        *------- Count the records with that part number.
        SEEK Search
        COUNT WHILE Part_No = Search TO HowMany
```

If the requested part number does not exist, the program gives the user a warning:

```
        DO CASE
            *------- If part not found, warn user.
            CASE HowMany = 0
                ? "          No such part number!!"
                ? CHR(7)
```

If several records in the NewStock file have the requested part number, the program displays them all and asks the user to pick one by number:

```
            *------- If part number found, proceed.
            CASE HowMany > 0
                *------- If several records have that part number,
                *------- display them and get correct record number.
```

```
IF HowMany > 1
   CLEAR
   SEEK Search
   LIST WHILE Part_No = Search;
    Part_No, Qty, Cost, Date, Vendor
   ?
   INPUT "Edit which record (enter record number)? ";
    TO RecNo
   GOTO RecNo
```

If only one record in the NewStock file has the requested part number, that record is located and its record number is stored to the variable RecNo:

```
ELSE
   SEEK Search
   RecNo = RECNO( )
ENDIF (HowMany > 1)
```

The program then stores some of the original field data for the record to be edited to memory variables. Once again, this is so the command file can make decisions about updating the Master file after editing is completed:

```
*------ Store original field values to memory variables.
Old_Part = Part_No
Old_Qty = Qty
Old_Cost = Cost
```

Next, the program displays the selected record so the user can edit or delete it:

```
*------ Display edit screen and allow edit.
CLEAR
Deleted = " "
@ 1,1 SAY "Edit New Stock Transaction . . . "
@ 3,1 SAY "Part Number " GET Part_No PICT "!!!!!"
@ 5,1 SAY "Quantity " GET Qty
@ 5,20 SAY "Purchase Price " GET Cost
@ 7,1 SAY "Date " GET Date PICT "99/99/99"
@ 7,15 SAY "Vendor " GET Vendor
@ 9,2 SAY "Delete this record? (Y/N) " GET Deleted PICT "!"
READ
```

Now the command file needs to decide what adjustments to make to the Master file. First, if the cost has been changed in the NewStock file, it should be changed in the Master file:

```
*------- After editing, adjust Master file.
*------- First, handle change in cost.
IF Cost # Old_Cost
    New_Part = Part_No
    New_Cost = Cost
    USE Master INDEX Master
    SEEK New_Part
    IF FOUND( )
        REPLACE Cost WITH New_Cost
        USE NewStock INDEX NewStock
        GOTO RecNo
    ENDIF
ENDIF (Cost # Old_Cost)
```

If the record is deleted from the NewStock file after the update has taken place, the corresponding record in the Master file has too many items in its quantity field (Qty) and too few items on order (On_Order). A CASE statement takes care of this adjustment:

```
DO CASE
    *------- If new stock transaction to be deleted,
    *------- subtract its quantity from the Master file,
    *------- and add it to the On_Order field.
    CASE Posted .AND. Deleted = "Y"
        DELETE
        No_Dels = No_Dels + 1
        USE Master INDEX Master
        SEEK Old_Part
        IF FOUND( )
            REPLACE Qty WITH Qty - Old_Qty
            REPLACE On_Order WITH On_Order + Old_Qty
        ENDIF
```

If the user changes the part number in a NewStock record that was already updated, the Master file has too many items in the quantity field for the old part number and too few items for the new part number. Also, it has too few items on order for the old part number and too many for

the new one. The second CASE statement adjusts the Master file for this
situation:

```
*------- If part number changed, subtract the
*------- quantity from the old part number,
*------- and add to the new. Do the opposite
*------- for the On_Order field.
CASE Posted .AND. Part_No # Old_Part
    New_Qty = Qty
    New_Part = Part_No
    USE Master INDEX Master
    SEEK Old_Part
    IF FOUND()
        REPLACE Qty WITH QTY - Old_Qty
        REPLACE On_Order WITH On_Order + Old_Qty
    ENDIF
    SEEK New_Part
    IF FOUND()
        REPLACE Qty WITH Qty + New_Qty
        REPLACE On_Order WITH On_Order - New_Qty
    ENDIF
```

If the user changed only the quantity, the Master file Qty and On _Order
fields have to be adjusted for the difference between the quantity originally used in the update and the corrected quantity. The third CASE statement handles this situation:

```
            *------- If user just changed the quantity,
            *------- adjust the Master file quantity.
            CASE Posted .AND. Qty # Old_Qty
                Diff = Qty - Old_Qty
                USE Master INDEX Master
                SEEK Old_Part
                IF FOUND()
                    REPLACE Qty WITH Qty + Diff
                    REPLACE On_Order WITH On_Order - Diff
                ENDIF
            ENDCASE
        ENDCASE
    ENDIF (Search # 0)
ENDDO (while Search # 0)
```

The lines above also close the DO CASE, IF, and DO WHILE clauses. When the user chooses to exit a program, the command file first packs any records that have been marked for deletion, then closes the databases and returns to NMenu.PRG, from which it was called:

*--- If records have been deleted, pack the NewStock data file.
IF No_Dels > 0
    CLEAR
    ? "Deleting unwanted records from the NewStock file . . . "
    USE NewStock INDEX NewStock
    PACK
ENDIF
*------- Done. Return to NewStock Menu.
CLOSE DATABASES
RETURN

The entire NewEdit command file is displayed in Figure 15.4.

```
**************************************************** NewEdit.PRG
*   Edit the NewStock file and update Master.
*   Called from NMenu.

*------- Set up memory variables.
No_Dels = 0
Search = "1"

*------- Get part number for data to edit.
DO WHILE Search # "0"
    USE NewStock INDEX NewStock
    CLEAR
    @ 2,1 SAY "Edit New Stock Transactions"
    @ 2,60 SAY DTOC(T_Date) + "    " + TIME()
    @ 3,0 SAY ULine
    ACCEPT "Enter part number to edit (0 if none) " TO Search
    Search = UPPER(Search)

    *------- If user did not request exit, continue with edit.
    IF Search # "0"

        *------- Count the records with that part number.
        SEEK Search
        COUNT WHILE Part_No = Search TO HowMany

    DO CASE

        *------- If part not found, warn user.
        CASE HowMany = 0
            ? "       No such part number!!"
            ? CHR(7)
```

Figure 15.4 – The completed NewEdit command file

```
*------- If part number found, proceed.
CASE HowMany > 0

    *------- If several records have that part number,
    *------- display them and get correct record number.
    IF HowMany > 1
        CLEAR
        SEEK Search
        LIST WHILE Part_No = Search;
          Part_No, Qty, Cost, Date, Vendor
        ?
        INPUT "Edit which record (enter record number)? ";
          TO RecNo
        GOTO RecNo

    ELSE
        SEEK Search
        RecNo = RECNO()
    ENDIF (HowMany > 1)

    *------- Store original field values to memory variables.
    Old_Part = Part_No
    Old_Qty = Qty
    Old_Cost = Cost

    *------- Display edit screen and allow edit.
    CLEAR
    Deleted = " "
    @ 1,1 SAY " Edit New Stock Transaction..."
    @ 3,1 SAY "Part Number " GET Part_No PICT "!!!!!"
    @ 5,1 SAY "Quantity " GET Qty
    @ 5,20 SAY "Purchase Price " GET Cost
    @ 7,1 SAY "Date " GET Date PICT "99/99/99"
    @ 7,15 SAY "Vendor " GET Vendor
    @ 9,2 SAY "Delete this record? (Y/N) " GET Deleted PICT "!"
    READ

    *------- After editing, adjust Master file.

    *------- First, handle change in cost.
    IF Cost # Old_Cost
        New_Part = Part_No
        New_Cost = Cost
        USE Master INDEX Master

        SEEK New_Part
        IF FOUND()
            REPLACE Cost WITH New_Cost
            USE NewStock INDEX NewStock
            GOTO RecNo
        ENDIF
    ENDIF (Cost # Old_Cost)

    DO CASE

        *------- If new stock transaction to be deleted,
        *------- subtract its quantity from the Master file,
        *------- and add it to the On_Order field.
        CASE Posted .AND. Deleted = "Y"
            DELETE
            No_Dels = No_Dels + 1
```

Figure 15.4 – *The completed NewEdit command file (continued)*

```
                        USE Master INDEX Master

                        SEEK Old_Part
                        IF FOUND()
                            REPLACE Qty WITH Qty - Old_Qty
                            REPLACE On_Order WITH On_Order + Old_Qty
                        ENDIF

                *------- If part number changed, subtract the
                *------- quantity from the old part number,
                *------- and add to the new.  Do the opposite
                *------- for the On_Order field.
                CASE Posted .AND. Part_No # Old_Part
                    New_Qty = Qty
                    New_Part = Part_No
                    USE Master INDEX Master

                    SEEK Old_Part
                    IF FOUND()
                        REPLACE Qty WITH Qty - Old_Qty
                        REPLACE On_Order WITH On_Order + Old_Qty
                    ENDIF

                    SEEK New_Part
                    IF FOUND()
                        REPLACE Qty WITH Qty + New_Qty
                        REPLACE On_Order WITH On_Order - New_Qty
                    ENDIF

                *------- If user just changed the quantity,
                *------- adjust the Master file quantity.
                CASE Posted .AND. Qty # Old_Qty
                    Diff = Qty - Old_Qty
                    USE Master INDEX Master

                    SEEK Old_Part
                    IF FOUND()
                        REPLACE Qty WITH Qty + Diff
                        REPLACE On_Order WITH On_Order - Diff
                    ENDIF

            ENDCASE

        ENDCASE
        ENDIF (Search # 0)


ENDDO (while Search # 0)

*------- If records have been deleted, pack the NewStock data file.
IF No_Dels > 0
    CLEAR
    ? "Deleting unwanted records from the NewStock file..."
    USE NewStock INDEX NewStock
    PACK
ENDIF

*------- Done. Return to NewStock menu.
CLOSE DATABASES
RETURN
```

Figure 15.4 – The completed NewEdit command file (continued)

The Inventory System we've developed is fairly complex from a programming point of view, but very powerful and easy for a novice to use. The system provides a great deal of power for storing data about sales and incoming stock transactions and for printing useful reports. It also allows the store manager to update the Master file from these transaction files with a simple menu choice. Should a user discover an error in either the Sales or NewStock file, it is easy to edit the transaction, and the system automatically takes care of making all the proper corrections to the Master file.

With only minor modifications, you should be able to tailor this system to fit the needs of any specific business, whether your own or that of a consulting client.

Accounts Receivable System Design

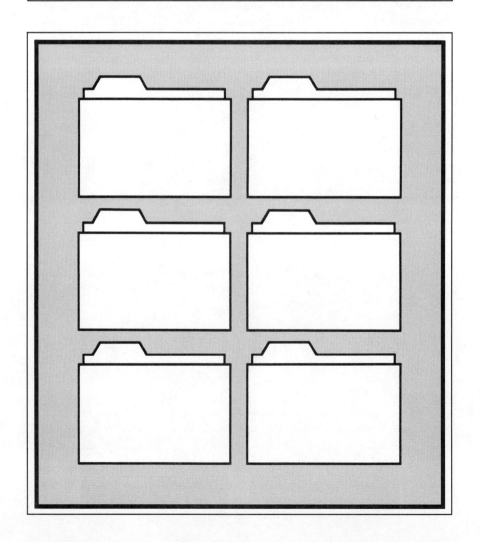

Beginning with this chapter, we'll design and develop an Accounts Receivable System that includes automatic billing. The system will store customer names and addresses, as well as the current and aged balances, in one database. It will store individual charges and payments in separate databases. Managing these files will allow us to explore more of the power of relational databases and learn some sophisticated dBASE programming techniques.

We're going to move a little faster in this section, since many of the techniques are second nature by now. We'll use detailed programmer comments and structured code to describe familiar routines, and we'll devote the step-by-step discussions to clarifying those powerful new techniques we're using for the first time.

Accounts Receivable Problem Definition

The primary goal of the Accounts Receivable System is to maintain a database of customer information and records of monthly charges and payments for each account. Each month, we want the system to prepare invoices that display the starting balance for the month, a list of individual transactions (both charges and payments), and the current balance due. We also want a summary report of monthly activity for each customer and an aging report showing the current, 30-, 60-, 90-, and over-90-day balances. We'll need a "quick-lookup" feature as well, to display a duplicate of the customer invoice when the user receives inquiries about an account.

And, of course, we want the system to be completely menu-driven for ease of use and to include options for editing data in all the databases.

Accounts Receivable I/O Specification

The most important output of the Accounts Receivable System will be the basic monthly statement, or invoice. This will include the customer's name and address, credit terms, starting balance, charges, payments, and current balance. Other outputs we will need are an aging report to display aged balances and a monthly summary report to provide a synopsis of the current month's activity, including balance, charges, and payments for each customer. In addition, the system should provide some historical reports to permit the user to check data from previous months.

Inputs to the Accounts Receivable System will be divided into three main categories. First, we'll need the following information about each customer:

Account number
Name
Address
City
State
Zip code
Phone number
Date of last bill
Starting balance for the month
Current charges for the month (total)
Current payments for the month (total)
Balance last month
Balance 2 months old

Balance 3 months old
Balance over 3 months old
Credit terms

Then we'll need this information about individual charge transactions for each customer:

Account number
Invoice number
Part number of item purchased
Description of item purchased
Quantity purchased
Unit price of item purchased
Total amount of purchase
Date purchased
Whether customer has been billed for this transaction

Finally, we'll need the following information about each customer's payments and any adjustments made to the account:

Account number
Check number
Amount of payment/adjustment
Date of payment/adjustment
Description of payment/adjustment
Whether payment/adjustment has been posted to account

With this outline of the reports we want the system to produce and the information we need to enter into the system, we can begin the actual database design.

Accounts Receivable Database Design

The Accounts Receivable System provides a good relational database model. Because there may be hundreds of individual charges and payments for each customer during the year, it makes sense to store all basic

customer information in one file and information about charges and payments in separate files. This allows more efficient use of disk space, especially on a floppy-disk system, and it also speeds the process of locating
information by keeping individual databases as small as possible.

The Main System

Customer information will be stored in the Customer database. Its structure, with a brief description of each field, is shown in Figure 16.1.

We'll use the Cust_No (customer account number) field as the key field to
relate data in the Customer database to data in the individual Charges and
Payments databases. So once you've created the database, go ahead
and index it on this field. We'll call the index file CustNo.NDX. Create it with
the following command:

INDEX ON Cust_No TO CustNo

From time to time, the user may need to look up customers by name, so
we'll create a second index file keyed on customer name. We'll call it

```
Structure for database : Customer.DBF

Field   Field name  Type         Width  Dec     Description

    1   CUST_NO     Numeric         4    0      Customer number
    2   LNAME       Character      15           Last name
    3   FNAME       Character      10           First name
    4   ADDRESS     Character      25           Address
    5   CITY        Character      20           City
    6   STATE       Character       2           State
    7   ZIP         Character      10           Zip code
    8   PHONE       Character      13           Phone number
    9   LAST_UPDAT  Date            8           Date of last billing
   10   START_BAL   Numeric         8    2      Starting balance
   11   CHG_CURR    Numeric         8    2      Current charges
   12   PAY_CURR    Numeric         8    2      Current payments
   13   BAL_30      Numeric         8    2      Balance last month
   14   BAL_60      Numeric         8    2      Balance 2 months ago
   15   BAL_90      Numeric         8    2      Balance 3 months ago
   16   BAL_90PLUS  Numeric         8    2      Balance 4 months ago
   17   TERMS       Character      20           Credit terms
```

Figure 16.1 – Structure of the Customer database

CustName.NDX, and to ensure consistency for sorting and searching, we'll use all uppercase for the names. Create the CustName index with this command:

INDEX ON UPPER(LName) ¦ UPPER(FName) TO CustName

Next, we can create the database for recording individual charges, Charges.DBF. Figure 16.2 shows the structure of this database, along with a brief description of each field.

Notice that the Cust_No field is identical in name, type, and width to the Cust_No field in the Customer database. That's because this is the field that relates each charge to information in Customer.DBF. Whenever a field is used to relate information from one database to information in another, the field must be identical in both databases. Also notice that Charges.DBF has a Logical field called Billed. This is actually a safety device built into the system to ensure that a customer is never billed twice for the same goods. We'll see how this field is used as we develop the programs.

Since the Cust_No field is the key field for relating this database to the Customer database, it must be indexed. After you've created the database, create the index file ChrgNo.NDX by typing this command:

INDEX ON Cust_No TO ChrgNo

Payments to each customer's account will be recorded in a database called Payments.DBF, with the structure shown in Figure 16.3. The Payments database again has the Cust_No field for relating payments to

```
    Structure for database : Charges .DBF

    Field   Field name   Type        Width Dec      Description

        1   CUST_NO      Numeric        4   0   Customer number
        2   INVOICE_NO   Numeric        6   0   Invoice number
        3   PART_NO      Character      5       Part number
        4   QTY          Numeric        4   0   Quantity purchased
        5   UNIT_PRICE   Numeric        9   2   Unit price
        6   AMOUNT       Numeric        9   2   Total amount charged
        7   DATE         Date           8       Date of purchase
        8   DESCRIPT     Character     20       Description
        9   BILLED       Logical        1       Has customer been billed
                                                yet?
```

Figure 16.2 – Structure of the Charges database

```
Structure for database : Payments.DBF

Field  Field name  Type       Width Dec    Description

    1  CUST_NO     Numeric        4 0       Customer number
    2  CHECK_NO    Character      5          Check number
    3  AMOUNT      Numeric        9 2        Amount of payment
    4  DATE        Date           8          Date of payment
    5  DESCRIPT    Character     30          Description
    6  POSTED      Logical        1          Has this payment
                                             been noted on a bill?
```

Figure 16.3 – Structure of the Payments database

individual accounts in the Customer database and the Posted field to act as a safety device to ensure that each payment is recorded only once.

The Payments database will be indexed on the Cust_No field using an index file called PayNo.NDX. Once you've created the database, create the index file with the usual command:

INDEX ON Cust_No TO PayNo

Historical Data

This system, like most accounts-receivable systems, is designed to run on a month-to-month basis. That is, during the course of the month, individual charges and payments are recorded as they occur. At the end of the month, the accumulated transactions are printed on invoices and the bills are mailed to the customers.

But what do we do with charges and payments on file once they've been recorded and the invoice has been mailed? There are three ways to handle these data:

1. Delete all charges and payments immediately after the billing takes place. The advantage of this approach is that it saves disk space. The disadvantage is that the historical information about individual transactions is lost at the end of each month.

2. Leave all charges and payments in the files, but mark them as having been posted already. This method has the advantage of keeping a cumulative history of charges and payments, but it has the

disadvantage of letting the Charges and Payments databases grow endlessly.

3. Move all charges and payments that have been accounted for out of the Charges and Payments databases into separate historical files. This approach has the advantage of keeping the Charges and Payments files relatively small, while still maintaining a history of individual transactions.

For our Accounts Receivable System, we'll use the third method, moving all transactions that have been accounted for to separate history files on separate disks. To create a history file for the Charges database, just copy the structure of the Charges file to another file. In this case, we'll store charges that have already been billed to a file called BillHist.DBF. You can use these commands:

USE Charges
COPY STRUCTURE TO BillHist

To make a similar history file called PayHist.DBF, type these commands:

USE Payments
COPY STRUCTURE TO PayHist

In the next few chapters, we'll see how the system automatically sends transactions that are no longer needed in the Charges and Payments databases to their respective history files.

Accounts Receivable Software Structure

The Accounts Receivable System will consist of options for adding new data, printing reports (including invoices), editing data, and performing monthly postings. The hierarchical relationships among the various command files needed to manage this system are shown in Figure 16.4.

To speed up programming for this complex system and standardize as many of the routine procedures as possible, we'll use two new dBASE III PLUS programming techniques: procedures and parameter passing. Since these are new concepts, we'll take time to study them in detail in Chapter 17.

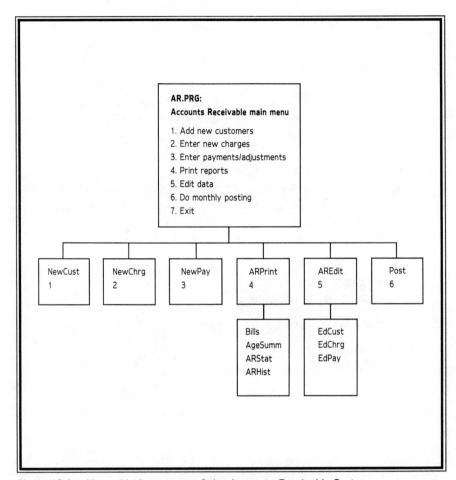

Figure 16.4 – Hierarchical structure of the Accounts Receivable System

Procedures and Parameters

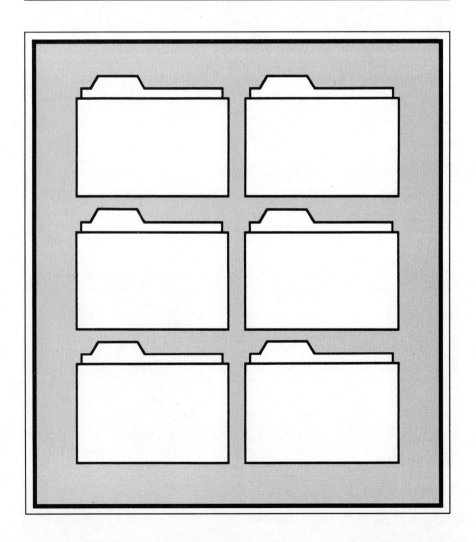

In this chapter we'll have a chance to look at some more advanced programming techniques using the PROCEDURE and PARAMETERS commands in dBASE III PLUS. By developing a *library* of routines that can be used over and over in different portions of the Accounts Receivable System and storing them all in one file, we'll be able to simplify the overall programming task considerably and speed up program execution throughout the system.

The A/R System Procedure File

A dBASE III PLUS procedure file is like a collection of command files within a single large command file. The advantage of a procedure file is that once it is opened with the SET PROCEDURE command, all of the individual "command files" within the procedure file are loaded into RAM, where they can be accessed much faster than from disk (even a hard disk). This, of course, dramatically improves the overall speed of a large system.

Standardizing Title Formats

Any procedure (any single routine in a procedure file) can be turned into a general-purpose routine by using the PARAMETERS command. Parameters are used to send data to and from procedures without requiring the use of specific variable names or specific data in the procedure itself. To make this clearer, let's take a close look at a procedure for printing titles on menu screens, as shown in Figure 17.1.

The first line of the procedure contains the required command PROCEDURE plus the procedure name (in this case, Title). The second line, PARAMETERS Title, informs dBASE that there is one parameter assigned to this procedure, and its name is Title. The remaining lines print the title, system date, and system time at row 1, ULine (a PUBLIC memory variable of 80 underline characters, defined in AR.PRG) at line 2, and a couple of blank lines. Then the RETURN command restores control to the file or routine that called the procedure.

Now the beauty of this procedure is that at any point in the program where we want to print a title with the date, time, and an underline, we just use the DO command and specify the title to print:

DO Title WITH "Accounts Receivable Main Menu"

The WITH option alerts dBASE that the data following it are parameters. The PARAMETERS Title command in the procedure itself assigns "Accounts Receivable Main Menu" to its own Title variable, then uses

```
PROCEDURE Title
PARAMETERS Title
   * ---------------------- Display screen title.
  CLEAR
  @ 2,1 SAY Title
  @ 2,60 SAY DTOC(DATE()) + "      " + TIME()
  @ 3,0 SAY ULine
  ?
  ?
RETURN
```

Figure 17.1 - Procedure for displaying screen titles

this information as needed in the rest of the procedure. The results look like this:

Accounts Receivable Main Menu   **06/01/86**   **12:00**

Standardizing Error Messages

Another useful procedure for a user-oriented application like the Accounts Receivable System would be one that prints error messages on the screen, as shown in Figure 17.2.

The Error procedure uses a single parameter, Message. When called from a program by the DO command, this procedure clears the screen from line 20 down, presents the Message variable at line 20, rings the bell (CHR(7)), and waits for the user to press a key before it returns to the calling program. Hence, the command

DO Error WITH "No such Customer Number!"

displays this error message on the screen and waits for the user to tell the program to try again:

No such Customer Number!
Press any key to try again

These two procedures demonstrate not only an easy way to ensure uniform display formats in a system but also a means of streamlining the

```
PROCEDURE Error
PARAMETER Message
   * ----------- Display error message.
   @ 20,0 CLEAR
   @ 20,3 SAY Message
   ? CHR(7)
   WAIT "    Press any key to try again"
   RETURN
```

Figure 17.2 – *Procedure for displaying error messages*

overall programming effort. Any title or error message can be displayed in a standard format with a single command (DO . . . WITH). There is no need to repeat all the @ . . . SAY . . . GETs that would otherwise be needed for formatting the many titles and error messages in the system. Should you decide to alter the format of the prompts or titles later, you would only have to change the procedure to reformat all the prompts and titles in the entire system.

Customer-Number Validation Procedure

The Accounts Receivable System uses a third procedure that allows the user to provide either a customer name or a customer number. With the single command

DO GetCust WITH M_Cust_No, M_Name, M_Address, Exiting

this procedure will accomplish the following tasks:

1. Display a screen for the user to enter a customer name or number (as in Figure 17.3)

2. Let the calling program know if the user chose to exit the procedure altogether

3. Automatically look up and display a list of customer account numbers for the customer name entered

4. Reject all invalid numbers, present an error message, and allow the user to try again

5. Return the customer number (M_Cust_No), first and last names (M_Name), and address (M_Address) from the Customer database (allowing the user to verify that the correct customer has been accessed)

The GetCust procedure does a great deal to streamline the programming effort, because many modules in the Accounts Receivable System need to allow the user to look up customers quickly by either name or account number. We'll discuss the GetCust procedure in detail later in the chapter. It performs a lot of work, so it's fairly long (for a procedure). But it is better to write it once and put it in a procedure file than to repeat the same program lines over and over again in separate command files!

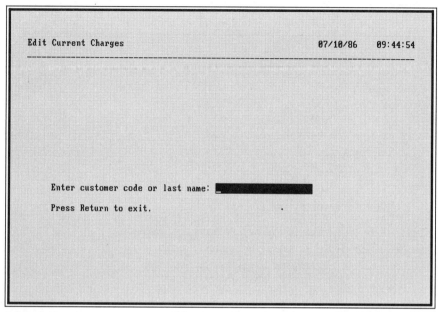

```
 Edit Current Charges                              07/10/86    09:44:54
 ----------------------------------------------------------------------




           Enter customer code or last name: 
           Press Return to exit.                          .
```

Figure 17.3 – Custom screen for entering customer name or number in the GetCust procedure

Creating the Procedure File

Creating a procedure file is just like creating a command file. You simply use the MODIFY COMMAND editor (or an external word processor). Assign the file any name you like; dBASE will add the usual .PRG extension. In this example I've named the procedure file ProcLib1.PRG (for Procedure Library 1). A procedure file can contain up to 32 procedures. Each must start with a PROCEDURE command and name and end with the RETURN command. If you want to pass parameters to and from a procedure, as with the Title and Error procedures already discussed, the PARAMETERS command must be listed *immediately below* the PROCEDURE command (*nothing* is allowed in between). Figure 17.4 shows the entire ProcLib1 procedure file used in the Accounts Receivable System. Notice that Title, Error, and GetCust are all contained within the file, and that each begins with the PROCEDURE and PARAMETERS commands. After entering the procedures into the file, save it as you would any regular command file (^End or ^W).

```
*************************************************** ProcLibl.PRG
* General procedures for the AR System.

*------- Display screen title.
PROCEDURE Title
PARAMETERS Title
    CLEAR
    @ 1,0 SAY Title
    @ 1,60 SAY DTOC(DATE()) + "   " + TIME()
    @ 2,0 SAY ULine
    ?
    ?
RETURN
*------- Display error message.
PROCEDURE Error
PARAMETERS Message
    @ 20,0 CLEAR
    @ 20,3 SAY Message
    ? CHR(7)
    WAIT "    Press any key to try again"
RETURN

* ------------ Look up customer by number or name.
PROCEDURE GetCust
PARAMETERS M_Cust_No, M_Name, M_Address, Exiting

  *------- Set up loop for validating customer code.
  *------- Enter customer number or last name and scan for it.
  Valid = .F.
  DO WHILE .NOT. Valid

    * --------- Get customer name or number.
    Lookup=SPACE(20)
    @ 4,0 CLEAR
    @ 15,5 SAY "Enter customer code or last name:" GET Lookup
    @ 17,5 SAY "Press Return to exit."
    READ

    * ----------- If nothing entered, return "Exiting"
    IF Lookup = " "
       Exiting = .T.
       RETURN
    ENDIF (Lookup is blank)

    * ------------ Look up by name, if name entered.
    IF ASC(Lookup) >= 65
       Lookup = UPPER(TRIM(Lookup))
       SET INDEX TO CustName, CustNo
       SEEK Lookup

       *------- If name found...
       IF FOUND()
          * ---- Display customers with requested name.
          M_Cust_No = Cust_No
          @ 5,0 CLEAR
          @ 6,0 SAY "Number Last Name     First Name    Address"
          ?
          DISPLAY OFF WHILE UPPER(LName) = Lookup;
             Cust_No, LName, FName, Address
          @ 22,2 SAY "Enter customer code: ";
             GET M_Cust_No PICTURE "9999"
          READ
          Lookup = STR(M_Cust_No,4)
       ELSE (if name not found)
          DO Error WITH "Not found!"
       ENDIF (name not found)

    ENDIF (name entered)
```

Figure 17.4 – The ProcLib1 procedure file

```
      * ---------- Look up by customer number.
     IF VAL(Lookup) > 0
        M_Cust_No = VAL(Lookup)
        SET INDEX TO CustNo, CustName
        SEEK M_Cust_No

        *------- If found, continue, else ask again.
        IF FOUND()
           Valid = .T.
           M_Name=TRIM(FName)+" "+TRIM(LName)
           M_Address = TRIM(Address)
        ELSE
           DO Error WITH "Not found!"
        ENDIF (not eof)

     ENDIF (number entered)

  ENDDO (While invalid entry)
RETURN
```

Figure 17.4 – The ProcLib1 procedure file (continued)

Using the Procedure File

Now let's discuss how to get at the procedures from within another command file.

A procedure file needs to be opened before any of the procedures within it can be accessed. The command to do this is SET PROCEDURE TO plus the name of the procedure file, for example:

SET PROCEDURE TO ProcLib1

Once this command is entered, all the procedures in the ProcLib1 file are stored in RAM and can be accessed quickly with the DO command from any other program or procedure, or even from the dot prompt.

When a procedure file is no longer needed, or when you want to switch to a different procedure file, you must close the open file with the command

CLOSE PROCEDURE

At that point, the procedures in the file become inaccessible until the SET PROCEDURE TO command is issued again. dBASE will not allow more than one procedure file to be open at a time.

In the next chapter we'll use the SET PROCEDURE command to open the ProcLib1 procedure file from the Accounts Receivable System main-menu program, so that its procedures will always be available to the entire system.

A Note on Parameter Passing

The PARAMETERS command is used to assign variable names that are *local* to a procedure. Whatever data are sent to a procedure with the DO . . . WITH command are automatically assigned consecutively to the specific variables listed in the PARAMETERS statement.

A procedure can contain any number of variables, separated by commas, in its PARAMETERS list. The PARAMETERS command must be the first executable command in the procedure. That is, only the PROCEDURE command itself (and programmer comments) may be listed above the PARAMETERS command.

When several parameters are used in a procedure, both the calling DO . . . WITH command and the receiving PARAMETERS command must have exactly the same number of parameters listed. For example, the following procedure, named GetArea, uses the variables Length, Width, and Area in its PARAMETERS statement:

```
PROCEDURE GetArea
PARAMETERS Length, Width, Area
    Area = Length * Width
RETURN
```

So you must send back the same parameters (Length, Width, and Area) from your DO . . . WITH statement. You must always send exactly the same number of parameters listed in the PARAMETERS statement. In the following example, only two variables were sent to GetArea, so dBASE responded with an error message, wondering where the third parameter was:

```
L = 100
W = 277
DO GetArea WITH L, W
Syntax Error
    ?
PARAMETERS Length, Width, Area
```

   Actually, there are several ways to pass information to and from a procedure (first, of course, the procedure file must be opened with the SET PROCEDURE TO command):

   1. Data can be passed from *existing* memory variables, as follows:

```
X = 5
Y = 10
Z = 0
DO GetArea WITH X, Y, Z
```

   If you now print the value of Z, you get the results of the calculation Area = Length x Width:

```
? Z
   50
```

   The calling variables may also have the same names as the receiving variables:

```
Length = 20
Width = 25
Area = 0
Do GetArea WITH Length, Width, Area
? Area
   500
```

   If you attempt to pass variables that do not exist, dBASE will return an error message:

```
Do GetArea WITH J, K, L
Variable not found
      ?
```

   2. *Constants* can be passed to a procedure, as in the Title and Error procedures discussed earlier:

```
Result = 0
DO GetArea WITH 30, 20, Result
? Result
   600
```

3. *Calculations* can be passed to a procedure:

```
Area = 0
DO GetArea WITH (27 ^(1/3)), (5 * 5), Area
? Area
     75.00
```

Incidentally, parameter passing is not limited to procedures. You can pass values between command files in the same fashion.

The GetCust Procedure

Before closing this chapter, let's take a moment to discuss the GetCust procedure in detail. It appears in the ProcLib1 command file, starting with these lines:

```
PROCEDURE GetCust
PARAMETERS M_Cust_No, M_Name, M_Address, Exiting
```

GetCust employs techniques similar to those used to validate part numbers in the Inventory System. However, it allows the user to enter *either* a customer name *or* a customer number, which requires a little more effort on the programmer's part. Whenever this procedure is accessed, Customer.DBF as well as the CustNo and CustName index files are opened, so that the procedure can use the SEEK command in either index. (The SEEK and WHILE commands are used to increase processing speed even further.)

Notice that four parameters are assigned: M_Cust_No (customer number), M_Name (customer name), M_Address (customer address), and Exiting (did the user decide to exit from the calling routine?). These are used primarily to pass information back to the program that called the procedure.

The DO WHILE .NOT. Valid loop ensures that the procedure will keep asking for a customer name or number until a valid customer number is entered or the user decides to exit. The @ . . . SAY . . . GET and READ commands display a screen asking for the user's request and store the answer to the variable Lookup.

Several IF clauses in the procedure file then decide how to handle the user's entry. If the user presses Return without entering a name or number, the Exiting variable is set to True (.T.) and control returns to the calling program, as shown in the routine below:

```
*----------- If nothing entered, return "Exiting"
IF Lookup = " "
    Exiting = ,T,
    RETURN
ENDIF (Lookup is blank)
```

If the user enters a customer name, the routine below translates the name to uppercase and attempts to find the name in the CustName index:

```
*----------- Look up by name, if name entered.
IF ASC(Lookup) >= 65
    Lookup = UPPER(TRIM(Lookup))
    SET INDEX TO CustName, CustNo
    SEEK Lookup
```

The ASCII code of the letter A is 65; all other letters have higher ASCII values, while numeric characters have ASCII values below 65.

If the name is found in the CustName index, the routine displays all individuals with that last name on the screen and asks the user to enter the appropriate customer number. The Lookup variable then takes the customer number as its value, as shown in the following routine:

```
* ------- If name found . . .
IF FOUND( )
    * ------- Display customers with requested name.
    M_Cust_No = Cust_No
    @ 5,0 CLEAR
    @ 6,0 SAY "Number Last Name        First Name;
      Address"
    ?
    DISPLAY OFF WHILE UPPER(LName) = Lookup;
      Cust_No, LName, FName, Address
    @ 22,2 SAY "Enter customer code: ";
      GET M_Cust_No PICTURE "9999"
    READ
    Lookup = STR(M_Cust_No,4)
```

If the entered name is not found, the routine below displays an error message (yes, one procedure can call another, as long as they are in the same procedure file):

```
    ELSE (if name not found)
        DO Error WITH "Not found!"
    ENDIF (name not found)
ENDIF (name entered)
```

At this point, the procedure has a customer number to work with, because the user entered either a valid customer name or a customer number directly. The next routine attempts to find the customer number in the CustNo index:

```
* ----------- Look up by customer number.
IF VAL (Lookup) > 0
    M_Cust_No = VAL(Lookup)
    SET INDEX TO CustNo, CustName
    SEEK M_Cust_No
```

If the customer name is found, the Valid variable is set to "True," M_Name takes on the value of the first and last names, and M_Address takes on the value of the address. If the customer number is not found, the routine displays an error message:

```
    * ------- If found, continue, else ask again.
    IF FOUND( )
        Valid = .T.
        M_Name = TRIM(FName) + " " + TRIM(LName)
        M_Address = TRIM(Address)
    ELSE
        DO Error WITH "Not found!"
    ENDIF (not eof)
ENDIF (number entered)
```

The end of the procedure marks the end of the DO WHILE .NOT. Valid loop and returns control to the calling program when a valid customer number has been entered:

```
    ENDDO (While invalid entry)
RETURN
```

You may have noticed that GetCust has no USE command. That's actually part of the reason for its portability. The appropriate USE command is issued by the calling program *before* the GetCust procedure is begun.

Once a procedure file has been created to handle these routine but lengthy tasks, developing programs for entering and editing data is quick and easy, as we'll see in Chapter 18.

Main Menu, Data Entry, and Editing

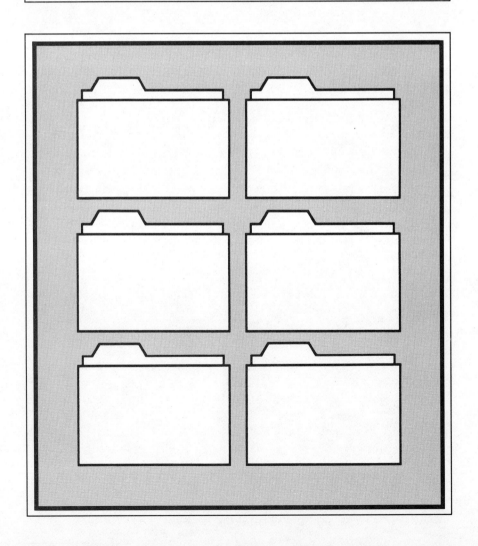

In this chapter we'll develop the main-menu program for the Accounts Receivable System and the programs for entering and editing data in the Customer, Charges, and Payments databases. These programs will all look very familiar, since they follow the same basic logic as their counterparts in the Inventory System. The custom screens will also look much like those in the Inventory System, so we won't spend a great deal of time repeating the detailed, step-by-step explanations. Instead, we'll concentrate on the new commands and techniques we're using for the first time.

A/R System Main Menu

The A/R System main-menu program, like most menu programs, sets up some initial system parameters and then presents a list of options to the user (see Figure 18.1).

However, in this menu program we need to include the command

SET PROCEDURE TO ProcLib1

to open the procedure file we developed in the last chapter. We also need to include the CLOSE PROCEDURE command near the bottom of the program, to close the file when the user exits the system.

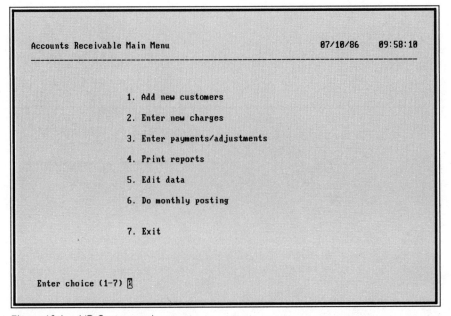

```
Accounts Receivable Main Menu                         07/10/86   09:58:10
------------------------------------------------------------------------


                      1. Add new customers

                      2. Enter new charges

                      3. Enter payments/adjustments

                      4. Print reports

                      5. Edit data

                      6. Do monthly posting


                      7. Exit



  Enter choice (1-7) ▯
```

Figure 18.1 – A/R System main menu

We'll use the Title procedure to display a title on the screen and the PUB-LIC command to make the M_Cust_No, M_Name, M_Address, and Exiting memory variables accessible at all levels throughout the system. (This isn't necessary from a technical standpoint; it just keeps these variables active so that we don't have to recreate them each time we access the GetCust procedure.)

The SET COLOR option, which we haven't used before, sets up a fancy display on color monitors: in this case, a blue background with yellow print on the main screen and a magenta background with white print for the highlights. (If that seems a bit flamboyant to you, feel free to change the color codes.) If you don't have a color monitor, the IF ISCOLOR() clause will ignore the SET COLOR command.

The SET DEVICE TO SCREEN option is used in the main-menu program to restore the default setting after the monthly invoices have been printed or a status check has been performed.

The RUN DATE command executes the DOS DATE program from within dBASE, to allow the user to change the system date if necessary. (Remember, though, that the RUN command requires about 320K RAM and the presence of DOS COMMAND.COM on the same disk as dBASE.EXE.)

Figure 18.2 shows the entire Accounts Receivable main-menu program, AR.PRG.

```
********************************************** AR.PRG
*   Accounts Receivable main menu.
*
CLEAR ALL

*-- Declare variables as public for passing to procedures.
PUBLIC M_Cust_No, M_Name, M_Address, Message, Exiting

*------- Open Procedure file ProcLib1.PRG
SET PROCEDURE TO ProcLib1

*------- If color monitor in use, set colors.
IF ISCOLOR()
    SET COLOR TO GR+/B, W+/RB
ENDIF

*--------------------------- Set parameters.
* SET DEFAULT TO B
SET BELL OFF
SET DELETED ON
SET DEVICE TO SCREEN
SET HEADING OFF
SET STATUS OFF
SET TALK OFF

*--- Get the date (RUN needs about 320K RAM).
CLEAR
? "Press Return to use suggested date, or enter new date"
?
RUN DATE

*---------- Create underline variable, ULine.
ULine = REPLICATE("_",80)

*------------ Set up a loop for the main menu.
Choice = 0
DO WHILE Choice # 7
    CLEAR

    *------- Print screen title.
    DO Title WITH "Accounts Receivable Main Menu"
    TEXT
                    1. Add new customers

                    2. Enter new charges

                    3. Enter payments/adjustments

                    4. Print reports

                    5. Edit data

                    6. Do monthly posting


                    7. Exit
    ENDTEXT

    @ 24,1 SAY "Enter choice (1-7)" GET Choice PICT "9" RANGE 1,7
    READ
```

Figure 18.2 – The Accounts Receivable main-menu command file

```
          *------- Branch accordingly.
          DO CASE
               CASE Choice = 1
                    DO NewCust
               CASE Choice = 2
                    DO NewChrg
               CASE Choice = 3
                    DO NewPay
               CASE Choice = 4
                    DO ARPrint
               CASE Choice = 5
                    DO AREdit
               CASE Choice = 6
                    DO Post
          ENDCASE

          ENDDO (while Choice # 7)

          *------- Close procedure file and exit.
          CLOSE PROCEDURE
          CLEAR
          *QUIT
```

Figure 18.2 – The Accounts Receivable main-menu command file (continued)

Adding New Customers

In a relational system such as the one we're developing now, it's essential that no two records in the Customer database have the same account number. Therefore, we'll include a built-in error-checking routine in the New-Cust program to ensure that every customer number is unique. As an added convenience to the user, we'll also have the program automatically increment the account number with each new customer and suggest this number on the entry screen.

When the user selects option 1 from the main menu, we'll have the program clear the screen and ask for a number for the new customer:

Enter customer number (0 to quit): 1001

The user can press Return to use the suggested number, enter a zero and press Return to exit to the main menu, or type in a different account number. If the user enters a number that already exists, the computer will beep, display the message

Number already in use!

and allow another try.

Once the user enters a valid (unused) customer number, the program uses the APPEND command to add a blank record to the Customer database and displays a custom screen for entering the new data, as shown in Figure 18.3.

Figure 18.4 shows how the custom screen looks when drawn with the Screen Painter. Use these commands to enter the Screen Painter:

USE CUSTOMER
CREATE SCREEN FNewCust

Choose the Select Database File option to assign the screen to Customer.DBF, then select Load Fields to bring the fields to the Blackboard. (You need not bring the Last_Updat, Chg_Curr, or Pay_Curr fields to the Blackboard.) Use the usual keys and commands to arrange the screen however you wish.

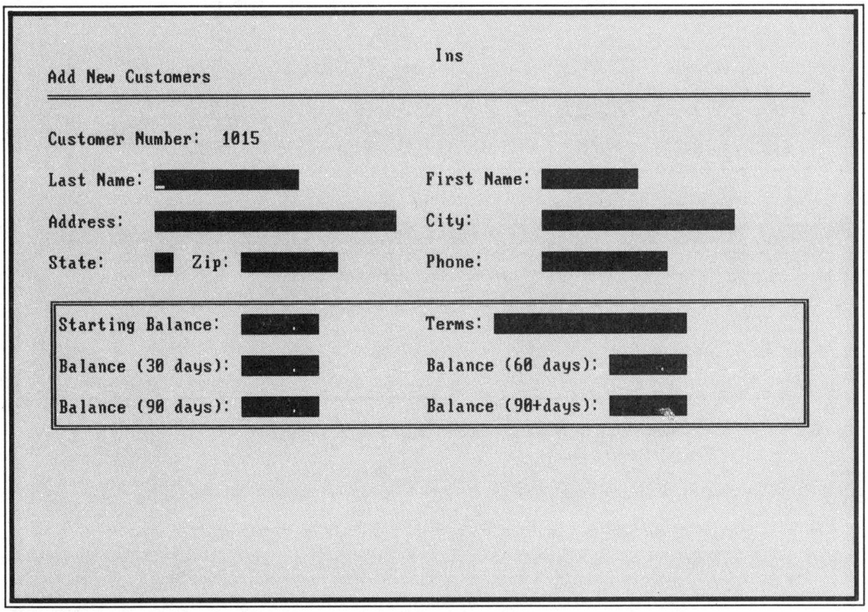

Figure 18.3 – Custom screen for adding new customers

Since the customer number is controlled by the program, you do not want the user to change the customer number on this screen. Therefore, move the cursor to the 9999 highlight (for Cust_No), call up the menu (F10), and press Enter so that the Action changes to Display/SAY. Press F10 to return to the Blackboard. Remember to highlight Exit and select Save to save the screen and generate the format (.FMT) file.

The program for entering new customers into the system is named NewCust.PRG: it is listed in Figure 18.5. Notice that the technique used to verify that the customer name is not a duplicate is similar to the technique used in the Inventory System for checking the uniqueness of part numbers. NewCust uses the Next_No variable both to increase the customer number and to check the uniqueness of the user's entry.

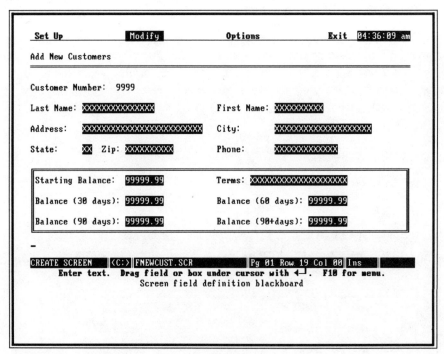

Figure 18.4 – The FNewCust screen on the Blackboard

```
*************************************************** NewCust.PRG
*   Add new customers to the A/R System.
*   Called from AR main menu.

USE Customer INDEX CustNo, CustName

  *------- Store largest customer number to memory variable Next_No.
  GO BOTT
  Next_No = Cust_No

  *------- Print screen title.
  DO Title WITH "Add New Customers"

  *------- Set up loop for adding customers.
  Exiting = .F.
  DO WHILE .NOT. Exiting

      *------- Increment customer number by 1.
      Next_No = Next_No + 1

      *------- Suggest next number, but allow user to change it.
      @ 15,5 SAY "Enter customer number (0 to quit): ";
        GET Next_No PICT "9999"
      @ 17,5 SAY "Press Return to accept number displayed."
      READ

      *------- If zero entered, return to main menu.
      IF Next_No = 0
         Exiting = .T.
         LOOP
      ENDIF

      *------- Check to see if number is already taken.
      *------- If it is, loop and ask for another number.
      SEEK Next_No
      IF FOUND()
         ? "Number already in use!", CHR(7)
         LOOP
      ENDIF

      *------- If new number isn't taken, add new record,
      *------- using FNewCust format screen.
      APPEND BLANK
      REPLACE Cust_No WITH Next_No
      REPLACE Terms WITH "Net 30"
      REPLACE Last_Updat WITH DATE()
      SET FORMAT TO FNewCust
      READ
      SET FORMAT TO
      @ 4,0 CLEAR

  ENDDO (while not exiting)

  *------- End of program.
  CLOSE DATABASES
  RETURN
```

Figure 18.5 – The NewCust command file

Adding New Charges

Next we'll develop the program for adding transactions to the Charges database. First we'll need to design a custom screen, as in Figure 18.6.

To create the screen, enter these commands at the dot prompt:

USE Charges
CREATE SCREEN FNewChrg

Use the Select Database File option to attach Charges.DBF. Then use Load Fields to pull in all the fields except Amount and Billed. You can move things around on the screen in the usual fashion.

To keep the Cust_No field from being edited, move the cursor to the Cust_No highlight (9999), press F10, and press Return so that the Action option changes to Display/SAY.

We'll want to display a couple of memory variables on this screen, but the Screen Painter won't allow this. So we'll improvise. Once you're satisfied with the design of your screen, save it with the usual Exit and Save options from the menu.

```
  Set Up              Modify            Options         Exit  05:10:21 am

  Add New Charges


  Customer Number: 9999          Name:
                                 Address:

  Invoice No.: 99999999          Date: 99/99/99

  Part No.:    XXXXX    Qty.:9999  Unit Price: 999999.99


  Description:XXXXXXXXXXXXXXXXXXX

  ┌──────────────────────────────────────────────────────────────────┐
  │ CURSOR MOVEMENT: Up, Down, Left, and Right arrow keys.             │
  │                                                                    │
  │ INSERT MODE:       Ins        │ DELETE CHARACTER:        Del       │
  │ SAVE:              ^End or ^W  │ ABANDON                  ^Q        │
  └──────────────────────────────────────────────────────────────────┘

  MODIFY SCREEN    <C:> FNEWCHRG.SCR            Pg 01 Row 20 Col 00
        Enter text.  Drag field or box under cursor with ◄─┘.  F10 for menu.
                          Screen field definition blackboard
```

Figure 18.6 – The FNewChrg screen on the Blackboard

To add memory variables to the screen, you need to modify the .FMT file. At the dot prompt, enter the commands

CLOSE FORMAT
MODIFY COMMAND FNewChrg.FMT

and change the lines that read

@ 4, 33 SAY "Name:"
@ 5, 33 SAY "Address:"

to

@ 4, 33 SAY "Name: " + M_Name
@ 5, 33 SAY "Address: " + M_Address

(The row and column positions in the @ commands may be different in your format file.) Save the changes with ^W or ^End.

To test the new screen from the dot prompt, enter these commands:

M_Name = "Adam Jones"
M_Address = "123 Apple Valley Way"
USE Charges
SET FORMAT TO FNewChrg
APPEND

If your edits to the format file were okay, you'll see the custom screen appear. If not, you probably need to correct the format file, again using MODIFY COMMAND FNewChrg.FMT. Press ^Q to abandon the screen, then enter the command

CLOSE FORMAT

to close the format file.

The program for adding new charges to the system is called New-Chrg.PRG. It uses the GetCust procedure we developed in Chapter 17 to look up the customer to whom the transaction is being charged and verify the account number. Figure 18.7 shows the entire NewChrg command file.

To automatically add sales tax to the Amount field in NewChrg.PRG, just increment the Amount variable by your local tax rate before the last ENDDO command. For example, if your local tax rate is 6 percent, you'd use the command

Amount = 1.06 * Amount

```
*************************************************** NewChrg.PRG
*   Add individual charges to the Charges file.
*   Called from AR main menu.

*------- Print the screen title.
DO Title WITH "Enter New Charges"

*------- Open both Charges and Customer databases.
SELECT 1
USE Customer INDEX CustNo, CustName
SELECT 2
USE Charges INDEX ChrgNo

*------- Set up loop for adding entries.
Exiting = .F.
DO WHILE .NOT. Exiting

    *------- Get customer name or number, and validate.
    SELECT 1
    DO GetCust WITH M_Cust_No, M_Name, M_Address, Exiting

    *------- Allow user to enter transaction data using FNewChrg screen.
    IF .NOT. Exiting
        SELECT 2
        APPEND BLANK
        REPLACE Cust_No WITH M_Cust_No
        REPLACE Date WITH DATE()
        REPLACE Billed WITH .F.
        SET FORMAT TO FNewChrg
        READ
        CLOSE FORMAT
        REPLACE Amount WITH Qty * Unit_Price
    ENDIF
    @ 3,0 CLEAR

ENDDO (while adding new transactions)

*------- Done; return to main menu.
CLOSE DATABASES
RETURN
```

Figure 18.7 – The NewChrg command file

Adding New Payments

The program for adding new payments to the system is called New-Pay.PRG. It's almost the same as the NewChrg program, except that it allows the user to record transactions in the Payments database.

The custom screen for adding payment transactions is generated using the usual techniques with the Screen Painter. Enter the following commands:

USE PAYMENTS
CREATE SCREEN FNewPay

Use the Select Database File option to attach Payments.DBF, and use Load Fields to load all the fields except Posted. Use the F10 menu to change the action of the Cust_No field on the Blackboard to Display/SAY. Use the usual keys to move things around on the Blackboard, and select Exit and Save when you are satisfied with your screen. Figure 18.8 shows the FNewPay screen on the Blackboard.

When you get back to the dot prompt, enter the commands

CLOSE FORMAT
MODIFY COMMAND FNewPay.FMT

to add memory variables to the format file. Change the lines that read

@ 5, 35 SAY "Name:"
@ 6, 35 SAY "Address:"

to

@ 5, 35 SAY "Name: " + M_Name
@ 6, 35 SAY "Address: " + M_Address

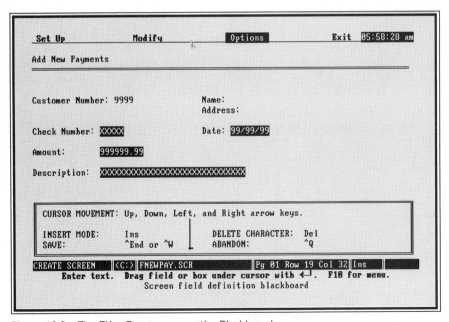

Figure 18.8 – The FNewPay screen on the Blackboard

(Again, the row and column coordinates in your format file may be different.) Save the new format file using ^W or ^End.

You may need to create the memory variables M_Name and M_Address to test the screen from the dot prompt. (Use the same basic procedure we used to test the FNewChrg screen.)

This same screen can be used both for entering regular payments and for making adjustments to an account. For example, suppose a customer returns a box of floppy disks and wants the amount of the purchase credited to his account. The screen can be filled out to indicate the amount of the credit, and the description field can be used to describe the reason for the adjustment, as in Figure 18.9.

Like the NewChrg command file, the NewPay program uses the GetCust procedure to get and verify customer numbers. In fact, it's so nearly identical with NewChrg.PRG that you can just use ^KR to read a copy of NewChrg into the empty NewPay.PRG file and make the necessary changes. The completed NewPay.PRG file is shown in Figure 18.10.

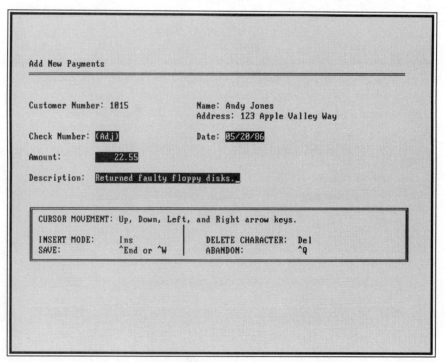

Figure 18.9 – Adjustment transaction filled out on Payments screen

```
************************************************** NewPay.PRG
*  Add individual payments to the Payments file.
*  Called from AR main menu.

*------- Print the screen title.
DO Title WITH "Enter New Payments"

*------- Open both Payments and Customer databases.
SELECT 1
USE Customer INDEX CustNo, CustName
SELECT 2
USE Payments INDEX PayNo

*------- Set up loop for adding entries.
Exiting = .F.
DO WHILE .NOT. Exiting

    *------- Get customer name or number, and validate.
    SELECT 1
    DO GetCust WITH M_Cust_No, M_Name, M_Address, Exiting

    *------- Allow user to enter transaction data, using FNewPay screen.
    IF .NOT. Exiting
        SELECT 2
        APPEND BLANK
        REPLACE Cust_No WITH M_Cust_No
        REPLACE Date WITH DATE()
        REPLACE Descript WITH "Payment"
        REPLACE Posted WITH .F.
        SET FORMAT TO FNewPay
        READ
        CLOSE FORMAT
    ENDIF

    @ 3,0 CLEAR
ENDDO (while adding new transactions)

*------- Done; return to main menu.
CLOSE DATABASES
RETURN
```

Figure 18.10 – The NewPay command file

A/R System Edit Programs

Edits to the Accounts Receivable database are handled by the EdCust, EdChrg, and EdPay command files. These are accessed from a menu program, as shown in Figure 18.11. The AREdit command file is shown in Figure 18.12.

```
Accounts Receivable Edit Menu                        07/10/86      10:05:45
------------------------------------------------------------------------------



                    1. Edit customer file

                    2. Edit current charges

                    3. Edit current payments


                    4. Return to main menu





Enter choice (1-4)  ▯
```

Figure 18.11 – The A/R System Edit menu

```
************************************************** AREdit.PRG
*   Menu for editing the A/R System.
*   Called from AR main menu.

EChoice = 0
DO WHILE EChoice # 4
    CLEAR
    DO Title WITH "Accounts Receivable Edit Menu"

    TEXT
                    1. Edit customer file

                    2. Edit current charges

                    3. Edit current payments


                    4. Return to main menu
    ENDTEXT
    @ 24,1 SAY "Enter choice (1-4) " GET EChoice PICT "9" RANGE 1,4
    READ

    *------- Branch accordingly.
    DO CASE
        CASE EChoice = 1
            DO EdCust
        CASE EChoice = 2
            DO EdChrg
        CASE EChoice = 3
            DO EdPay
    ENDCASE

ENDDO (EChoice # 4)

*------- Done; return to main menu.
RETURN
```

Figure 18.12 – The AREdit command file

Editing the Customer Database

We'll use the custom screen in Figure 18.13 to edit data in the Customer database. Figure 18.14 shows the FEdCust screen on the Blackboard. To

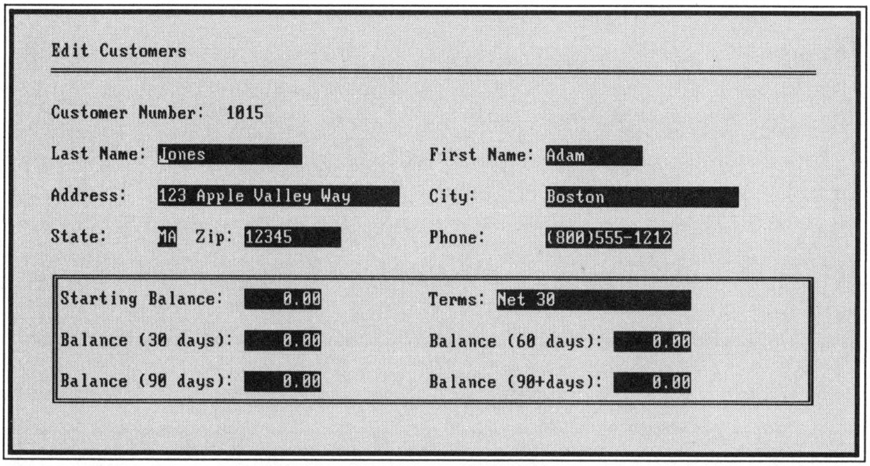

Figure 18.13 – Sample screen for editing customer data

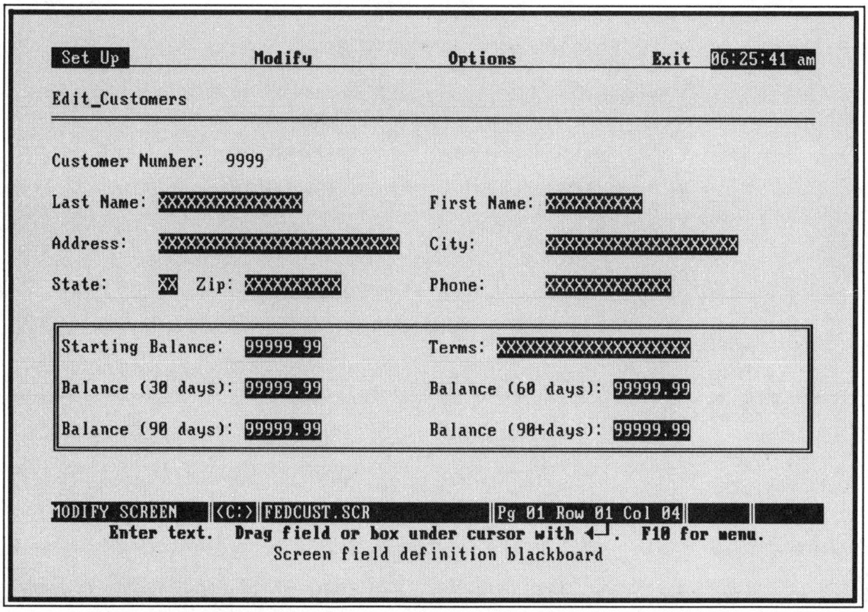

Figure 18.14 – The FEdCust screen on the Blackboard

facilitate creating the screen, first copy FNewCust.SCR to FEdCust.SCR by entering the command

COPY FILE FNewCust.SCR TO FEdCust.SCR

at the dBASE dot prompt. Then use the command

MODIFY SCREEN FEdCust

to bring the copied screen onto the Blackboard. (Press F10 to see the Blackboard.) Change the heading "Add New Customers" to "Edit Customers", and save the file.

The program for editing customer data is named EdCust.PRG. Like the preceding data-entry programs, it uses the GetCust procedure to look up and verify customer numbers. Figure 18.15 shows the entire EdCust command file.

```
**************************************************** EdCust .PRG
*  Edit customer information.
*  Called from A/R Edit menu.

*------- Print the screen title.
DO Title WITH "Enter Customer File"

USE Customer INDEX CustNo, CustName

*------- Set up loop for editing.
Exiting = .F.
SET DELETED OFF
DO WHILE .NOT. Exiting

    *------- Get customer by name or number.
    DO GetCust WITH M_Cust_No, M_Name, M_Address, Exiting

    *------- Edit using the FEdCust screen (if not exiting).
    IF .NOT. Exiting
        SEEK M_Cust_No
        SET FORMAT TO FEdCust
        EDIT
        SET FORMAT TO
        @ 4,0 CLEAR
    ENDIF

ENDDO (while not exiting)

*------- Done with program.
SET DELETED ON
CLOSE DATABASES
RETURN
```

Figure 18.15 – The EdCust command file

Editing Current Charges

The programs for editing the Charges and Payments databases allow the user to enter either a customer name or a customer number to locate a particular account, then use the PgUp and PgDn keys to scroll through the records to find a specific transaction.

We'll use a custom screen called FEdChrg for editing the Charges and Payments databases. To create the FEdChrg screen, first copy the FNewChrg screen to FEdChrg.SCR using this command at the dot prompt:

COPY FILE FNewChrg.SCR TO FEdChrg.SCR

Then enter the command

MODIFY SCREEN FEdChrg

to bring the copied screen to the Screen Painter. Press F10 to view the Blackboard, change the title to Edit Charges, and add instructions for scrolling, as shown in Figure 18.16. Call up the menu and select Exit and Save.

Now, to keep the name displayed on the screen as the user scrolls through records with PgUp and PgDn, we need to have the format file

```
 Set Up           Modify          Options         Exit  07:03:10 am

 Edit Charges
 _____

 Customer Number: 9999       Name:
                             Address:

 Invoice No.: 99999999       Date: 99/99/99

 Part No.:    XXXXX   Qty.:9999  Unit Price: 999999.99

 Description:XXXXXXXXXXXXXXXXXX

 ┌─────────────────────────────────────────────────────────────┐
 │ CURSOR MOVEMENT: Up, Down, Left, and Right arrow keys.        │
 │ SCREEN SCROLLING:  PgUp, PgDn_                                 │
 │ INSERT MODE:    Ins          DELETE CHARACTER:    Del         │
 │ SAVE:           ^End or ^W    ABANDON             ^Q          │
 └─────────────────────────────────────────────────────────────┘

MODIFY SCREEN  <C:> FEDCHRG.SCR          Pg 01 Row 16 Col 31
       Enter text.  Drag field or box under cursor with ←┘.  F10 for menu.
                    Screen field definition blackboard
```

Figure 18.16 – The FEdChrg screen on the Blackboard

point to the appropriate record on the Customer database. To accomplish this, the first step is to enter the commands

CLOSE FORMAT
MODIFY COMMAND FEdChrg.FMT

and change the lines that read

@ 4, 33 SAY "Name:"
@ 5, 33 SAY "Address:"

to

@ 4, 33 SAY "Name: " + TRIM(A–>FName) + " " + TRIM(A–>LName)
@ 5, 33 SAY "Address: " + TRIM(A–>Address)

as shown in Figure 18.17. (The row and column coordinates in the @ commands may be different in your format file.) Save the format file with ^W or ^End. (We could have performed the same task using a View (.VUE) file, but this technique is much quicker and simpler.)

```
@  1,  0   SAY "Edit Charges"
@  4,  0   SAY "Customer Number:"
@  4, 17   SAY  CHARGES->CUST_NO
@  4, 33   SAY "Name: "+TRIM(A->FName)+" "+TRIM(A->LName)
@  5, 33   SAY "Address: "+TRIM(A->Address)
@  7,  0   SAY "Invoice No.:"
@  7, 13   GET  CHARGES->INVOICE_NO  PICTURE "99999999"
@  7, 33   SAY "Date:"
@  7, 39   GET  CHARGES->DATE
@  9,  0   SAY "Part No.:"
@  9, 12   GET  CHARGES->PART_NO
@  9, 22   SAY "Qty.:"
@  9, 27   GET  CHARGES->QTY
@  9, 33   SAY "Unit Price:"
@  9, 45   GET  CHARGES->UNIT_PRICE
@ 12,  0   SAY "Description:"
@ 12, 12   GET  CHARGES->DESCRIPT
@ 15,  2   SAY "CURSOR MOVEMENT: Up, Down, Left, and Right arrow keys."
@ 16,  2   SAY "SCREEN SCROLLING:  PgUp, PgDn"
@ 17,  2   SAY "INSERT MODE:      Ins              DELETE CHARACTER:     Del"
@ 18,  2   SAY "SAVE:             ^End or ^W       ABANDON               ^Q"
@  2,  0   TO  2, 78    DOUBLE
@ 14,  0   TO 19, 78    DOUBLE
@ 16, 35   TO 18, 35
```

Figure 18.17 – The modified FEdChrg format file with A –> pointers

In the program, we'll need to set up a relationship between the Charges and Customer databases so that the appropriate customer name and address can be displayed on the screen as the user scrolls through records in the Charges database. The commands below set up such a relationship linking the two databases by customer number:

*------- Open both Charges and Customer databases.
SELECT 1
USE Customer INDEX CustNo, CustName
SELECT 2
USE Charges INDEX ChrgNo
*------- Set up relationship.
SET RELATION TO Cust_No INTO Customer

The SET RELATION TO command ensures that dBASE will always *point to* the appropriate record in the Customer database, based on the customer number associated with the transaction being edited. The A- > symbols in the format file refer the program to the LName, FName, and Address fields in the Customer (SELECT 1) database.

The program to perform the edits, EdChrg.PRG, is listed in Figure 18.18. In addition to the SET RELATION TO command just discussed, notice the

IF FOUND() .AND. .NOT. Billed

```
**************************************************** EdChrg .PRG
*   Edit individual charges in the Charges file .
*   Called from AR Edit menu .

*------- Print the screen title .
DO Title WITH "Edit Current Charges"

*------- Open both Customer and Charges databases .
SELECT 1
USE Customer INDEX CustNo, CustName
SELECT 2
USE Charges INDEX ChrgNo

*------- Set up relationship .
SET RELATION TO Cust_No INTO Customer

*------- Set up memory variables and loop for editing .
SET DELETED OFF
Exiting = .F.
DO WHILE .NOT. Exiting

    *------- Get customer by name or number .
    SELECT 1
    DO GetCust WITH M_Cust_No, M_Name, M_Address, Exiting
```

Figure 18.18 – The EdChrg command file

```
       *------- Edit the transaction, if valid and not exiting.
      IF .NOT. Exiting
           SELECT 2
           SEEK M_Cust_No
           IF FOUND() .AND. .NOT. Billed
               SET FORMAT TO FEdChrg
               EDIT
               CLOSE FORMAT
           ELSE
               Do Error with "Already posted! Make adjustment transaction!"
           ENDIF
      ENDIF (not exiting)

         @ 4,0 CLEAR
      ENDDO (while not exiting)

      *------- Recalculate Amount field.
      SELECT 2
      REPLACE ALL Amount WITH Qty * Unit_Price
      SET DELETED ON
      CLOSE DATABASES

      *------- Done; return to Edit menu.
      RETURN
```

Figure 18.18 – The EdChrg command file (continued)

statement. This statement prevents the re̶̶ ̶ d from being edited *after* the invoice has already been sent or the transaction has been posted. The program to print the monthly statements makes the Billed field True as soon as a transaction is printed on an invoice. When Billed = .T., changes to the Charges database must be made through adjustment transactions in the NewPay database, as discussed earlier.

After editing is completed, the command

REPLACE ALL Amount WITH Qty * Unit_Price

is used to ensure that any edits to either the Qty or the Unit_Price field are immediately calculated into the Amount field.

Editing Payments

The program for editing current payments is almost identical to the program for editing current changes. The custom screen for editing payments is named FEdPay. Use the dBASE COPY FILE command to copy FNewPay-.SCR to FEdPay.SCR. Then use MODIFY SCREEN FEdPay, press F10, change the title to Edit Payments, and enter instructions for scrolling the screen, as shown in Figure 18.19. Call up the menu and select Exit and Save to save the new screen.

Use the MODIFY COMMAND editor to edit FEdPay.FMT to include pointers into the Customer database. Change the lines that read

@ 5, 35 SAY "Name:"
@ 6, 35 SAY "Address:"

to

@ 5, 35 SAY "Name: " + TRIM(A–>FName) + " " + TRIM(A–>LName)
@ 6, 35 SAY "Address :" + TRIM(A–>Address)

as shown in Figure 18.20. (Once again, the exact row and column coordinates in the @ commands may be different in your format file.)

The EdPay command file is shown in Figure 18.21. Notice the use of the SET RELATION TO command again to set up a relationship between the Payments and Customer databases.

Now that we've developed all the programs for entering and editing information in the A/R System, we can turn our attention to getting information *out* of the system. In the next chapter we'll develop the programs to print the A/R invoices and reports.

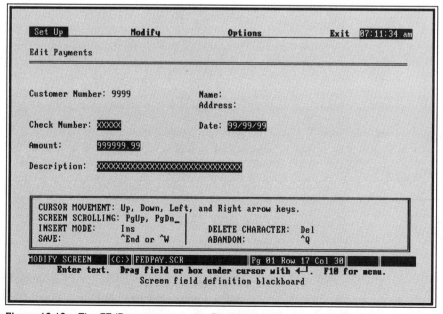

Figure 18.19 – *The FEdPay screen on the Blackboard*

```
@  1,  0   SAY "Edit Payments"
@  5,  0   SAY "Customer Number:"
@  5, 17   SAY  PAYMENTS->CUST_NO
@  5, 35   SAY "Name: "+TRIM(A->FName)+" "+TRIM(A->LName)
@  6, 35   SAY "Address: "+TRIM(A->Address)
@  8,  0   SAY "Check Number:"
@  8, 14   GET  PAYMENTS->CHECK_NO
@  8, 35   SAY "Date:"
@  8, 41   GET  PAYMENTS->DATE
@ 10,  0   SAY "Amount:"
@ 10, 14   GET  PAYMENTS->AMOUNT
@ 12,  0   SAY "Description:"
@ 12, 14   GET  PAYMENTS->DESCRIPT
@ 16,  2   SAY "CURSOR MOVEMENT: Up, Down, Left, and Right arrow keys."
@ 17,  2   SAY "SCREEN SCROLLING: PgUp, PgDn"
@ 18,  2   SAY "INSERT MODE:      Ins            DELETE CHARACTER:  Del"
@ 19,  2   SAY "SAVE:             ^End or ^W     ABANDON:           ^Q"
@  2,  0   TO  2, 77      DOUBLE
@ 15,  0   TO 20, 78      DOUBLE
@ 17, 32   TO 19, 32
```

Figure 18.20 – The modified FEdPay format file with A -> pointers

```
************************************************* EdPay .PRG
*  Edit individual payments in the Payments file.
*  Called from AR Edit menu.

* --------- Print the screen title.
DO Title WITH "Enter Current Payments"

*------- Open both Customer and Payments databases.
SELECT 1
USE Customer INDEX CustNo, CustName
SELECT 2
USE Payments INDEX PayNo

*------- Set up relationship.
SET RELATION TO Cust_No INTO Customer

*------- Set up loop for editing entries.
*------- Enter a name and then scan.
SET DELETED OFF
Exiting = .F.
DO WHILE .NOT. Exiting

    *------- Get customer by name or number.
    SELECT 1
    DO GetCust WITH M_Cust_No, M_Name, M_Address, Exiting

    *------- If not exiting and transaction not already posted,
    *------- proceed with edit.
    IF .NOT. Exiting
        SELECT 2
        SEEK M_Cust_No
```

Figure 18.21 – The EdPay command file

```
         IF FOUND() .AND. .NOT. Posted
            SET FORMAT TO FEdPay
            EDIT
            CLOSE FORMAT
         ELSE
            DO Error WITH "Already posted! Make adjustment transaction!"
         ENDIF
      ENDIF (not exiting)

      @ 4,0 CLEAR
   ENDDO (while not exiting)

   *------- Done; close databases and return to Edit menu.
   SET DELETED ON
   CLOSE DATABASES
   RETURN
```

Figure 18.21 – The EdPay command file (continued)

A/R System Reports

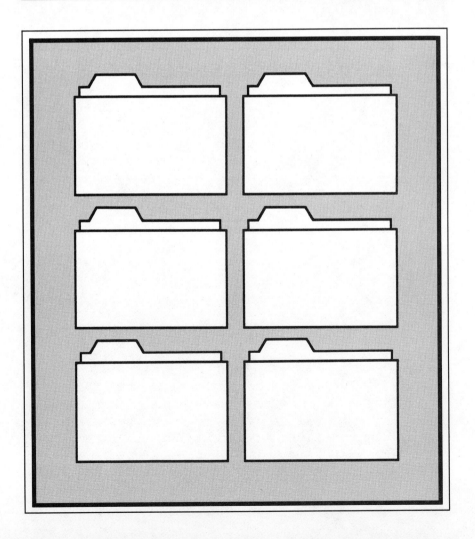

A great deal of the activity in an accounts-receivable system centers around printed output: monthly invoices, summary and aging reports for fiscal control, quick lookups for customer service, and historical reports for planning and administration. Obviously, all these different types of output are going to require some skillful programming on our part if we're to keep our processing fast and efficient. So we'll use procedures and parameters for some routines, and we'll design the programs to produce more than one type of report wherever possible.

Accounts Receivable Report Menu

First we'll set up a menu to route all this reporting activity. When the user selects option 4 from the main menu, a menu of report options will appear, as in Figure 19.1.

Option 1 on the menu of report options prints the invoices and should be run only once a month, whenever the business does its billings. Generally, options 2 and 3 are also used only once a month, after invoices have been printed, to get summaries of each customer's billing status. Option 4 is used for a quick look at the current status of an account, in case a customer should have questions. Option 5 provides a review of historical data, to let the user see a customer's billing and payment history, review information for a particular range of dates, or even see how a particular product has been selling.

The program for displaying the Reports menu in the Accounts Receivable System is named ARPrint.PRG. It's a straightforward menu program, so there is no need to discuss it in detail, other than to note that both options 2 and 3 branch to a program called AgeSumm.PRG. As you'll see shortly, this one program is designed to print both the monthly summary and the aging reports. The entire ARPrint program is shown in Figure 19.2.

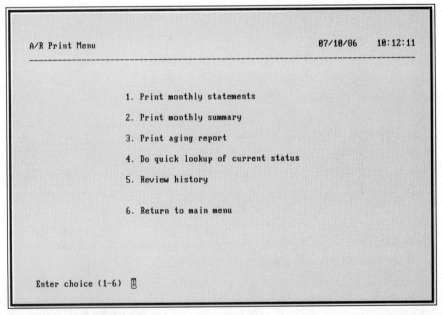

```
A/R Print Menu                                    07/10/86    10:12:11
-----------------------------------------------------------------------



               1. Print monthly statements

               2. Print monthly summary

               3. Print aging report

               4. Do quick lookup of current status

               5. Review history


               6. Return to main menu




    Enter choice (1-6)  0
```

Figure 19.1 – A/R Reports menu

```
************************************************* ARPrint .PRG
* Menu of print options for the A/R System.
* Called from A/R main menu.

PChoice = 0
SET DELETED ON

DO WHILE PChoice #6
    CLEAR
    DO Title WITH "A/R Print Menu"
```

Figure 19.2 – The ARPrint command file for A/R System reports

```
        TEXT
                        1. Print monthly statements

                        2. Print monthly summary

                        3. Print aging report

                        4. Do quick lookup of current status

                        5. Review history


                        6. Return to main menu
        ENDTEXT
        @ 24,1 SAY "Enter choice (1-6) " GET PChoice PICT "9" RANGE 1,6
        READ

        *------- Branch accordingly.
        DO CASE

            CASE PChoice = 1
                DO Bills

            CASE PChoice = 2
                RepForm = "ARSumm"
                DO AgeSumm

            CASE PChoice = 3
                RepForm = "Aging"
                DO AgeSumm

            CASE PChoice = 4
                DO ARStat

            CASE PChoice = 5
                DO ARHist

        ENDCASE

    ENDDO (PChoice # 6)

    *------- Done; return to main menu.
    SET DELETED OFF
    RETURN
```

Figure 19.2 – The ARPrint command file for A/R System reports (continued)

Printing Invoices

Two programs in the system allow the user to print an invoice: Bills.PRG, which prints *all* invoices at the end of the month and then flags all charges and payments as posted (Billed = .T. and Posted = .T.), and ARStat.PRG, which prints an invoice for a single customer without flagging any transactions as already billed. The ARStat program can be used either to check a customer's current billing status at any time during the month or to produce a duplicate invoice.

The BillProc Procedure File

Both the Bills and the ARStat programs use a command file named BillProc.PRG (see Figure 19.3) to format and print the invoices. To speed processing and avoid duplication of program code, BillProc is treated as a procedure file by simply using the PROCEDURE command and naming the first procedure PrintBills. Notice that BillProc also contains a procedure called RowCheck. Since the invoices are formatted with @ . . . SAY commands and we don't know in advance how many rows will be printed for a given bill, the RowCheck procedure keeps track of the number of rows displayed on the screen or printer and handles screen pauses and page ejects accordingly. (Ordinarily, we'd put the PrintBill and RowCheck procedures directly into the ProcLib1 procedure file, but they won't fit if we use the MODIFY COMMAND editor. We'd need to use an external word processor.)

```
*************************************************** BillProc .PRG
*  Prints a bill, using procedures PrintBills and RowCheck .
*  Called from Bills .PRG and ARStat .PRG.

PROCEDURE PrintBills
PARAMETERS M_Cust_No, Printer, Status

*------- If printer, print return address, date in English.
CLEAR
Page = 1
IF Printer
    EngDate = CMONTH(DATE()) + STR(DAY(DATE()),3);
        + ", " + STR(YEAR(DATE()),4)
    @ 1,0 SAY "My Company, Inc."
    @ 1,60 SAY EngDate
    @ 2,0 SAY "123 Mystreet"
    @ 3,0 SAY "Mycity,  CA 90000"
    Row = 6
ELSE
    Row = 1
ENDIF

*------- Print customer name and address,
*------- using Row variable to control display and eject.
SELECT 1
IF FName # " "
    @ Row,0 SAY TRIM(FName) + " " + LName
ELSE
    @ Row,0 SAY LName
ENDIF
@ Row+1,0 SAY Address
@ Row+2,0 SAY TRIM(City) + ", " + State + " " + Zip
Row = Row + 4

*------- Print customer number, terms,
*------- and starting balance from the Customer file.
@ Row,0 SAY "Customer No.  :" + STR(Cust_No,4)
@ Row+1,0 SAY "Terms         :" + Terms
@ Row+2,0 SAY "Balance as of :" + DTOC(Last_Updat) + ": "
@ Row+2,30 SAY Start_Bal PICT "999,999.99"
@ Row+3,0 SAY ULine

Start = Start_Bal
Row = Row + 5
```

Figure 19.3 – The BillProc procedure file for invoices and status checks

```
*------- Print heading for charges.
@ Row,0 SAY "Inv. # Part  Description                    Qty"
@ Row,43 SAY "Price      Total Date"

ROW = ROW + 2
*------- Select Charges database: list and total current charges.
SELECT 2
SEEK M_Cust_No

Tot_Charge = 0
DO WHILE Cust_No = M_Cust_No .AND. .NOT. EOF()
    IF Status .OR. .NOT. Billed
        @ Row,0 SAY Invoice_No
        @ Row,7 SAY Part_No
        @ Row,13 SAY Descript
        @ Row,34 SAY Qty
        @ Row,39 SAY Unit_Price PICT "999,999.99"
        @ Row,50 SAY Amount PICT "999,999.99"
        @ Row, 62 SAY Date
        Tot_Charge = Tot_Charge + Amount
        Row = Row + 1

        *------- Mark as billed if not a status check.
        IF .NOT. Status
            REPLACE Billed WITH .T.
        ENDIF
    ENDIF (not status report and not already billed)
    SKIP
ENDDO (Cust_No = M_Cust_No)

*------- Print Payments heading.
@ Row+1,0 SAY ULine
@ Row+2,1 SAY "Payments/Adjustments"
Row = Row + 4

*------- Check row position if displayed on screen.
DO RowCheck WITH 20,64

*------- Select Payments file: list and total payments/adjustments.
SELECT 3
SEEK M_Cust_No
Tot_Pay = 0
DO WHILE Cust_No = M_Cust_No .AND. .NOT. EOF()
    IF Status .OR. .NOT. Posted
        @ Row,0 SAY "Check # "
        @ Row,9 SAY Check_No
        @ Row,16 SAY Descript
        @ Row,50 SAY Amount PICT "999,999.99"
        @ Row,62 SAY Date
        Tot_Pay = Tot_Pay + Amount
        Row = Row + 1

        *------- Check row position if displayed on screen.
        DO RowCheck WITH 20,64

        *------- Mark as billed if not status report.
        IF .NOT. Status
            REPLACE Posted WITH .T.
        ENDIF
    ENDIF (not status report and not already posted)
    SKIP
ENDDO (while Cust_No = M_Cust_No)

*------- Check row position if displayed on screen.
@ Row,0 SAY ULine
DO RowCheck WITH 17,56
```

Figure 19.3 – The BillProc procedure file for invoices and status checks (continued)

```
*------- Print starting balance, total charges,
*------- payments, ending balance, and thank you note.
SET FIXED ON
@ Row+1,5   SAY "Previous balance  :"
@ Row+1,25  SAY Start PICT "999,999.99"
@ Row+2,5   SAY "Total charges     :"
@ Row+2,25  SAY Tot_Charge PICT "999,999.99"
@ Row+3,5   SAY "Payments received :"
@ Row+3,25  SAY Tot_Pay PICT "999,999.99"
@ Row+4,5   SAY "Balance due       :"
@ Row+4,25  SAY (Start + Tot_Charge) - Tot_Pay PICT "999,999.99"
SET FIXED OFF

IF Printer .AND. Status
    @ Row+8,10 SAY "*** Duplicate Invoice ***"
ENDIF
IF Printer .AND. .NOT. Status
    @ Row+8,5 SAY "Thank you"
ENDIF

*------- Pause if not going to the printer.
IF .NOT. Printer
    @ 22,0 CLEAR
    WAIT
ENDIF

*------- Done printing bill. Return to menu.
RETURN

*------- Procedure for checking row positions on screen or printer.
PROCEDURE RowCheck
PARAMETERS ScreenMax, PrintMax

IF .NOT. Printer .AND. Row >= ScreenMax
    @ 23,0 CLEAR
    WAIT "Press any key for next page..."
    Row = 1
    CLEAR
ENDIF (row too big for screen)

IF Printer .AND. Row >= PrintMax
    @ Row+2,70 SAY "Page " + STR(Page,1)
    Page = Page + 1
    EJECT
    Row = 5
ENDIF (row too big for printer)

RETURN
```

Figure 19.3 – The BillProc procedure file for invoices and status checks (continued)

Several important memory variables are used in BillProc to determine how the billing process is handled. If the user is just performing a status check, the Status variable is True and transactions are printed regardless of whether they've already been included in a monthly billing. The transactions are not marked as Billed or Posted after a status check, but if the user is indeed printing the monthly statements, the Status variable is False, and transactions printed on the invoice are flagged as True to ensure that they aren't repeated on the next month's statements. Figure 19.4 shows a sample invoice printed by the BillProc procedure file.

```
My Company, Inc.                        December 1, 1986
123 Mystreet
Mycity,  CA 90000


Wilbur Watson
345 Jaybird St.
San Diego, CA 92122

Customer No. :1000
Terms        :Net 30
Balance as of :11/01/86:       27.50
-------------------------------------------------------------

Inv. # Part  Description             Qty    Price     Total Date

   881 AAA   DSDD Floppy Disks         5    22.50    112.50 11/15/86
   881 BBB   Printer Ribbon           12     4.95     59.40 11/15/86


-------------------------------------------------------------
Payments/Adjustments

Check # 1661  Payment                                100.00 11/24/86
Check # (Adj) (Returned faulty box of disks)          22.50 11/30/86
-------------------------------------------------------------
Previous balance  :      27.50
Total charges     :     171.90
Payments received :     122.50

Balance due       :      76.90


Thank you
```

Figure 19.4 – A sample invoice produced by BillProc.PRG

Once again, notice that the database and index files are opened by the calling program (Bills.PRG) before beginning the procedure, thereby making the procedures *portable* to any number of programs.

The Monthly Billing Cycle

Figure 19.5 shows the Bills command file for printing monthly statements. The SET DEVICE TO PRINT command sends all @ . . . SAY commands to the printer. Notice that the command file uses the BillProc procedure to print bills, then reopens the ProcLib1 procedure before ending. The closing command, RETURN TO MASTER, terminates the Bills program and returns control directly to AR.PRG, rather than to the Reports menu.

Status Checks and Duplicate Invoices

The ARStat command file allows the user to check the current billing status of a customer or print a duplicate invoice. It displays the data in the

```
****************************************************** Bills.PRG
*  Prints monthly statements.
*  Called from AR Print menu.

*------- Have user prepare printer (or cancel).
Proceed = " "
DO Title with "Print Monthly Bills"
@ 15,5 SAY "Prepare printer and press any key to proceed."
@ 17,5 SAY "(Type X to cancel)..." GET Proceed PICT "!"
READ

*------- Return to menu, if requested.
IF Proceed = "X"
   RETURN
ENDIF

*------- Open files and delete records with "0" amount.
SELECT 1
USE Customer INDEX CustNo
SELECT 2
USE Charges INDEX ChrgNo
DELETE ALL FOR Amount = 0
SELECT 3
USE Payments INDEX PayNo
DELETE ALL FOR Amount = 0

*------- Set decimal places to 2, send @...SAYs to printer,
*------- and open bill-printing procedure file.
CLEAR
SET DECIMALS TO 2
SET DEVICE TO PRINT
SET PROCEDURE TO BillProc

*------- Set parameters to printer and "not status" report.
Printer = .T.
Status = .F.

*------- Loop through Customer database and print a bill for everyone.
SELECT 1
DO WHILE .NOT. EOF()
   Lookup = Cust_No
   DO PrintBill WITH Lookup, Printer, Status
   EJECT

   *------- Get next customer.
   SELECT 1
   SKIP
ENDDO
*------- Done: close files.
SET DEVICE TO SCREEN
CLOSE DATABASES
CLOSE PROCEDURE

*------- Open ProcLib1 procedure file.
SET PROCEDURE TO ProcLib1

*------- Print reminder about posting, then return to main menu.
CLEAR
TEXT
                Monthly postings (main-menu option # 6)

                should be performed immediately after

                printing the monthly statements.
ENDTEXT
?
@ 22,10 SAY "Press any key to return to main menu..."
WAIT " "
RETURN TO MASTER
```

Figure 19.5 – The Bills command file for printing monthly statements

monthly-invoice format. Notice that the Status variable is set to True in this program, so that the PrintBills procedure knows the user is just per-forming a status check and not a monthly billing. Figure 19.6 lists the entire ARStat program.

```
************************************************* ARStat.PRG
*   Quick lookup of a single statement.
*   Called from A/R Print menu.

*------- Open files and delete records with "0" amounts.
SELECT 1
USE Customer INDEX CustNo
SELECT 2
USE Charges INDEX ChrgNo
DELETE ALL FOR Amount = 0
SELECT 3
USE Payments INDEX PayNo
DELETE ALL FOR Amount = 0

*------- Set up memory variables for status report.
Status = .T.
Printer = .F.
M_Cust_No = 0
M_Name = " "
Exiting = .F.
DO WHILE .NOT. Exiting

     *------- Print screen title.
     DO Title WITH "Quick Lookup of Current Status"

     *------- Get customer by number or name.
     SELECT 1
     DO GetCust WITH M_Cust_No, M_Name, M_Address, Exiting

     *------- Proceed with bill.
     IF .NOT. Exiting

         *------- Ask about printer.
         @ 5,0 CLEAR
         LP = " "
         @ 15,5 SAY "Send statement to printer? (Y/N) " GET LP PICT "!"
         READ
         CLEAR

         *------- Set up printer if necessary.
         IF LP = "Y"
             Printer = .T.
             SET DEVICE TO PRINT
         ENDIF

         *------- Print current statement for customer.
         SET PROCEDURE TO BillProc
         DO PrintBill WITH M_Cust_No, Printer, Status
         CLOSE PROCEDURE
         SET PROCEDURE TO ProcLibl

         *------- Handle printer.
         IF Printer
             EJECT
             SET DEVICE TO SCREEN
         ENDIF
     ENDIF (not exiting)

ENDDO (while not exiting)

*------- Done: Close files and return to A/R Print menu.
CLOSE DATABASES
RETURN
```

Figure 19.6 – The ARStat command file for status checks and duplicate invoices

Summary and Aging Reports

Options 2 and 3 from the Accounts Receivable Print menu allow the user to print the aging and monthly summary reports. These reports are usually printed immediately after the monthly billing is completed.

The Monthly Activity Summary report displays the current balance, charges, and payments for each customer, as shown in Figure 19.7. We'll use dBASE's CREATE REPORT command to design the monthly report. The report format is stored in a file named ARSumm.FRM. To create this form file, type these commands:

USE Customer
CREATE REPORT ARSumm

You can design the report any way you wish. To create the format in Figure 19.7, fill out the REPORT FORM parameters and column information as in Figure 19.8.

The Accounts Receivable Aging report displays data from the Customer database in the format shown in Figure 19.9. Once again, use the commands USE Customer and CREATE REPORT Aging to design the form, and fill in the first page of the questionnaire and the individual columns of information as shown in Figure 19.10.

Use the second page of the questionnaire to display the customer-number heading and the actual customer number above each line of the

```
    Page No.     1
    11/21/84
                              Monthly Activity Summary

    Cust.                     Current  Current  Current  Last
      No. Name                Balance  Charges Payments Posted


      1000 Mike Miller            50.00   100.00    50.00 04/30/84
      1001 Wilbur Watson           0.00     0.00   150.00 04/30/84
      1002 Sheri Stone           100.00   200.00   250.00 04/30/84
    *** Total ***

                                 150.00   300.00   450.00
```

Figure 19.7 – Monthly Activity Summary report

```
Page title                Monthly Activity Summary
Page width (positions)    80
Left margin               0
Right margin              0
Lines per page            58
Double space report       No
Page eject before printing Yes
Page eject after printing Yes
Plain page                No

Column contents:

   Contents              Heading        Width   Decimals   Total?

1  Cust_No               Cust.; No.       5        0        N
2  TRIM(FName)+" "+LName  ;Name           26        0
3  Start_Bal             Current;Balance  9        2        Y
4  Chg_Curr              Current;Charges  8        2        Y
5  Pay_Curr              Current;Payments 8        2        Y
6  Last_Updat            Last;Posted      8        0
```

Figure 19.8 – Format for ARSumm.FRM

```
Page No.     1
11/13/85
                       Accounts Receivable Aging Report

                       Current
Name                   Balance  30 Days  60 Days  90 Days 90+ Days


** Customer Number 1000
Wilbur Watson           139.25   49.40    27.50     0.00     0.00

** Customer Number 1001
Julie Cusey              32.61   87.06     0.00     0.00     0.00

** Customer Number 1002
Frankly Unctuous        212.31  237.06    71.80     0.00     0.00

** Customer Number 1003
 ABC Company            194.25   70.00   164.10     0.00     0.00
```

Figure 19.9 – The Accounts Receivable Aging report

```
Page title                Accounts Receivable Aging Report
Page width (positions)    80
Left margin               0
Right margin              0
Lines per page            58
Double space report       No
Page eject before printing Yes
Page eject after printing Yes
Plain page                No

Column contents:

   Contents              Heading        Width   Decimals   Total?

1  TRIM(FName)+" "+LName  ;Name           26
2  Start_Bal             Current;Balance  9        2        N
3  Bal_30                ;30 Days         8        2        N
4  Bal_60                ;60 Days         8        2        N
5  Bal_90                ;90 Days         8        2        N
6  Bal_90Plus            ;90+ Days        8        2        N
```

Figure 19.10 – Format for Aging.FRM

report. To do this, enter Cust_No as the field to group on and "Customer Number:" as the group heading.

Both reports are printed using the AgeSumm program. Recall that the Accounts Receivable Print menu contains the following CASE statements:

CASE PChoice = 2
    RepForm = "ARSumm"
    DO AgeSumm
CASE PChoice = 3
    RepForm = "Aging"
    DO AgeSumm

If the user selects option 2, the word ARSumm is stored to a memory variable called RepForm. If the user selects option 3, the word Aging is stored to RepForm. Hence the RepForm variable contains the name of the report form (.FRM) file to be used. The ARPrint program then branches to AgeSumm.PRG, which is listed in Figure 19.11.

```
********************************************************** AgeSumm .PRG
*  Prints aged balances or summary report.
*  Called from A/R Print menu.

@ 5,0 CLEAR

*------- Ask about printer
STORE " " TO LP, Mac
@ 15,5 SAY "Send report to printer? (Y/N) " GET LP PICTURE "!"
READ

*------- Set up for printing, if necessary.
IF LP = "Y"
    Mac = "TO PRINT"
    WAIT "Prepare printer, then press any key to print."
ENDIF

*------- Use Customer database and report stored in RepForm.
CLEAR
USE Customer INDEX CustNo
REPORT FORM &RepForm &Mac

*------- Pause, if necessary, then return to menu.
IF LP # "Y"
    WAIT "Press any key to return to A/R Print menu..."
ELSE
    EJECT
ENDIF

RETURN
```

Figure 19.11 – The AgeSumm command file for printing summary reports

History Reports

The Accounts Receivable history reports allow the user to search both the historical and current files for various types of information. When the user selects option 5 from the Print menu, the screen displays the data-selection menu shown in Figure 19.12.

If the user selects option 1 and then enters a customer account number, all historical data for that customer are displayed in the format shown in Figure 19.13. Option 2 from the History menu allows the user to type in a product code. The program then displays all transactions involving that specific item. (This report is helpful for seeing how well an item is moving, as well as for resolving inventory discrepancies.) Figure 19.14 shows a sample history report by product code. Option 3 produces a similar report that displays all transactions for a particular month or specific date.

Once again, each report is printed using the dBASE REPORT FORM command. The report by customer account number and the report by date actually require *two* format files each. These files are simply called up sequentially, without a page eject, by ARHist.PRG.

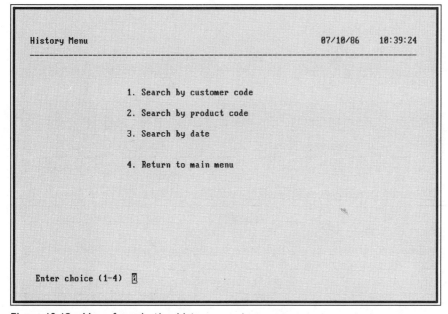

Figure 19.12 – Menu for selecting history reports

```
Page No.       1
04/02/84
                                Customer History

Cust Part   Qty Description                    Unit    Total Date
  #  No.                                        Price

1001 AAA     5 Floppy disks                     22.50   112.50 01/21/84
1001 ZZZ     1 Disk alignment                   12.50    12.50 03/17/84
1001 MMM     5 Floppy disks                     24.50   122.50 03/31/84
*** Total ***
                                                        247.50


Cust Check Description                   Amount Date
 No.  No.
1001 1331   Payment                      100.00 02/15/84
1001 1775   Payment                      100.00 03/15/84
*** Total ***
                                         200.00
```

Figure 19.13 – Sample history report by customer account number

```
Page No.       1
03/31/84
                          Product Code History

Part  Description              Qty    Unit    Total Date
No.                                   Price

ASD   SSSD Floppy disk (1 Unit)    5    .89     4.45 02/21/84
ASD   SSSD Floppy disk (1 Unit)   15    .89    13.35 01/27/84
ASD   SSSD Floppy disk (1 Unit)   25    .89    22.25 03/01/84
ASD   SSSD Floppy disk (1 Unit)    2    .79     1.58 03/15/84
ASD   SSSD Floppy disk (1 Unit)    1    .79      .79 03/21/84
ASD   SSSD Floppy disk (1 Unit)   12    .74     8.88 03/30/84
*** Total ***
                                  60   4.99    51.30
```

Figure 19.14 – Sample history report by product code

The top portion of the customer-number report is printed with a report format named CusHist1.FRM. To design the CusHist1 report format, use BillHist and enter the command CREATE REPORT CusHist1. Enter Customer History as the page heading, and Cust_No, Part_No, Qty, Descript, Unit_Price, Amount, and Date as the contents of the columns. dBASE's default column-width and decimal settings need not be changed. The bottom portion of the report is printed with the CusHist2 report format. Once again, type

USE PayHist
CREATE REPORT CusHist2

to design the report format. No page heading is needed, so just enter Cust_No, Check_No, Descript, Amount, and Date as the contents of the columns. The default width and decimal settings need not be changed.

The product-code history report is printed with the CodeHist report format. To design this report, type

USE BillHist
CREATE REPORT CodeHist

Enter Product Code History as the page heading, and use the fields Part_No, Descript, Qty, Unit_Price, Amount, and Date for the column contents.

The date history report is printed using the DatHist1 and DatHist2 report formats. Enter the commands

USE BillHist
CREATE REPORT DatHist1

to design the format for the top of the report. Enter Product Code History for the page heading, and use the fields Date, Part_No, Descript, Qty, Unit_Price, Amount, and Cust_No for the column contents. To design the bottom portion of the report, type

USE PayHist
CREATE REPORT DatHist2

Omit the page heading, and use the fields Date, Check_No, Amount, Descript, and Cust_No for the report columns.

Of course, the formats presented above are merely suggestions. You can design these reports any way you please, to suit the specific needs of your business. By all means, experiment; try out a variety of formats to see which works best for you and to learn what you can do with the REPORT command.

Once you've designed all the necessary report formats with the CREATE REPORT command, you can develop the ARHist command file to actually print the reports. The completed ARHist command file is presented in Figure 19.15.

Now that we've created the programs to enter and edit data and to produce all the reports we're going to need, we'll complete our auto-mated Accounts Receivable System by developing a program for monthly updating.

```
****************************************************** ARHist.PRG
*   Search history, and current charges and
*   payments files, and display summary data.
*   Called from AR Print Options menu.

HChoice = 0
DO WHILE HChoice # 4
    CLEAR
    DO Title WITH "History Menu"

    TEXT
                    1. Search by customer code

                    2. Search by product code

                    3. Search by date


                    4. Return to main menu
    ENDTEXT
    @ 24,1 SAY "Enter choice (1-4) " GET HChoice PICT "9" RANGE 1,4
    READ

    *------- Set up search macro accordingly.
    @ 4,0 CLEAR
    DO CASE
        CASE HChoice = 1
            M_Cust_No = 0
            @ 15,5 SAY "Enter customer number " GET M_Cust_No PICT "99999"
            READ
            LookAt = "Cust_No"
            LookFor = M_Cust_No
            RepForm1 = "CusHist1"
            RepForm2 = "CusHist2"
            SET EXACT ON

        CASE HChoice = 2
            M_Code = SPACE(5)
            @ 15,5 SAY "Enter product code " GET M_Code
            READ
            LookAt = "UPPER(Part_No)"
            LookFor = UPPER(M_Code)
            RepForm1 = "CodeHist"
            SET EXACT ON
```

Figure 19.15 – The ARHist command file

```
        CASE HChoice = 3
            M_Date = SPACE(8)
            @ 15,5 SAY "Enter Date " GET M_Date
            READ
            LookAt = "DTOC(Date)"
            LookFor = TRIM(M_Date)
            RepForm1 = "DatHist1"
            RepForm2 = "DatHist2"
            SET EXACT OFF

        CASE HChoice = 4
            SET EXACT OFF
            RETURN

    ENDCASE

    *------- Ask about printer .
    @ 5,0 CLEAR
    STORE " " TO LP, Mac
    @ 15,5 SAY "Send report to printer? (Y/N) " GET LP PICT "!"
    READ
    IF LP = "Y"
        Mac = "TO PRINT"
    ENDIF

    *------- Search billing history file.
    USE BillHist
    SET FILTER TO &LookAt = LookFor
    COPY TO Temp
    USE Temp
    APPEND FROM Charges FOR &LookAt = LookFor
    SET FILTER TO &LookAt = LookFor
    REPORT FORM &RepForm1 &Mac

    *------- If not searching for product code, search Payments files.
    IF HChoice # 2
        USE PayHist
        SET FILTER TO &LookAt = LookFor
        COPY TO Temp
        USE Temp
        APPEND FROM Payments
        SET FILTER TO &LookAt = LookFor
        REPORT FORM &RepForm2 &Mac PLAIN NOEJECT
    ENDIF

    *------- If report not going to printer, pause.
    IF LP # "Y"
        ?
        ?
        WAIT
    ENDIF

ENDDO (HChoice # 4)
```

Figure 19.15 – The ARHist command file (continued)

Monthly System Updates

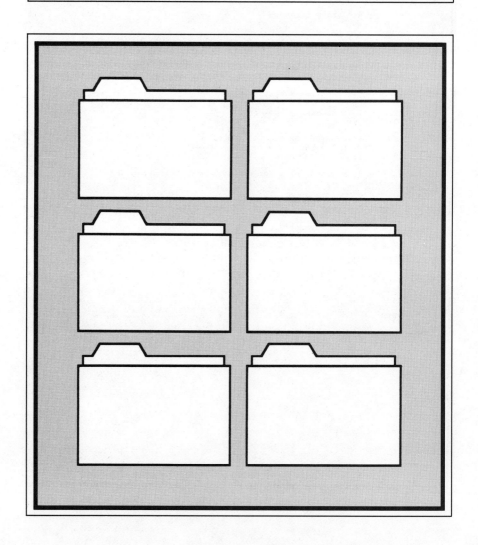

At the end of each month, after all invoices have been printed, the user should perform the monthly updating procedure to copy all current transactions to the history files and update the current and aged balances in the Customer file. Main-menu option 6 performs the update, using the Post.PRG command file.

In the interest of safety, the Post program requires that the user enter a password to perform the update. This helps to ensure that the user doesn't accidentally perform the update by inadvertently selecting the wrong menu option, and it also ensures that only authorized personnel are able to perform the update. Our password is literally the word PASSWORD, but of course you can change that to anything you like.

The update process works like this. First all current, 30-, 60-, and 90-day balances are shifted back one month, using the REPLACE command. Then all current charges that have already been printed on invoices are summarized in a database named Summary, and the update is performed using the Summary file with the UPDATE FROM command. Finally, all current billed charges (Billed = .T.) are added to the BillHist database and deleted from Charges, emptying the Charges database for the new month.

This same process is then repeated for the Payments database, with all posted payments (Posted = .T.) being transferred to the PayHist database.

After the updates from the transactions are performed and the old transactions are transferred to the history files, the starting balance and last update fields are updated, using a couple of REPLACE commands.

Then the process of calculating the aged balances begins. Since this process could take quite a while on a large database, the lines

*---------- Show progress.
@ 20,1 SAY "Aging the balances: Record " + ;
  STR(RECNO(),4) + " of " + STR(RECCOUNT(),4)

display a message such as

  Aging the balances: Record 2 of 100

As each record is processed, the counter (at 2 in this example) increases until the job is done (at 100 records in this example).

The actual calculations for aging the balances are performed with a series of IF clauses. If no payments were made (Pay_Curr < = 0), there is nothing to recalculate, so the command file skips over all the aging calculations using the LOOP command. (The LOOP command passes control directly to the ENDDO command, ignoring any commands in between.) Otherwise, the command file adjusts the 90 + -, 90-, 60-, and 30-day balances based on the current payment. The payment is incrementally subtracted from the aged balances beginning with the oldest positive balance.

When all updating is complete, the program displays a message about printing reports, waits for the user to press a key, closes the databases, and returns to the main menu. The entire Post command file is shown in Figure 20.1.

```
*************************************************** Post .PRG
*   Posts summarized monthly accounts to the Customer file
*   and ages the receivables .
*   Called from AR main menu .

SET DELETED ON
CLEAR
Do Title with "Monthly Posting"

*------- Display reminder and get password .
TEXT
            This is the program to post payments and charges .

            Be sure you have printed all the monthly invoices

                before proceeding with this program .
ENDTEXT

Password = SPACE(8)
@ 15,12 SAY "Enter password to proceed " ;
  GET Password PICT "!!!!!!!!"
READ
```

Figure 20.1 – The Post command file for updating the A/R System

```
*------- If proper password not entered, return to the menu.
IF Password # "PASSWORD"
    ? "Illegal password!", CHR(7)
    SET DELETED OFF
    RETURN
ENDIF

*------- Do the posting. First, shift all current, 30-, 60-, and 90-
*------- day billings "back" one field in the Customer file.
@ 20,1 SAY "Working..."
CLOSE DATABASES
USE Customer

REPLACE ALL;
  Bal_90plus WITH Bal_90Plus + Bal_90,;
  Bal_90 WITH Bal_60,;
  Bal_60 WITH Bal_30,;
  Bal_30 WITH Chg_Curr - Pay_Curr

REPLACE ALL;
  Chg_Curr WITH 0,;
  Pay_Curr WITH 0

*------- Now, create summary of the Charges database by customer number.
SET SAFETY OFF
USE Charges INDEX ChrgNo
COPY STRUCTURE TO Summary
TOTAL ON Cust_No TO Summary FIELDS Qty, Unit_Price, Amount FOR Billed

*------- Now update the Customer database current balances
*------- with data from the charges summary file.
SELECT 1
USE Customer INDEX CustNo
SELECT 2
USE Summary
SELECT 1
UPDATE ON Cust_No FROM Summary REPLACE Chg_Curr WITH B->Amount

*------- Move all posted transactions to the billing history file.
SELECT 2
USE BillHist
APPEND FROM Charges FOR Billed

*------- Then empty the current Charges file.
CLOSE DATABASES
USE Charges INDEX ChrgNo
DELETE ALL FOR Billed
PACK

*------- Now, summarize payment totals for each customer.
USE Payments INDEX PayNo
COPY STRUCTURE TO Summary
TOTAL ON Cust_No TO Summary FIELDS Amount FOR Posted

*------- Now update the Customer database current balances
*------- with data from the Payments summary file.
SELECT 1
USE Customer INDEX CustNo
SELECT 2
USE Summary
SELECT 1
UPDATE ON Cust_No FROM Summary REPLACE Pay_Curr WITH B->Amount

*------- Put all posted transactions in the payment history file.
SELECT 2
USE PayHist
APPEND FROM Payments FOR Posted
```

Figure 20.1 – The Post command file for updating the A/R System (continued)

```
*------- Then empty the current payments file.
CLOSE DATABASES
USE Payments INDEX PayNo
DELETE ALL FOR Posted
PACK

*------- Then update the 'last billed' and 'starting balance' fields
*------- in the Customer database.
USE Customer
REPLACE ALL Start_Bal WITH Start_Bal + Chg_Curr - Pay_Curr
REPLACE ALL Last_UpDat WITH DATE()

*------- Adjust aged balances.
GO TOP
DO WHILE .NOT. EOF()

   *---------- Show progress.
   @ 20,1 SAY "Aging the balances: Record "+ ;
     STR(RECNO(),4)+" of "+STR(RECCOUNT(),4)

   *------- If no payment, skip calculations.
   IF Pay_Curr <= 0
      SKIP
      LOOP
   ENDIF  (Pay_Curr <= 0)

   *--- Otherwise, incrementally subtract the payment.
   More = .F.
   NextBal = .T.
   IF Bal_90Plus > 0
      Remain = Pay_Curr - Bal_90Plus
      IF Remain >= 0
         REPLACE Bal_90Plus WITH 0
         More = .T.
      ELSE
         REPLACE Bal_90Plus WITH ABS(Remain)
         NextBal = .F.
      ENDIF ( >= 0)
   ENDIF (90+ > 0)

   *--------------------------- 90 days.
   IF NextBal .AND. Bal_90 > 0
      IF More
         Remain = Remain - Bal_90
      ELSE
         Remain = Pay_Curr - Bal_90
      ENDIF (More)
      IF Remain >= 0
         REPLACE Bal_90 WITH 0
         More = .T.
      ELSE
         REPLACE Bal_90 WITH ABS(Remain)
         NextBal = .F.
      ENDIF (>=0)
   ENDIF (nextbal & bal90>0)
   *--------------------------- 60 days.
   IF NextBal .AND. Bal_60 > 0
      IF More
         Remain = Remain - Bal_60
      ELSE
         Remain = Pay_Curr - Bal_60
      ENDIF (More)
      IF Remain >= 0
         REPLACE Bal_60 WITH 0
         More = .T.
      ELSE
         REPLACE Bal_60 WITH ABS(Remain)
         NextBal = .F.

      ENDIF (Remain >= 0)
   ENDIF (nextbal & bal60>0)
```

Figure 20.1 – The Post command file for updating the A/R System *(continued)*

```
       *-------------------------- 30 days .
       IF NextBal .AND. Bal_30 > 0
          IF More
             Remain = Remain - Bal_30
          ELSE
             Remain = Pay_Curr    Bal_30
          ENDIF (More)
          IF Remain >= 0
             REPLACE Bal_30 WITH 0
             More = .T.
          ELSE
             REPLACE Bal_30 WITH ABS(Remain)
             NextBal = .F.
          ENDIF (<0)
       ENDIF (Nextbal & bal90>0)
       SKIP
   ENDDO (eof customer)

   *------- Done.  Display closing messages
   CLEAR
   ? CHR(7)
   TEXT
                  The posting procedure is complete.

                  Use option 4 from the main menu

          to print current monthly summary and aging reports.

   ENDTEXT
   *------------ Get rid of any old keypresses.
   CLEAR TYPEAHEAD
   WAIT "Press any key to return to main menu..."

   *------- Return to the main menu
   SET DELETED OFF
   CLOSE DATABASES
   RETURN
```

Figure 20.1 – The Post command file for updating the A/R System (continued)

The Post command file is the last one in the Accounts Receivable System. By judicious use of procedures and parameter passing, and by careful planning of the user interface, we've created a completely automated system whose actual process is completely *transparent* (invisible) to the end user. Not only that, we've developed such tight programming code that we'll have no problem running this complex system on a personal computer.

Be sure to test the overall system by adding some accounts to the databases and running through a couple of months of hypothetical transactions.

With any custom software system, there are always peripheral functions you can add to make the system more sophisticated or to tie it to other systems. In Chapter 21, I'll present such a linking program, along with some tips on modifying existing systems and a utility program to help you debug your command files, just to give you an idea of the tremendous range of activities dBASE III PLUS command files can handle.

Useful Programs
and Techniques

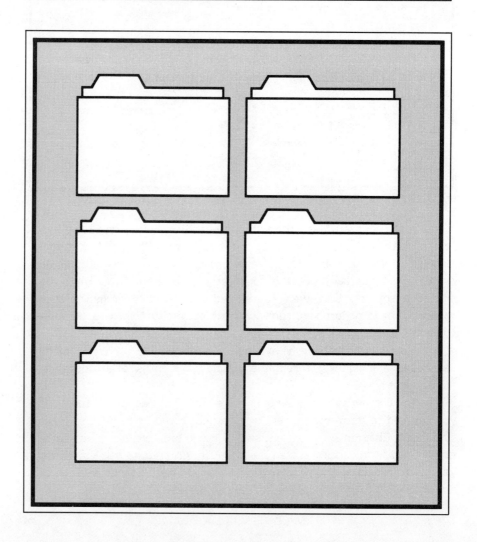

At the end of Chapter 20, I mentioned that there will always be ways to enhance and streamline any system we might design. I neglected to say that dBASE III PLUS is also flexible enough to allow us to write nondatabase programs (utility programs) in dBASE code. In this chapter, I'll discuss ways you can approach the problem of modifying existing, undocumented dBASE III PLUS software systems. Then I'll show you a couple of examples of the enhancements mentioned above: a program for linking the Inventory and Accounts Receivable Systems, as well as a utility program for formatting and debugging the command files you write.

Modifying Existing Software

It seems that just about every dBASE programmer is eventually faced with the task of modifying software that someone else wrote. This is usually a pretty tricky problem, because most of the time you don't have a clue as to what database, index, command, and format files are involved. But if you know the name of the main-menu program, you can usually at least locate a specific routine that needs editing.

Minor Modifications

Some modifications can be made through the "quick-and-dirty" method of pressing the Esc key at just the right moment. Find out how to run the main-menu program (*someone* must at least know how to get started in the system!) and make the appropriate menu selections so that the routine that needs modification is running. As soon as the area that needs to be changed is displaying its feedback on the screen, start pressing the Esc key and keep pressing it until the command file terminates. dBASE will display a prompt such as

Called from – B:ARStat.PRG
Called from – B:ARPrint.PRG
Called from – B:AR.PRG
Cancel, Ignore, or Suspend? (C, I, or S)

From this prompt, you can see that the program that needs modification is called ARStat.PRG, and that it was called from ARPrint.PRG, which in turn was called from AR.PRG. Jot down these bits of information on a piece of paper, then type C to select Cancel.

Caution: This won't work if the original programmer used SET ESCAPE OFF to disable the Esc key. If that is the case, see the subsection on major modifications for other solutions.

Next, use the DISPLAY STATUS command to find out which files are open at the moment, as well as the status of the various SET parameters. Notice that the file that is currently selected (the one in use at the moment you pressed the Esc key) is specified (Customer.DBF, in this example), along with all active index files and their key fields, as in Figure 21.1. If necessary, use the SET PRINT ON command and then the DISPLAY STATUS command again to get a hard copy of the status screen.

Next, get a hard copy of the structure of each of the databases. Just type SET PRINT ON, then SELECT 1 and DISPLAY STRUCTURE, SELECT 2 and DISPLAY STRUCTURE, and so forth, until you have them all.

Armed with this knowledge, you can use the dBASE TYPE command to make a hard copy of the actual command file that needs editing. (If the previous programmer removed all prior indentations, you might want to make your task easier by putting them back in, using the MODIFY COM-MAND editor or the Debug program described later in this chapter.) Study the hard copy thoroughly, to become as familiar as possible with the command file you need to modify *before* you make any changes. From that point on, you're on your own.

```
. DISPLAY STATUS

Currently Selected Database:
Select area:  1, Database in Use: C:Customer.dbf   Alias: CUSTOMER
     Master index file:  C:CustNo.ndx  Key: Cust_No

Select area:  2, Database in Use: C:Charges.dbf    Alias: CHARGES
     Master index file:  C:ChrgNo.ndx  Key: Cust_No

Select area:  3, Database in Use: C:Payments.dbf   Alias: PAYMENTS
     Master index file:  C:PayNo.ndx  Key: Cust_No

File search path:
Default disk drive: C:
Print destination:  PRN:
Margin =      0
Current work area =    1

Press any key to continue..._
```

Figure 21.1 – Sample screen from DISPLAY STATUS command

Major Modifications

Unfortunately, the "quick-and-dirty" method won't work in all situations. If you're planning on a major overhaul, it is best to begin by becoming as familiar with the overall system as possible. If there is documentation available, read it. If there is none, create some. A little reverse engineering will help do the trick here.

First, find out the name of the main-menu program and call the file onto the screen. Note all calls to other programs through the DO command, and jot them down in hierarchical order, as in Figure 21.2. Then repeat this process for each of the lower-level programs and add any new files to the hierarchy, as in Figure 21.3.

As you may have guessed, we're reconstructing a software design from the existing software. If you have a sophisticated word processor like WordStar or Microsoft Word, you might want to use it to do this reverse-engineering step. Then you can use the word processor's FIND option to locate each DO quickly. (Be sure to use the "ignore case" option. Not all programmers write code in uppercase.)

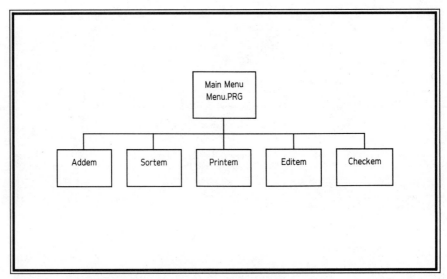

Figure 21.2 – Sample hierarchy of programs in a system

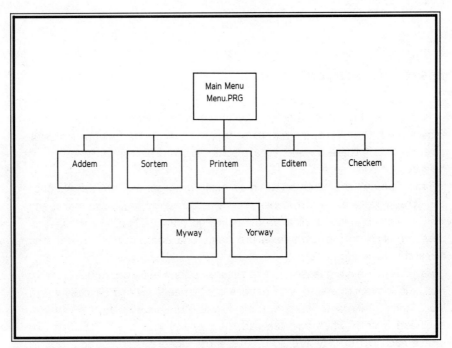

Figure 21.3 – More detailed hierarchy of programs in a system

You should also search for all the USE and INDEX (or INDE, in case of abbreviations) commands in each program. Make notes of which command files use which databases and which databases use which index files. And, of course, search for ESCA in each program, so you can find any SET ESCAPE OFF commands and get rid of them (which will allow you to return to the quick-and-dirty method outlined above).

After you've determined which databases the system uses, load each one from the dot prompt with the USE command, then type the SET PRINT ON and DISPLAY STRUCTURE commands. This will give you a hard-copy reference to all fields in the system.

At this point you have some rudimentary documentation: database structures and an overall software structure. If you have eliminated any SET ESCAPE OFF commands while working through the programs, you also now have the option to cancel command-file execution with the Esc key and return to the minor-modifications approach.

I can't really help you much more than that. The possibilities for modifications to software systems are nearly infinite. Of course, the more familiar you are with the dBASE language itself, the easier your task will be. And the more documentation you have to work with, whether it is the previous programmer's or that created through the reverse-engineering process, the better. But I might make these additional suggestions:

1. Try not to eliminate any fields from any database in the system. If you eliminate a field from a database, you'll have to eliminate all references to it in every command file in the entire system. If you're just trying to keep the field out of a report, change the command file or report (.FRM) file instead. Conversely, it's OK to *add* a field to a database at any time, since this won't have any effect on existing command files or reports.

2. Use the ECHO, STEP, and DEBUG parameters. If you know which program in a system needs modification but you're not sure you understand the code, set the ECHO, STEP, and DEBUG commands on to watch the program run. You can also use the SET ECHO ON command to trace dBASE command-file execution from a main-menu program down to a lower-level program. Use ^S to start and stop the echoing so you can see what's going on.

3. If the programs contain few comments (and that's usually the case), add some detailed remarks of your own after you've

analyzed the code. Not only will this help you once you actually begin your modifications, but it will also save the next consultant the necessity of dealing with the same mysteries.

An Inventory/Accounts Receivable Linker

One software modification you might want to try lets you link the Accounts Receivable and Inventory Systems presented in this book. This modification requires the following changes:

1. Transactions from the Charges database must be subtracted from quantities in the Master inventory file.

2. Records from the Charges database that have already been taken into account in the Master inventory file must be marked some-how, so they're not accidentally counted twice.

3. Transactions in the Charges history file, BillHist, must be checked when updating the Master inventory file, since there is no easy way of synchronizing accounts receivable posting dates with inventory updates.

Before we begin writing the program, we'll need to load the Charges database and add a field to tell the program whether the record has already been posted to the Master inventory file (the Customer file has already been taken care of in Post.PRG). To do this, just use the MOD-IFY STRUCTURE command and add a logical field named InPost. The struc-ture of Charges.DBF will now look like Figure 21.4. Next, use BillHist and add the same field, so that its structure looks exactly like the new struc-ture for Charges.DBF.

For safety's sake, we need to make sure that each new record added to the Charges database shows the InPost field as False. To do this, type MODIFY COMMAND NewChrg. When the program appears on the screen, scroll to the bottom of the file and find the routine for adding a new record. Then add the command REPLACE InPost WITH .F. at the position indicated by the arrow:

```
*------- Allow user to enter transaction data
*------- using FNewChrg screen.
```

```
Structure for database : C:Charges .DBF

Field  Field name  Type        Width   Dec
   1   CUST_NO     Numeric        4      0
   2   INVOICE_NO  Numeric        6      0
   3   PART_NO     Character      5
   4   QTY         Numeric        4      0
   5   UNIT_PRICE  Numeric        9      2
   6   AMOUNT      Numeric        9      2
   7   DATE        Date           8
   8   DESCRIPT    Character     20
   9   BILLED      Logical        1
  10   INPOST      Logical        1
```

Figure 21.4 – New structure for the Charges database

```
IF .NOT. Exiting
    SELECT 2
    APPEND BLANK
    REPLACE Cust_No WITH M_Cust_No
    REPLACE Date WITH DATE( )
    REPLACE Billed WITH .F.
    REPLACE InPost WITH .F. ◄─────
    SET FORMAT TO FNewChrg
    READ
    CLOSE FORMAT
    REPLACE Amount WITH Qty * Unit_Price
ENDIF
```

Now we need to write the routine that will update the Inventory System Master file from all nonposted (InPost = .F.) records in the Charges and BillHist files, and also mark those records as posted (InPost = .T.) once the task is finished. The Updater command file handles updates to the Master file, so let's just add a line to Updater.PRG, near the bottom of the program, that tells it to run a program called ARUpdate.PRG to update from the Accounts Receivable Charges and BillHist files. Just above the lines where Updater.PRG closes all databases and returns to the Master menu, add the command USE ARUpdate, as shown in the following program segment:

```
    *--- Use original NewStock file, make Posted fields "True".
    CLOSE DATABASES
    USE NewStock
    REPLACE ALL POSTED WITH .T.
        *------- New lines added to Updater.PRG for
        *------- interfacing with A/R System begin here.
        DO ARUpdate
        *------- And end here.
    ENDIF (record number > 0)
    *------- Free up all work areas and return to Master menu.
    CLOSE DATABASES
    RETURN
```

Now create the ARUpdate command file for updating the Master file from Charges and BillHist. Figure 21.5 shows the entire ARUpdate program.

```
************************************** ARUpdate .PRG
** Update the master file from Charges and BillHist.
CLEAR
? "Updating from the A/R system..."
**** Use the Charges database.
USE Charges

**** Copy all nonupdated records to Temp file.
COPY STRUCTURE TO Temp
COPY TO Temp FOR .NOT. InPost

**** Now get the records from BillHist.
USE Temp
APPEND FROM BillHist FOR .NOT. InPost
**** Get the Temp file sorted by part number.
INDEX ON Part_No TO ARIndex

**** Use the Master file for updating.
SELECT 1
USE Master INDEX Master
SELECT 2
USE Temp INDEX ARIndex

**** Update master from the temporary A/R file.
SELECT 1
UPDATE ON Part_No FROM Temp REPLACE Qty WITH Qty-Temp->Qty

**** Go back to the original charges file
**** and make all Posted fields "True"
CLOSE DATABASES
USE Charges
REPLACE ALL InPost WITH .T.
*** Do the same with the BillHist file.
USE BillHist
REPLACE ALL InPost WITH .T.

*** Then return to the Updater command file.
RETURN
```

Figure 21.5 – The ARUpdate command file

This program modification was easy, because the part-number fields in the Charges, BillHist, and Master databases all had the same name (Part_No), type (Character), and Width (5). Therefore, Part _No could serve as a key field to link the three databases. The moral of this story is this: If, when you are first designing a system, you think you might eventually want to link data between systems, it is a good idea to plan your key fields accordingly.

A Debugging Tool

Two of the biggest impediments to the debugging process in any programming language are lack of proper indentations, which makes it difficult to locate "chunks" of logic in a program, and missing ENDDO, ENDIF, and ENDCASE commands, which many high-level programming languages like dBASE III PLUS can't tell you about. To help deal with these problems, I've written a dBASE utility program that can put proper indentations into any command file. It will also inform you of any missing or extraneous ENDIF, ENDDO, or ENDCASE commands.

When you run the Debug program, it will ask you to

Enter name of command file

If the file you wish to debug already has the extension .PRG, you can type just the file name (for example, Test). Otherwise, specify the extension as well (Test.FMT). Be sure to include the drive specifier, if necessary (B:Test). The screen will display the prompt

Working . . .

and then display each line of the command file as it puts in the proper indentations. Next, the program will display a count of all commands that involve clauses, as in Figure 21.6. Note that the screen in Figure 21.6 points out an unmatched DO WHILE . . . ENDDO pair; also, note that the new command file, with proper indentations, is now stored under the original file name, Test.PRG, and the original program is stored under the file name Test.OLD.

Figure 21.7 shows the Test command file (Test.PRG) before it was run through the Debug program (it's a mess, I know). Figure 21.8 shows the same command file *after* it has been run through Debug.PRG and the missing ENDDO command has been added.

```
Command File statistics:

DO WHILE statements  :          1
ENDDO statements     :          0   <--- Whoops!  Unmatched pair.

IF statements        :          0
ENDIF statements     :          0

DO CASE statements   :          1
ENDCASE statements   :          1


     The original command file is now stored under Test.OLD

     The modified, indented version is stored under Test.PRG
```

Figure 21.6 – Screen from the Debug command file

```
**************************************** Test.PRG
*--------------------- Test the Debug.PRG program.
SET TALK OFF

*---------------- Display menu and get user's choice.
STORE 0 TO Choice
DO WHILE Choice # 5
CLEAR
TEXT

              Membership System main menu

                   1. Add new members
                   2. Print membership information
                   3. Change/delete data
                   4. Check for duplicates

                   5. Exit Membership System

ENDTEXT
@ 12,22 SAY "Enter choice (1-5) " GET Choice
   READ

*------------------ Branch to appropriate program.
DO CASE

CASE Choice = 1
DO AddNew

CASE Choice = 2
        DO Reports

     CASE Choice = 3
DO EditDel

CASE Choice = 4
   DO DupCheck

   ENDCASE

   ENDDO (while Choice # 5)
       CLOSE DATABASES
*QUIT
```

Figure 21.7 – Sample program before using Debug.PRG

```
**************************************** Test.PRG
*-------------------- Test the Debug.PRG program.
SET TALK OFF

*--------------- Display menu and get user's choice.
STORE 0 TO Choice
DO WHILE Choice # 5
   CLEAR
   TEXT

             Membership System main menu

                  1. Add new members
                  2. Print membership information
                  3. Change/delete data
                  4. Check for duplicates

                  5. Exit Membership System

   ENDTEXT
   @ 12,22 SAY "Enter choice (1-5) " GET Choice
   READ

   *----------------- Branch to appropriate program.
   DO CASE

      CASE Choice = 1
           DO AddNew

      CASE Choice = 2
           DO Reports

      CASE Choice = 3
           DO EditDel

      CASE Choice = 4
           DO DupCheck

   ENDCASE

ENDDO (while Choice # 5)
CLOSE DATABASES
*QUIT
```

Figure 21.8 – The same sample program after using Debug.PRG

The Debug program works by first storing the original name and then renaming the program to the same file name with the extension .PRG (if it wasn't already a .PRG file). Then it reads the command lines from the .PRG file into a database file named Debug.DBF. Each line in your command file becomes a single record in the Debug.DBF file. Using a standard DO WHILE .NOT. EOF() loop, the debugger stores each line of the program to a memory variable called MemVar and checks for the abbreviations of various commands (DO WHIL, ENDD, DO CASE, ENDC, TEXT, and so forth). (It checks for abbreviations, but it will find the command even if it isn't abbreviated, because an exact match is not used in the comparison.) For each command that involves a programming clause, Debug increments a counter and makes determinations about indentation. After each line is analyzed, it is placed back into the Debug database with proper indentations. When the analysis is complete, the original .PRG file is renamed, using the extension .OLD, and the new version of the program is copied from Debug.DBF to the original file name, using the DELIMITED WITH BLANK option. This creates a file in the "straight ASCII" format dBASE uses to store all command files.

Before you can run Debug.PRG, you'll need to create a database named Debug.DBF, with the structure shown in Figure 21.9. Notice that the file contains only one field, Line, and that it is 254 characters wide. Each record in this database contains a single line from the command file being debugged. The APPEND FROM command with the SDF option is used to read the "straight ASCII" command file into the Debug database.

Figure 21.10 shows the entire Debug command file. Comments within the program describe the function of each routine.

Caution: Don't use the Debug program on an important command file until the Debug program itself is fully tested and debugged. Your best bet is to create a test program specifically for working with Debug.PRG (perhaps by copying a good file to another name and then messing it up a bit). Once you're sure that the Debug program is running properly, you can use it as a debugging tool with any command file you wish.

Keep in mind that the Debug program calculates the amount of indentation based on the commands in the command file you're debugging. If the program is missing an ENDDO, ENDIF, or ENDCASE command, the indentations will probably be inaccurate in the newly indented program. This may help you locate the exact spot in the program where the missing ENDIF, ENDCASE, or ENDDO command belongs.

You can run any command file through the Debug program as many times as you wish. However, each time you do, the existing .OLD file will be replaced with the latest "original" file, and the true original will be lost (unless you rename it before running Debug).

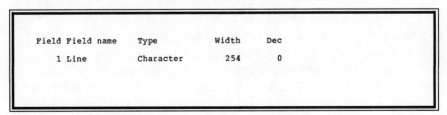

```
        Field Field name    Type        Width     Dec
            1 Line          Character     254       0
```

Figure 21.9 – Structure of the Debug database

```
************************************************** Debug .PRG
*   Test for unmatched clauses in command files,
*   and insert indentations.

SET TALK OFF
SET EXACT OFF
SET SAFETY OFF
CLEAR

*------- Get name of program to debug.
FileName = SPACE(12)
@ 5,5 SAY "Enter name of command file " GET FileName
READ
CLEAR
? "Working..."

*------- Add .PRG extension if necessary.
IF .NOT. "." $(FileName)
   FileName = TRIM(FileName) + ".PRG"
ENDIF

*------- Store FileName without extension to FName.
FileName = UPPER(FileName)
FName = SUBSTR(FileName,1,AT(".",FileName)-1)

*------- Pull a copy of the program into Debug.DBF.
USE Debug
ZAP
APPEND FROM &FileName SDF
GO TOP

*------- Start counters for clause commands.
STORE 0 TO Indent, Amt, DoWhile, If, DoCase, EndDo, EndIf, EndCase

*------- Loop through each line of the command file.
DO WHILE .NOT. EOF()
   MemVar = TRIM(Line)
   *------ Peel off leading blanks
   MemVar = LTRIM(MemVar)

   *------- Set flags to false.
   STORE .F. TO Increase, Decrease, NewElse, NewCase, Text

   *------- Check for clause commands: handle counters and indents.
   DO CASE

      CASE UPPER(MemVar) = "DO WHIL"
           DoWhile = DoWhile + 1
           Amt = 3
           Increase = .T.

      CASE UPPER(MemVar) = "IF "
           STORE If + 1 TO If
           Amt = 3
           Increase = .T.

      CASE UPPER(MemVar) = "DO CASE"
           DoCase = DoCase + 1
           Amt = 8
           Increase = .T.

      CASE UPPER(MemVar) = "CASE" .OR. MemVar = "OTHE"
           NewCase = .T.

      CASE UPPER(MemVar) = "ENDD"
           STORE EndDo + 1 TO EndDo
           Indent = Indent - 3
```

Figure 21.10 – The Debug command file

```
      CASE UPPER(MemVar) = "ENDI"
          STORE EndIf + 1 TO EndIf
          Indent = Indent - 3

      CASE UPPER(MemVar) = "ENDC"
          STORE EndCase + 1 TO EndCase
          Indent = Indent - 8

      CASE UPPER(MemVar) = "ELSE"
          NewElse = .T.

      CASE UPPER(MemVar) = "TEXT"
          Store .T. TO Text

  ENDCASE

*------- Add new indent to line.
REPLACE Line WITH SPACE(Indent) + MemVar

*------- If command was "ELSE", unindent the one line.
IF NewElse
    Indent = Indent - Amt
    REPLACE Line WITH SPACE(Indent) + MemVar
    Indent = Indent + Amt
ENDIF

*------- If command was a CASE or OTHERWISE, unindent.
IF NewCase
    Indent = Indent - 5
    REPLACE Line WITH SPACE(Indent) + MemVar
    Indent = Indent + 5
ENDIF

    *------- If remaining lines to be indented, increase indent.
    IF Increase
        Indent = Indent + Amt
    ENDIF

    REPLACE Line WITH TRIM(Line)
    ? TRIM(Line)

    *------- Don't modify anything in TEXT...ENDTEXT block.
    IF Text
        SKIP
        DO WHILE .NOT. "ENDT" $ (UPPER(Line))
            ? TRIM(Line)
            SKIP
        ENDDO
    *------- Otherwise, skip to next line.
    ELSE
        SKIP
    ENDIF (MemVar=Text)

ENDDO (while not eof)

*------- Store original command file with .OLD as the extension.
OldName = FName + ".OLD"
IF FILE(OldName)
    ERASE &OldName
ENDIF
RENAME &FileName TO &OldName

*------- Copy new version of program to original FileName.
COPY TO &FileName DELIM WITH BLANK
CLOSE DATABASES
```

Figure 21.10 – The Debug command file (continued)

```
*------- Display command file stats.
CLEAR
Whoops = "  <--- Whoops!  Unmatched pair."
? "Command File statistics:"
?

*------- Print DO WHILE...ENDDO stats.
? "DO WHILE statements  :", DoWhile
? "ENDDO statements     :", EndDo
IF DoWhile # ENDDO
   ?? Whoops
ENDIF
?

*------- Print IF...ENDIF stats.
? "IF statements        :", If
? "ENDIF statements     :", EndIf
IF If # EndIf
   ?? Whoops
ENDIF
?

*------- Print DO CASE...ENDCASE stats.
? "DO CASE statements   :", DoCase
? "ENDCASE statements   :", EndCase
IF DoCase # EndCase
   ?? Whoops
ENDIF
?
?

*------- Print closing statements.
? "The original command file is now stored under &OldName"
?
? "The modified, indented version is stored under &FileName"

*------- Done.
```

Figure 21.10 - The Debug command file (continued)

A Check-Writing Procedure

Chances are, if you write many dBASE command files, you'll eventually have to write a program that prints checks. This can be a tricky problem when it comes time to translate the dollar amount (for example, $1,234.76) to English (One thousand two hundred thirty four and 76/100 dollars). I've included here a procedure named Translat.PRG that can translate any number up to 999,999.99 to its proper English equivalent.

The sample program reads data from a database named Checks that has the structure shown in Figure 21.11.

The command file also needs to have the unique English equivalent for all numbers. For convenience, I've stored these in a memory file named English.MEM. To create the English.MEM file, type in the English command file shown in Figure 21.12. Then simply run the program, and it will create the memory file for you.

```
Field   Field name   Type        Width   Dec
    1   CHECK_NO     Numeric         5    0
    2   TO_WHOM      Character      25
    3   AMOUNT       Numeric         9    2
    4   DATE         Date            8
** Total **                        48
```

Figure 21.11 – Structure of the Checks database

```
******************************************** English.PRG
*-------------- Sets up memory file for
*-------------- storing English equivalents.

CLEAR
? "Creating English.MEM with English words for numbers..."
?
SET DEFA TO C
SET TALK ON
CLEAR MEMORY

U = " "
U1 = "ONE"
U2 = "TWO"
U3 = "THREE"
U4 = "FOUR"
U5 = "FIVE"
U6 = "SIX"
U7 = "SEVEN"
U8 = "EIGHT"
U9 = "NINE"
U10 = "TEN"
U11 = "ELEVEN"
U12 = "TWELVE"
U13 = "THIRTEEN"
U14 = "FOURTEEN"
U15 = "FIFTEEN"
U16 = "SIXTEEN"
U17 = "SEVENTEEN"
U18 = "EIGHTEEN"
U19 = "NINETEEN"
U20 = "TWENTY"
U30 = "THIRTY"
U40 = "FORTY"
U50 = "FIFTY"
U60 = "SIXTY"
U70 = "SEVENTY"
U80 = "EIGHTY"
U90 = "NINETY"

*-------- Save all variables to English.MEM file.
SAVE TO English
CLEAR
?
?
? "Done.  English.MEM now has all English words for numbers."
SET TALK OFF
```

Figure 21.12 – The English command file

After running the English command file, check to make sure it ran correctly by typing in these commands:

RESTORE FROM English
DISPLAY MEMORY

You should see all of the English words stored to memory variables. Each memory variable name begins with the letter U and ends with the number that it represents (for example, U20 is "TWENTY", U9 is "NINE", and so forth). Figure 21.13 shows how the screen looks after you type the RESTORE FROM English and DISPLAY MEMORY commands.

The procedure file that translates the numeric dollar amount to English is named Translat.PRG. Create and save it as you would any other command file. Translat.PRG is shown in Figure 21.14.

Any program can access the Translat procedure, as long as the program uses this command:

SET PROCEDURE TO Translat

```
     U          pub    C    " "
     U1         pub    C    "ONE"
     U2         pub    C    "TWO"
     U3         pub    C    "THREE"
     U4         pub    C    "FOUR"
     U5         pub    C    "FIVE"
     U6         pub    C    "SIX"
     U7         pub    C    "SEVEN"
     U8         pub    C    "EIGHT"
     U9         pub    C    "NINE"
     U10        pub    C    "TEN"
     U11        pub    C    "ELEVEN"
     U12        pub    C    "TWELVE"
     U13        pub    C    "THIRTEEN"
     U14        pub    C    "FOURTEEN"
     U15        pub    C    "FIFTEEN"
     U16        pub    C    "SIXTEEN"
     U17        pub    C    "SEVENTEEN"
     U18        pub    C    "EIGHTEEN"
     U19        pub    C    "NINETEEN"
     U20        pub    C    "TWENTY"
     U30        pub    C    "THIRTY"
     U40        pub    C    "FORTY"
     U50        pub    C    "FIFTY"
     U60        pub    C    "SIXTY"
     U70        pub    C    "SEVENTY"
     U80        pub    C    "EIGHTY"
     U90        pub    C    "NINETY"
       28 variables defined,      209 bytes used
      228 variables available,   5791 bytes available
```

Figure 21.13 – Memory variables restored from English.MEM

```
*******************************************  Translat .PRG
*--- Procedure to convert a number to English equivalent.

PROCEDURE Translat
PARAMETERS Number,English

*---------- Set up memory variables.
Counter = 1
Start = 1
String = STR(Amount,9,2)

*------------------------- Loop through thousands and hundreds.
DO WHILE Counter < 3

   *------------------------ Split out hundreds, tens, and ones.
   Chunk = SUBSTR(String,Start,3)
   Hun = SUBSTR(Chunk,1,1)
   Ten = SUBSTR(Chunk,2,2)
   One = SUBSTR(Chunk,3,1)

   *-------------------- Handle hundreds portion.
   IF VAL(Chunk) > 99
      English = English + U&Hun + ' HUNDRED '
   ENDIF (chunk > 99)

   *-------------------- Handle second 2 digits.
   T = VAL(Ten)
   IF T > 0

      DO CASE

         *--------- Case 1: Handle even tens and teens.
         CASE (INT(T/10.0)=T/10.0) .OR. (T>9 .AND. T<20)
            English = English + U&Ten

         *--------- Case 2: Handle greater than 10,
         *--------- but not evenly divisible.
         CASE T > 9 .AND. (INT(T/10.0)#T/10.0)
            Ten = SUBSTR(Ten,1,1) +'0'
            English = English + U&Ten+' '+U&One

         *--------- Case 3: Handle less than 10.
         CASE T < 10
            English = English + U&One

      ENDCASE

   ENDIF (T > 0)

   *--------------- Add "Thousand" if necessary.
   IF Amount > 999.99 .AND. Counter = 1
      English = English +' THOUSAND '
   ENDIF (need to add "Thousand")

   *--------------- Prepare for pass through hundreds.
   Start = 4
   Counter = Counter + 1

ENDDO (while Counter < 3)

*--------------- Tack on cents.
IF INT(Amount) > 0
   English = English + " AND "
ENDIF

English = English + SUBSTR(String,8,2)+"/100"

*--------------- End procedure.
RETURN
```

Figure 21.14 – The Translat procedure file

If another procedure is already open, it must first be closed (CLOSE PRO-
CEDURE). The calling program must also contain the command

RESTORE FROM English

to get the English memory variables from the English.MEM file into memory. At the point where you need to translate a number to English, use the
following commands:

Mem_Amount = Amount

English = " "

DO Translat WITH Mem_Amount, English

(Amount is the name of the field that contains the dollar amount for the
check in the database.)

The sample program, Checks.PRG, shown in Figure 21.15, uses the

```
*********************************** Checks .PRG
*--------------- Sample program to write checks.
CLEAR
SET TALK OFF
SET SAFETY OFF

SET PROCEDURE TO Translat

*--------------- Save existing memory variables to THOUGHT,
*--------------- and bring in English-equivalent variables.
SAVE TO Thought
RESTORE FROM English

*------------- Use the Checks database.
USE Checks
INDEX ON Check_No TO CheckNos
?
? "First check to be printed will be ",Check_No
?
?
WAIT "Press any key to begin writing checks"

CLEAR
*SET PRINT ON
GO TOP
DO WHILE .NOT. EOF()

    *-------------------------- Translate Amount to English.
    M_Amount = Amount
    English = " "
    DO Translate WITH M_Amount,English

    *---------- Print the check (will require modification
    *---------- for most preprinted check formats).
    ? "                                       ",DTOC(Date)
    ?
    ? To_Whom,"      ",Amount
    ?
    ? English
    ?
    ?
    ?
    SKIP
ENDDO (not eof)
SET PRINT OFF
```

Figure 21.15 – *The Checks command file to print checks*

```
*--------------- Get rid of "English" memory
*--------------- variables, and bring back originals.
CLOSE PROCEDURE
CLEAR MEMORY
RESTORE FROM Thought
CLOSE DATABASES
RETURN
```

Figure 21.15 – *The Checks command file to print checks (continued)*

Translat procedure to print checks from the sample Checks database. Before running the Checks command file, be sure to create the Checks database and add some test data to it, so the program has a database to print from. And don't forget to create the English memory file first, too.

A Word-Wrap Procedure

In some programming situations, you might find that you want to use a fairly long Character field (up to 254 characters) in a database. You could use a Memo field, which automatically *word wraps* the string when displayed on the screen or printer. However, Memo fields do not allow searching, and they require a great deal of disk space. In this section, we'll develop a procedure that can word wrap any regular Character field using any right margin you wish.

Figure 21.16 shows the Wrap procedure. To create it, use the command MODIFY COMMAND ProcLib2 to create the ProcLib2 procedure file. Then type in the Wrap procedure as shown in Figure 21.16. To test the Wrap procedure, you can enter the command file shown in Figure 21.17 with the command MODIFY COMMAND WrapTest.

After entering both command files, type in the command DO WrapTest. The screen will ask that you enter a long character string (up to 254 characters) and a right margin. The Wrap procedure then displays the character string with a ragged right margin. Figure 21.18 shows a long string of word-wrapped text with a right margin of 35.

```
*********************************** ProcLib2.PRG
*
*---------- Procedure to word wrap long strings.
*---------- (with ragged right margin).
PROCEDURE Wrap
PARAMETERS String, Margin

*-------------------- Set up loop through string.
Length = LEN(TRIM(String))
DO WHILE Length > Margin
   Spot = Margin

   *------ Find blank nearest right margin (Spot).
   DO WHILE SUBSTR(String,Spot,1) # " "
      Spot = Spot - 1
   ENDDO (until blank space found)

   *---- Print portion, and assign rest to String.
   ? LEFT(String,Spot-1)
   String = SUBSTR(String,Spot+1,Length-Spot)
   Length = LEN(String)
ENDDO (while Length > Margin)

*--------- Print remainder of string, then return.
? String
RETURN
```

Figure 21.16 – The Wrap procedure in ProcLib2.PRG

```
*********************************** WrapTest.PRG
*------------ Program to test the word-wrap procedure.
SET TALK OFF
CLEAR

*------------ Open procedure file.
SET PROCEDURE TO ProcLib2

*------------ Get test data.
TestString=SPACE(254)
Right = 80
@ 2,1 SAY  "Type in any character string up to 254 characters:"
@ 4,2 GET TestString
@ 10,1 SAY "Enter right margin (up to 80) " GET Right
READ
?
?

DO Wrap WITH TestString,Right


CLOSE PROCEDURE
```

Figure 21.17 – The WrapTest command file

```
This is a long string typed in to
test the Wrap.PRG procedure.  The
right margin was set to 35, and
the procedure will break this
string between words to fit this
margin.  Any program can access
Wrap.PRG using the syntax DO Wrap
WITH <string>,<margin>.
```

Figure 21.18 – Sample long string with ragged right margin

The Wrap procedure can, of course, be included in any procedure file you wish. Once the procedure file is open, use this command:

DO Wrap WITH <string>, <margin>

(String is a memory variable containing the string to be wrapped, and margin is a number or variable representing the right margin.) The commands below word wrap a field named Abstract using a right margin of 72:

WrapString = Abstract
DO Wrap WITH WrapString,72

Handy Business Formulas

One of the beauties of procedure files is that in a sense they allow you to add new commands and functions to the dBASE language. For example, dBASE does not have a built-in capability to perform financial calculations such as future value, present value, or mortgage payment. But with the appropriate procedure file, you can add these calculations to dBASE.

Let's look at an example. Figure 21.19 shows a procedure file named BusProcs.PRG. It contains formulas for future value (FV), payment on a loan (PMT), and present value (PV).

To use the procedure file, you must first make the memory variables FV, PMT, and PV public by entering this command:

PUBLIC FV,PMT,PV

```
************************************** BusProcs .PRG
*------------- Procedures for calculating financial data.

*------------------- FV procedure calculates future value.
PROCEDURE FV
PARAMETERS Payment,Interest,Term
   FV = Payment * ((1+Interest)^Term-1)/Interest
RETURN

*------------- PMT procedure calculates payment on a loan.
PROCEDURE Pmt
PARAMETERS Principal, Interest, Term
    PMT = Principal * Interest/(1-1/(1+Interest)^Term)
RETURN

*---- PV procedure calculates present value of an annuity.
PROCEDURE PV
PARAMETERS Payment, Interest, Term
    PV = Payment * (1-1/(1+Interest)^Term)/Interest
RETURN
```

Figure 21.19 – The BusProcs procedure file

Next, open the procedure file using the SET PROCEDURE TO BusProcs command.

Now suppose you wanted to calculate the future value of an investment of equal monthly payments of $500.00, at an annual interest rate of 16 percent, for five years. The FV formula is calculated on the per-period interest rate, so you'll need to divide the annual interest rate by 12 (.16/12). Also, you'll need to multiply the number of years by 12 to reflect the true number of months (5 x 12). Perform this conversion in the WITH portion of the DO command by entering this command:

DO FV WITH 500,.16/12,5 * 12

To see the result of the calculation, enter the command

? FV

and dBASE displays the result:

45517.76

To calculate the payment of a loan of $15,000, at a 15 percent annual interest rate, for 10 years, use the PMT procedure. Again, you need to convert the interest rate to months (.15/12) and the years to months (10 x 12), so enter this command:

DO PMT WITH 15000,.15/12,10 * 12

To see the results of the calculation, type

? PMT

and dBASE displays the monthly payment for the loan:

242.00

To calculate the present value of equal, regular payments on a loan, use the PV procedure. For example, to calculate how large a loan you can pay off at $1,000 per month, at 12.5 percent annual interest, for 30 years, enter the following command:

DO PV WITH 1000,.125/12,30 * 12

Note that, once again, we've converted to monthly data (.125/12,30 * 12). To see the results of the calculations, enter

? PV

and dBASE displays

93698.07

which means that you can borrow $93,698.07 at $1,000 per month at 12.5 percent APR. When you are done with the procedure file, remember to close it.

You can access these formulas from any command file or dBASE system. Just be sure that either a menu, program, or general command file includes the commands

PUBLIC FV, PMT, PV
SET PROCEDURE TO BusProcs

to activate the procedure file.

Statistical Procedures

With procedure files, you can also add some statistical capabilities to dBASE III PLUS, such as highest value, lowest value, variance, and standard deviation. Figure 21.20 shows a procedure file named StatProc.PRG that contains formulas for these calculations. These formulas also provide for *filtering* equations.

```
**************************************** StatProc.PRG
*-------------- Procedures for calculating statistics

*------------------- Max finds largest value in field.
PROCEDURE Max
PARAMETERS FieldName,Condition
     SET FILTER TO &Condition
     GO TOP
     Max = -99999
     DO WHILE .NOT. EOF()
        IF &FieldName > Max
           Max = &FieldName
        ENDIF (&FieldName)
        SKIP
     ENDDO

     *-- Return to nonfilter condition.
     SET FILTER TO
RETURN

*------------------- Min finds smallest value in field.
PROCEDURE Min
PARAMETERS FieldName,Condition
     SET FILTER TO &Condition
     GO TOP
     Min = 9999999
     DO WHILE .NOT. EOF()
        IF &FieldName < Min
           Min = &FieldName
        ENDIF (&FieldName)
        SKIP
     ENDDO

     *-- Return to nonfilter condition.
     SET FILTER TO
RETURN

*------------------- Var finds the variance.
PROCEDURE Var
PARAMETERS FieldName,Condition
     SET FILTER TO &Condition
     GO TOP
     COUNT TO N
     SUM(&FieldName) TO TOT
     SUM(&FieldName ^2) TO TOTSq
     Correction = TOT^2/N
     Var = (TOTSq-Correction)/(n-1)

     *-- Return to nonfilter condition.
     SET FILTER TO
RETURN

*---------- Std finds the standard deviation.
PROCEDURE Std
PARAMETERS FieldName,Condition
     SET FILTER TO &Condition
     GO TOP
     COUNT TO N
     SUM(&FieldName) TO TOT
     SUM(&FieldName ^2) TO TOTSq
     Correction = TOT^2/N
     Variance = (TOTSq-Correction)/(n-1)
     Std = SQRT(Variance)

     *-- Return to nonfilter condition.
     SET FILTER TO
RETURN
```

Figure 21.20 – The StatProc procedure file

To test the procedure, we'll use a database called Test.DBF, which has the structure shown in Figure 21.21 and contains the records shown in Figure 21.22.

To use the statistical procedures, be sure to load the database on which you wish to perform calculations (use Test in this example). Then, make the Max, Min, Var, and Std variables public and open the StatProc procedure file:

PUBLIC Max,Min,Var,Std
SET PROCEDURE TO StatProc

```
Structure for database : C:Test.DBF

Field  Field name   Type        Width    Dec
    1  LNAME        Character      15
    2  FNAME        Character      10
    3  CITY         Character      15
    4  SALE         Numeric        10      2
    5  COMMISS      Numeric         5      3
```

Figure 21.21 – Structure of the Test database

```
 #   LNAME        FNAME        CITY              SALE COMMISS
 1   Adams        Andy         San Diego      1234.56   0.150
 2   Adams        Andy         San Diego       555.55   0.100
 3   Adams        Andy         San Diego       999.90   0.100
 4   Adams        Andy         San Diego      8765.43   0.200
 5   Johnson      Jeremy       Los Angeles     222.55   0.100
 6   Johnson      Jeremy       Los Angeles    1232.55   0.150
 7   Johnson      Jeremy       Los Angeles    6655.33   0.200
 8   Watson       Wanda        San Diego      5463.87   0.200
 9   Watson       Wanda        San Diego       765.33   0.100
10   Watson       Wanda        San Diego      9595.99   0.200
```

Figure 21.22 – Contents of the Test database

The general syntax for any statistical procedure is

DO <formula> WITH "<field name>", "<condition>"

For example, to find the largest value in the Sale field for San Diego residents, type the following command:

DO Max WITH "Sale", "City = 'San Diego' "

Note the use of the single quotation marks inside the double quotation marks. This is only necessary when the search condition involves a character field. To see the results of the calculation, enter the command

? Max

and dBASE responds with

9595.99

For San Diego residents, $9,595.99 is the largest sale.

Let's try another. Suppose you want to find the smallest commission for sales over $5,000. Enter the following command:

DO Min WITH "Commiss","Sale > 5000"

(Note the absence of single quotes in the "Sale > 5000" condition; Sale is a Numeric field.) To see the results, enter the command

? Min

dBASE responds with

0.200

indicating that 20 percent is the smallest commission on a sale over $5,000.

If you wish to get statistics on all the records in a database, substitute a blank space for the <condition> portion for the formula. For example, to find the smallest sale in the entire database, enter this command:

DO Min WITH "Sale", " "

To see the result, enter

? Min

and dBASE responds by displaying the smallest Sale amount in the entire database:

222.55

To calculate and see the variance of the Sale field for individuals with the last name "Adams", type

DO Var WITH "Sale","LName = 'Adams' "
? Var

dBASE then displays

15427762.96

To see the standard deviation (the square root of the variance), enter the command

? SQRT(Var)

or use the Std procedure, as below:

DO Std WITH "Sale","LName = 'Adams' "

Display the result with the command

? Std

and dBASE responds with

3927.82

When you are finished with the StatProc procedure file, close the procedure file as usual.

You can include the StatProc and BusProcs procedures in a single procedure file, thus making them all accessible simultaneously. In fact, you could include *all* of the procedures we've used in this book in a single procedure file, but watch out for MODIFY COMMAND's 4,000-line limit and the limitations of procedure files (32 procedures per file, maximum). Be sure to assign public variables as necessary.

Light-Bar Menus

You've no doubt noticed how the dBASE III PLUS Assistant allows you to select an item on the pull-down menu by either highlighting it or typing in the first letter of the menu option. You can create somewhat similar menus for your own dBASE applications. Figure 21.23 shows a sample *light-bar* menu that lets the user select an item by either moving the highlighter, using ↑ and ↓ and pressing Return, or typing the item number.

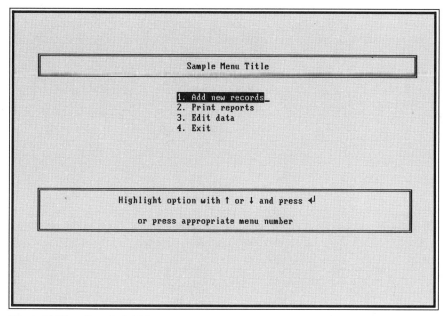

Figure 21.23 – Sample light-bar menu

The command file to display this menu is shown in Figure 21.24. Notice that the command file stores all menu items to the variables Opt1, Opt2, Opt3, and Opt4 in the following lines:

```
*------------- Create menu options (Opt1–Opt4).
Opt1 = "1. Add new records"
Opt2 = "2. Print reports"
Opt3 = "3. Edit data"
Opt4 = "4. Exit"
```

Then the program displays the menu items along with some instructions, graphic characters, and double-bar boxes:

```
*---------------------------- Display the menu.
@ 1,1 TO 3,79 DOUBLE
@ 2,32 SAY "Sample Menu Title"
@ 5,30 SAY Opt1
@ 6,30 SAY Opt2
@ 7,30 SAY Opt3
@ 8,30 SAY Opt4
```

```
***************************************** Menu.PRG
*    Sample menu with movable "light bar"
CLEAR
SET TALK OFF

*-------------- Create menu options (Opt1-Opt4).
Opt1="1. Add new records"
Opt2="2. Print reports"
Opt3="3. Edit data"
Opt4="4. Exit"

*----------------------------- Display the menu.
@ 1,1 TO 3,79 DOUBLE
@ 2,32 SAY "Sample Menu Title"
@ 5,30 SAY Opt1
@ 6,30 SAY Opt2
@ 7,30 SAY Opt3
@ 8,30 SAY Opt4

*- Display instructions with graphics characters.
@ 14,1 TO 18,78 DOUBLE
@ 15,18 SAY "Highlight option by using "
@ 15,40 SAY CHR(24)+" or "+CHR(25)+" and press ";
   +CHR(17)+CHR(217)
@ 17,22 SAY "or press appropriate menu number"


*------------------- Initialize memory variables.
Opt=1
Sub=STR(Opt,1)
KeyPress=0
Choice=0

*--------------------- Reverse-video on option 1.
@ 5,30 GET Opt1
CLEAR GETS

*--------------- Loop for selecting menu options.
DO WHILE Choice < 4

   *------------------------ Wait for a keypress.
   KeyPress=0
   DO WHILE KeyPress=0
      KeyPress=INKEY()
   ENDDO (KeyPress)


   *----------------------- Arrow key pressed.
   IF KeyPress=24 .OR. KeyPress=5
      @ Opt+4,30 SAY Opt&Sub
      Opt=IIF(KeyPress=24,Opt+1,Opt-1)
      Opt=IIF(Opt>4,1,Opt)
      Opt=IIF(Opt<1,4,Opt)
      Sub=STR(Opt,1)
      @ Opt+4,30 GET Opt&Sub
      CLEAR GETS
      LOOP
   ENDIF

   *---------------------- Option number entered.
   IF KeyPress >= 49 .AND. KeyPress <= 52
      Choice=KeyPress-48
   ENDIF

   *--------------------------- Return pressed.
   IF KeyPress=13
      Choice=Opt
   ENDIF
```

Figure 21.24 – Program to display a light-bar menu

```
        *-------------------- An option was selected.
        IF Choice > 0
           CLEAR
           ? "Choice=",Choice
           Choice=5
        ENDIF

     ENDDO (Choice)
```

Figure 21.24 – Program to display a light-bar menu (continued)

*- Display instructions with graphics characters.
@ 14,1 TO 18,78 DOUBLE
@ 15,18 SAY "Higlight option by using "
@ 15,40 SAY CHR(24) + " or " + CHR(25) + " and press ";
+ CHR(17) + CHR(217)
@ 17,22 SAY "or press appropriate menu number"

Several memory variables are initialized: Opt, which is the number of the option currently highlighted; Sub, the string equivalent of Opt; KeyPress, which stores the ASCII code of the user's keypress; and Choice, the menu item eventually selected:

*------------------ Initialize memory variables.
Opt = 1
Sub = STR(Opt,1)
KeyPress = 0
Choice = 0

Next the program uses the GET command to redisplay the menu choice in reverse video or the color set with the SET COLOR command. Immediately, the CLEAR GETS command disallows changes in the highlighted area, but the highlight remains:

*------------------ Reverse-video on option 1.
@ 5,30 GET Opt1
CLEAR GETS

A simple DO WHILE loop redisplays the menu until the user decides to exit:

*-------------- Loop for selecting menu options.
DO WHILE Choice < 4

A second DO WHILE loop waits for a keypress with the INKEY( ) function. INKEY( ) can intercept presses on noncharacter keys such as arrow keys. It stores a code representing the key pressed in the memory variable (Key-Press in this example):

```
*------------------------- Wait for a keypress.
KeyPress = 0
DO WHILE KeyPress = 0
    KeyPress = INKEY()
ENDDO (KeyPress)
```

If the user presses ↓ (24) or ↑ (5), the program redisplays the currently highlighted menu option with SAY (so the highlight disappears), then adds or subtracts one from the Opt number. IIF functions keep the highlighter in the range of one to four (for the four menu choices). The Sub variable, which receives the new value of Opt as a string, is used to display the next menu item with GET. (For example, if Opt = 4, then Sub = "4" and Opt&Sub becomes Opt4):

```
*------------------------- Arrow key pressed.
IF KeyPress = 24 .OR. KeyPress = 5
    @ Opt + 4,30 SAY Opt&Sub
    Opt = IIF(KeyPress = 24,Opt + 1,Opt – 1)
    Opt = IIF(Opt > 4,1,Opt)
    Opt = IIF(Opt < 1,4,Opt)
    Sub = STR(Opt,1)
    @ Opt + 4,30 GET Opt&Sub
    CLEAR GETS
    LOOP
ENDIF
```

If a number between one and four is entered (which uses the code 49, 50, 51, or 52) the variable Choice is assigned the appropriate value by subtracting 48 from the KeyPress code:

```
*---------------------- Option number entered.
IF KeyPress > = 49 .AND. KeyPress < = 52
    Choice = KeyPress – 48
ENDIF
```

If the user presses Return (13), the Choice variable is assigned the current value of Opt:

```
*------------------------- Return pressed.
IF KeyPress = 13
    Choice = Opt
ENDIF
```

At this point, the variable Choice will have some value greater than zero only if the user selected an item (rather than pressing an arrow key). In an actual menu program, a DO CASE clause would then be used to branch to the selected command file. Here, the sample program merely displays the user's choice:

```
*-------------------- An option was selected.
IF Choice > 0
    CLEAR
    ? "Choice = ",Choice
    Choice = 5
ENDIF
```

The menu repeats until the user selects Exit:

```
ENDDO (Choice)
```

Some of the codes used with INKEY() are displayed in Table 21.1. You can also enter the small command file below, run it, and press any key to see the INKEY() code for that key:

```
* * * * * * * * * * * * * * * * * * * * * * * * * * * * * * * InKey.PRG
CLEAR
@ 5,5 SAY "Press any key to see code "
@ 7,5 SAY "(Ctrl-key combinations work too)"
?
KeyPress = 0
DO WHILE KeyPress = 0
    KeyPress = INKEY()
ENDDO
?
? "The code for that key is ",KeyPress
```

Noncharacter Keys	Equivalent Ctrl Key	INKEY() Code
↑	Ctrl-E	5
↓	Ctrl-X	24
→	Ctrl-D	4
←	Ctrl-S	19
Ins	Ctrl-V	22
Del	Ctrl-G	7
Home	Ctrl-A	1
End	Ctrl-F	6
PgUp	Ctrl-R	18
PgDn	Ctrl-C	3

Table 21.1 – INKEY() codes for special keys

Well, that brings us to the end of our tour of dBASE III PLUS programming techniques and business applications. I hope the experience has been rewarding and that you're now as enthusiastic about this powerful software package as I am. Try out some ideas of your own, and don't be afraid to experiment. You can't hurt anything, and you could very well come up with a slick new solution to an old problem.

Runtime + and Compilers

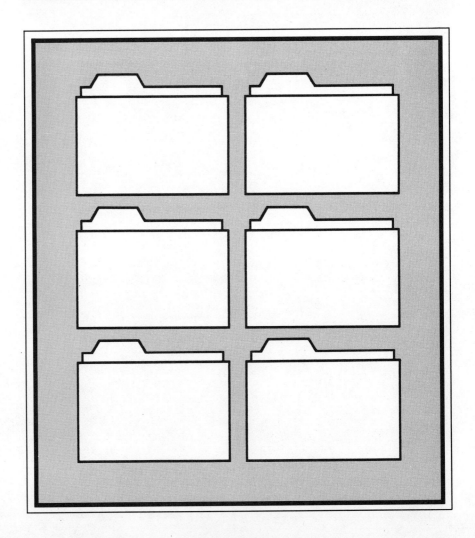

In this appendix we'll discuss topics that are primarily of interest to those who either are considering marketing the programs they create or need maximum speed and performance in their custom dBASE III PLUS systems. We'll discuss two different types of marketing aids: the RunTime + package provided by Ashton-Tate and the compilers offered by third-party companies.

RunTime +, which is included in your dBASE III PLUS package, allows you to encrypt your command files, improve their speed slightly, and market your programs to people who do not own dBASE III PLUS. (Your potential customers can buy dBRUN at a reduced cost to run your system.)

The compilers, discussed later in this appendix, allow you to convert your programs to machine language instructions. This also makes it impossible for unauthorized persons to tamper with your original programs. Furthermore, the compilers offer significant improvement in speed and complete independence from dBASE III PLUS and dBRUN. Your potential customers can run your programs directly from the DOS prompt. (In fact, with the compilers, you don't even need dBASE III PLUS to create the programs.)

RunTime +

RunTime + consists of two programs that come with your dBASE III PLUS package: dBCODE and dBLINKER. dBCODE will encrypt your command files so that unauthorized users cannot access the original command files (called *source code*). dBLINKER can combine several command files (*not* procedure files) into a single large file that is more compact and runs a bit more quickly than standard dBASE III PLUS programs.

Command files that are encrypted with dBCODE (and optionally combined with dBLINKER) can be run either from dBASE III PLUS directly or from a separate product named dBRUN. This means that you can market your custom system to users who do not own dBASE III PLUS. Instead, the potential customer can purchase a copy of dBRUN from Ashton-Tate at a reduced cost. This might make your product more appealing to those who wish to use only your custom system, without going to the added expense of purchasing dBASE III PLUS.

To use dBCODE and dBLINKER, you need to move files around and create new directories. A good understanding of basic DOS file management techniques is a must, but we'll work through an example here that covers every step. Keep in mind that dBCODE and dBLINKER are run from the DOS prompt, so you need not have dBASE III PLUS running or even available until you have completely encrypted the command files.

Let's encrypt the Membership System we developed earlier in this book, just to get a feel for how RunTime + works. Recall that the Membership System consists of the command files Members.PRG, AddNew.PRG, Reports.PRG, EditDel.PRG, and DupCheck.PRG. (There are also format, label, and report files, but these are excluded from the encryption process. The optional PrintDir program can be included, if you've created it, because it is a command file.)

Creating the Directories

Create two directories named Source and RunTime on either your hard disk or a blank, formatted disk in drive B. On a hard disk, log onto your root directory and enter these commands from the DOS C> prompt (remember to press Return after typing each command):

```
MD\Source
MD\RunTime
```

On a floppy-disk system, log onto drive A and at the DOS A> prompt enter these commands:

MD B:\Source
MD B:\RunTime

Copying the Command Files

Next, you need to copy all the files that you want to encrypt to the Source directory. First log onto the Source directory. On a hard disk, enter this command:

CD\Source

On a floppy disk, enter these commands:

B:
CD\Source

To help keep track of where you are, enter the command PROMPT PG at the DOS prompt. The DOS prompt will show both the currently logged drive and the directory (for example, C:\Source> or B:\Source>).

Next you need to use the DOS COPY command to copy all the .PRG files to the Source directory. If *only* the Membership System command files are on the disk or directory you are copying from, you can enter the command

COPY C:*.PRG *.SRC

On a floppy-disk system, enter this command:

COPY A:*.PRG *.SRC

This will copy *all* the .PRG files from drive C (or drive A) onto the Source directory and change the file name extensions to .SRC (which dBCODE requires). If you are using a hard disk and the .PRG files are stored on a separate directory, include the directory name in the COPY command. For example, the command below copies all the .PRG files from a directory named DB onto the Source directory and renames them to .SRC:

COPY C:\DB*.PRG *.SRC

If there are more than just the Membership System command files on the disk you are copying from, you must copy the files individually. On a hard disk, where the command files are stored on a directory named DB, enter these commands:

```
COPY  C:\DB\Members.PRG
COPY  C:\DB\AddNew.PRG
COPY  C:\DB\Reports.PRG
COPY  C:\DB\EditDel.PRG
COPY  C:\DB\DupCheck.PRG
COPY  C:\DB\PrintDir.PRG
RENAME  *.PRG  *.SRC
```

(If you are not using the PrintDir.PRG program, don't copy it.) The last command, RENAME, changes the extension of all .PRG files to .SRC, which dBCODE requires.

On a floppy-disk system, enter these commands:

```
COPY  A:Members.PRG
COPY  A:AddNew.PRG
COPY  A:Reports.PRG
COPY  A:EditDel.PRG
COPY  A:DupCheck.PRG
COPY  A:PrintDir.PRG
RENAME  *.PRG  *.SRC
```

(Again, leave out PrintDir.PRG if you're not using that program.) While still logged onto the Source directory, enter the DIR command to ensure that the .SRC files are there.

If you are confused about how to use COPY and RENAME, read up on the DOS MKDIR, CHDIR, COPY, and RENAME commands in your DOS manual. It will be time well spent.

Incidentally, if you develop a system in the future that you know you are going to encrypt, you can save a little time by naming the files with identical leading characters (for instance, MemMenu.PRG, MemAdd.PRG, MemRep.PRG, MemEdit.PRG, MemDup.PRG). That way you can use a single command such as

```
COPY  C:\DB\:Mem*.PRG  Mem*.SRC
```

to copy and rename all the appropriate files.

When all the necessary .PRG files are copied to the Source directory and renamed to .SRC extensions, you are ready to create a response file.

Creating a Response File

A *response file* is an ASCII text file that contains the names of the command files to encrypt. You can use any word processor (with a non-document mode), line editor, the dBASE III PLUS MODIFY COMMAND editor, or even the DOS COPY CON command to create this file. The response file must have the extension .RSP, and it must list the root command file (usually the main menu) first. In this example we'll name the response file MemProgs.RSP. Probably the easiest way to create the response file is to stay logged onto the Source directory and enter the command

COPY CON MemProgs.RSP

Then carefully type in the names of the command files to encrypt, without the .PRG extensions. Be sure to list the root (main menu) program, Members, first. Also, be sure to press Return after typing in each file name, *including* the last file name. (Leave out PrintDir if you're not using it.) To save the file, press F6 (or ^Z) after typing in all the file names. Your screen should look like this when you're done:

COPY CON MemProgs.RSP
Members
AddNew
Reports
EditDel
DupCheck
PrintDir
^Z
    1 File(s) copied

To verify that the .RSP file exists, enter this command at the DOS prompt:

TYPE MemProgs.RSP

You should see the Membership System file names appear on the screen. If you use a word processor to create the .RSP file, be sure to copy it to the Source directory and to use CD\Source to log onto the Source directory again when done.

Copying RunTime +

Your next task is to find the dBCODE and dBLINKER programs (named DBC.COM and DBL.COM) on your dBASE III PLUS Utilities disk and copy them to the Source directory. While still logged onto the Source directory, put the appropriate dBASE III PLUS disk in drive A and enter the following command:

COPY A:DB?.COM

You should see the message

2 file(s) copied

(If you don't, try a different dBASE III PLUS disk in drive A.) When the copy is successful, you're ready to use dBCODE to encrypt the command files. (NOTE: You can run the RunTime+ programs from any disk or directory. We've copied them in this example only to simplify matters.)

Using dBCODE

The general syntax for using dBCODE at the DOS prompt is

DBC -r<response file> -s\<source> -o\<runtime>

where <response file> is the name of the .RSP file, <source> is the name of the source directory, and <runtime> the name of the runtime directory. In this example, stay logged onto the Source directory and enter the command

DBC -rMemProgs.RSP -s\Source\ -o\RunTime

You'll see a copyright notice and the names of files appear on the screen as the encryption progresses. When done, the DOS prompt will reappear.

Verifying the Encryption

To verify that the command files have been encrypted, log onto the Run-Time directory with the following command:

CD\RUNTIME

Then enter the DIR command to verify that all the command files are there. (The encrypted files will have the extension .PRG.) Now enter the command

TYPE Members.PRG

to view the Members command file. You'll see encrypted code that appears to be nonsense; nobody will be able to tamper with it to suit their own

purposes. Your original .PRG command files are still on the original disk or
directory.

Caution: Never copy these encrypted .PRG files to the disk or directory
that contains your original command files. The encrypted files will overwrite the originals, and even you won't be able to access your original command files! To play it safe, you might want to make extra backups of your
command files when working with dBCODE.

Now you could stop at this point and market the encrypted files in this
format. You can run these encrypted files with either dBASE III PLUS or
dBRUN. However, you might as well go ahead and link the encrypted files
into a single file with dBLINKER.

Using dBLINKER

The dBLINKER program (DBL.COM) provides several options in the command line. To see these options, log onto the Source directory again with
this command:

    CD\Source

Then enter the command

    DBL ?

You'll see the copyright notice and the options as listed below:

    dBLINKER (2.05) MS-DOS/PC-DOS * * *
    COPYRIGHT (c) ASHTON-TATE 1984, 1985.
    AS AN UNPUBLISHED LICENSED PROPRIETARY WORK.
    ALL RIGHTS RESERVED.
    dBASE III RunTime + Linker
    Usage: dbl [-cfile -foutfile -i[prefix] -p -rfile -sprefixfile...]
      FLAGS (order arbitrarily, don't concatenate!)
      -c ASCII copyright header file
      -f output filename (.prg)
      -i generate information file (.map)
      -p prefix significant in filename compare
      -r response file
      -s source directory
      file . . .   dBCODE code file(s) (.prg)

The optional -c flag allows you to put a copyright notice in your program.
To do so, you must first create an ASCII text file with the extension .HDR.

Again, use a word processor or the COPY CON command, and place the file on the Source directory.

The optional -i flag will create an information file, which we'll demonstrate in a moment. The required -f flag contains the name of the linked file, -r contains the name of the response file, and -s contains the name of the source directory.

For this example, we'll use a simple linking command. At the DOS prompt (on the Source directory) enter the following command:

DBL -rMemProgs.RSP -fMail -s\RunTime\ -i

This command line specifies MemProgs.RSP as the response file, Mail as the name for the linked files, RunTime as the directory containing the encrypted files to be linked, and -i to create an information file. You'll see the dBLINKER copyright notice appear, the names of the command files as they are linked, and the DOS prompt when done.

Caution: dBLINKER cannot link procedure files. If your system uses a procedure file, eliminate its name from the response file before using dBLINKER. The procedure file must be included on the disk that you plan to market, but it must be separate from the linked files.

To verify the link, enter the command

DIR Mail. *

at the DOS prompt (while still on the Source directory). You should see (at least) the file names Mail.PRG, the file containing all the linked, encrypted files for the Membership System, and Mail.MAP, the information file. If you attempt to list the Mail.PRG file, you'll see only encrypted code. You can use the TYPE command to list the Mail.MAP file to see the contents of the information file, which shows the names of the original .PRG files and the calling relationships among them.

Testing the Encrypted File

You can run the Mail.PRG file directly from the dBASE III PLUS dot prompt. First you need to copy Mail.PRG from the Source directory to the disk or directory containing dBASE III PLUS and all the database, index, format, label, and report files for the Membership System. (Copy *only* the linked file, Mail.PRG, not the encrypted .PRG files on the RunTime directory!)

Once you have Mail.PRG and the various other files associated with the Membership System together on a disk or directory, run dBASE III PLUS in the usual manner to get to the dot prompt, and use SET DEFAULT to set up a default drive if necessary. Then just enter the command

DO Mail

to run the program. The Membership System will run just as it did before, except that rather than accessing the original .PRG command files, dBASE III PLUS will use only the linked, encrypted files in Mail.PRG. When it comes time to distribute your custom system, be sure to leave the original .PRG files off of the distribution disk (unless you want the users to have access to the original source code).

If you attempt to use dBASE TYPE or MODIFY COMMAND to view or edit the Mail.PRG command file, you'll find that these files are invisible! (If you do use MODIFY COMMAND, use ^Q to abandon Mail.PRG. Don't save it after calling it into the MODIFY COMMAND editor.)

Marketing Your Creation

When it comes time to distribute or market your work, be sure to copy all the associated database (.DBF), index (.NDX), report-format (.FRM), label (.LBL), format (.FMT), and any procedure (.PRG) files associated with the system to a floppy disk.

To be sure that you haven't forgotten any files or left any bugs in the system, test every feature in the system before you start distributing. Any errors that slip by at this point will certainly come back to haunt you later.

Be sure to include some documentation that explains to the customer how to use the system, as well as instructions for making backups. You should also contact Ashton-Tate about the dBRUN program, so that you can market the product to customers who do not own dBASE III PLUS.

Needless to say, you can't encrypt and market any of the systems presented in this book. These are part of a published work to which SYBEX owns the copyright. Therefore, any unauthorized redistribution of the command files presented here would be a copyright infringement.

RunTime + Limitations

Before using RunTime+ for serious work, make sure you understand its limitations and rules thoroughly. Refer to the appropriate sections in the dBASE III PLUS manual. In this section, we'll just summarize the important rules and limitations.

Illegal Commands

RunTime+ cannot process these commands:

    SET
    ASSIST
    HELP

The SET command without any parameters is the only illegal SET command. You can use SET with specific parameters such as SET COLOR and SET DEFAULT. RunTime+ will, however, ignore the following SET commands:

    SET DEBUG
    SET DOHISTORY
    SET ECHO
    SET STEP
    SET SUSPEND

File Size Restrictions

Clause commands, such as DO WHILE, IF, and DO CASE, must fit within 32K of space. With this restriction, you can encrypt files of any size.

Macro Resrictions

You cannot use macros as command verbs or as SET parameters. For example, the sequence

    Z = "LIST"
    &Z LName, FName, Address

is illegal because LIST is a command verb. The sequence

    Z = "TALK"
    SET &Z OFF

is illegal because TALK is a SET parameter.

You can use macros in the DO command only if the file you are calling is *not* linked. It must be external to the linked programs. For example, the sequence

    ProgNam = "PrintDir"
    DO &ProgNam

is legal only if PrintDir.PRG is external to the linked programs. (It can, however, still be encrypted.)

All other uses of macros are legal. For example, the sequence

```
PMacro = "TO PRINT"
REPORT FORM Director &PMacro
```

is legal because "TO PRINT" is neither a command verb (the first word on a line) nor a SET parameter, and it is not used as a file name.

Procedure Files

As mentioned earlier, procedure files cannot be linked with dBLINKER. They can be encrypted with dBCODE, but they must be excluded from the linking process. Be sure to put a copy of the procedure file (encrypted or not) on the distribution disk so that the linked files can find it.

Compilers

Compilers offer the programmer who is considering marketing his software many advantages. These advantages are listed briefly here:

1. Better performance: Compiled dBASE programs run up to 20 times faster than dBASE command files (though in most applications, the increased speed will not be quite so dramatic).

2. Stand-alone performance: Since a compiled program can be run directly from the DOS A > or C > prompt, a potential user need not own dBASE III PLUS or dBRUN. The compiled programs are completely independent.

3. Program security: Since the compiled version of a dBASE command file contains only machine language commands, unauthorized users cannot access the original dBASE program.

4. More power: The compilers include additional commands and functions that the original dBASE language does not offer. (However, they generally lack some commands as well, such as BROWSE and EDIT.)

At the time this book was written, there were two compilers available for dBASE III. (Both were still in the stage of upgrading to dBASE III PLUS, so some of the information presented in this appendix is probably changing as you read.)

The compilers are dBlll Compiler, manufactured by WordTech Systems in Orinda, CA, and Clipper, manufactured by Nantucket in Culver City, CA. We'll discuss both compilers in this appendix. But first, let's talk about assembly language, machine language, and compilation to get some background.

High-Level Languages, Low-Level Languages, and Compilers

Figure A.1 shows a dBASE III PLUS command file that can display all the ASCII characters, with a space between each, on the screen. The command file takes up about 215 bytes of disk space, and it takes about 22 seconds to run. However, since you need to have dBASE readily available to run the program, the actual disk space required to run this program is closer to 451,275 bytes (or 440K).

Figure A.2 shows the same program written in assembly language. The leftmost column contains commands for the assembler, and the middle column contains the assembly language proper (starting at the mov cx,100h command, and ending at the int 20h command); the lines preceded

```
*----------------------- ASCII.PRG
*----------------------- Display all ASCII codes.
SET TALK OFF
Counter = 0
DO WHILE Counter <= 255
   ?? CHR(Counter)+" "
   Counter = Counter + 1
ENDDO (Counter = 0)
```

Figure A.1 – dBASE program to display ASCII codes

```
;----------------------- ASCII.ASM
;----------------------- Display all ASCII codes
prog      segment            ;start of segment
          assume cs:prog     ;assume code segment

          org 100h           ;originate location counter
start:    mov cx,100h        ;start counter at 256 dec.
          mov dl,0           ;start with 0 ASCII character
next:     mov ah,2           ;call DOS Output function
          int 21h            ;call to DOS function
          push dx            ;save last value in dx
          mov dl,20h         ;put in ASCII space
          int 21h            ;call DOS function
          pop dx             ;get back last dx value
          inc dl             ;next ASCII character
          loop next          ;repeat until done
          int 20h            ;return to DOS

prog      ends               ;end of segment
          end start          ;end of assembly
```

Figure A.2 – Assembly language program to display ASCII codes

with semicolons (;) are programmer comments. Even though the sample dBASE and assembly programs perform exactly the same task, they obviously look very different.

Before you can run the assembly language program, you need to *assemble* it into *machine language*. The IBM ASM or MASM assemblers will take care of that process for you. Figure A.3 shows the assembly program after assembling it into machine language.

There are two very big advantages to the assembly language version of the ASCII program: it uses up only 21 bytes of disk space, as opposed to 451,275 bytes in dBASE, and it takes only about 1 second to run, as opposed to 22 seconds in dBASE. That's about 22 times faster using about 1/20,000 of the disk space.

The big disadvantage to assembly language is that it is difficult to learn, read, and produce. While dBASE has many English-like commands, such as APPEND, EDIT, UPDATE, and so forth, assembly language has only very primitive commands like mov, int, push, and pop. Assembly language has no built-in commands for managing data files or even screen displays. To

```
B90001
B200
B402
CD21
52
B220
CD21
5A
FEC2
E2F2
CD20
```

Figure A.3 – Machine language program to display ASCII codes

produce an assembly language program that performs what dBASE does with a single command (such as INDEX) could take days or even weeks.

The compromise between dBASE and assembly language is a compiler. A compiler takes your dBASE command file(s) and makes a copy that is, in essence, written in assembly language. Like all assembly language programs, the compiled programs can be run directly from the DOS prompt.

When you run a dBASE program, the computer needs lots of help translating the English-like dBASE commands into machine language. That extra help is a big program named dBASE III PLUS (or dBRUN). dBASE contains an interpreter that reads a single line from your dBASE program, checks it for errors, translates it to machine language, and then executes it. It repeats this process for every line in the command file. All these steps take time, and hence the program runs relatively slowly.

An assembled (machine language) program requires no overhead and no translation. The computer (with the help of DOS) can read and execute the program immediately. You just type in the name of the program at the DOS A> or C> prompt, and the program runs.

A compiled program is never quite as efficient as one that is actually written in assembly language. But then again, it's much easier to write a program in dBASE and compile it (using two simple commands) than it is to write a program in assembly language. Therefore, the compiler acts as sort of a compromise between the convenience of·a high-level language (like dBASE) and the efficiency of a low-level language (like assembly language). Table A.1 compares the size and speed of a program written and

	dBASE III PLUS	Clipper Compiled	Assembly Language
Seconds	??	10	1.5
Bytes	451,275	127,872	22

Table A.1 – Comparison of dBASE, compiled, and assembly programs

executed with dBASE, a compiled copy of the program (using the Clipper compiler), and the assembly language version of the program.

The In-Between Languages

At the risk of digressing, I might mention that there are many languages between the high-level dBASE and low-level assembly language. Such languages do not generally offer an interpreter at all. You write your program using a text editor (like WordStar), and then you must compile it to run it. Furthermore, these languages generally don't offer the high-level file and screen handling features of dBASE, such as INDEX, @, SET FILTER, and so forth. You have to write such routines yourself or purchase them from somebody who has already taken the time to do so.

The mid-level languages have the (perhaps familiar) names of C, Pascal, CB86, CBASIC, COBOL, FORTRAN, and many others. (In fact, there are about 250 documented programming languages floating about.)

Languages that are designed to be compiled generally compile and run more efficiently. For example, a sample program to display all the ASCII characters, written in CB86, (a compiled language with a syntax similar to BASIC) is shown in Figure A.4.

When compiled, this program takes up 8,074 bytes of disk space (about 8K), and it takes about 3 seconds to run. The same program written in C or Pascal would probably run faster and require less disk space (depending on the particular compiler used).

Why are there so many languages? Well, different languages are good for different things. Assembly language is especially well suited for writing real-time software to control external machines that require critical timing.

```
REM --------------------------- ASCII.BAS
REM ------ Program to display ASCII codes.
FOR X% = 0 TO 255
    PRINT CHR$(X%);" ";
NEXT X%
```

Figure A.4 – *CB86 version of ASCII program*

The C language is generally used for writing operating systems (like UNIX), compilers, spreadsheets, word processors, and database management systems (dBASE is written in C). Languages like Pascal are also good for writing word processors and database managers, but they are high level enough to write applications software like general ledger and payroll.

Database managers, like dBASE, are specifically designed for writing business applications software. Of course, there is considerable overlap in the uses of the languages, but suffice it to say that one would not likely write a payroll system in C or assembly language. The long development time would not justify the quicker runtime speed.

Another class of languages is designed for artificial intelligence applications. LISP and PROLOG fall into this category and are used for Expert Systems and other programs that mimic human thinking and learning. LISP is an acronym for *list processor*, and PROLOG is an acronym for *programming in logic*. Most versions of LISP are interpretive (like dBASE). Turbo PROLOG, by Borland, is compilable.

But enough digression. Now that we have an idea about high- and low-level languages and what compilers are all about, let's get down to more specifics.

The Clipper Compiler

The Clipper compiler allows you to compile any command file or group of command files from the dBASE .PRG to the DOS .EXE executable format. Because Clipper is a true *native code* compiler (which means it generates EXE files that require no further interpretation), significant increases in speed are virtually guaranteed. (The last section in this appendix provides examples of performance improvements.) Clipper is copy protected (though, of course, the programs you compile with it are not).

Complete compilation of a command file requires two commands. First, to compile a program named Test1.PRG, you would enter the following command:

CLIP Test1

The second step is to link the compiled program using the command

PLINK86 FILE Test1

Optionally, you can use a batch file provided with Clipper to compile and link the program with this single command:

CL Test1

Compilation and linking time on a small program (about 10 lines of code) is a little under four minutes.

You can compile and link groups of command files, procedure files, and *user-defined functions.* (A user-defined function is similar to a normal dBASE function such as TRIM() or RECNO(), except that it is a function you create and define yourself.)

At the time this book was written, Clipper was still being updated to include new dBASE III PLUS commands and functions. Therefore, be sure to check with Nantucket for the latest information.

Clipper Enhancements

In several respects, Clipper provides more flexibility than dBASE III PLUS. Clipper allows up to 2,048 memory variables, 1,024 fields per record, and up to eight children to one parent in a SET RELATION definition (as opposed to one in dBASE). Clipper also provides the capability to add custom help screens that the user can access by pressing F1.

Clipper also allows you to store Memo fields in memory variables, which means that you can search and manipulate the Memo field. Clipper provides liberal use of macros, including macros as conditions in DO WHILE loops and recursive macros. Macros cannot be used in place of commands (like USE, LIST, DISPLAY, and so forth).

User-defined functions provide more flexibility than procedures. For example, in Chapter 21, we created some business procedures that could accept parameters such as

DO PMT WITH (150000,.16/12,30 * 12)

In Clipper, you could easily change the procedure into a user-defined function and treat it as you would any other function, using the syntax

Payment = PMT(15000,.16/12,30 * 12)

or

? PMT(15000,.16/12,30 * 12)

During editing on a screen, Clipper allows the user to press Ctrl-U to undo a change. For example, if during editing the user changes the part number from A-111 to Z-999, typing Ctrl-U immediately converts the part number back to A-111.

Clipper can call assembly language subroutines with up to seven parameters (as opposed to one in dBASE). Clipper can save and restore screens displayed with @ SAY commands, so that they "pop up" on the screen instantly.

The Clipper DECLARE statement allows you to use arrays (subscripted variables) in your programs, such as the following:

DECLARE Day[7]
Day[1] = "Sunday"
Day[2] = "Monday"
Day[3] = "Tuesday"
Day[4] = "Wednesday"
Day[5] = "Thursday"
Day[6] = "Friday"
Day[7] = "Saturday"

Once declared, you can use numbers to access the array elements. For example,

? Day[3]

displays Tuesday. If variable XYZ = 7, then the command

? DAY[XYZ]

displays Saturday. An array can contain up to 2,048 elements.

Clipper Functions

All of the dBASE III PLUS functions are supported by Clipper, though some are supported through an external file that you must link into your compiled program. (This is easily achieved.) Clipper contains some additional functions that dBASE III PLUS does not include:

ALLTRIM()	Trims both leading and trailing blanks from a character string.
AMPM()	Displays time based on a 12-hour clock with "am" or "pm".
DAYS()	Calculates days based on a number of seconds.
DTOS()	Converts a date to yyyymmdd format as a character string (e.g. 19861201). This is very useful for combining dates and character strings in index files.
ELAPTIME()	Calculates elapsed time between two times.
EMPTY()	Returns True (.T.) if a variable or expression is blank.
LENNUM()	Returns the length of a number.
PROCLINE()	Returns the line number of the current program or procedure file.
PROCNAME()	Returns the name of the current program or procedure file.
SECS()	Returns the number of seconds in a time string.
SOUNDEX()	Returns the Soundex code for a word, which helps find data of similar sound but different spelling.
STRZERO()	String equivalent of a number with leading zeros rather than leading blanks.
TSTRING()	Converts seconds to a time string.
UPDATED()	Returns True if a value was changed during a READ command.

Clipper Commands

Most of the general programming commands from dBASE III Developer's Release are supported by Clipper. However, commands that are unique to dBASE III PLUS were not fully supported at the time this book was written.

The following commands are not supported by Clipper. Again, keep in mind that some of this information is likely to change with future releases of Clipper. As we'll discuss in a moment, most of the listed commands are excluded because they are virtually useless in a compiled program:

APPEND *	ON <key>,<escape>,<error>
ASSIST	RELEASE MODULE
BROWSE	RETRY
CHANGE	RETURN TO MASTER
CLEAR FIELDS	SET
CLEAR TYPEAHEAD	SET CARRY
CREATE <filename> * *	SET DATE
CREATE/MODIFY LABEL	SET DEBUG
CREATE/MODIFY QUERY	SET DOHISTORY
CREATE/MODIFY REPORT	SET ECHO
CREATE/MODIFY SCREEN	SET FIELDS
CREATE/MODIFY VIEW	SET HEADING
DISPLAY/LIST HISTORY	SET HELP
DISPLAY/LIST FILES	SET HISTORY
DISPLAY/LIST MEMORY	SET MEMOWIDTH
DISPLAY/LIST STATUS	SET MENUS
DISPLAY/LIST STRUCTURE	SET ORDER
EDIT	SET SAFETY
EXPORT	SET STATUS
HELP	SET STEP
IMPORT	SET TITLE
INSERT	SET TYPEAHEAD
LOAD	SET VIEW
MODIFY COMMAND	SET TALK
MODIFY STRUCTURE	SUSPEND

* APPEND FROM and APPEND BLANK are supported.
* * CREATE <NewFile> FROM <OldFile> is supported.

Debugging Commands

The dBASE III PLUS debugging commands (such as SET ECHO and SET DEBUG) are not supported by Clipper for two reasons. First, you wouldn't want to compile a program until it was fully tested and debugged. (If it didn't work in dBASE III, it isn't going to work in Clipper.) Secondly, Clipper has its own debugger to help you debug compiled programs.

Create/Modify Commands

Generally, you create and modify database files, format files, report formats, and label formats while you are creating your custom system. Rarely would you ever include a CREATE or MODIFY command in your finished custom system.

Keep in mind that Clipper does support the DO, REPORT FORM, LABEL FORM, SET FORMAT, and USE commands, so that the compiled program can access previously created command, report, mailing label, format, and database files. In addition, Clipper provides utilities that allow you to create the various format files, and therefore you need not even use dBASE III PLUS to create them.

Full-Screen Operations

Commands such as APPEND, EDIT, BROWSE, and INSERT are not supported, partly because most systems use custom screens rather than standard dBASE screens. You can use SET FORMAT and READ, instead, to provide editing capabilities to the user.

dBASE III PLUS Commands

Features that are unique to dBASE III PLUS, such as query forms, catalogs, and view files, were not supported by Clipper at the time this book was written. Similarly, unique commands such as CLEAR TYPEAHEAD, SET MEMOWIDTH, and SET FIELDS are not supported yet, but may well be in a future release of Clipper.

Index Files

Clipper creates its own index files with the extension .NTX. After creating your database, you can run a special Clipper utility to create index files directly from the DOS prompt. Also, if a command file should contain an INDEX ON command, Clipper will create the .NTX index file rather than the dBASE .NDX index file.

The PUBLIC Clipper command

Now you may be wondering how one goes about working with dBASE programs that contain features unique to Clipper. A simple and elegant solution to this problem is the PUBLIC Clipper command. You can place the command

PUBLIC Clipper

near the top of any command file. dBASE will create the variable Clipper, assigning it the value False (.F.). (dBASE always initializes PUBLIC memory variables as False.) Then, you can place Clipper-specific commands inside IF statements. For example, since dBASE uses .NDX for index file names and Clipper uses .NTX, you could enter a routine such as the following:

```
PUBLIC Clipper
IF Clipper
   USE MyFile INDEX MyFile.NTX
ELSE
   USE MyFile INDEX MyFile.NDX
ENDIF
```

dBASE III PLUS will use the .NDX file.

Unlike dBASE III PLUS, Clipper always sets the PUBLIC Clipper variable to True (.T.) when it first encounters it. (It does this *only* with the variable specifically named "Clipper".) Therefore, the compiled version of the routine would use the .NTX index file.

dBIII Compiler

dBIII Compiler, manufactured by WordTech Systems Inc. of Orinda, CA, is more of a *pseudocompiler* than a true compiler. Rather than generating true machine language (or assembly language), the compiler generates a form of pseudocode that is much closer to machine language than dBASE is. (WordTech, however, is planning on releasing a "true compiler" in the summer of 1986.)

dBIII Compiler comes with several optional *linkers* that allow you to be specific about the type of machine the compiled program will run on. You can select from among PC-DOS machines (IBM PC and 100 percent compatible) and MS-DOS machines (any MS-DOS machine, including the IBM PC). There is also an option that allows the compiled program to use both dBASE II and dBASE III data.

Full compilation is a simple two-step process. For example, to compile a program named Test1.PRG, enter this command:

dB3C Test1.PRG

Then, to link the compiled file into a DOS-executable .EXE file, enter the command

dB3L Test1

Total compilation time for a small program with 10 lines of code is about 55 seconds. The end result is three files with the extensions .EXE, .OVL, and .DBC, which can be run directly from the DOS prompt.

Even if your custom system consists of a dozen command (.PRG) and format (.FMT) files, it can be compiled into these three files automatically. dBIII Compiler will use the DO and SET FORMAT commands already in the custom system to combine the required command and format files automatically.

dBIII Compiler Enhancements

dBIII Compiler offers several features that are not available in dBASE III PLUS. One is the SET DEVICE TO ALTERNATE command. This allows a program to store text printed with @ . . . SAY commands on a file. (dBASE III PLUS allows @ . . . SAY commands to be displayed on the screen or printer only.) Similarly, the SET FEED command allows the programmer to have control over page ejects sent to the printer from @ . . . SAY commands.

The SET DBF and SET NDX commands allow you to specify drives and directories for database files and index files. Programs and other files can exist on a separate drive or directory.

The SET FLASH command allows you to determine whether format files are "painted" on the screen (slowly) or presented instantaneously.

The SET TIME command allows a program to change the system time from within a command file.

For more advanced programmers, the BITSET, IN, OUT, and DOSINT commands provide control over low-level functions, such as the speaker or an external port. BITSET returns a True if the bit at a specified position is set on. IN returns a single numeric value from a specified port. OUT sends a single value to the specified port. DOSINT allows data to be sent to and read from DOS interrupt vectors.

dBIII Compiler (version 2.0) supports local area networks. A faster native-code compiler is scheduled for release in the summer of 1986. Another new product scheduled for release is dBXL. This product performs the same tasks as the dBASE III PLUS interpreter, so that programs written for dBIII Compiler can be tested and run interactively without the use of dBASE III PLUS.

dBIII Compiler Functions

dBIII Compiler supports all dBASE III functions, but at the time this book was written, it did not support the functions that are unique to dBASE III PLUS. The dBIII Compiler CLEAR KEY and INKEY() commands, however, duplicate the CLEAR TYPEAHEAD and INKEY() commands from dBASE III PLUS.

dBIII Compiler Commands

Like the Clipper compiler, dBIII Compiler does not support interactive (dot prompt) commands or debugging aids. (dBIII Compiler also has its own debugger.) The following commands are among those not supported by dBIII Compiler (the reasons for the exclusion of all these commands are discussed in the section on Clipper in this appendix):

APPEND *	ON \<key\>,\<escape\>,\<error\>
ASSIST	RELEASE MODULE
BROWSE	RETRY
CHANGE	SET
CLEAR FIELDS	SET CARRY
CREATE * *	SET DATE
CREATE/MODIFY LABEL	SET DEBUG
CREATE/MODIFY QUERY	SET DOHISTORY
CREATE/MODIFY REPORT	SET ECHO
CREATE/MODIFY SCREEN	SET FIELDS
CREATE/MODIFY VIEW	SET HEADING
DIR	SET HELP
DISPLAY/LIST HISTORY	SET HISTORY
DISPLAY/LIST FILES	SET MEMOWIDTH
DISPLAY/LIST STATUS	SET MENUS
EDIT	SET ORDER
EXPORT	SET SAFETY
HELP	SET STATUS
IMPORT	SET STEP
INSERT	SET TITLE
LOAD	SET TYPEAHEAD
MODIFY COMMAND	SET VIEW
MODIFY STRUCTURE	SET TALK
	SUSPEND

 * APPEND FROM and APPEND BLANK are supported.
 * * CREATE \<NewFile\> FROM \<OldFile\> is supported.

dBIII Compiler Index Files

Index files created and maintained in dBASE III PLUS are completely compatible with dBIII Compiler index files, and vice versa.

The *\ Comment

To keep dBASE III PLUS from attempting to execute a command unique to dBIII Compiler, simply precede the command line with the characters *\. dBASE will treat the line as a comment; dBIII Compiler will ignore the *\ characters and compile the line. For example, dBASE III PLUS will ignore the illegal SET DEVICE TO ALTERNATE command in the following command sequence:

```
*\ SET DEVICE TO ALTERNATE
SET ALTERNATE TO AltFile
SET ALTERNATE ON
```

Macro Restrictions

Macros can be used in place of all file names and as conditions in DO WHILE loops. Keywords and commands cannot be stored in macros. For example, the following sequence is not allowed:

```
Mac = "ON"
SET FLASH &MAC
```

Performance Comparisons

Compiling a custom system does not guarantee that the entire system is suddenly going to run at the speed of light. Keep in mind that a compiler basically just *preinterprets* your command files and stores these already interpreted commands in a separate file. It does not make the *physical* attachments to the basic computer move any quicker.

When you compile a program, you can expect major speed improvements in routines that do not access the screen, printer, or disk. (That's because these external devices won't slow down the execution speed.) dBASE III PLUS commands that in themselves manage data already in RAM (like SEEK and FIND) are likely to show no apparent improvement in performance when compiled. (Arguably, 0.8 seconds is 20 percent faster than 1.0 second, but few people are going to notice the 0.2 second difference.)

Processes that are heavily disk bound, such as a LOCATE command, will probably not show a major increase in performance. That's because most of the time spent in a LOCATE command is spent in physically searching the disk for data. The compiled program cannot speed up the physical movement of the disk drive.

To demonstrate the effect of the compilers, I compiled and tested four different programs. The first, named Test1.PRG, is shown in Figure A.5. This program simply displays a starting time, repeats a loop 1,000 times, and displays the time when done. Since it does not access the screen or disk, its speed will be most improved when compiled.

The second program, Test2.PRG, also repeats a loop 1,000 times, but displays a number on the screen each time through the loop. In this case, the screen will slow down the brute-force execution of the compiled program, so the performance improvement will not be as dramatic as in the case of Test1.PRG. (Obviously, a printer would slow things down even more.) Test2.PRG is shown in Figure A.6.

```
*************************************** Test1.PRG
*---- Program that accesses no external devices.
SET TALK OFF
? TIME()
Counter = 1
DO WHILE Counter <= 1000
    Counter = Counter + 1
ENDDO
? TIME()
```

Figure A.5 – *The Test1 command file*

```
*************************************** Test2.PRG
*-------- Program that accesses only the screen.
SET TALK OFF
StartTime = TIME()
Counter = 1
DO WHILE Counter <= 1000
    Counter = Counter + 1
ENDDO
? StartTime
? TIME()
```

Figure A.6 – *The Test2 command file*

The third program, Test3.PRG, attempts to locate the last name Smith in an unindexed database named CTest.DBF. (In this example, Smith was stored at the 1,000th record.) Since the primary job of this program is to search the disk for a particular piece of information, there will be little speed difference when this program is compiled. Test3.PRG is shown in Figure A.7.

Test4.PRG, shown in Figure A.8, accesses both the screen and disk through a LIST command. The effect of the compiler on the speed of this program will be sort of an averaging of the Test2 and Test3 programs.

```
*********************************** Test3.PRG
*-------- Program that is heavily "disk bound".
SET TALK OFF
? TIME()
*-------- Locate the 1,000th record.
USE CTest
LOCATE FOR LName = "Smith"
? RECNO()
? TIME()
```

Figure A.7 - The Test3 command file

```
*********************************** Test4.PRG
*-------- Program that is disk and screen bound.
SET TALK OFF
StartTime = TIME()
*-------- Locate the 1,000th record.
USE CTest
LIST LName, FName, Company, Address
? StartTime
? TIME()
```

Figure A.8 - The Test4 command file

The actual processing times on an IBM XT with 640K RAM and a 10-megabyte hard disk are shown in Table A.2. (These processing times will differ on other computers.) Keep in mind that the dBIII Compiler used was a prereleased Beta test version of the native-code compiler. You can probably expect faster and smaller compiled programs from the final release in the summer of 1986. The winter 1985 version of Clipper was used.

The sizes of the files are also shown in the table. For the dBASE III PLUS row, you need to add 440K if dBASE III PLUS is used to run the program, or about 340K if dBRUN is used.

As would be expected, Test1.PRG showed the most significant improvement when compiled. The 49-second dBASE program was reduced to nine seconds with dBIII Compiler and eight seconds with Clipper.

The screen accessing (with the ? command) in Test2.PRG slowed down all three versions as expected. However, both the Clipper and dBIII Compiler versions were definitely faster than the dBASE III PLUS version.

The Test3.PRG program, which used the LOCATE command to locate the thousandth record on the database, ran slightly slower with dBIII Compiler, and the same when compiled with Clipper.

Test4.PRG, which accesses both the disk and screen, was significantly improved with the Clipper compiler and slowed down slightly with the WordTech compiler. (Again, since a prereleased Beta test version of the WordTech native-code compiler was used, these processing times should not be considered final results.)

	Test 1	Test 2	Test 3	Test 4	
dBASE III PLUS	49	117	9	154	Seconds
	209 +	256 +	256 +	256 +	Bytes
Clipper Compiled	8	50	9	115	Seconds
	127,904	127,920	127,952	127,968	Bytes
dBIII Compiled	9	66	10	166	Seconds
	114,096	114,160	115,440	115,978	Bytes

Table A.2 – Comparison of source and compiled code

Conclusions

In some ways, these results bring us back to the earlier chapters in this book where we discussed speed and performance in relation to index files. Notice that, even when compiled, programs that are heavily disk bound run slowly. Therefore, if a system runs too slowly in dBASE III PLUS because of poor use of index files, it will probably still run too slowly when compiled.

Any processes that perform calculations will speed up dramatically. For example, Translat.PRG, Debug.PRG, and the various procedures discussed in Chapter 21 all run extraordinarily fast when compiled.

When several command files are linked together in a compiled application, there are no disk accesses required to perform a DO command, therefore the system switches from menu to menu more quickly. Even though this trims off only a second or two in processing time, it gives the appearance of great speed and is a nice convenience if one has grown tired of the pause when switching from menu to menu. (Of course, you could accomplish this without a compiler: just put your entire application in a large procedure file.)

In terms of independence from dBASE III PLUS and Ashton-Tate products in general, the compilers offer the most advantage. Even dBRUN adds some overhead to the cost of your product. There are thousands of "user-created" applications packages for sale in the world, and you probably don't need extraneous costs added to yours to compete. You need to buy a compiler only once. You can compile and copy as many programs as you like. Anyone with the right computer can then use your software.

Interfacing with Other
Software Systems

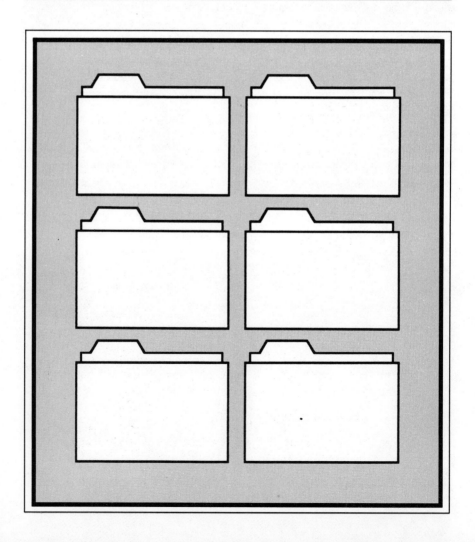

The dBASE III PLUS COPY and APPEND FROM commands allow you to interact with data from word processors, VisiCalc, Multiplan, and Lotus 1-2-3. The IMPORT and EXPORT commands let you interact with PFS:FILE data. Many programs, such as Framework, Symphony, Paradox, and R:base 5000 have their own options for interfacing with dBASE data.

Interfacing with PFS:FILE

To import a PFS file into dBASE III PLUS, first make sure the PFS file is readily available on the disk in drive B or on your hard disk. Then enter the command

IMPORT FROM <filename> TYPE PFS

substituting the name of the PFS file where <filename> is shown. Also, be sure to use the correct drive. For example, to import a PFS file named Accounts stored on drive B, you would enter the command

IMPORT FROM B:Accounts TYPE PFS

dBASE III PLUS will separate the PFS file into several manageable files. Each file will be named the same as the PFS file, but it will include a dBASE III PLUS extension. The three files will be a database file (.DBF), a format file for custom screens (.FMT), and a view file for combining the screen and data files (.VUE).

To export data to a PFS file, use the command

EXPORT TO <filename> TYPE PFS

where <filename> is the name of the dBASE III PLUS file that you want to export. If the file is on drive B, use the B: drive specification:

EXPORT TO B:ExpFile TYPE PFS

You must open the database (.DBF) file with the USE command before entering the EXPORT command. Also, if the database to be exported has a custom screen associated with it (.FMT file), you should activate that screen before you export the file, using the SET FORMAT TO command from the dot prompt.

Note that options to import and export PFS files are also available from the Tools option under the Assistant menu.

Interfacing with Spreadsheets

You can interface dBASE III PLUS data with a variety of spreadsheet packages. To copy a database file to VisiCalc format, load the database and enter the command

COPY TO <filename> TYPE DIF

where <filename> is the name of the new file. dBASE will add the extension .DIF to the exported file.

To export data to Multiplan spreadsheets, use the SYLK option with the COPY command:

COPY TO <filename> TYPE SYLK

Again, the file being exported must have been opened with the USE command before issuing the COPY command. The copied file will not have an extension.

To copy data to Lotus 1-2-3 format, use the .WKS option with the COPY command:

COPY TO <filename> TYPE WKS

The new file will have the extension .WKS.

For stubborn transfers that are difficult to accomplish, you can experiment with the SDF and delimited options. For example, the command

COPY TO <filename> TYPE SDF

makes a file in *system data format*. This is often called an *ASCII text* file because it contains no special codes. Most spreadsheets can *import* a file stored in system data format if an importing option is available. The file name extension .TXT will be added to the file name automatically, unless you supply another.

The DELIMITED option for copying files might also work for exporting to spreadsheets. We'll discuss the DELIMITED option under interfacing with word processors in this appendix.

To import spreadsheet data, you need to first create a database that has the structure you want for your .DBF file. (Of course, you can use an existing database if you wish.) You then need to open the database with the USE command and use the APPEND FROM (rather than COPY TO) option to import the foreign data.

To import from a text (SDF) file, you would use this syntax:

APPEND FROM <filename> TYPE SDF

You must fully identify the file being imported. For example, to import MailData.TXT from drive B, you would enter this command:

APPEND FROM B:MailData.TXT SDF

To import data from a VisiCalc DIF file, you would use the command

APPEND FROM <filename>.DIF TYPE DIF

(assuming that the file was stored with DIF as the extension).

To import a Multiplan spreadsheet, you would use this command:

APPEND FROM <filename>. TYPE SYLK

If the Multiplan file has no extension, use a period after the file name in the APPEND FROM command. For example, to import a Multiplan spreadsheet on drive B named Accounts, enter this command:

APPEND FROM B:Accounts. TYPE SYLK

To import Lotus 1-2-3 worksheets, use the .WKS option with the APPEND FROM command:

APPEND FROM Accounts.WKS TYPE WKS

Again, be sure to use the B: drive designator on a file name if you are using a floppy-disk system. Also, be sure to pay attention to the extension of the file you are importing, and to use that extension in the file name of the APPEND FROM command.

Interfacing with Word Processors

You can send dBASE reports to word processing systems for further editing or inclusion in other documents. To do so, design your report using the MODIFY REPORT command in dBASE. Then print the report with the TO <filename> option. You can then load up your word processor and read the report into the word processing system. Here is a typical scenario using the WordStar program as the word processor:

```
A> dBASE
USE Mail
MODIFY REPORT ByName
(Define report format)
REPORT FORM ByName TO Transfer
QUIT
```

The TO Transfer option with the REPORT FORM command sends a copy of the report to a disk file named Transfer.TXT. When you quit dBASE, the A> reappears on the screen. Now you can load up WordStar. Let's say you want to pull the dBASE report into a document called Manual.TXT. Type

WS Manual.TXT

When the document appears on the screen, position the cursor at the place you want the dBASE report to appear. Then press ^KR. The WordStar program asks

NAME OF FILE TO READ?

Reply with

Transfer.TXT

That's all there is to it. The report, which appeared on the screen when you asked dBASE to

REPORT FORM ByName

is now in a WordStar document and also in a disk file called Transfer.TXT.

Now, you may want to send your dBASE file to WordStar's MailMerge option for printing form letters. In this case, you need to create a database in MailMerge format. Let's say that you want to send a database named Mail.DBF to a MailMerge file from which to print form letters. After loading up dBASE, type

USE Mail

Then you need to copy it to another data file in MailMerge-readable form. The command is

COPY TO MM DELIMITED

This creates a data file called MM.TXT, which the MailMerge file can access to create form letters. Then you have to create the form letter in Word-Star. Assume that the Mail database contains the fields LName, FName, Address, City, State, Zip, and Phone. You have to quit dBASE and load up the WordStar program. Then you can create a document called Form.LET. Figure B.1 contains a sample form letter that can read the data file you've just created.

```
.OP
.DF  MM.TXT
.RV  LName,FName,Address,City,State,Zip,Phone
&FName& &LName&
&Address&
&City&, &State&       &Zip&


Dear &FName&,
     How do you like getting these form letters? You
probably wouldn't know the difference if it were not
for my dot-matrix printer.
                    Ta ta for now,
                    Zeppo
.PA
```

Figure B.1 – Sample MailMerge form-letter file

Notice that Phone was included in the .RV command, even though it is not used in the form letter anywhere. This is essential if the Phone variable exists. The .RV command is expecting a certain number of fields, so it must have the same number of fields as the data file, regardless of whether you plan on using that field in your form letter. Even if you wanted only the first name for your form letter, you would still have to read in all of the fields. If you forget this important tidbit, your form letter might come out in a most unpleasant format.

After you create and save the form letter, you merely need to merge print it using the appropriate MailMerge command. That is, select WordStar option M from the WordStar Main menu, and when it asks NAME OF FILE TO MERGE PRINT?, tell it Form.LET. A letter for each individual in the Mail database will then be printed. The first one should appear as in Figure B.2.

You could use a dBASE .LBL file to print mailing labels for all these individuals, or you could create a WordStar MailMerge document to print names and addresses directly on envelopes, one envelope at a time. Figure B.3 is a MailMerge file (named Envel.TXT) to print envelopes from your MM.TXT data file.

After you create and save Envel.TXT, you can merge print it in the usual WordStar fashion. However, when the merge print option asks

PAUSE FOR PAPER CHANGE BETWEEN PAGES (Y/N)

be sure to answer Y. Then you can insert each individual envelope, lining it up so that the print head is right where you want the printing to start.

```
Andy Appleby
123 A St.
San Diego, CA 92123

Dear Andy,
     How do you like getting these form letters? You
probably wouldn't know the difference if it were not
for my dot-matrix printer.
                   Ta ta for now,
                      Zeppo
```

Figure B.2 – Sample form letter produced by MailMerge

```
.MT 0
.OP
.DF  MM.TXT
.RV  LName,FName,Address,City,State,Zip,Phone
                &FName& &LName&
                &Address&
                &City&,  &State&      &Zip&
.PA
```

Figure B.3 – MailMerge file to print envelopes

The MailMerge option will print one envelope, eject it from the printer, and wait for you to put in the next envelope.

If you want your form letter to go to certain individuals only, you can specify this in your dBASE COPY command. Let's assume you want your form letters to go to San Diego residents only. With the dBASE dot prompt showing and the Mail database in use, type this command:

COPY TO MM FOR City = 'San Diego' DELIMITED

Only San Diego residents would appear on the MailMerge file, hence only individuals in San Diego would have form letters printed.

If you already have a MailMerge file and want to use some dBASE commands to manage it, you can send a copy of it to dBASE. To do so, you need to load up dBASE and create an empty file with the CREATE command. Structure it so that it has the same fields as your MailMerge file. When dBASE asks INPUT DATA NOW?, respond with N. Then load the newly created database, and issue the command

APPEND FROM MM.DAT DELIMITED

You can now sort your MailMerge file or do whatever you please with it in dBASE III PLUS. (This example assumed that the name of your existing MailMerge file was MM.DAT.) To get the dBASE database back into MailMerge-readable form, just load the dBASE file and issue the command

COPY TO MM.DAT DELIMITED

dBASE III PLUS Vocabulary

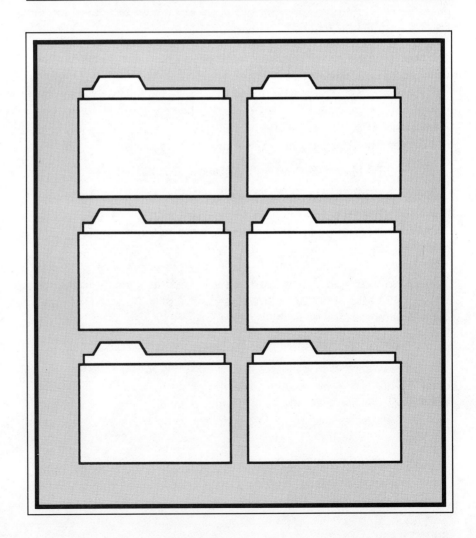

Command	Definition
!	Converts character to uppercase in @ . . . SAY . . . GET commands (@ 5, 5 GET Answer PICTURE "!").
#	Not equal to. Also used in templates of @ . . . SAY . . . GET statements to allow entry of only numbers, blanks, and symbols.
$	Substring function, used for finding a character string embedded within a larger character string (LIST FOR 'Lemon' $ADDRESS). In @ . . . SAY statements, $ displays dollar signs in place of leading zeros.
&	Used as a prefix on a name to declare that name as a macro function instead of as a literal.
()	Used for logical and mathematical grouping [?(10 + 10) * 5].

Command	Definition
*	Multiplies two numbers (? 10 * 10), or acts as a "wild card" in a DIR command. As a template symbol in @ . . . SAY statements, * displays asterisks in place of leading zeros.
* *	Exponent symbol. ? 99 * *2 displays 99 squared. X = 1234 * *(1/3) stores the cube root of 1234 to memory variable X.
;	Splits long command lines into two separate lines.
^	Exponent symbol. ? 34 ^5 displays 34 raised to the fifth power (45435424.00). In text, the ^ symbol usually means "hold down the Ctrl key."
+	Adds two numbers or links two character strings.
−	Subtracts two numbers or links two character strings with trailing blanks removed.
.AND.	Tests whether two things are true simultaneously (LIST FOR 'Oak' $ADDRESS .AND. City = 'San Diego').
.NOT.	Tests whether a condition is not true (DO WHILE .NOT. EOF).
.OR.	Tests whether one or another of two conditions is true (LIST FOR City = 'San Diego' .OR. City = 'Los Angeles').
/	Divides two numbers (? 10/5).
<	Less than (LIST FOR LName < 'Smith').
< =	Less than or equal to (LIST FOR LName < = 'Smith').
=	Equal to (LIST FOR LName = 'Smith').
>	Greater than (LIST FOR LName > 'Appleby').

Command	Definition
> =	Greater than or equal to [LIST FOR Date > = CTOD("03/01/86")].
?	Moves to the beginning of a new line and displays the contents of a field, memory variable, or the results of a mathematical equation (? 1 + 1).
??	Displays the contents of a field, memory variable, or expression at the current cursor position [?? SQRT(X)].
@	Displays information in specified format on screen or printer (@ 5,1 SAY 'Hi').
ABS	Returns the absolute value of a number [? ABS(–234) displays 234].
ACCEPT	Displays a prompt on the screen and waits for a response. Stores answer to a memory variable as Character data (ACCEPT 'Do you want more?' TO YN).
ALIAS	Allows a database to be accessed through two different names (USE Mail ALIAS Names).
ALL	Refers to all records in the database (DISPLAY ALL, DELETE ALL, REPLACE ALL).
APPEND	Adds new records of data to the end of the currently opened database.
APPEND BLANK	Adds a new record to the bottom of a database, with all fields blank.
APPEND FROM	Reads the records from another database and adds them to the bottom of the database in use (APPEND FROM Temp). If the source file is not a dBASE III or dBASE III PLUS file, use the SDF or DELIMITED options with APPEND FROM to import the database.

Command	Definition
ASC	Displays the ASCII value of a character [? ASC("A") displays 65].
ASSIST	Activates the menu-driven interface to access dBASE III PLUS.
AT	Shows the position at which one character string starts in another [? AT("B","AABBCC") displays 3 because B appears as the third character in "AABBCC"].
AVERAGE	Computes the average of a Numeric field in a database [AVERAGE AMOUNT FOR MONTH (Date) = 12].
B:	Signifies drive B for storing data files (CREATE B:Mail).
B->	Refers to a field from a database opened in work area 2 (or B) with the SELECT command. C-> refers to a field opened in work area 3 or C, and so forth (LIST Code, B->Title,Qty, Amount).
BOF()	Function that determines whether the beginning of the file has been reached. Opposite of EOF() [? BOF()].
BROWSE	Displays a "screenful" of the database and allows you to scan and make changes to the database.
/C	Used with the SORT command to ignore upper-/lowercase in a sort (SORT ON LName/C, FName/C TO Temp).
CALL	Executes an assembly language program (binary file) that has been placed into memory with the LOAD command.
CANCEL	Aborts command file execution and returns to the dot prompt.

Command	Definition
CDOW()	Displays the day of the week as a character (Sunday, Monday, etc.) for a Date field or memory variable [? CDOW(Date)].
CHANGE	Globally edits a specific field in a database (CHANGE FIELD Phone FOR City = "San Diego").
CHR()	Displays the ASCII character for a number [? CHR(65) displays "A", ? CHR(7) rings the bell].
CLEAR	Clears the screen and repositions the cursor to the upper-left corner.
CLEAR ALL	Closes all database, index, format, and relational databases. Undoes all SELECT commands. Frees all memory used by memory variables.
CLEAR FIELDS	Releases all fields from all work areas originally set with the SET FIELDS command.
CLEAR GETS	Releases GET variables from READ access.
CLEAR MEMORY	Erases all current memory variables.
CLEAR TYPEAHEAD	Empties the typeahead buffer so that old keypresses do not affect current prompts.
CLOSE	Closes open files, of either alternate, database, format, index, or procedure types (CLOSE DATABASES).
CMONTH()	Displays the month for a Date field or memory variable as a Character string (e.g. January) [? CMONTH(Date)].
COL()	Returns the current column position of the cursor [? COL()].
COMMAND	Indicates a command or text file (MODIFY COMMAND Menu).

Command	Definition
CONTINUE	Used with the LOCATE command to find the next record with a particular characteristic specified by the LOCATE command.
COPY	Copies the contents of one database into another database, including any associated Memo fields.
COPY FILE	Copies a file to another file (COPY FILE MyProg.PRG TO MyProg.BAK).
COPY STRUCTURE	Copies the structure of a database to another database without copying the contents (COPY STRUCTURE TO Mail2).
COUNT	Counts how many records in a database meet some criterion [COUNT FOR MONTH(Date) = 12 TO December].
CREATE	Allows you to create a database and define its structure (CREATE Mail).
CREATE LABEL	Creates a format file for mailing labels (same as MODIFY LABEL) (CREATE LABEL B:TwoCol).
CREATE REPORT	Creates a custom report format (same as MODIFY REPORT) (CREATE REPORT ByName).
CREATE QUERY	Creates a query form and allows the user to fill in a query.
CREATE SCREEN	Accesses the Screen Painter for creating custom forms.
CREATE VIEW	Creates an editable and displayable screen, pulling together data from several linked databases.
CTOD()	Converts a date stored as a Character string ("01/01/86") to a Date data type [LIST FOR Date = CTOD("01/01/86")].
/D	Used with SORT to sort in descending order (largest to smallest) (SORT ON Zip/D TO Temp).

Command	Definition
DATE()	Displays dBASE internal date [? DATE()].
DAY()	Displays the day of the month for a Date data type as a number [? DAY(Date)].
DBF()	Returns the name of the database file currently in use [? DBF()].
DELETE	Marks a record for deletion (DELETE RECORD 7).
DELETED()	Evaluates to True if record is marked for deletion [LIST FOR DELETED()].
DELIMITED	Copies dBASE databases to other data file formats (COPY TO MM.TXT. DELIMITED).
DIR	Shows files on disk (DIR B: *.PRG displays command file names on drive B).
DISKSPACE()	Returns the amount of space available, in bytes, on the currently logged disk drive [IF DISKSPACE() < 200].
DISPLAY	Shows information about a database or its contents (DISPLAY ALL, DISPLAY STRUCTURE).
DISPLAY HISTORY	Displays the last 20 commands typed in at the dot prompt.
DISPLAY MEMORY	Displays the name, type, size, and status of all current memory variables.
DISPLAY STATUS	Displays the current status of databases and index files in use, SET parameters, and function key (F1–F10) assignments.
DO	Runs a command file or procedure (DO Mail).
DO CASE	Sets up a clause of mutually exclusive options in a command file. Terminated with the END-CASE command.
DO WHILE	Used with ENDDO to set up a loop in a command file [DO WHILE .NOT. EOF()].

Command	Definition
DTOC()	Converts a Date field or memory variable to a Character data type [LIST FOR DTOC(Date) = "01/01/86"].
EDIT	Displays existing data in a record and allows you to change its contents (EDIT 17).
EJECT	Advances paper in printer to top of new page.
ELSE	Performs a set of commands if the criterion in an IF statement is false.
ENDDO	Used with the DO WHILE command to mark the bottom of a loop in a command file.
ENDIF	Marks the end of an IF clause in a command file.
EOF()	Function that returns True if the end of the database file has been reached and passed. Used primarily in DO WHILE loops in command files [DO WHILE .NOT. EOF()].
ERASE	Deletes a specific file from the directory (ERASE Temp.DBF).
ERROR()	Returns a number indicating the error caught by an ON ERROR command.
EXIT	Escapes from a DO WHILE loop without terminating execution of the command file. Control is transferred to the statement immediately following the ENDDO statement.
EXP()	Natural exponent of a number [? EXP(1)].
EXPORT	Copies data from a dBASE III PLUS database into another file in PFS format.
FIELD()	Returns name of a field in a database file [? FIELD(3) displays the name of field number 3 in the currently open database].

Command	Definition
FILE	Refers to a disk file. DISPLAY FILES shows disk files.
FILE()	Returns True if the named file exists on disk, otherwise returns False. [IF FILE("My-Data.DBF")].
FIND	Looks up information rapidly in an indexed database file (FIND "Miller").
FKLABEL()	Displays the names of function keys on a computer. [? FKLABEL(1) would display F2, the name of the key on an IBM keyboard. On another computer, FKLABEL(1) might display another label.]
FKMAX()	Determines the number of programmable function keys on a given terminal [? FKMAX( ) returns 9 on an IBM keyboard, for programmable function keys F0 through F9].
FOUND()	The FOUND() function is True (.T.) when a FIND, SEEK, LOCATE, or CONTINUE command finds the requested record. Otherwise, FOUND() returns False (.F.).
GET	Used with the READ command to accept field and memory variable data from the screen (@ 5,1 SAY 'Last name' GET LName).
GETENV()	Returns information about the operating system environment [? GETENV("COMSPEC") might display C:Command.COM, indicating that the Command.COM file is on the root directory of drive C].
GO BOTTOM	Goes to the last record in a database.
GO TOP	Starts at the first record in a database.
HELP	Provides help on the screen for a command or function [HELP RECNO()].

Command	Definition
IF	Determines whether to perform commands in a command file based on some criteria (IF ZIP = '92122').
IIF()	Abbreviated version of the IF command using the syntax IIF(<this is true>, <do this>, <otherwise do this>). Unlike IF . . . ENDIF constructs, you can execute IIF() at the dBASE III PLUS prompt. [ROOT = SQRT(IIF(X>0,X,ABS(X))) takes the square root of the absolute value of X if X<0.]
IMPORT	Reads data from a PFS:FILE database into dBASE III PLUS format.
INDEX	Creates an index file of sorted data (INDEX ON LName TO Names) or uses an existing index to display data in sorted order (USE Mail INDEX Names).
INKEY()	Scans the keyboard to see whether a key has been pressed and returns the keypress as an ASCII code between 0 and 255. Does not interrupt program execution to scan the keyboard.
INPUT	Displays a prompt on the screen and waits for a response terminated by pressing the Return key. Used with Numeric data (INPUT 'How many labels per page' TO PER:PAGE).
INSERT	Puts a new record into the database at the current record location. Also, INSERT BEFORE.
INT()	Returns the integer portion of a number, with decimal places truncated (not rounded) [? INT(1.99999) displays 1].
ISALPHA()	Determines whether the first letter of a variable is a letter. Example: ? ISALPHA("123 A St.") returns .F.

Command	Definition
ISCOLOR()	Returns .T. if color monitor is in use; otherwise returns .F.
ISLOWER()	Determines whether the first letter of a character string is a lowercase letter [? ISLOWER("alan") returns .T.].
ISUPPER()	Determines whether the first letter of a character string is uppercase [? ISUPPER("Snowball") returns .T.].
JOIN	Creates a third database based on the contents of two existing databases (JOIN TO NewDB FOR CODE = B->Code).
LABEL	Displays or prints mailing labels in the format specified in a file created with the MODIFY LABEL command (LABEL FORM TwoCol TO PRINT).
LEFT()	Returns the specified left portion of a character string [? LEFT("Snowball",4) returns Snow].
LEN()	Returns the length of a string [? LEN("Word") would display 4].
LIST	Shows the contents of a database.
LIST FOR	Lists data that have some characteristic in common (LIST FOR LName = 'Smith').
LOAD	Places an assembly language (binary) file into memory where it can be executed with a CALL command.
LOCATE	Finds a record with a particular characteristic (LOCATE FOR LName = 'Smith').
LOG()	Calculates the natural logarithm of a number [? LOG(2.72)].
LOOP	Skips all commands between itself and the ENDDO command in a DO WHILE loop.

Command	Definition
LOWER()	Converts uppercase letters to lowercase [? LOWER(Name)].
LTRIM()	Removes leading blanks from character strings [? LTRIM(" Hello") displays Hello without leading blanks].
LUPDATE()	Returns the date of the last update for the currently open database file [? LUPDATE()].
M->	Specifies a memory variable. Useful when a field and memory variable share the same name (? M->LName).
MAX()	Returns the higher of two numbers [? MAX (20,40) returns 40].
MEMORY	Displays memory variables in RAM (DISPLAY MEMORY or LIST MEMORY).
MIN()	Returns the lower of two numbers [? MIN(20,40) returns 20].
MOD()	Returns the modulus (remainder) of two numbers [? MOD(5,3) returns 2].
MODIFY	Used to create or change a command file, database structure, label format, report format, screen, view file, or query file (MODIFY COMMAND, MODIFY STRUCTURE, MODIFY LABEL, and so forth).
MONTH()	Returns the month of a Date field or variable as a number (1-12) [LIST FOR MONTH(Exp-Date) = 12].
NDX()	Displays the names of active index files (1-7). To display the name of the master index file, enter the command [? NDX(1)].
OFF	Leaves record numbers out of displays (LIST OFF). Also, turns off parameters (SET PRINT OFF).

Command	Definition
ON	Sets dBASE parameters into ON mode (SET PRINT ON).
ON ERROR	Executes a dBASE command when an error occurs.
OS()	Returns the name of the operating system in use [? OS()].
PACK	Permanently deletes records marked for deletion from the database.
PARAMETERS	Command used to define variables passed by a DO . . . WITH command.
PCOL()	Displays the current column position of the printer head [? PCOL()].
PICTURE	Used with the GET command to make templates and define acceptable character types [@ 12,1 SAY 'Phone number' GET PHONE PICTURE'(999)999-9999'].
PRIVATE	Specifies memory variables that are automatically erased when a command file terminates (PRIVATE ALL LIKE M *).
PROCEDURE	An advanced programming technique whereby tasks are broken down into flexible routines accessed throughout a system. The PROCEDURE command names a procedure; SET PROCEDURE loads a procedure file into memory for global access.
PROW()	Displays the current row position of the printer head [? PROW()].
PUBLIC	Specifies memory variables that are not to be erased when command file terminates (PUBLIC CHOICE, LP, X, Y, Z).
QUIT	Closes all files and exits dBASE III PLUS back to the operating system's A > prompt.

Command	Definition
RANGE	Specifies a range of acceptable values with @ . . . SAY . . . GET and READ commands (@ 12,5 SAY "Enter choice" GET CHOICE RANGE 1,5).
READ	Used with @ . . . SAY . . . GET statements to read in field and memory variable data from the screen.
READKEY()	Returns the key pressed to exit a full-screen operation like APPEND, BROWSE, CHANGE, CREATE, EDIT, INSERT, MODIFY, or READ. Keypress is stored as an integer in the range of 0 to 255.
RECALL	Brings back a record marked for deletion (RECALL RECORD 14) but not yet permanently deleted with PACK.
RECCOUNT()	Displays the number of records in the open database file [? RECCOUNT()].
RECNO()	Returns the current record number [LIST FOR RECNO() > = 10 .AND. RECNO() < = 20 lists all records in the range of records 10 to 20].
RECORD	Refers to a single record (DELETE RECORD 4).
RECSIZE()	Returns the number of bytes in each record in a database [? RECSIZE()].
REINDEX	Recreates all active index files.
RELEASE	Erases current memory variables to free memory space for other use (RELEASE ALL).
RENAME	Changes the name of a disk file (RENAME Old.DBF TO New.DBF).
REPLACE	Changes the current contents of a field with new data. Used in global changes (REPLACE ALL LName WITH 'Smith' FOR LName = 'SMITH').

Command	Definition
REPLICATE()	Replicates a character in a variable up to 255 times [ULine = REPLICATE("·",80) creates a memory variable named ULine consisting of 80 hyphens].
REPORT	Allows you to either create a report format (MODIFY REPORT) or display data in report format (REPORT FORM ByName).
RESTORE	Recalls memory variables that were saved to disk with the SAVE command back into RAM (RESTORE FROM Thought).
RESUME	Continues running a program that has been temporarily suspended for the purposes of debugging.
RETRY	Used in networking to retry executing a command that failed because of a locked record or file.
RETURN	Returns control from a command file to the dot prompt or to the calling command file.
RETURN TO MASTER	Returns control from a subprogram back to the first-run program (usually the main-menu program).
RIGHT	Takes characters from the right side of a character string [? RIGHT("Snowball",4) displays ball].
ROUND()	Rounds a number to a specified number of decimal places [? ROUND(Rate * Hours),2].
ROW()	Returns the current row position of the cursor on the screen [? ROW()].
RTRIM	Same as the TRIM function below.
RUN	Executes a program outside of dBASE III PLUS. For example, RUN WS runs the WordStar program. The RUN command can also be represented with an exclamation point (! WS).

Command	Definition
SAVE	Stores a copy of memory variables to a disk file (SAVE TO Thought).
SAY	Used with @ to position output on the screen or printer (@ 5,2 SAY 'Hi').
SDF	Standard data format. Copies dBASE files to other database formats (COPY TO Basic.DAT SDF FOR RECNO() < 100).
SEEK	Looks up the contents of a memory variable in an indexed database file [STORE CTOD ("01/01/86") TO Lookup ⏎, SEEK Lookup].
SELECT	Assigns databases in use to any one of ten work areas numbered 1 through 10 or lettered A through J (SELECT 1, SELECT A).
SET	Displays a menu of SET parameters and allows changes to be made via a menu of options.
SET ALTERNATE	Transfers all screen activity (except @ ... SAY commands) to a text file, after the file name is specified and the alternate is on (SET ALTE TO file, SET ALTE ON).
SET BELL	Determines whether the bell sounds when a field is filled on an APPEND, EDIT, or custom screen (SET BELL OFF).
SET CARRY	When the CARRY option is on, a newly appended record automatically receives the contents of the previous record, which can then be edited.
SET CATALOG	Creates catalog files and sets recording of file names either ON or OFF.
SET CENTURY	ON displays the century in date displays; OFF hides the century.
SET COLOR	Changes the color of the screen foreground, background, and border.

Command	Definition
Command	**Definition**
SET CONFIRM	Determines whether pressing the Return key is necessary after filling a screen prompt (SET CONFIRM ON).
SET CONSOLE	When console is off, nothing is displayed on the screen (SET CONSOLE OFF).
SET DATE	Determines the format for displaying Date data. Options are AMERICAN, ANSI, BRITISH, ITALIAN, FRENCH, GERMAN.
SET DEBUG	Determines whether the SET ECHO command directs output to the printer or the screen. With SET DEBUG ON, SET ECHO ON directs debug output to printer while execution goes to screen.
SET DECIMALS	Sets the minimum number of decimals displayed in the results of mathematical calculations (SET DECIMALS TO 2).
SET DEFAULT	Determines which disk drive dBASE uses when looking for disk files with the USE, DO, INDEX, SELECT, and other commands that access files (SET DEFAULT TO B). Can be overridden by using drive designators in file names.
SET DELETED	Determines whether records marked for deletion are displayed with LIST, DISPLAY, ?, REPORT, and LABEL commands (SET DELETED ON hides deleted records).
SET DELIMITER	Determines how field entries are displayed on the screen with APPEND, EDIT, and custom screens (SET DELIMITER TO "[]" encloses fields in brackets).
SET DEVICE	Determines whether @ . . . SAY commands display data on the screen or on the printer (SET DEVICE TO PRINTER, SET DEVICE TO SCREEN).

Command	Definition
SET DOHISTORY	When ON, lines from command files are recorded in the HISTORY file. When OFF, only lines typed in from the dot prompt are recorded.
SET ECHO	A debugging aid that displays each line of a command file as it is being processed (SET ECHO ON).
SET ESCAPE	Determines whether a command file terminates when Esc is pressed (SET ESCAPE OFF aborts the power of the Esc key).
SET EXACT	Determines whether dBASE compares two values with an exact match or with first letters only. With EXACT off, Smith will match Smithsonian.
SET FIELDS	Determines which fields will be displayed.
SET FILTER	Limits display of data to those records that match a criterion (SET FILTER TO LName = "Smith" will limit output of LIST, REPORT, LABEL, etc. to Smiths).
SET FILTER TO FILE	Uses the contents of a query (.QRY) file to set up a filter condition. (SET FILTER TO NotBilld gets filtering information from the NotBilld.QRY file. SET FILTER TO with no file name clears all filter conditions.)
SET FIXED	Sets the number of decimal places that will appear with all numeric displays. Usually used in conjunction with the SET DECIMALS command (SET FIXED ON).
SET FORMAT	Specifies a custom screen display stored in a format (.FMT) file to be used with an EDIT or APPEND command (SET FORMAT TO AddNames, SET FORMAT TO).

Command	Definition
SET FUNCTION	Reprograms the function keys (F1–F10) to perform custom tasks (SET FUNCTION 10 TO 'BROWSE'). DISPLAY STATUS shows current settings.
SET HEADING	Determines whether field names will be displayed above data in DISPLAY, LIST, SUM, and AVERAGE commands (SET HEADING OFF removes field names from displays).
SET HELP	Determines whether the message "Do you want some help? (Y/N)" appears during an error (SET HELP OFF removes the prompt).
SET HISTORY	Specifies the number of commands stored in the HISTORY file or the status of HISTORY. (SET HISTORY TO 50 stores 50 lines in the history file. SET HISTORY OFF stops recording command lines.)
SET INDEX	Specifies index file(s) to make active with a database (SET INDEX TO NAMES, ZIPS).
SET INTENSITY	Determines whether field entries on full-screen EDIT and APPEND operations are displayed on the screen in reverse video (SET INTENSITY OFF removes reverse video).
SET MARGIN	Adjusts the left margin for printer displays (SET MARGIN TO 5).
SET MEMOWIDTH	Determines the width of Memo field displays.
SET MENUS	Determines whether cursor-control commands appear in a menu above APPEND, EDIT, BROWSE, and other displays (SET MENUS ON displays the menus).
SET MESSAGE	Displays a message at the bottom of the screen (SET MESSAGE TO "How are you today?").

Command	Definition
SET ORDER	Selects an index file from a list to make primary.
SET PATH	Specifies directory paths to search for disk files (SET PATH TO \C:DBIII will cause dBASE to search path DBIII on drive C if a file is not found on the current drive).
SET PRINT	Determines whether displays will be echoed to the printer (SET PRINT ON causes all screen displays to be printed; SET PRINT OFF returns to normal mode).
SET PROCEDURE	Advanced programming technique whereby subprograms are combined into a single file and assigned procedure names (SET PROCE-DURE TO Routines).
SET RELATION	Sets up a relationship between two data files in use, based on a field they have in common (SET RELATION TO Code INTO Master).
SET SAFETY	Determines whether the message "(file name) already exists—overwrite it? (Y/N)" appears when a file is about to be overwritten (SET SAFETY OFF disables).
SET SCOREBOARD	Determines whether massages in the top line or status bar appear.
SET STATUS	Turns the status bar at the bottom of the screen on or off.
SET STEP	Debugging aid used to limit command file execution to a single line at a time (SET STEP ON).
SET TALK	Determines whether dBASE displays a response to various commands. Usually, SET TALK OFF is used in command files to eliminate dBASE messages.

Command	Definition
SET TITLE	Determines whether prompts for titles appear in active catalogs.
SET TYPEAHEAD	Determines the number of characters to be held in the type-ahead buffer. The default is 20; the possible range is 0 to 32000 (SET TYPEAHEAD TO 9999).
SET UNIQUE	Used with the INDEX command to display an ordered listing of unique field values (SET UNIQUE ON). Can be used to temporarily delete records with duplicate key values.
SET VIEW	Opens a view (.VUE) file (SET VIEW TO AcctRec).
SKIP	Skips to next record in the database. Can also skip more or less than 1 record (SKIP 10, SKIP -3).
SORT	Rearranges records in a database into sorted order. Requires that records be sorted to another database (SORT ON LName TO Temp).
SPACE()	Generates a string of blanks [LName = SPACE(20) creates a memory variable called LName that consists of 20 blank spaces].
SQRT()	Displays the square root of a number [? SQRT(64), STORE SQRT(64) TO X].
STORE	Assigns a value to a memory variable (STORE 1 TO Counter).
STR()	Converts a number to a string. Useful for complex sorting with index files [INDEX ON Code + STR(AMOUNT,12,2) TO Test].
STRUCTURE	Refers to the structure rather than the contents of a database (DISPLAY STRUCTURE).

Command	Definition
STUFF()	Allows you to put data into an existing character string without dismantling the original string [? STUFF("HaHoHa",3,2,"Ha") returns HaHaHa—because Ha was stuffed at the 3rd character, replacing 2 characters].
SUBSTR()	Isolates a portion of a string [? SUBSTR("ABC-DEFG",3,2) displays CD, a substring starting at the third character, 2 characters long].
SUM	Adds a column of fields and displays the total (SUM AMOUNT).
SUSPEND	Halts execution of a command file and returns control to the dot prompt. The RESUME command restarts execution.
TEXT	Starts a block of text in a command file, terminated with the command ENDTEXT.
TIME()	Displays the current system time in the form hh:mm:ss [? TIME()].
TOTAL	Summarizes and totals a database to another database. Files must be either presorted or preindexed (TOTAL ON Code TO SaleSumm).
TRANSFORM()	Like a PICTURE statement, lets you define formats for data displayed with the LIST, DISPLAY, REPORT, and LABEL commands[LIST TRANSFORM(AMOUNT,"###,###,###.##") displays all amounts in ###,###,###.## format].
TRIM()	Removes trailing blanks from a character string [LIST TRIM(FName),LName].
TYPE	Displays the contents of a DOS ASCII (text) file (TYPE MyReport.TXT).
UPDATE	Revises the file in use by adding or replacing data from another database (UPDATE ON Code FROM Sales REPLACE Price WITH B->Price).

Command	Definition
UPPER()	Converts lowercase letters to uppercase [INDEX ON UPPER(LName) TO Names].
USE	Tells dBASE which database to work with (USE Mail).
VAL()	Changes character strings to numerics [? VAL(Address)].
VERSION()	Displays the version number of dBASE III PLUS in use [? VERSION()].
WAIT	Stops execution of a command file and waits for user to press a key. Keypress is stored to a memory variable (WAIT TO Data).
YEAR()	Displays the year of a Date field or variable in 19XX format [LIST FOR YEAR(Date) = 1986].
ZAP	Permanently removes all records from a database and active index files.

Index

!, 97, 425
#, 97, 425
$, 425
&, 37, 425
( ), 425
*, 46–47, 54, 60, 81, 426
* *, 426
*\ comment, 411
+, 426
−, 426
/, 426
/C command, 428
/D command, 430
;, 16, 426
<, 426
< =, 426
=, 426
>, 426
> =, 427
?, 43, 51, 427
??, 427
@ command, 45, 80, 155, 311, 427
^ , 426

A

ABS command, 427
ACCEPT command, 44, 427
Accounts. *See also* Accounts
  Receivable System
    adjusting, 314
    assigning numbers to, 306–307
    checking status of, 330–335
    payments and balances, 279–280

Accounts Receivable System
  adding new customers, 306–308
  adding payments, 312–314
  adding sales tax, 311
  adding transactions, 310–311
  current balances, 336
  designing, 279–286
  developing main-menu program,
   303–306
  editing, 315–323
  handling charges and payments,
   284
  hierarchical structure of, 286
  historical reports, 339–342
  history files, 284–285
  input-output specification,
   280–281
  library of routines, 289
  linking to Inventory System,
   356–359
  looking up customers, 292
  monthly activity summary, 336
  printing invoices, 329–330
  printing monthly statements,
   333–334
  procedure file, 289
  reports, 280–281, 327–329,
   336–342
  software structure, 285–286
  speeding program execution, 285,
   289
  standardizing error messages,
   291–292
  updating procedures, 345–346

AddNames.FMT file, 85, 99, 102
AddNames.TXT file, 99
AddNew program, 100–101
AddNumbs program, 181, 184–187
Address index, 145–146
AgeSumm program, 328, 338
ALIAS command, 427
ALL command, 427
Alphabetical order, 29
.AND. extension, 426
APPEND command, 5, 22, 36–37, 95,
  307, 417, 427
AREdit program, 315–316
ARHist program, 342–343
ARPrint program, 328–329
Arrow keys, 43
ARStat program, 329–330, 335, 352
ARUpdate program, 358
ASC command, 428
ASCII characters, 103
  displaying, 398–400
  text file, 419
Ashton-Tate, 387–388
ASSIST command, 428
Asterisks, 46–47, 54, 60, 81, 426
AT command, 428
AVERAGE command, 31, 428

B

B-> command, 428
B: command, 428

Billings
  automatic, 279
  cycles, 333
Bills command file, 334
Bills program, 329-333
Blackboard. *See* Screen Painter, Blackboard
BOF() command, 428
Boxes, 91-93
BROWSE command, 428
BROWSE screen, 33-34
BusProcs procedure file, 372-373

C

CALL command, 428
CANCEL command, 428
Cancel option, 56
CaseTest program, 51
CDOW() command, 429
CHANGE command, 429
Character data, 44-45, 61-64, 71
Characters
  ASCII, 103
  graphic, 102-103
  numbers in Memo field, 5
Charges database, 283, 303, 357. *See also* Accounts Receivable System
  adding transactions to, 310-311
  editing, 319
  history files, 285
  relating to Customer database, 321
Check-writing procedure, 365-370
Checks program, 369-370
CHR() command, 102, 429
CLEAR commands, 47, 49-50, 59-60, 155, 429
  ALL, 429
  FIELDS, 429
  GETS, 429
  MEMORY, 429
  TYPEAHEAD, 155-156, 429
Clipper compiler, 402-407, 414
CLOSE command, 59-60, 429
CLOSE PROCEDURE command, 303
CMONTH() command, 429
COL() command, 429
Color monitors, 304
COMMAND command, 429

Command lines
  length of, 16
  printing, 61
  viewing, 60
Commands, 425-447
  displaying, 59
  misspelling, 63
  naming, 53
Common fields, 8
Compilers, 397-415
  advantages, 397-398
  Clipper, 402-407, 414
  dBIII, 408-411
  effect of, 412-413
Config.SYS file, 65
Constants, 297
CONTINUE command, 430
COPY commands, 32, 417, 430
  FILE, 430
  STRUCTURE, 430
COUNT command, 430
Count program, 46-47
Crashes, 56, 59
CREATE commands, 2, 430
  LABEL, 430
  QUERY, 430
  REPORT, 32, 190-191, 430
  SCREEN, 430
  VIEW, 430
CTOD() command, 234, 430
Cursor movement, 43, 90, 109
Custom forms. *See* Custom screens
Custom screens, 85-87, 90-91, 98
  adding picture templates to, 96-97
  creating with Screen Painter, 98
  for editing, 133-136
  for Inventory System, 181-182
  for Membership System, 85-92, 94-96
  modifying, 95
  saving, 94
  selecting fields for, 182
  testing, 94
  using graphics characters in, 102-103
  viewing, 95-96
Customer database, 282-283, 303
  adding blank records to, 307
  editing, 317-318, 320
  relating to Charges database, 321

Customers. *See also* Accounts Receivable System
  adding, 306-308
  assigning identification numbers, 306-308
  checking status of, 329-333, 336
  directory, 110-115
  storing information about, 279, 282
  validating identification numbers, 292

D

Data
  avoiding duplication of, 8
  character, 44-45, 61-63, 71
  field, 45
  historical, 284
  memory-variable, 45
  modifying, 5
  numeric, 44-45, 61-63, 71
  passing to and from procedures, 297
  searching ranges of, 26
  types of, 57, 62, 71
Data entry
  correcting errors, 214
  for recording sales, 212-213
  simplifying by using templates, 96
Data files
  master, 161, 163, 166
  multiple, 163
  sales, 167
  transaction, 162-163, 166
Data type mismatch, 57, 61-62
Databases
  designing, 71
  determining, 17
  master-file/transaction-file, 1, 13-17
  relating, 321
  relational, 1, 8
  single, 1-2
  single with Memo field, 3-8
DATE() command, 431
Dates, 44-45, 57, 62, 64
  assigning in Inventory System, 170
  concatenating to spaces, 114
  displaying, 26-27, 80
  entering as character strings, 114, 234

DAY( ) command, 431
dBCODE program, 392
DBF( ) command, 431
.DBT extension, 5
dBIII Compiler, 408–411, 414
dBLINKER program, 393
DEBUG command, 60
Debug program, 360–365
Debugging, 56–61, 65, 359–365
Default disk drive, 58, 79, 166
DELETE command, 431
DELETED( ) command, 431
DELIMITED command, 431
DIR command, 431
Directory, 107, 115
    creating with report generator,
        110
    grouping expression, 112–114
    printing, 35, 154
    sample of, 111
Directory program, 149–154
DISKSPACE( ) command, 431
DISPLAY commands, 3, 57, 431
    HISTORY, 59, 431
    MEMORY, 57, 62–63, 431
    STATUS, 58, 63, 353, 431
    STRUCTURE, 57, 62–63
DO CASE . . . ENDCASE commands,
    51–55, 431
DO command, 43, 431
DO WHILE command, 46–48, 146, 431
DOS TYPE command, 115
DTOC( ) command, 62, 80, 114, 432
DupCheck program, 143–148
Duplicate records, 143–147

E

EdChrg program, 321–322
EDIT command, 5, 34, 95, 432
EditDel program, 133–136
    listing, 140–141
    modifying, 137–139
    testing, 141
Editing, 32, 133–136
    current charges, 319–320
    current payments, 322–323
    customer data, 317–320
    keys, 87
    with MODIFY COMMAND, 41, 57
    sales transactions, 259–262

EdPay command file, 324–325
EJECT command, 50, 432
ELSE command, 432
Encrypting programs, 387–388, 394
ENDCASE command, 51–55, 61
ENDDO command, 46–47, 61, 432
ENDIF command, 50, 61, 432
EOF( ) command, 432
ERASE command, 432
Error procedure, 291–292
ERROR( ) command, 432
Errors, 38, 56–57, 59–60, 63
    caused by misplaced commands,
        61
    correcting data, 214
    data type mismatches, 61–62
    debugging, 56–58
    invalid function arguments, 63
    logical, 60, 65
    misspellings, 58, 63
    of omission, 65
    programming, 61
    records out of range, 38, 65
    reducing likelihood with templates,
        96
    too many files open, 65
    typographical, 65
Esc key, 352
EXIT command, 432
EXP( ) command, 432
EXPORT command, 417, 432

F

Field data, 45
Field highlights, 86, 92
    locations, 93
    repositioning, 89–90
Field labels, 86, 90
Field names, 57, 89–90
Field prompts, 93
FIELD( ) command, 432
Fields
    for address information, 2
    common, 8
    key, 3, 12, 163
    loading into Screen Painter, 87
    logical, 167
    maximum length in dBASE, 4
    in membership database, 71
    Memo, 3–8

Fields (continued)
    selecting for custom form, 86
    space requirements, 71
FILE command, 433
Files
    creating and editing with MODIFY
        COMMAND, 41
    format, 98, 102, 107
    text, 98
    viewing status of, 57
Filter condition, 121, 157
FIND command, 25, 27, 30–31, 36–38,
    433
FKLABEL( ) command, 433
FKMAX( ) command, 433
Floppy disks, 2, 17, 41
.FMT extension, 98, 102
FNewChrg program, 310
FOR command, 27–28
Form letters, 119
Format files, 98, 102, 107
FOUND( ) command, 433
Framework, 417
Function keys, 58
Functions and argument types, 64

G

GET command, 45, 433
GetCust procedure, 292–293,
    298–300
GETENV( ) command, 433
GO BOTTOM command, 433
GO TOP command, 433
Graphics characters, 102–103

H

Hard copy, 61
Hard disks, 17
HEADING command, 145
HELP command, 433
HISTORY commands, 59

I

IF . . . ELSE . . . ENDIF commands,
    48–51
IF command, 434
IfTest program, 49
Ignore option, 56

IIF command, 50–51, 434
IMenu program, 169–170, 173, 177
IMPORT command, 417, 434
Indentations, 52–54
INDEX command, 22, 29, 434
Index files
    adding records to, 22–23
    copying, 35
    corrupted, 38, 65
    creating, 19–20, 23
    determining need for, 72
    displaying names and contents of, 58
    to increase speed, 24–26, 31–32, 34
    master, 36
    primary, 36–37
    reconstructing, 65
    searching ranges of dates in, 26–27
    sorting records in, 35–36
    technicalities of, 27
    using multiple, 35–36
    using to store sort orders, 3
    viewing status of, 57
INDEX ON command, 20, 23, 65
Indexed fields, 8, 37
INKEY() command, 384, 434
INPUT command, 44, 434
Input-output (I/O) specification, 70, 164, 280
INSERT command, 22, 434
INT() command, 434
Invalid function argument, 63
Inventory control. *See* Inventory System
Inventory System, 13, 17, 161. *See also* New Stock system
    adding part numbers, 181, 184
    adding sales data, 209–213
    automatic price feature, 226
    capability for storing data and printing reports, 277
    checking part numbers, 185–186
    command file, 173
    correcting data-entry errors, 214
    creating custom screens, 181–183
    creating and printing purchase orders, 192
    creating sales program, 215–226

Inventory System (continued)
    current-stock reports, 187–189
    designing, 161–168
    editing, 203–205, 237, 259–262
    linking to Accounts Receivable System, 161, 351, 356
    main menu, 169–172, 178–180
    master file, 177–179, 187
    orders, 191–195, 200–203
    recording sales transactions, 217, 223–226
    reports, 187–195, 210–211, 248
    sales reports, 210–211, 227–236
    software design, 168–169
    testing program for, 174
    updating, 205, 237, 253–256, 259, 269, 357–358
    using key fields to relate files, 163
Inventory/Accounts Receivable linker, 356–359
Inventry.DBF master file, 14
Invoices, 209, 212–226, 280, 327
    automatic price feature, 226–227
    duplicate, 333, 335
    printing, 217, 221, 329–330
    reports, 228, 231
    sample produced by BillProc, 333
ISALPHA() command, 434
ISCOLOR() command, 435
IScreen1.FMT file, 182–183
ISLOWER() command, 435
ISUPPER() command, 435

J

JOIN command, 435
Joint listing from two databases, 12

K

Key fields, 3, 12, 163

L

LABEL command, 435
Label Contents screen, 109–110
LABEL FORM command, 109
Labels, 107–110, 119, 148–149
LEFT() command, 435
LEN() command, 435

Library of routines, 289
Library reference system, 3–5
Library program, 7
Light-bar menus, 378–381
LIST commands, 3, 5, 12, 15, 36, 145, 435
    FOR, 24, 435
    HISTORY, 59
LOAD command, 435
LOCATE command, 22, 435
LOG() command, 435
Logical errors, 60, 65
Logical fields, 167
Lookup table, 11–12
LOOP command, 346, 435
Loops, 46–48, 54, 79–80, 137–138, 146, 200
Lotus 1-2-3, 417
LOWER() command, 436
LTRIM() command, 436
LUPDATE() command, 436

M

M–> command, 436
Macros, 411
Mailing labels. *See* Labels
Mailing lists, 1–3, 68–69. *See also* Membership System
MailMerge, 421–423
Margins, 58
Master-file/transaction-file databases, 1, 13–17
MAX() command, 436
MEdit program, 203–206
Members program, 77
Membership System
    adding new records to, 85, 100–101
    checking for duplicate records in, 143–144
    command files, 73, 77–79, 82
    creating, 68-70, 73, 77–83
    custom screens for, 85–96
    custom templates, 96–98
    deleting records in, 139
    directory, 107, 110–115, 149–154
    editing, 133–141
    encrypting, 388
    enhancing, 143
    entering data, 85

Membership System (continued)
  index files for, 72
  index of zip codes and addresses, 145–146
  input-output specification, 70
  mailing labels, 107–110
  menu, 73, 77–83
  modular design of, 74
  printing information from, 119
  querying, 119–121
  Reports program, 129–131
  sorting, 119
  testing program, 81
Memo fields, 3–8
MEMORY command, 436
Memory variables
  adding to screen, 311
  checking, 63
  hard copy of, 57
  viewing status of, 57
Memory-variable data, 45
MIN( ) command, 436
Misspellings, 58, 63
MMenu program, 179–180, 253
MOD( ) command, 436
MODIFY commands
  COMMAND, 41–43, 293, 436
  QUERY, 128
  REPORT, 115
  SCREEN, 95
Modular program design, 73–74
MONTH( ) command, 436
MReports program, 187, 192–197
Multiplan, 417

N

Names
  for commands and variables, 53
  length of, 113
  uppercase, 269, 283
NDX( ) command, 436
New Stock system, 249–251
  command file, 245–246
  data-entry program, 242–244
  menu, 241
  reports, 246–247
  software structure, 239–240
NewChrg program, 311–312
NewCust program, 306–309
NewEdit program, 270–276

NewPay program, 312–315
NewReps program, 249–251
NewStock data file, 168, 239, 269
NMenu command file, 241
.NOT., 426
Numeric data, 44–45, 61–64, 71

O

OFF command, 436
ON command, 437
ON ERROR command, 437
ON KEY command, 156
.OR., 426
Orders program, 195–203
OS( ) command, 437
OTHERWISE command, 52

P

PACK command, 437
Paradox, 417
Parameters, 290
  controlling with SET commands, 58, 79
  passing to and from procedures, 285, 293–298
PARAMETERS command, 289–290, 293, 296, 437
Password, 345
Payments database, 284, 303, 313–314
  adding new payments, 312
  editing, 319, 322–323
PCOL( ) command, 437
PFS:FILE data, 417–418
PICTURE command, 80, 437
Picture templates, 96–98
Point-of-sale routine, 209, 212, 215, 223
Pos program, 212–226
Post command file, 345–349
.PRG extension, 43, 293
Primary index file, 36–37
PrinStop program, 155–156
PrintBills procedure, 335
PrintDir program, 149–158
Printer, 50, 61, 154–158
Printing, 126–127
  characters per inch, 107
  commands, 61

Printing (continued)
  invoices, 228
  mailing labels, 107–108
  purchase orders, 192
  sales reports, 228
  stopping, 50, 154–158
PRIVATE command, 437
PROCEDURE command, 289–290, 293, 437
Procedure files, 289–290
  BillProc, 330–333
  creating, 293
  RowCheck, 330
  using, 295, 374
Procedures, 285, 298
  calling one another, 300
  for check writing, 365–366, 369–370
  customer-number validation, 292
  making portable to other programs, 333
  modifying, 292
  number in procedure file, 293
  for printing error messages on screen, 291
  for printing titles on menu screens, 290
  using, 296–297
  using parameters to send data to, 290
  word-wrap, 370–372
ProcLib1 program, 293–298
Programmer comments, 47, 53–54
Programming, 41, 47, 67–69
  advanced techniques, 52–55, 143, 279, 285, 289
  debugging, 52, 56–61, 65
  designing database, 71
  errors, 56–65
  with modular design, 73–74
  procedures and parameter passing, 285
  speed, 289, 292
  structured, 52–55
Programs
  controlling progress of, 60
  creating, 55–56
  creating self-documenting, 52
  debugging, 52
  to display screen, 85
  echoing, 60–61

Programs (continued)
hierarchical structure of, 74, 354
interacting with user, 44
linking, 349, 351
marketing, 387, 395–398
for membership-management
system, 73, 77–78
modifying, 351–353, 356
modular design of, 73–75
testing, 43, 60
utility, 349, 351
writing and testing, 75
PROW( ) command, 437
Pseudocode, 77–78
PUBLIC command, 437
Purchase orders, 192, 197

Q

Querying, 119, 121, 126
QUIT command, 81, 437
Quotation marks, 44

R

R:base 5000, 417
RANGE command, 80, 83, 438
READ command, 45–46, 80, 438
READKEY( ) command, 438
RECALL command, 438
RECCOUNT( ) command, 438
RECNO( ) command, 438
RECORD command, 438
Records
adding, 3, 5, 22–23
checking for duplicate, 143–147
comparing, 146
deleting, 127, 133, 139
displaying, 3, 21, 121
editing, 5, 133, 136, 259–260
listing by date, 26–27
locating, 2
nonexistent, 65
packing for deletion, 139
presenting in report format, 32
out of range, 65
searching with FOR option, 28
seeking to edit, 138
sorting, 21, 29, 36, 72
"unhiding", 157
viewing, 5

RECSIZE( ) command, 438
REINDEX command, 65, 438
Relational databases, 1, 8, 279–281
RELEASE command, 438
RENAME command, 438
REPLACE command, 36, 438
REPLICATE( ) command, 439
REPORT command, 3, 36, 115, 439
Report generator, 110–111
Reports
creating, 32, 190–191, 336–337
formats of, 187–191
historical, 327, 339–342
in inventory system, 187
menu for selecting format of,
120
modifying format of, 115
organizing, 119
parameters for, 229–230
printing, 154–157, 193–194, 338
sales, 227–230
stock, 246–247
summary, 336–338
using in word processing
document, 115
verifying, 115
Reports program, 119, 122–131,
148–149
Response files, 391
RESTORE command, 439
RESUME command, 439
RETRY command, 439
RETURN command, 439
Reverse video, 86
RIGHT command, 439
ROUND( ) command, 439
ROW( ) command, 439
RowCheck procedure, 330
RTRIM command, 439
RUN command, 439
RUN DATE command, 304
RunTime +, 387–397
copying, 391–392
limitations, 395

S

SalEdit program, 261–269
Sales data file, 167, 259–262
Sales database system, 15

Sales files
editing records in, 259–262
transferring data from, 16
Sales system. See also Inventory
System
correcting data-entry errors, 214
editing files, 237
entering selling price, 226
menu, 210–211
recording transactions, 167, 217
reports, 227–236
software structure, 209–210
Sales tax, 311
Sales.DBF, 167, 209
SalReps program, 230–236
SAVE command, 440
SAY command, 45, 440
.SCR extension, 98
Screen Painter, 85–86, 91
Blackboard, 86–88, 94
creating files with, 98
SDF command, 440
Search string, 138
Searching, 2, 72, 128–129
with FIND and SEEK commands,
38
with FOR option, 28
Memo fields, 8
range, 26–28
speed, 24–27, 30
SEEK command, 25, 27, 30, 36–38,
138, 440
SELECT command, 12, 440
Semicolon notation, 16
SET commands, 58
ALTERNATE, 440
BELL, 440
CARRY, 440
CATALOG, 440
CENTURY, 440
COLOR, 304, 440
CONFIRM, 441
CONSOLE, 155, 441
DATE, 441
DEBUG, 61, 441
DECIMALS, 441
DEFAULT, 2, 79, 441
DELETED, 157, 441
DELIMITER, 441
DEVICE, 441
DEVICE TO PRINT, 333

SET commands (continued)
    DOHISTORY, 442
    ECHO, 60, 442
    ESCAPE, 442
    EXACT, 442
    FIELDS, 442
    FILTER, 157, 442
    FIXED, 442
    FORMAT, 94, 442
    FUNCTION, 443
    HEADING, 443
    HELP, 443
    HISTORY, 59, 443
    INDEX, 128, 157, 443
    INTENSITY, 443
    MARGIN, 443
    MEMOWIDTH, 6, 443
    MENUS, 443
    MESSAGE, 443
    ORDER, 444
    PATH, 444
    PRINT, 50, 444
    PROCEDURE, 295–297, 444
    RELATION, 12, 321, 444
    SAFETY, 444
    SCOREBOARD, 444
    STATUS, 79, 444
    STEP, 60, 444
    TALK, 47, 60, 444
    TITLE, 445
    TYPEAHEAD, 445
    UNIQUE, 445
    VIEW, 445
Single databases, 1–3
SKIP command, 445
SMenu program, 209–211
Software
    designing, 73–75
    modifying, 351–356
    writing custom system, 67–70
SORT command, 21, 34–35, 445
Sort orders, 21, 72, 119–120, 125, 128

Sorting, 2–3, 21, 129
    in alphabetical order, 29
    index files, 20, 23, 32, 36
    by last name, 2
    Memo fields, 8
    speed, 20, 23, 32, 34
Source directory, 388–389
SPACE( ) command, 445
Speed, 35
    of dBASE III PLUS applications, 19
    of searches, 30
    of sorts, 20, 23, 32, 34
Spreadsheets, 418–419
SQRT( ) command, 445
StatProc.PRG procedure file, 374–375
Status bar, 79
Status checks, 333
STEP option, 60
Stock
    orders, 191–192, 195, 200
    recording new, 239
    reordering, 197–199
    report on current, 187
    reviewing status of, 246–247
    updating records of, 253–256
STORE command, 47, 445
STR( ) command, 445
STRUCTURE command, 445
Structured programming, 52–55
STUFF( ) command, 446
SUBSTR( ) command, 446
SUM command, 31, 446
SUSPEND command, 446
Suspend option, 56
Symphony, 417
System data format, 419

T

.T., 54
Telephone numbers, 71
Test database, 376

Test programs, 43–44
TEXT command, 80, 446
Text editor, 41
Time, 80
TIME( ) command, 446
Title procedure, 290, 304
TO PRINT option, 61
TOTAL command, 446
Transaction files, 13–14, 162–163, 166
TRANSFORM( ) command, 446
Translat procedure file, 368
TRIM( ) command, 446
.TXT extension, 98, 115, 419
TYPE command, 61, 115, 446
Typeahead buffer, 155–157

U

UPDATE command, 15–16, 34, 446
Updater program, 254–259
Updating, 16–17, 253–259, 345–346
UPPER( ) command, 269, 447
USE command, 16, 36, 38, 447

V

VAL( ) command, 45, 447
Values, 298
Vendor codes, 8–11
VERSION( ) command, 447
VisiCalc, 417

W

WAIT command, 45, 447
WHILE command, 26–27, 30–32
Word processors, 417, 420
Word-wrap procedure, 370–372
WordTech compiler, 414

Y

YEAR( ) command, 447

Z

ZAP command, 447
Zip codes, 3, 35–36, 38, 71–72, 145–146

ADVANCED TECHNIQUES IN dBASE III PLUS

Sample Programs Available on Disk

If you'd like to use the programs in this book but don't want to type them in yourself, you can send for a disk containing all the sample systems in the book. To obtain this disk, complete the order form and return it along with a check or money order for $35.00. California residents add 6 percent sales tax.